IT'S NATION TIME

IT'S
NATION
TIME

A Progressive Defence

JERRY WHITE

McGill-Queen's University Press

Montreal & Kingston • London • Chicago

ISBN 978-0-2280-2296-1 (cloth)
ISBN 978-0-2280-2342-5 (ePDF)
ISBN 978-0-2280-2343-2 (ePUB)

Legal deposit fourth quarter 2024
Bibliothèque nationale du Québec

Printed in Canada on acid-free paper that is 100% ancient forest free
(100% post-consumer recycled), processed chlorine free

This book has been published with the help of a grant from the
Federation for the Humanities and Social Sciences, through the
Awards to Scholarly Publications Program, using funds provided
by the Social Sciences and Humanities Research Council of Canada.

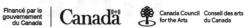

We acknowledge the support of the Canada Council for the Arts.
Nous remercions le Conseil des arts du Canada de son soutien.

McGill-Queen's University Press in Montreal is on land which
long served as a site of meeting and exchange amongst Indigenous
Peoples, including the Haudenosaunee and Anishinabeg nations.
In Kingston it is situated on the territory of the Haudenosaunee and
Anishinaabek. We acknowledge and thank the diverse Indigenous
Peoples whose footsteps have marked these territories on which
peoples of the world now gather.

Library and Archives Canada Cataloguing in Publication

Title: It's nation time : a progressive defence / Jerry White.
Other titles: It is nation time
Names: White, Jerry, 1971- author.
Description: Includes bibliographical references and index.
Identifiers: Canadiana (print) 20240390962 | Canadiana (ebook)
    2024039108X | ISBN 9780228022961 (cloth) | ISBN 9780228023425
    (ePDF) | ISBN 9780228023432 (ePUB)
Subjects: LCSH: Nationalism—Case studies. | LCSH: National
    characteristics—Case studies. | LCGFT: Case studies.
Classification: LCC JC311 .W45 2024 | DDC 320.54—dc23

This book was designed and typeset by studio oneonone
in Minion 11/14

For the "un-seminar" – Katie Lawrence, Connor Morris, Malorie Urbanovitch, and Kai Woolner-Pratt: in the darkness of the lockdown, a pedagogical north star.

And for the parishioners of Saint Eugene's Church: true believers and keepers of the faith.

In Newark, when we greet each other on the streets, we say, "what time is it?" We always say "It's nation time!" ... Nationalism is about land and nation, a way of life trying to free itself."

– Amiri Baraka, at the Congress of African People, September 1970, as reproduced on *Black Journal*, episode 56, first broadcast 1972

Contents

Acknowledgments

I hope I do not sound flippant when I say that this book would not have come about without the COVID-19 pandemic. I am surely not the only person to have been provoked into a quasi–midlife crisis by all of that, towards a sense that maybe the time had come to change the kind of work that I did. But more specifically, as the lockdown really took hold, I found myself very worried about the prospect of teaching online, something I had never done before and had blithely assumed I would be able to avoid forever. Faced with the need to get comfortable with both the technology and the pedagogical difference, I asked a few recent and not-so-recent former students from the University of Alberta and the University of King's College if they wanted to be part of a series of little dry runs so I could get used to it all. We ended up convening a weekly seminar, ostensibly devoted to contemporary Europe but in fact going way further afield, which met throughout that darkest period, often going over the three-hour time limit we set for its sessions. Out of that came the desire to write a book-length defence of the nation, a process that led to my reconvening most of that group (and, at the end, all of it) as I put drafts of each chapter into their supportive, patient, and unspeakably generous hands. It was the best experience of teaching I have ever known. Katie Lawrence, Connor Morris, Malorie Urbanovitch, and Kai Woolner-Pratt: this book must be dedicated to you.

On somewhat more prosaic notes, I am happy to thank a number of colleagues who supported this writing in different ways. Gérard Bouchard read the full manuscript and his uncompromisingly generous response was exactly what I needed to get this thing into shape. I feel the same way about the late Garry Watson; he read all of these chapters as I drafted them, pulled no punches, and reminded me of why I loved being part of the same department as him during our shared Alberta days. Intellectually speaking he died with his boots on, working for as long as he could on a book about Susan Sontag, Alexandre Kojève, and much in between. It was a great blessing that he in turn shared those chapters with me, sending them on as he finished them. What luck, to reconnect with a colleague such as that, while there was still a bit of time.

In my new home of Saskatchewan it has been wonderful to have the intellectual fellowship of William Bartley and Matthew Neufeld, both of whom provided much sustenance as I got this thing done; I think of them together as *les vrais*. In my old home of Halifax/Dartmouth, Chris Elson reminded me of some of the best parts of living and working in that part of the world; much the same is true of Pádraig Ó Siadhail, who continues, for his sins, to try and keep me honest on matters Irish. In Montreal I thank Kyla Madden, who was supportive at an early stage in just the right ways, and Jonathan Crago, who took this thing in hand in ways that only he could.

Sasha and Bubba have heard no small part of the conceptual framework of this book, whether they knew it or not. Sometimes they pushed back, sometimes they corrected my French, and sometimes they offered the happiest surprise of all, which was seeming to think that I was right about some stuff. They made me think about all of it in ways I could have never even imagined before they came along. And Sara Daniels, as always, deserves the biggest thanks of all.

IT'S
NATION
TIME

Introduction

In terms of its value for a progressive view of the world, "the nation" has seen better days. The post–Cold War conflicts in Yugoslavia and throughout the post-Soviet world seemed to set the stage for a twenty-first century that would see the rise of right-wing and far-right governments in Europe, the United States, Central and South America, and Asia who all depended on a toxic mix of populism and nationalism to shore up their authoritarian ways.

With this book, I want to make the case that this does not tell the whole story. Specifically, I want to make the case that the concept of "the nation" still has some life left, and moreover can be a positive force in a way that most contemporary progressives can recognize. What I want to do with this book is argue that national formations – large and globally influential nations such as England or India, "small nations" such as Georgia or New Zealand, stateless nations such as Catalonia or the Métis – remain relevant in a globalized world, and moreover deserve to have their relevance defended by those who believe in the possibility of cultural diversity in such a world. Throughout this book I will argue that nations are always complex, heterogeneous structures, but that this does not mean that an appeal to the infinite diversity so prized by contemporary liberalism is the only way to understand cultural identity. In some ways I am informed here by what Charles Tilly, in a 1995 paper titled "Citizenship, Identity, and Social History," saw as an incipient alternative to such an understanding: "The emerging view is *relational* in the sense that it locates identities in connections among individuals and groups rather than in the minds of particular persons or whole populations. It therefore breaks with both the sorts of individualism that have dominated recent analyses of social life: both (1) methodological individualism with its independent, self-contained, self-propelling rational actors, and (2) phenomenological individualism with its deep subjectivity ad well as its penchant for solipsism."[1] The solipsistic temptation of liberalism is a topic I will return to.

In some ways I am responding to George Orwell throughout. His 1941 book-length essay *The Lion and the Unicorn: Socialism and the English Genius* is seminal in terms of my considerations, especially hard-headed, Second World War–bound statements therein such as "[O]bviously the snobbishness and political ignorance of people like airmen and naval officers will be a very great difficulty … An intelligent Socialist movement will *use* their patriotism, instead of merely insulting it, as hitherto"[2] (his italics). Orwell's use of the word "patriotism" is perhaps a preview of his 1945 essay "Notes on National-ism," in which he is acidicly critical of the concept, writing that "[b]y 'nation-alism' I mean first of all the habit of assuming that human beings can be classified like insects and that whole blocks of millions or tens of millions of people can be confidently labelled 'good' or 'bad.'"[3] It was patriotism that he wished to defend, something he described as "devotion to a particular place and a particular way of life, which one believes to be the best in the world but has no wish to force upon other people."[4] But Orwell muddies the waters con-siderably when he writes that "[n]ationalism, in the extended sense in which I am using the word, includes such movements and tendencies as Commu-nism, political Catholicism, Zionism, Antisemitism, Trotskyism and Pacifism. It does not necessarily mean loyalty to a government or a country, still less to one's own country, and it is not even strictly necessary that the units in which it deals should actually exist."[5] As I hope will become especially clear when we reach the section of the book that deals with England, my work here is very much in the spirit of *The Lion and the Unicorn*, which displays a geniuine affection for Englishness that I find moving. I have tried to retain, in the back of my mind, the considerations of "Notes on Nationalism" as a sort of cau-tionary, all the while hoping that my definition of "nationalism" is really just closer to Orwell's definition of "patriotism."

In the main I will try to articulate this argument for the continued validity of the concept of "nation" via a series of case studies. These are literally all over the map: Africa and its diaspora, France, Georgia, India, New Zealand, Quebec, England, Ireland, Catalonia, the Métis Homeland, English Canada, the circumpolar Inuit homeland and especially Greenland, and the Mohawk territories of Kahnawake, Kanesatake, and Akwesasne. There is a certain Euro-American bias in this list, one that reflects my own experience and linguistic abilities, but that roll call also offers a chance to talk about every continent except for Antarctica (my discussion of Catalonia will engage with Cuba, which in terms of South America I am hoping will be, as my grandfather used to say, "close enough for government work"). These case studies are essays in thinking about how national identities manifest in a globalized world, essays that try as much as possible to evoke the situations in specific places during specific historical periods. What brings these seemingly disparate case studies together is a common sense that an attention to the reality of nation, via whatever manner of governance, is not only consistent with the left's historical political prerogatives but in most cases a prerequisite for this politics. I will walk through a number of such governance arrangements, but will spend the most time with federalism, largely because I believe that it offers the most space for the robust recognition of the multinational reality that defines the globalized twenty-first century. Before getting to federalism, though, I will also seek to explain how different political and cultural regimes (ethnos, republic, and commonwealth) can also recognize that reality in ways consistent with the historical prerogatives of the left.

All to say, I want to offer a *progressive* defence of the nation. I believe that a defence of the national idea is also a defence of the historical (and, I hope, the contemporary) ideals of the left. I take these generally to include rationalism, a faith in collective action that is coupled with a robust defence of difference, a vision of social justice that calibrates its concerns by attention to the situation of the most marginal figures in society, and a belief that sustained progress towards such goals is possible. In some ways, I am led by a statement made by the Irish writer Desmond Fennell in that most revolutionary year of 1968:

> If the Republic [of Ireland] were not governed by practising Catholics who profess allegiance to the social encyclicals of Pope John and if the terms "right" and "left" were taken seriously in Irish politics (which they are not), then the present Irish State-society would be described as "leftist." The circumstances of its origin, the decisive role of public ownership in the economy (much greater than in Sweden, say, after thirty years of "Socialist" government), the Church-State relationship, the commitment to social redistribution of income and control of private business, the virtual abolition of capital punishment, the relative classlessness of society, Irish loyalty to the UNO, and Irish policies in the United Nations Assembly on Communist China, nuclear disarmament, and the Afro-Asian nations, Ireland's non-membership of NATO – all these factors would qualify the Irish State-society as "left," and consideration of this fact helps to characterize the human circumstances in which Irish Catholicism is developing.[6]

I think this is an enunciation of left politics that is startling for many rea
sons. One is its simple precision: there are specific issues that can be clearly
named, issues that are completely consistent with leftism's historical commitment to the protection of the most vulnerable in society, from one's
neighbours ("the commitment to social redistribution of income") all the
way up to the level of geopolitics ("The circumstances of its origin"; "Irish
loyalty to the UNO"; "the Afro-Asian nations, Ireland's non-membership of
NATO"), and everywhere in between ("the decisive role of public ownership
in the economy"; "control of private business, the virtual abolition of capital
punishment," etc.). It is also startling because it gives the lie to the absurd
fiction that until about five years ago the Republic of Ireland was some sort
of right-wing hellscape. That sense, too widespread among Ireland's youth
especially, comes from an assumption that justice is only meaningful when
couched in individualist terms. That sort of liberal individualism, however
one might feel about it as an ideology, is obviously not the *only* way to see
the world. A critique of such an approach to liberalism will also play a central
role in this book.

Fennell has generally (although perhaps erroneously) been understood by
his Irish readers as being on the right; thus it is appropriate to invoke him before saying that throughout this book (although especially in this introduction) I will temper some of this idealism about what the left could be with a
general sense of gloominess that I have come to see as, more or less, "conservative." Anyone who reads mainstream conservative thought cannot fail to be
struck by the overall sense of a tragic view of history, one that accounts for
conservative scepticism towards the projects of progressivism. This is particularly true in Catholic circles; readers of *First Things*, the leading magazine
of the American Catholic right, will know that this tragic view infuses everything in their pages, and that this view is inseparable from a broader religious
analysis that begins with the fact of humankind's fallen nature (this is one of
the things to which the magazine's title refers). But left circles have long been
home to a defence of nation as well. David Edgerton's sprawling 2018 history
The Rise and Fall of the British Nation recalls of the immediately post-WWII
Labour Party that "[i]t wanted a classless nation, one in which the working
class would dissolve into its proper place in the nation. But the nation was a
higher thing than class, or socialism."[7] Elsewhere he writes that "British capitalism put class before nation, while the left put nation before class"[8] and that
"on the left especially, but not exclusively, the failure to be national enough

was seen as the central problem with the United Kingdom in the past, and into the present."[9] These are the kinds of perspectives that inform the arguments of this book, even though I differ sharply from Edgerton about the specific nation in question. His history is of a liberal, outward-looking "British nation" that gradually replaced an older imperial model. He has relatively little to say about England, Scotland, and Wales as such (although he devotes one of his twenty chapters to Northern Ireland), and that is the order of nation that this book will be concerned with. I more or less understand what Edgerton means by "the British nation," but I think that is a very approximate sense of the national reality of the United Kingdom, before or after WWII.[10] Edgerton's description of the left's defence of nation, however, is entirely consistent with what will follow here. In some ways, my analyses are closest of all to Timothy Brennan's classic 1990 essay "The National Longing for Form." I am very much in sympathy with Brennan's statement that "[t]his impatience with the apparently divisive and warlike character of 'nation-statism' is very common among European critics in the postwar period, who work either within a Marxist tradition of 'internationalism' or a liberal tradition of sensible 'patriotism,' perhaps most of all in England and the United States where even Left social critics (until very recently) have ritually denounced 'imperialism' while withdrawing their support from the oppositional forces that imperial legacy has inevitably unleashed."[11]

That tradition of anti-national internationalism is alive and well in contemporary Marxist discourse, at least in English, and this book stands in (more-or-less) friendly opposition to it. Overall that opposition is strongly motivated by Jawaharlal Nehru's sense, offered in his 1946 prison memoir *The Discovery of India* (which I will discuss in more detail later on in this book), that "a real internationalism is not something in the air without roots or anchorage. It has to grow out of national cultures and can only flourish to-day on the basis of freedom and equality and true internationalism."[12] Contrast this with Thomas Miley's 2023 book *Self-Determination Struggles*, where he draws a hard line between such struggles and nationalism as such. Early on he writes hopefully of "the emergence, from below, of a new, direct-democratic, and anti-statist conceptualization and praxis of struggle for self-determination."[13] Miley sees the Kurdish movement as exemplary; praising the imprisoned leader of the Kurdistan Worker's Party Abdullah Öcalan (PKK), he writes that "he manages an impressive re-articulation of self-determination, away from the goal of an independent nation-state, instead positioning himself in favour of a form of radical, direct democracy against the state."[14] I can see how such an analysis is consistent with a suspicion of authority and coercion that is always part of state or for that matter national solidity, a suspicion that has certainly been central to much thought on the progressive left.

But I also think that it is no minor matter that Miley's rejection of national identity and state formations comes from a *Turkish* context. Turkey has kept Abdullah Öcalan in prison as long as it has as part of a larger project of brutal repression against any enunciations of Kurdish nationalism. The Kurds have it very, very bad under the Turkish state, and they have for a long time. The Kurds in Iraq, on the other hand, have achieved a near-total devolution for the area now legally known as the "Kurdistan Region" (هەرێمی کوردستان) in in Kurdish; إقليم کردستان in Arabic). The Kurdish language has official status there; its parliament in Erbil makes most of the decisions that affect the everyday lives of the Kurdish people living there. The matter of rejecting all state formations and the national identities that sometimes enable them as a matter of being either disempowered or complicit in the crimes of "the plutocrats, the tyrants and the war-mongers," which is what Miley argues will be the case "so long as the cult of the nation continues to mystify our consciousness,"[15] can seem always and tragically true from the perspective of a Turkish prison cell. From the perspective of a devolved parliament where deputies can speak their own language and know that their region is *by far* the best-functioning part of a state that has been otherwise shattered by an American invasion, the significance of national identity in achieving the historical goals of the progressive left looks very different indeed.

This sense of nations (and not just states) as being a check against the idealist sensibilities of internationalists of various stripes, Marxists and imperialists alike, is particularly present in contemporary Europe, where conservative critics of the European Union often use the figure of sovereign nation-states as a foil for what they see as the overreach of a liberal-technocratic Bruxelles elite. This analysis is becoming more and more prominent in eastern Europe, that is to say the "Visegrád Group" of the Czech Republic, Poland, Hungary, and Slovakia, all of which have been recent homes to right-wing governments that have been causing the social-democratic and liberal-leaning forces of western Europe no small amount of concern. This is clearly not what Brennan had in mind in terms of "the oppositional forces that imperial legacy has inevitably unleashed," but it is folly to ignore them. Anne Applebaum has written about exactly this tension in her recent book *Twilight of Democracy*, which is an extended version of her cover story in the October 2018 issue of *The Atlantic*. Both are instructive inasmuch as they are explicit about the degree to which her critique is from a right-liberal perspective, even though throughout she presents that critique as a more simplistically moral distinction between "open" and "closed" visions of national belonging. I am no fan of Hungary's right-wing premier Viktor Orbán or his fellow travellers in *Mitteleuropa*, but Appelbaum's sense of the present state of central and eastern Europe strikes me as (1) far too enthusiastic about the terrific things that await all those who embrace a mishmash of Euro-American liberalism and (2) too patronizing by half towards those who remain sceptical.[16]

To put matters in a more Canadian context, I am strongly motivated in this defence of the nation by the tradition of the "Red Tory." Gad Horowitz famously defined this distinctively northern political animal in his review of George Grant's 1965 book *Lament for a Nation*: "a conscious ideological conservative with some 'odd' socialist notions … or a conscious ideological socialist with some 'odd' tory notions."[17] My work in this book will proceed more or less from the latter position: in defence of the broad contours of democratic socialism, but with some "odd" notions, some of which are derived from thinkers that seem to be more right than left.

Grant was writing as part of a long tradition of English-language conservatism. G.K. Chesterton's 1904 novella *The Napoleon of Notting Hill* is a dystopic fantasy set in a future where nations no longer exist, until the titular neighbourhood of London declares independence. Summoning the image of comparably impractical national formations, Chesterton writes:

"But Nicaragua …" began Barker, with great hesitation, "Nicaragua is no longer a …"

"Nicaragua has been conquered like Athens. Nicaragua has been annexed like Jerusalem," cried the old man, with amazing fire. "The Yankee and the German and the brute powers of modernity have trampled it with the hoofs of oxen. But Nicaragua is not dead. Nicaragua is an idea."[18]

That *idée qui ne sait pas mourir*, to invoke Louis Hémon's *Maria Chapdelaine*, is what Grant is seeking to defend, more from Athens than from Jerusalem but definitely from the Yankee and the German alike. He, like Chesterton, is looking to literally *conserve* cultural difference from the forces of a totalizing modernity. In this way, both are clearly in the line of an anti-capitalist form of conservatism that is enjoying something of an unlikely

American renaissance in the form of neo-traditionist intellectual journalists of the right, such as Ross Douthat (in *The New York Times*) and Rod Dreher (in *The American Conservative*).

By way of giving a taste of ways progressive nationalists might learn from a certain kind of conservative, an *amuse-bouche* if you will, I would point to a thinker who, before his death in 2019, had made a profession of angering the left through much merciless ridicule. Roger Scruton was in many ways a "conservative's conservative," forever arguing, always in cool tones, for the importance of high culture, historical awareness, better architecture, traditional modes of family life, and so on.[19] He was a dyed-in-the-wool Cold Warrior, having done serious and often dangerous cultural work in communist-era Poland, Hungary, and Czechoslovakia (Applebaum recalls in *Twilight of Democracy* how she was one of his couriers in those days);[20] he was subsequently honoured by all three post-Communist national governments. I will discuss him in greater detail when we reach the chapter that deals with England and the United Kingdom. For our present introductory purposes, however, his work devoted to defending the idea of the nation is significant. In a 1990 essay called "In Defence of the Nation" (collected in his 1990 book *Philosopher on Dover Beach*), he sets out four preconditions for national belonging: shared language, shared associations, shared history, and common culture. I disagree that the first is imperative, as I hope that my discussions in later chapters of multilingual nations such as India, Ireland, and the Métis will bear out (to say nothing of a country I don't spend much time with in this book, Switzerland). The other three preconditions, on the other hand, should not be seen as out of place in an analysis informed by the historic priorities of the international left. Indeed, a figure no less significant than the aforementioned Jawaharlal Nehru wrote as much in *The Discovery of India* when he asserted that "[n]ationalism is essentially a group memory of past achievements, traditions and experiences, and nationalism is stronger to-day [1946] than it has ever been."[21] These definitions of nationalism seem wholly logical, in no small part because they are also inseparable from the other aspect of national identity that Scruton discusses, which is *territorial.* As he winds down the argument of "In Defence of the Nation," Scruton points to the failure of the Ottoman Empire, writing that "its subject peoples, having (apart from the Turks and the Lebanese) no national but only a confessional loyalty, showed no disposition to defend their territory collectively, or to recognize a common jurisdiction over the people who resided there."[22] For Scruton, as for many progressives, this sort of monological view is inadequate; it is a *national* view, one that can encompass Christians, Muslims, and countless others in its sense of a group whose shared memory, associations, history, and culture come from the experiences found in specific territories, not cosmologies.

Scruton echoes this sense of nations as the defenders of *diversity* in a booklet published in 2004 (and then revised in 2006) called *England and the Need for Nations*. He writes there that "the first-person plural of nationhood, unlike those [pronouns] of tribe or religion, is intrinsically tolerant of difference."[23] By insisting on this, he seems to implicitly answer a question that the sociologist Charles Tilly asked in a 1993 article titled "National Self-Determination as a Problem for All of Us": "In a more utopian vein, by what means other than establishing one independent state per mobilized nation can might we guarantee cultural variability, civic connectedness, protection of minorities, and other desiderata commonly portrayed as benefits of national self-determination?"[24] The answer I, following Sir Roger, would offer goes something like: "by making a habit of recognizing more than one nation in a state, and by in turn recognizing that those nations themselves are the repository of cultural variability, civic connectedness, minorities worthy of protection, and other desiderata of national *recognition*." Perhaps I could say it more briefly: by the means of always distinguishing "the nation" from "the state." Tilly says as much elsewhere, writing in a 1994 article called "States and Nationalism in Europe 1492–1992" that "precious few of the world's existing states have approximated the homogeneity and commitment conjured up by the label 'nation-state,'"[25] and in a paper of the same year titled "Time of States" that the early states of the eighteenth century "created the powerful idea, although rarely anything like the reality, of the nation-state: the coherent, homogeneous people matched to its own state."[26]

Scruton's language in the *England* pamphlet also clearly anticipates the more sociological treatment of Gérard Bouchard. Conservatives like Scruton and progressives like Bouchard (Tilly seems to more or less come up the middle) have historically defended difference in what may seem like competing ways, many of which have to do with the role that the state should play in that defence (and as I will show in this book, the matter has by no means been as simple as the left reliably being either for or against such a role). But that defence of difference is a genuine point of intersection.

That defence is also core to the work done by Tom Nairn in *Faces of Nationalism* (1997). Some of that book is dated now, being heavily invested in the experience of eastern Europe of the 1990s and the pre-devolution era of

Scottish politics. But much of it remains relevant for present-day considerations, something that is true of Nairn's work overall, including his even-
more-dated *The Break-Up of Britain* (originally published in 1977 and
subsequently revised several times, most recently in 2015). Particularly important is his sense, offered at the opening of *Faces of Nationalism*, that "there
is, naturally, nothing left-wing about internationality. It is bourgeois, capitalist
Progress incarnate."[27] I can hear echoes there of Kimberlé Crenshaw's statement that "[a]t this point in history, a strong case can be made that the most
critical resistance strategy for disempowered groups is to occupy and defend
a politics of social location rather than to vacate and destroy it."[28] That is to
say, there is no reason to believe that vacating and destroying a sense of *location* will do anything for the constituencies that the left has sought to defend,
either at this point in history or when Crenshaw was writing (in 1991). That
sort of evasion will only benefit the powerful in the way that it seizes a he-
gemonic position without acknowledging that it is a position at all. Everyone
has a location, something that is at the heart of Crenshaw's conceptualization
of "intersectionality." A rational view of the world will acknowledge that
simple fact instead of pretending to rise above it on the way to Mount Olym-
pus. Nationality is part of that location. In an essay about Scotland, Nairn
writes explicitly about the agendas that hide behind national indifference:

> A fear of philosophical relativism often attaches to any admission of just
> how biased speculation normally is by a theorist's or historian's national
> background. In my view, this is wholly unfounded. It nearly always ema-
> nates from some metropolitan thought-world within which the thinker
> assumes his or her privileged and instinctive access to the universal. Its
> standard accompaniment is cant about the Enlightenment (menaced,
> sinking, to be saved from the masses without delay, etc.).[29]

Given Nairn's acidic sense of a widespread reluctance to acknowledge what
hipper scholars call "positionality," at this point I should put my own cards
on the table. I primarily identify as an English Canadian, and most of what I
am writing here comes from that perspective. But there are some caveats. The
first is that I am originally American (born in Philadelphia, raised in Colorado,
and with a BA from the University of Oregon). A certain amount of my sense
of English-Canadian culture derives from my upbringing in a country with
a sometimes-boisterous sense of patriotism. In coming to Canada (I arrived
in 1996 to do an MA at the University of Alberta and have not lived in the US

since) I was not seeking to leave patriotism as such behind, but rather to find a country where I felt better about adhering to it (in a non-boisterous way, of course). Over time I have evolved from that more-or-less liberal "sensible patriotism" that Timothy Brennan mentions in his aforementioned chapter towards a more fiery, zeal-of-the-converted English-Canadian nationalism. And while I have never properly lived in the province of Quebec, I have spent a lot of time there since my first trip to Montreal in 1993 (by coincidence I arrived the day before the federal election that made the Bloc Québécois the official opposition). I have never known a life in Canada that did not involve being an enthusiastic student of Quebec culture. Specifically, I was indelibly formed by the historical memory of the sort of Quebec nationalism that Francine Pelletier has (in a book-length lament for the ethnocentric turn of such nationalism) ascribed specifically to the Parti Québécois as founded by René Lévesque: "The nationalism that the PQ promoted and which calls to me is a step beyond a strictly 'civic' nationalism: it is progressive. It actively promotes diversity"[30] (my translation; hereafter m.t.).

Indeed, I am convinced that what English Canada needs is a strong dose of Quebec-style, diversity-infused cultural nationalism. That is a position that would have been commonplace in Canadian nationalist circles of the 1960s and '70s. Scott Symons[31] enunciated my position in his (far from commonplace) 1967 novel *Combat Journal for Place d'Armes*:

> I can't say it in English, Luc … typically. But in French I can – "j'incarne un énorme besoin du Canada français" – just because I am English-Canadian … just because I love my own people, my own land, my own citizenship, my own family, so very much. You Canadiens are an essential part of my own will to live …[32] (ellipses in the original)

What I admire in Quebec culture is something that Nairn incorporates into his own political analyses: an awareness, not always explicit but always *there*, of a national identity. If I were being really honest, I'd likely admit that I miss that a little bit about the United States too. The widespread squeamishness about such matters in English Canada has been, along with hockey and poutine, the most serious barrier to my full integration up here. It is the great paradox of this place that the least English-Canadian thing about me is the force of my attachment to an English-Canadian identity. This defence of English Canada was once a more-or-less "left" position. In the second (1972) edition of his 1961 history of Canadian identity, W.H. Morton wrote that "it was

said by some continentalist Canadians that this outburst of Canadian nationalism was monopolized by the Left. In fact, the feeling was evident in all
parties and all aspects of Canadian society; it did not merely represent a
Socialist wish to 'nationalize.'"[33] In those 1960s and '70s a seemingly default-
left English-Canadian nationalism had to do with a locally controlled economy that seemed forever in danger of being taken over by the voraciously
imperialist capitalism of the United States, as well as with a desire to protect
a local culture that was forever in danger of being swamped by a no-less-
voraciously imperialist Anglophone mass entertainment manufactured in
that same southern republic. Today this progressive nationalism has vanished
from the landscape of the Canadian left, where it is much more common to
find either vehement denunciations of Canada as an illegitimate state built
upon genocide or vaguely embarrassed reactions to any talk of national identity, the latter of which is plainly an imitation of the progressive sensibilities
common in the United States.

Indeed, throughout this book I will evince an impatience with a "global"
political discourse that filters all manner of histories and present-day situations through an unspoken assumption that everything is understandable
as though it were happening in the United States. The frequency with which
Brexit was described by mainstream media commentators as a sort of British
Trumpism, even though the actual referendum happened four and a half
months before the real-estate salesman in question won the US presidential
election, is typical of this tendency to Yankify the entire planet. Canadian
commentators' total indifference to the specifics of Haitians in Quebec or of
African Nova Scotians in their coverage of the Black Lives Matter movement
is exemplary of the same phenomenon. American politics has come to be
understood by much of the mainstream media in Canada and the UK as a
kind of natural state of affairs. It's not so much that all politics are basically
global; increasingly, Anglophone media outlets assume that all politics are
basically American.

A critique of liberalism will also be a key theme throughout this book. I
want to make it clear that I am launching this critique from the left, and that
this is a well-worn path in modern left cultural criticism, particularly, it is
only fair to say it, in the United States.[34] Christopher Lasch's 1979 *The Culture
of Narcissism* is probably the most famous exemplar, but for me his more relevant works are the ones that came at the beginning and end of his career.
The New Radicalism in America 1889–1963: The Intellectual as Social Type, the
second monograph he published (his first was a revision of his dissertation

about American responses to the Russian Revolution), is a focussed historical study that is also deeply polemical, using detailed portraits of figures such as Jane Addams, Randolph Bourne, the editors of the Walter Lippman–era *New Republic*, and so on, as a means to critique the liberalism which he believed continued to define the American left of the 1960s. Something similar was going on in Lasch's longest book, 1991's *The True and Only Heaven: Progress and Its Critics*, which offered a series of in-depth studies of specific American-historical periods by way of arguing that progressive overreach has had an unmistakeably middle-class quality, something understood by many generations of populists more connected to an overall national consensus (Martin Luther King Jr among them). I will be seeking to follow this path via portraits of specific nationalist movements and manifestations, which will converge, I hope in the manner of *The New Radicalism in America* and *The True and Only Heaven*, in an overall argument: the nation remains a viable concept for progressives, despite the uneasiness evinced by the liberals who sometimes deceptively claim that political identity.

In so doing I will be making an argument for the validity of the sort of national identity that liberalism too often ignores because of the sometimes significant (but I believe generally legitimate) claims that such national identity makes on individuals. This rejection of any infringement on individual sovereignty was the subject of Lasch's final, posthumously published book (he died in 1994), the more explicitly polemical *The Revolt of the Elites and the Betrayal of Democracy*. Therein he traces the rise of an elite class utterly unhinged from the demands of locality, religion, nation, and to some extent family, all of which he argues had by the 1990s become increasingly disdained by upper-middle-class American professionals as unacceptable drags on the sovereignty of the individual. He argues, as I have mentioned above, that this "revolt" is little more than a justification of selfishness dressed up in the costume of liberation, something I will discuss when I come to Patrick Deneen, Lasch's "opposite number" on the American Catholic right.

Liberalism as defined by all of its major thinkers and texts (Locke, Paine, the *Federalist Papers*, and Mill, right up to Isaiah Berlin, Amartya Sen, and Martha Nussbaum) is based on the assumption of the individual as the basic repository of sovereignty. This is obviously at odds with the assumptions of the democratic left, again, going back to Marx, up through the French socialists such as Jean Jaurès, the Mensheviks of early Georgian independence, India's Congress Party, and the African socialism of the decolonizing and post-colonial period, all of which I will discuss at some point in this book. This broad left tradition has as a parallel·assumption the centrality of collective action, the imperative to work together as opposed to the protection of individual liberties. For liberals, of course, such action entails a potential (indeed likely) infringement on the sovereignty of individuals on the part of families, traditions, communities, nations, states, etc. This most liberals see as unacceptable, albeit not 100 per cent of the time. If an infringement of individual sovereignty is indeed acceptable, liberalism historically holds that the burden of proof for that legitimacy lies with the structure doing the infringing, never with the individual. Indeed, it is the individual who needs to finally benefit from such an infringement.

This is explicit in Locke, and in ways that are important for our considerations here. In his 1664 text *Essays on the Law of Nature*, he wrestled with the question of individual autonomy and its connection to a sense of communal good. He writes at one point of people who "have maintained that justice and equity should not be measured by extraneous law, but should be assessed by each individual in the light of his own interest. However, this unjust view has always been rejected by the wiser amongst mankind, those who retained some sense of common humanity, some concern with the welfare of society."[35] It is precisely this attention to "some sense of common humanity" as a force that tempers individualist excess that is important for this consideration of national identity. Extraneous forces (such as national cohesion) can bear down upon an individual, and if that individual is wise then she will reject the idea that this must be illegitimate purely because these forces are external to her. But in that same letter, Locke reveals the final motivation for this adhesion to such force: "Self-interest is not the foundation of the law of nature, or the reason for obeying it, although it is the consequence of obedience to it ... Thus the test of the rightness of an action is not whether it is self-interested; but rather a moral action is also self-interested, but only if it is right."[36] Here we can see the degree to which Locke really is the father of modern liberalism, as any course in political philosophy will teach you. An insistence on the primacy of the individual doesn't solely determine every decision about justice, but that primacy remains inseparable from those questions nevertheless. There is an exquisite oscillation at work here, a sense that of course one cannot just think of oneself, and yet one can't stop thinking of oneself either. That is the condition of much modern liberalism, particularly in the Anglophone world. This book is motivated instead by positions such as Charles Tilly's, enunciated in a 2003 article called "Political Identities in Changing Polities," which he concludes by writing that "[i]dentity processes, in short, do not merely concern people's individual states of mind. They figure centrally in the world's great political struggles today, as they did in sixteenth-century England."[37]

What I am keen to emphasize for our purposes here is that the term "liberal," in nearly every political culture, has long been incompatible with a left position; casual evocations of a "liberal left" are a product of a specifically American political climate.[38] The global spread of such evocations is a fairly recent, and I would argue incoherent, phenomenon. Applebaum, with whose analyses I generally disagree, is admirably lucid on this matter, no doubt as a result of her many years in eastern Europe. Distinguishing the group of post–Cold War European liberals with whom she identified from the current manifestations of the European hard-right, she writes in *Twilight of Democracy* that "perhaps devotion to Reagan is a bit too specific. What really held this group together – and what drew me to it as well – was a kind of post-Cold-War optimism, a sense that 'we had won' … This wasn't the nostalgic conservatism of the English; this was something more buoyant, more American, an optimistic conservatism that wasn't backward-looking at all."[39] Indeed not: it was *liberal*.

The way in which these kinds of statements fit neither into left nor right configurations are indicative of the degree to which Applebaum is a near-perfect embodiment of what Erica Benner calls "liberal-postnationalists." Discussion of this political animal comes at the end of her 1995 book *Really Existing Nationalisms*, which she revised in 2018 by way of taking a full account of the aftermath of the fall of the Berlin Wall. Most of that work is devoted to explaining the degree to which Marx and Engels's writings on national matters are more nuanced than most commentators have generally acknowledged, and the bulk of *Really Existing Nationalisms* has a quasi-exegetical quality when it comes to its attention to what that duo actually wrote.[40] But the concluding chapter, written for the 2018 edition, seems to be directly addressing figures such as Applebaum, as we can see when Benner says that "[f]oreign friends of post-communist liberalizers would … do well to remember that the freedoms they espouse are a luxury of the relatively secure and well-fed."[41] What she is alluding to there is a breezy liberalism that doesn't worry too much about the ravages of newly opened markets and doesn't really have any sense of what it's like to be part of a nation whose right to self-determination has been denied for decades or centuries by an imperial power, all of which seems to such a postnational liberal as awfully abstract and airy in comparison to the greater material freedoms of consumer capitalism. That Applebaum would have seen "something more buoyant, more American" developing on the post-Communist right is entirely consistent with Benner's analyses. She writes, for instance:

> Because the regimes which had hitherto "frozen" national aspirations were imperial and repressive, it seemed logical to infer that all anti-communist nationalism must be the mirror-image of what it opposed: it must, that is, be liberal and westward-looking. As it happened, nationalism after communism turned out to be more than one thing. Some of it was tied to the construction of liberal democracies, and sought to forge cooperative links with the world outside. But much of it was illiberal and anti-democratic, while more than a few of the most zealous anti-communist nationalists turned out to be formerly zealous communist anti-nationalists.[42]

This is the situation particularly of Hungary but really of the aforementioned "Visegrád Group" (again, the Czech Republic, Poland, Hungary, and Slovakia), none of which have governments that are particularly liberal or westward-looking (despite the 2023 elections which produced a coalition led by Donald Tusk's centre-right Civic Platform). The critique of the liberal post-nationalism that Benner offers in *Really Existing Nationalisms* serves as a sharp rejoinder to the position embodied by Applebaum's *Atlantic* article and subsequent book, but it also offers a just-as-key cautionary reminder: nationalism after communism has turned out to be more than one thing. Some of what the Anglophone right has to say about nation is useful for progressives to consider, but their embrace of (or sometimes just sympathetic apology for) that "thing" that is going on in Hungary (strongman authoritarianism) is not consistent with an ethical conservatism,[43] any more than the cringe-inducing sympathy for Castroist or Chavista regimes that was once part of life on the left was consistent with a progressivism worthy of the name.

In following this line laid down by figures such as George Grant and Christopher Lasch, I am conscious of rigorous and ethically serious defences of liberalism from more or less the same period; the best example of such work is that of C.B. Macpherson. While he is most famous in Canada for his 1964 Massey Lectures, published as the book *The Real World of Democracy*, the book that is most relevant for our purposes here is his 1973 collection *Democratic Theory: Essays in Retrieval*. Therein one can see him taking full stock of the various challenges to liberalism that defined the 1960s and '70s, and trying to figure out how a just politics might emerge from them (something similar could be said of Samuel Moyn's 2023 book *Liberalism Against Itself*, which is critical of the thought of the same period but unlike Macpherson's work is explicitly written from *inside* of liberalism). Macpherson writes at one point that "[i]n the other two-thirds of the world the leaders, with willing enough followers, have concluded that for their countries at least it would be imposs-ible to move towards the ultimate humanistic goals by liberal-democratic methods ... It is time we reflected, more seriously than we have generally done, on their reading of our society."[44] What spurred this reflection of Macpherson's was the sense that liberalism had turned out to be more inti-mately connected to base consumerism than its Enlightenment-inflected the-orists would have intended. "No liberal-democratic justifying theory can hope to be adequate in our time unless it considers people primarily as exerters and enjoyers of their human capacities, rather than as consumers of utilities."[45] This image of "exerters and enjoyers of their human capacities" strongly recalls Charles Taylor's notion of "fullness," which he explained in a very different context: as an "Afterword" to the 2010 collection *Varieties of Secularism in a Secular Age*, devoted to his massive 2007 work, *A Secular Age*. Writing in the collection, Taylor (whose work as a whole is a major influence on this book's conceptual framework) offered a semi-confession: "Let me come out of the closet and tell you what it means to be my kind of Catholic. I think we have a calling to understand very different positions, particularly very different un-derstandings of fullness."[46]

Obviously Macpherson does not explain what kind of Catholic he is. Rather, he is explaining what kind of political theorist he is: one who is con-cerned with the full range of human experience rather than with that narrow range that can be precisely quantified in basically economic terms. His argu-ment is that it has been liberalism that has, historically, presented what he calls "a more rounded concept of the state, which would recognize and em-brace the claims of society as well as the individual."[47] I follow thinkers such as Grant and Lasch in holding that this is an overly optimistic view of what liberalism has *actually* done historically. Indeed, Macpherson seems to hold something close to that, and no small part of *Democratic Theory* is devoted to the prospect that "we *need* a post-liberal-democratic theory"[48] (his italics); contrast this to Moyn's concluding statement that "[t]he task for liberals in our time is to imagine a form of liberalism that is altogether original."[49] The younger American, in a manner that has become typical of academic political disourse there, finds it very difficult to step outside of a liberal framework;

the older Canadian is far more self-aware and flexible. For Macpherson, "a post-liberal-democratic theory" is mostly a matter of political economy: that is to say, of conceptualizing liberalism in a way that does not seek to express everything in quasi-monetary terms. One of the goals of this book is to explain how this "post-liberal-democratic theory" can move beyond liberalism without leaving behind democracy, in the manner of Orbán and Castro alike. A fully fleshed-out understanding of national identity is part of that move.

Castroism and Orbánism, as they actually existed or at the time of this writing exist as attempts to redefine specific states along politically repressive lines, are ultimately beside the point; it is imperative, as I said in response to Charles Tilly, to distinguish between nations and states. Having said that, it doesn't follow from this that state formations are irrelevant for considerations of the nation. Very much the opposite is in fact the case. The primary issue is that the word "state" is often casually taken as a synonym for "nation" (by, say, the United Nations, which is clearly a grouping of *states*). Rather, states are a set of forces which regulate issues such as borders, currency, diplomatic relations, etc., and which enjoy (in Max Weber's memorable formulation) a "monopoly on violence" in the form of military and police forces. The sociological literature on the state is massive (as massive as that on the nation), but overall I am strongly influenced by Bob Jessop's 2015 survey *The State: Past, Present, Future*, wherein he lays out many of the understandings of the concept that are mainstream in both Sociology and International Relations. He writes early in the book that "the constitutionalization as well as the territorialization of political power are key features of the modern state, especially if one wants to distinguish legitimate authority based on the rule of law from domination by warlords and mafia-style organizations with different codes of right and wrong."[50] The management of power is, for Jessop (himself following Weber), a key aspect of the work that states do; the state's ability to make that power both legible and potentially ethical is what makes it possible to mount a defence of the structure that does not rely on ultimately opportunistic appeals to that management's effectiveness (in the manner of Vito Corleone). Jessop also critiques these disciplinary assumptions, not the least of which is the Eurocentric quality of most state theory. Wrestling with East Asia, he concludes that "Enlightenment categories are not well-suited to grasping the complexity and interdependence of economic and extra-economic activities, organizations, and institutions. Indeed, there are also good grounds for arguing that, even in the West, these categories are fetishistic and inadequate."[51]

In searching for more flexible conceptions, he moves towards a discussion of the "state-nation," a term coined by Alfred Stepan, Juan J. Linz, and Yogendra Yadav in a 2010 article. They write that "'[n]ation-state' policies stand for a political-institutional approach that tries to make the political boundaries of the state and the presumed cultural boundaries of the nation match ... Some very successful contemporary democracies such as Sweden, Japan, and Portugal are close to the ideal type of a unitary nation-state. Some federal states such as Germany and Australia have also become nation-states."[52] I don't at all accept that either Sweden or Australia are as mono-national as they suggest, given the reality of both Sámi and Indigenous-Australian nationalities. I am more convinced when they go on to say:

> By contrast, "state-nation" policies stand for a political-institutional approach that respects and protects multiple but complementary sociocultural identities. "State-nation" policies recognize the legitimate public and even political expression of active sociocultural cleavages, and they include mechanisms to accommodate competing or conflicting claims without imposing or privileging in a discriminatory way any one claim. "State-nation" policies involve creating a sense of belonging (or "we-feeling") with respect to the statewide political community, while simultaneously creating institutional safeguards for respecting and protecting politically salient sociocultural diversities. The "we-feeling" may take the form of defining a tradition, history, and shared culture in an inclusive manner, with all citizens encouraged to feel a sense of attachment to common symbols of the state and some form of "constitutional patriotism."[53]

It is precisely these sociocultural diversities that I will deal with in this book, diversities that exist in a wide variety of relationships with the states that they are part of.

The tension between state and nation is acute in North American Indigenous communities. The Inuit, the Métis, or the Mohawk (to take only the examples I will deal with in this book) may seem to be the epitome of "stateless nations," but matters are not as simple as that, if for no other reason than all three of these groups cross the borders of one state-nation – that is to say, Canada – and another nation-state that the Inuit, Métis, and Mohawk (among nearly countless others) show to really be a state-nation – the US (the Inuit homeland doubles this figure, encompassing the territory between Russia's far east and Greenland). Indeed, the political militancy on the part of these groups has been about establishing something that looks like the workings of a state but which departs from that model in important ways as well (we can see this in Inuit politics, which I will discuss in the conclusion). This was as true for the Métis at the Red River Settlement (whose political life has been so thoroughly analyzed and documented by Dale Gibson's two-volume *Law, Life and Government at Red River*) as it was at Batoche or, later, at St-Paul-des-Métis in Alberta (originally conceived as a sort of "Metis reserve," it was eventually overrun by French-Canadian settlers but also served as a kind of precursor to the Métis Settlements of Alberta). The Inuit in both Canada and Greenland have made major strides since the 1970s in securing de facto "home rule" arrangements via the creation of the territory of Nunavut in 1999 and the establishment of the Inatsisartut or Greenlandic parliament in 1979 and the *Lov om Grønlands Selvstyre* (2008), known in English as the 2008 *Self Government Act*. I will discuss all of this in the conclusion. The Mohawk, whom I will also discuss in the conclusion, are well-known in Canada for their efforts to enter both the US and Canada using Haudenosaunee passports (issued by the five-nation Haudenosaunee Confederacy of which they are a part), and for the 1990 standoff at Oka where a militia drawn from three Mohawk communities engaged the Canadian army following the retreat of the Sûreté du Québec (Quebec's provincial police force). All of this quasi-state-building is consistent with efforts on the part of Sámi communities, for instance, to establish parliaments in countries where they have a historical presence (very much including Sweden, where the devolved parliament in Kiruna is called the Sametinget, or the Sámediggi in Sámi), even as they stop short of explicitly separatist aspirations. A pan-state body with representatives from Sweden, Norway, Finland, and Russia (that is to say, the territory known as Sápmi) exists as the body known in English as the Sámi Council and in Sámi as Sámiráđđi, but this is not a legislature or governing body as such; it is part of the world of NGOs. The Inuit have had much more success on that front in the form of the Inuit Circumpolar Council. The ICC stands as a cooperative body that is slowly trying to take back authority from the states in question, mostly in matters of language, culture, and land stewardship. Rather than being "stateless," I would posit that many Indigenous nations are seeking out something like a new kind of state, building apparatuses that are centred not in the Weberian "monopoly on violence" but rather in these matters that a group such as the ICC focusses on: language, culture, land management, etc. – that is to say, matters more traditionally tied to nationhood.

I am somewhat reluctant to invoke Benedict Anderson's 1983 book *Imagined Communities* here, given its status as an extremely over-quoted text. But his recollection of how nationality is dependent on "a deep, horizontal comradeship"[54] is indispensable, perhaps even more so than the so-widely quoted and to my eyes somewhat cryptic formulation of an "imagined community." A key part of my effort in this book will be to rescue the nation from the clutches of "the ethnic," a concept of belonging that is largely based on bloodlines. In so doing I am following the model of Hubert Aquin, whose collection *Blocs erratiques*, published in the year he died, 1977, had an indelible effect on me in my first year of graduate school, my first year of living in this country, in 1996 (my well-worn copy is the 1982 reprint). He writes in a celebrated essay collected therein called "La fatigue culturelle du Canada français":

> The nation is not, as Trudeau suggests, an ethnic reality. Ethnic homogeneity no longer exists, or at least is very rare … One has simply to look around among one's personal acquaintances to count the number of old-stock French Canadians who are not "real" French Canadians: Mackay, Johnson, Elliot, Aquin, Molinari, O'Harlety, Spénart, Esposito, Globenski, etc. … In fact, the French Canadian people has been replaced by a cultural-linguistic group whose common denominator is language. The same thing will happen to the Wolofs, Seres, and Fulani in Senegal who, if nothing interrupts the process of education and the resulting eventual formation of a cultural linguistic group of varied ethnic origin, will one day become Senegalese.[55]

To some extent this is as simple a matter as saying that I, like Aquin and countless others, favour a civic view of national identity. It is tempting to just do so and leave it at that. But "nation" and "ethnicity" are indeed entangled in the present imagination, and it is imperative to explain why this is, exactly. The only instance where this conflation is more common than popular misunderstandings of the Indigenous communities I have just discussed in passing is with the case of Black nationalism, the subject of the next chapter, devoted to "Ethnos." I will do my best in that chapter to explain that while I accept that ethnicity can be a meaningful identity marker (as it so obviously has been with Black people worldwide), the recent political histories of those communities have shown how much the rhetoric of the most important radicals inevitably shifts away from race or ethnicity and towards what Aimé Césaire so evocatively calls "that initiative of *nationalities*."

In this way I am also strongly influenced by Paul Gilroy, the founding director of the Centre for the Study of Race and Racism at University College
London and a major figure in the development of cultural studies. The key
text on this specific matter is clearly his 2000 book *Against Race: Imagining
Political Culture beyond the Culture Line*. He writes there that "[t]he order of
active differentiation that gets called 'race' may be modernity's most pernicious signature. It articulates reason and unreason. It knits together science
and superstition. Its specious ontologies are anything but spontaneous and
natural. They should be awarded no immunity from prosecution amid the
reveries of reflexivity and the comfortable forms of inertia induced by capitulation to the lazy essentialisms that postmodern sages inform us we cannot escape."[56] I am not exactly prosecuting this concept, as Gilroy suggests,
but nor am I granting it immunity in the manner of contemporary theoretical sages who either avoid or attack forms such as the nation because they
seem so predetermined and non-fluid while leaving concepts such as race
either unmentioned or uncritiqued. Rather, I am mostly refusing to engage
this most pernicious signature of modernity, this "specious ontology" that
"knits together science and superstition," by insisting throughout that concepts such as "race" or "ethnicity" must not be conflated with "nationality."
That said, I will spend the first chapter of this book arguing that the situation
of race and ethnicity is far more complex and that its discourse, at least in
the case of Africa and her diaspora, is much closer to that of *nation* than it
may at first appear.

In some ways that tale begins with a single capital letter. Capitalizing the
"B" in "Black" has become standard practice in progressive circles not simply
to give a typographical leg up to a minority who has had a hard time of things.
Rather, the capital "B" recognizes that "Black" is not just an adjective but rather
a specific community. African-American and African-Canadian communities
are highly diverse in terms of ethnic origins and always have been, but much
of the pre-wwii specifics of those diverse origins were lost in the experience
of enslavement, whose apparatus took no notice of such finer points of cultural belonging. Thus to say "Black" in North America or the Caribbean could
mean anything from Akan to Zulu, with Bambara, Bantu, Dogon, Ibo, Luba,
Yoruba, and countless others in between. For most African-Americans and
African-Canadians (at least of the "indigenous Black" heritage that I will discuss at greater length in the next chapter), this kind of detail is lost to history;
they are Black, which is their ethnic reality just as Akan might have been for
their early-nineteenth-century ancestors. In his essay on Steve McQueen's

2020 series of films known as *Small Axe*[57] (there are five in total), Gary Younge offers an optimistic view of this basic process, recalling how "[i]n time, a particular, hybrid cosmopolitan Black British identity emerged that borrowed and integrated a variety of influences from what one of its most prominent intellectual voices, the aforementioned Paul Gilroy, has called 'The Black Atlantic' (Gilroy was a consultant on the series). Through the sweep of *Small Axe*, we see that identity in the making but not yet quite made."[58] The emergence of this cosmopolitan but also cohesive identity *within* Britishness speaks to the kind of complexity and flexibility within contemporary manifestations of national identity that I am seeking to defend. So in British and North American English alike, "Black" gets a capital letter for the same reason "Akan" or "Jamaican" do. "White" tends not to attract such capitalization because for most white people in North America these origins are not lost, nor are they generally fused into the sort of cosmopolitan hybrid identity that Young, following Gilroy, is alluding to. I consider myself English Canadian, but I know that my mid-nineteenth- and early-twentieth-century heritage is mostly Irish and Italian, terms that I capitalize for exactly the same reasons I would capitalize "Yoruba," "English Canadian," or for that matter "Black." In an ethnic context, "white" really is an adjective, in a way that "Black," at least in North America, isn't.[59]

There is a comparable dynamic at work in most Indigenous nations, which get a capital "I" for similar reasons: to distinguish them as part of an experience specific to settler-colonial states, and thus distinct from, say, Iceland's long quest for an indigenous film industry (a situation where "indigenous" really is just an adjective) or, as we will see in the next chapter, Nova Scotia's "indigenous Black" community. Most Indigenous nations are heterogeneous in terms of ethnicity; the concept of "blood quantum" is colonial to the core, and has certainly been effective at diluting claims to Indigenous nationhood as generations progress. Having said that, Kim Tall Bear has written that "[t]here are problems with blood quantum, but the concept is not only about biological essentialism or an uncritical take-up of Eurocentric modes; ideas about relatedness that go to the heart of what is unique about the tribe also ground its continuing use."[60] Tall Bear is, however, well-known in Indigenous studies for her critiques of strictly genetic understandings of Indigenous belonging, and in various public fora was sharply critical of US presidential candidate Elizabeth Warren's claim to Cherokee identity.[61]

Perhaps ironically, for the purposes of this book it is actually most useful to quote the recent ruling by the Supreme Court of the Cherokee Nation, which was adjudicating on the matter of their constitution's deployment of the term "by blood," which undercut the citizenship rights of Black people who traced their ancestors to people enslaved by the Cherokees in the mid-nineteenth century. The "Discussion" section of Justice Shawna S. Baker's opinion for the court opens with this:

> On war-torn soil in Indian Territory during Reconstruction, thousands of miles from their respective homelands, the heartbeats of three First Nations, the Cherokees, the Shawnees, and the Delawares, and three continents of flesh tones and cultures, Native Americans, African Americans and adopted or intermarried European Americans, were forced to coalesce and weave together a single nation to be known by only one name henceforth: the Cherokee Nation.[62]

The distinction between "the Cherokees" and "the Cherokee Nation" is crucial for our purposes here. The former is an ethnic group, and thus bases its membership on an individual's essentially biological heritage. The latter formulation, on the other hand, is a *nation*: a community of people whose membership is based on a sense of both a common history and a shared future, a sense that can be offered to newcomers and thus to those newcomers' descendants in a way that ethnicity cannot.

Anderson is clear, almost poetically so, on this matter. In a chapter of *Imagined Communities* titled "Patriotism and Racism," he suggests a musical metaphor for national belonging, one that visualizes the communitarianism that I have been emphasizing: "No matter how banal the words and mediocre the tunes, there is in this singing an experience of simultaneity ... Singing the Marseillaise, Waltzing Matilda, and Indonesian Raya provide occasions for unisonality, for the echoed physical realization of the imagined community." In the next paragraph, he comes to the heart of the matter:

> Yet such choruses are joinable in time. If I am a Lett [a Latvian], my daughter may be an Australian. The son of an Italian immigrant to New York will find ancestors in the Pilgrim Fathers. If nationalness has about it an aura of fatality, it is nonetheless a fatality embedded in *history*. Here San Martin's edict baptizing Quechua-speaking Indians as "Peruvians" – a movement that has affinities with religious conversion – is exemplary. For it shows that from the start the nation was conceived in language, not in blood, and that one could be "invited into" the imagined com-

munity. Thus today, even the most insular nations accept the principle of *naturalization* (wonderful word!), no matter how difficult in practice they may make it.[63]

I think Anderson is being somewhat gestural when he says that "the nation was conceived in language," and I discuss examples where linguistic difference definitely does not signify national difference, Ireland being the clearest example, India being a more arguable case. In any event, the "not in blood" clause is key; nations are not at all the same as ethnicities, at least not in the modernity-enabled forms that Anderson argues are the real deal, so to speak. That is the kind of nation that I intend to defend in this book.

Although I can see Anderson's importance, my understanding of "the nation" as a concept is more fully underwritten by Gérard Bouchard. Here I am thinking especially of the work that he has done to enunciate "interculturalism" as an integration-centred alternative to "multiculturalism" (a term that has little support in Quebec because of a widespread sense that the government of Pierre Trudeau introduced it into Canadian life as a means of undercutting Quebec's claims to distinctiveness, effectively saying that they could get in line with the Irish and the Ukrainians and the Cree in an infinitely diverse but also fundamentally homogeneous state formation). I discuss "interculturalism" on multiple occasions in this book, as we will see in the "Federations" chapter where I discuss the degree to which I think it is actually as suitable a model for English Canada as for Quebec. But for introductory purposes, I turn to Bouchard's more recent book *Les nations savent-elles encore rêver?* which deals with the structures of "national myths" in numerous places. Explaining what he believes constitutes a nation, echoing Ernst Renan's famous line that "l'existence d'une nation est un plébiscite de tous les jours," Bouchard writes:

> I would offer a fairly consensual definition, a nation being a population that: (a) Perceives itself as a nation; (b) Shares an identity, that is to say a common vision of itself and of the Other, as well of its being; (c) Nourishes a feeling of belonging; (d) Adheres to the rule of law; (e) Has a recognized territorial seat; (f) Is endowed with any form of government, which does not necessarily need to be that of a sovereign state (one thinks of Catalonia, or Scotland, or Quebec) or (g) Aspires to a form of either autonomy or sovereignty.[64] (m.t.)

The most crucial of these for our present purposes are (f) and (g), and these points echo what a number of theorists of multiculturalism have set out in terms of the differing demands of various cultural groups, not all of which are necessarily nations. The best known such formulation is probably from Will Kymlicka's 1995 book *Multicultural Citizenship*, wherein he distinguishes between what he calls "Three forms of Group-Differentiated Rights,"[65] each of which he can identify in Canada: "(1) Self-government rights" (he gives Quebec and Indigenous nations as examples), "(2) Polyethnic rights" (he gives Sikhs as an example, specifically their desire to be exempt from motorcycle helmet laws so they can continue to wear the turban; elsewhere he mentions their desire to do so while still joining the RCMP),[66] and "(3) Special representation rights" (he presents arguments about "reserved seats" for "ethnic and racial minorities, women, the poor, the disabled, etc." in the House of Commons and Senate).[67] I understand that there can be some slippage between these formations, but for the purposes of this book we will be concerned almost exclusively with Kymlicka's (1), which is to say self-government rights, because it is only this group that fulfills Bouchard's (f) and (g), which is to say the desire for both a state or semi-state apparatus (which may stop short of achieving a fully independent nation-state, complete with an army, postage stamps, a seat at the UN, etc.) and some form of autonomy (which, again, may stop short of full separation). These are the considerations that distinguish nations (Sikh militants in India, whose collective quest for Khalistan is mostly but not exclusively separatist) from rights-seeking cultural groups (Sikh activists in English Canada or Quebec, whose desire for accommodation is based on exactly the opposite impulse, which is to more closely *integrate* into the nation via serving in the RCMP while wearing a turban or attending French-language schools while wearing the ceremonial dagger known as a kirpan). It is not correct to simply lump all of this under "minorities" and assume that these communities have more or less the same aspirations. Multicultural and intercultural considerations will come up in this book, but always in the context of how they form (or obscure the existence of, as we will see when we discuss the English, the Métis, etc.) the reality of *nations*.

In any event, Bouchard's definition of nations captures the combination of the ephemeral sense of togetherness and the concrete presence of *some* sort of political apparatus (not necessarily that of the classical state but maybe not so different from it either) that I have been alluding to throughout this introduction. But I have internalized a statement he makes towards the end of *Les nations savent-elles encore rêver?*: "It is unrealistic to think that humans can, one day, leave behind emotions, identity, memory, *solidarités de proximité*, dreams and myths. Faced with this impossible perspective, maybe we want to bet on nations that are capable of reforming themselves in accord with a world that is to be remade"[68] (m.t.). I'll take that bet, because I do indeed see the alternatives as sterile.

A search for connections beyond the sterile individualism of liberalism is the basis, I believe, for a defence of the nation that springs from the progressive traditions of the left in terms of a belief in the value of collective action. This vision of the nation also remains relevant in a globalized age where it sometimes seems inevitable that the universal, homogenized state of liberalism's dreams is just about to achieve its final dominion. I thus find myself in complete agreement with Yael Tamir's assessment that "[n]ational sentiments ... should be used to induce a readiness to rebuild a cross-class coalition, giving individuals worthwhile reasons to work together to promote the common good, securing a more just distribution of risks and opportunities."[69] That is from the conclusion to her 2019 book *Why Nationalism*, a work that goes a long way toward recovering a progressive view of national identity in the language of concrete political realities, much of which is obviously derived from her Israeli-socialist background (she has been active in the Israeli peace movement since the 1980s, and as a member of the Labour Party served as a minister in two governments). It comes from a different place politically than her countryman Yoram Hazony's *The Virtue of Nationalism*, published the same year, even if it shares with that more conservative book an openness to communitarian approaches that strikes me as distinctly Israeli. Tamir's book, a follow-up to her 1995 (arguably mistitled) study *Liberal Nationalism*,[70] is a breath of fresh air in a field of study that has for some while been preoccupied with insoluble and often circular arguments about unity vs diversity, imaginary vs concrete, etc. Like Gérard Bouchard and Roger Scruton, she and Yoram Hazony are ostensibly opposed but in fact similar thinkers who hover (mostly implicitly but from time to time via quotation) over a lot of what will follow in this book. These thinkers, opposed though they may seem, all support the fundamental argument I want to make in this book: the nation is far from dead, and the time is right to reconsider the ways in which it continues to live on.

CHAPTER 1

Ethnos

One of my fundamental assumptions about the definition of "nation" is that such a structure has nothing to do with ethnicity. It is easy to assume that nationalism goes hand in hand with ethnocentrism, something that has been visible in all too many cases, from American to Yugoslavian, A to Y, so to speak. No small part of why progressive thought has often been dismissive of nationality is precisely because of this mistaken conflation with "ethnicity." The national identities I will focus on in this book, on the other hand, are multiethnic in various ways. French, Irish, Georgian, Indian, New Zealander, Québécois, English, Catalan, English-Canadian, Métis, Inuit: all of these groups are complex and multifarious in terms of their ethnic makeup (think Catalans in France, Protestants in Ireland, people of Haitian descent in Quebec, the Greek community in Georgia, or the combination of Cree, Saulteaux, and Ojibwe that were part of the ethnogenesis of the Métis, all of which I will discuss as we move forward). The difference between "the Cherokees" and "the Cherokee Nation" that I discussed in the introduction is a distinction that will define most of this book. So I want to start out with the exception. That is to say, rather than the concept of multiethnic forms of nationality, which is what is going to form the core of this defence of the nation, I want to explain the reality of a multinational form of ethnicity.

Because if you are looking for a sense of how diverse and complex the concept of "nation" is, I would suggest that Africa and her diaspora provide a good starting place. This is a useful starting point because of my desire to separate the nation and the state as much as possible. Within Africa and her diaspora (an *ethnos* of sorts, but as we will see one that is diverse in *national* terms) we find a wide variety of understandings of "nation," understandings that are nevertheless evocations of *national* consciousness. One of these specificities is at the very least British, and more likely (as I will argue in chapter

4) English. That specificity was a key part of the flourishing of Black British cinema in the 1980s, led by avant-gardists such as John Akomfrah and somewhat more conventional figures such as Isaac Julien. Writing of this work, Paul Willemen has said that "[c]ompared to U.S. black films, black British films are strikingly British, yet in no way can they be construed as nationalistic. They are part of a British specificity, but not part of a British nationalism."[1] That is also true of Steve McQueen's *Small Axe*, which I mentioned in the introduction as being a series of 2020 films (five in all) that deal with various aspects of the Black British experience of the 1970s and '80s. In contrast, what we see in the négritude movement is precisely an effort to reclaim a series of *separate* and *national* identities – Senegalese, Martinican, and, it must not be forgotten, also French – from the generic, essentializing, and ultimately inadequate label of "nègre."

I should pause here to say that throughout this book I proceed from the assumption that the French word "nègre" generally has as its English equivalent "negro." I understand that there are some occasions where it might seem appropriate to translate it as the English term that I am only able to pronounce as "the n-word," but this is not generally the case. English translators of significant texts tend towards inconsistency, by way of drawing upon "the n-word's" hatefulness when the French original's use of "nègre" seems to be in that spirit. In their version of Césaire's *Cahier d'un retour au pays natal* – the version I will use throughout this book – John Berger and Anna Bostock sometimes translate "nègre" as the n-word,[2] and sometimes as "negro,"[3] depending on the context. In his version of Frantz Fanon's *Peau noir, masques blanques*, Richard Philcox translates "nègre" alternately as "Black man," "negro," and the n-word. The slipperiness of that book's most famous passage is indicative: for Fanon's "'Sale nègre!' ou simplement 'Tiens, un nègre!'"[4] Philcox gives "'Dirty [n-word]!' or simply, "Look! A Negro!"[5] Fanon's final two chapters use the word "nègre" in their titles ("Le Nègre et la psychopathologie" and "Le Nègre et la reconnaissance"), and in each case Philcox translates that as "Black man" ("The Black Man and Psychopathology" and "The Black Man and Recognition"), which doesn't seem right to me because it fails to capture what I read as Fanon's clinical and I believe ironic use of the term (as a practising clinician he'd have earned that irony).

I think the strongest support for my position that "nègre" should generally be translated as "negro" is the massive Pan-African event that unspooled in 1966 in Senegal under Léopold Senghor's patronage, which I will discuss later in this chapter: the Festival mondial des arts nègres. Of course it is not even remotely imaginable that such an event, sponsored by such a world-literary-political figure, could bear the name "The World Festival of N——r Arts." And indeed, the official English-language title of that event was "The World Festival of Negro Arts" (it was renamed the Festival mondial des arts noirs / World Festival of Black Arts for its second, 1977 edition in Lagos). Nor is it even remotely imaginable that the title of Senghor's pathbreaking collection *Anthologie de la nouvelle poésie nègre et malgache de langue française* would be correctly translated as *Anthology of the New French-Language Poetry by N——s and Malagasy*, either today or when it was first published in 1948. Senghor was not reclaiming that term ironically in either case, in the manner of contemporary enunciations such as the band NWA, and it is nothing more than naïve presentism to claim that this is the way the term "nègre" is being used in such contexts.

Philcox rightly translates Fanon's "Sale nègre!" as "Dirty [n-word]!" for the same reasons that it would be logical to translate "Sale juif!" as "Filthy k——e!" and not simply "Dirty Jew!" But it does not follow from that act of translation that the word "juif" is unpronounceably hateful in the manner of the word "k——e." That is equally true of the difference between the word "nègre" and the n-word. The casual conflation of the two is tone-deaf in the extreme because it fails to recognize the n-word's unique hatefulness in English. It seems clear to me that both the words "nègre" and "negro," on the other hand, carried in the pre-1980s period a certain fustiness that was clearly patronizing and thus racist in some contexts, while in other contexts serving as a respectable contrast to explicitly bigoted French-language slurs.

The fact that these French-language slurs do not begin with the letter "n" means that they are not as amenable to transplantation into a broadly Anglophone but in fact basically American context of racial tensions. The French language has its own history of now-unspeakable racist words, and the way in which Québécois activists have ignored that reality in favour of inserting themselves into those Anglo-American arguments must be seen as a product of an all-too-typical Canadian cultural insecurity when it comes to a sense that the real action, politically speaking, is to be found among the Yanks. If discussion of "le mot en n" were generally accompanied by engagement with "le mot en s" or "le mot en b" that would be one thing. In fact those first letters and the racial slurs they invoke are utterly illegible to an American audience and to many Québécois as well; thus discussion of them is basically absent from discourse north of the 49th. Discussion of both first letters can be found in recent French-language discourse in Quebec, but in ways that unmistakeably flow from various American cultural-freakouts-of-the-moment.[6] Suffice it to say that by "le mot en s" I am very much *not* referring to the word "systémique" (see Boucar Diouf's 20 February 2021 opinion piece in *La Presse*) nor do I mean by "le mot en b" the French townland of Bitche (see Pierre Chastenay's opinion piece in the 21 April 2021 issue of *Le Devoir*).[7]

Questions of translation aside, what we will see in this examination of Black nationalism between Africa and North America is a constant tension between conceptions of ethnicity that Loïc Wacquant has memorably called "thin" and "thick." In a 2022 *New Left Review* article, Wacquant wrote:

> At one end, "thin" ethnicity fully admits its arbitrariness: it is overtly "ethnic" in the sense that it is self-evidently grounded in the vagaries of *culture* and *history*, as with the variants of ethnoreligious, ethnonational and ethnoregional categories (Jews in contemporary France, Zainichi in postcolonial Japan, Toltecs in present-day-Mexico, for instance): at the other end, "thick" ethnicity denies its own historicity (which thus becomes covert) and claims to be rooted in the necessities of *nature* and *biology* (or its logical analogue, culture understood as hard-wired and virtually unchanging), materialized in its most extreme form by caste and caste-like arrangements.[8] (Italics his)

On the one hand, there is a clear presence of "thick" ethnicity in a lot of Black nationalism, very much including négritude: that is to say, a sense that the movement is meant to advocate for a group of people, and perhaps a group of *peoples*, defined at least in part by a difference that goes beyond historical specifics, and is rooted in a biologically based system of what Orlando Patterson calls an "ethno-somatic mode." Patterson deploys that term in a 2005 chapter where he argues that something like this belief in "thick" concepts of ethnicity is typically North American. He writes there that "North Americans developed what might be called a *binary* conception of race, more commonly known as the one-drop rule: the classification of all persons as 'white' or 'black,' including in the latter category all persons with any known African ancestry, however somatically light-skinned they may be."[9] He contrasts this with points south and east: "In South America and the Caribbean two different ethno-somatic systems emerged. They have in common that they are non-binary. 'Race' in these societies is conceived of in denotative terms, ranging on a continuum from white, through various mixed shades (each with a given name) to black."[10] This is close to Wacquant's sense of "thin" ethnicity, but not exactly the same thing. For Wacquant, a continuum of "mixed shades" is beside the point: ethnicity "is self-evidently grounded in the vagaries of *culture* and *history*," much like nation, and much like nation's *eveil* relation, caste.

Wacquant's discussion of ethnicity was published about a year after *New Left Review* featured a lively debate over whether or not Blackness should indeed be understood as a caste. Making the case that it should, Sujatha Gilda and Alan Horn wrote that "black people in America do not constitute a nation. They have no territory or economic life of their own; black culture is archetypically American."[11] Kheya Bag and Susan Watkins challenged the "caste" analysis in the next issue, having more sympathy with Abram Leon's term "people-class," which Gilda and Horn partially draw upon. I see why Gilda and Horn can't see African-Americans as a nation, and I suspect that they would have a similar analysis of African-Canadians; on the whole that is probably how a majority of Black people in twenty-first-century North American and Britain feel as well. This chapter, though, explores different historical moments when Black intellectuals could see their community as a nation, including in ways that were indeed "archetypically American" as well as archetypically Canadian. This chapter is thus more consistent with the Bag/Watkins sense of the argument (at least with the first word of its compound), seeing African-Americans and Africadians, for instance, as a "people," a term that is, for most observers, nearly indistinguishable from "nation."

I hope I am not using such terms too loosely, because overall I want to take seriously the imperative laid down early in Gilroy's aforementioned classic *The Black Atlantic*. There Gilroy asks his reader to "[c]onsider for a moment the looseness with which the term 'black nationalism' is used both by its advocates and by sceptics."[12] I want to use this chapter to make something of a virtue out of what I take Gilroy to understand as a vice. That is, I want to examine the ways that varying cultural formations that could be known as "Black nationalism" play off of one another in ways that leave their difference intact. What we can see (to put it in a self-consciously Canadian way) is a mosaic of nationalisms: at a distance they all seem to speak of a "Black nationalism," but closer inspection shows the reality of distinct elements, each one different in shape and functioning in different ways – each one, really, a different nation. I want to start here because it is precisely this *difference* that will frame all of the discussion of nation that I will be putting forward in this book.

I. Vicissitudes of Négritude: Sengor and Césaire

Vous souriez, Black Boy,	You smile, *Black Boy*,
vous chantez,	you sing,
vous dansez,	you dance,
vous bercez les générations	you cradle the generations
qui montent à toutes les heures	who, at all hours,
sur les fronts du travail et de la peine,	storm those sites of work and of pain,
qui montrez demain à l'assaut des bastilles	and who tomorrow will also storm the forts
vers les bastions de l'avenir	facing the battlements of the future
pour écrire dans toutes les langues,	so that they might write in every tongue
aux pages claires de tous les ciels,	on the blank pages of the heavens
la déclaration de tes droits méconnus	the declaration of your rights which have gone unacknowledged
depuis plus de cinq siècles,	for more than five centuries
en Guinée,	in Guinea,
au Maroc,	in Morocco,
au Congo,	in Congo,
partout enfin où vos mains noirs	finally everywhere where your Black hands
ont laissé aux murs de la Civilisation	have left, on Civilization's
des empreintes d'amour, de grâce et de lumière...	walls, traces of love, of grace, and of light ...

– Jean-F. Brière, "Black Soul," as collected in Léopold Sengor, ed., *Anthologie de la nouvelle poésie nègre et malagache de langue française*[13] (m.t.)

Difference was at the heart of the earliest movement that fits under what Paul Gilroy seems to mean as "Black nationalism," and that is négritude. I refer there to the literary and political movement that coalesced around the journal *Présence africaine* (founded in Paris in 1947 by the Senegalese writer Alioune Diop) and the writers Léopold Senghor of Senegal and Aimé Césaire of Martinique. The name of the movement indicates the degree to which a certain essentialism was always at work, as does the geographic distance between Senghor's and Césaire's home countries. The idea that Martinique and Senegal should share something meaningful by dint of their common "négritude," their common belonging to a global collective of Black people scattered throughout the world, is not a position that would attract much support in the twenty-first century. Part of the reason for négritude's emergence, of course, was that it was the colonialism of Paris (where the movement originated) which obscured this kind of difference, which patronizingly reduced people from Senegal and people from Martinique to the common status of "nègre," and thus forestalled any deeper inquiry into their culture or their humanity generally.

Looking back on négritude in 1988, Césaire explained the movement's goals in ways that square with the concept of nation that I am trying to defend in this book: something that is fundamentally separate from ethnicity (and so closer to "thin" concepts), even as it demands that individuals accept that identities are in some ways defined by certain kinds of singular identities (and so not entirely divorced from "thick"-inflected visions of "ethno-somatic modes"). For instance, Césaire told an audience at Florida International University:

> Thus I don't say *ethnicity* but *identity*, because that makes matters clear. That word designates what is fundamental, designates what everything that follows is built upon: designates a hard, irreducible core; designates that which gives to a man, a culture or a civilisation its own twist, its own style, its irreducible singularity.[14] (m.t.)

This, really, is where the movement invested most of its intellectual energy: in *son irréductible singularité*. Blackness was obviously part of that singularity, but Césaire is just as clear that "[j]e dirai donc non pas *ethnicity*." The concept is so foreign to his thought that he has to resort to English. Négritude proceeded from a sense of unity because that is what was forced onto colonized subjects in Africa and the Caribbean by colonizers as a response to that ethnicity; Blackness was where an individual's identity seemed to begin and end, particularly in the colonial metropolis of Paris. Négritude's attempt to recover identity proceeded from a rejection of the all-encompassing pseudo-pluralism of colonialism and a move towards what Mary McCarthy knew as "a singular" (she was writing about an American identity worthy of the name) and which Césaire in turn wanted to make *irréductible*. What négritude set the stage for was the pursuit of *nation*.

This may be part of why there is relatively little to be found about négritude in Anglophone Postcolonial Studies (although this is changing; see especially recent work by Merve Fejzula). To some extent, that Anglophone hostility, or at least scepticism, has been led by Wole Soyinka's famous (and possibly apocryphal) question "Does a tiger feel his tigritude?"[15] That is to say, the movement has often seemed to African intellectuals writing in English as a bit ponderous and preoccupied with identity, speaking to longstanding tensions between them and their Francophone counterparts.[16] Gilroy's problem with négritude, which *The Black Atlantic* briefly addresses via lost possibilities for analogies with Judaism and Diaspora,[17] seems to be more or less along these lines, and in turn along the lines of his impatience with what he regards as loose talk about what he writes as "black nationalism." He argues that the problem with this looseness is that it flattens out the political distinctiveness of Black cultural politics in the name of a vague pan-Africanism. He is especially irritated at the way that the Caribbean roots of popular music have recently been put in the service of an apparent pan-Africanism that is really just American:

> The musical components of hip hop are a hybrid form nurtured by the social relations of the South Bronx where Jamaican sound system culture was transplanted during the 1970s and put down new roots. In conjunction with specific technological innovations, this routed and re-routed Caribbean culture set in train a process that was to transform black America's sense of itself and a large portion of the popular music industry as well. Here we have to ask how a form which flaunts and glories in its own malleability as well as its transnational character becomes interpreted as an expression of some authentic African-American essence? How can rap be discussed as if it sprang intact from the entrails of the blues? Another way of approaching this would be to ask what it is about black America's writing elite which means that they need to claim this diasporic cultural form in such an assertively nationalist way?[18]

In later works Gilroy would find more to admire in négritude, writing in *Against Race* that in Senghor's work "fervent humanism is combined with, but somehow not contradicted by, a romantic ethnic particularity and an appreciation for cultural syncretism and transcultural symbiosis."[19] What those last two formulations are referring to is wholly consistent with the way in which I (following Roger Scruton, much to Gilroy's chagrin I'm sure!) am trying to define the word "nation."

But Gilroy is asking a reasonable question about why one part of the diaspora has such "need to claim this diasporic cultural form in such an assertively nationalist way," one worth offering some tentative answers to. To take the least charitable analysis possible, part of the reason for this elision that Gilroy mentions may stem from the reality that "black America's writing elite" is *American*. To follow what I said in the introduction, too much discourse from the United States, above all from the "writing elite," Black or not, avoids overt discussion of national identity for fear of seeming gauchely chauvinistic, favouring instead a casual universalism that erases (thinner and less-binary) distinctions (such as "Jamaican" or "Caribbean") in favour of a vaguely (and ultimately thicker and binary) ethnic understanding that obscures its American (that is to say obscures its *national*) origins. As with so much in pseudo-globalized discourse, it sometimes seems that all Blackness is basically American.[20] African-American intellectuals are, Gilroy seems to be arguing, very American indeed in their relative disinterest in anything that sits outside of the United States; this is a critique that has also, as I will discuss shortly, been offered by George Elliott Clarke.

A more generous answer to Gilroy's question would point to the longstanding history of African-American discourse that defends Black nationhood or something like it, a discourse that has, historically, been both internationalist in spirit and internationally influential. On the latter question, both of the key figures of négritude, Senghor and Césaire, have made a point of praising their American antecedents when looking back on the movement retrospectively. In a 1988 book titled *Ce que je crois*, Senghor recalled fondly that "I would be remiss if I failed to mention the influence that 'le mouvement culturel négro-américain' had on us as Black students in Paris, that movement of the *New Negro* and *Negro Renaissance*, the founders of which were Alain Locke but especially William Edward Burghard Du Bois ... In truth he is the historical founder of négritude, as we see from his first major work, written in 1903, *Souls of Black Folks*"[21] (m.t.). Césaire, in his Florida International University address, recalled how "négritude was born here, amongst you, in the United States. The first négritude was American négritude. We bear towards these men an enormous debt, and we need to recognize that, remember it and proclaim it"[22] (m.t.). Those first generations of African-American political and literary intellectuals – Frederick Douglass, W.E.B. Du Bois, Zora Neale

Hurston, etc. – were important not only for the ways that their writing and oratory combatted racism, but also for the ways in which it was pitched in explicitly internationalist ways. Although her 1937 novel *Their Eyes Were Watching God* is still a mainstay of the American secondary curriculum, Hurston (who died in 1960) was in the news recently because of the 2018 publication of her book-length interview with the man who was once believed to be the last surviving African-born American to have experienced enslavement, *Barracoon: The Story of the Last "Black Cargo,"* which had languished in her papers at Howard University. Her significant work as an ethnographer documented the folkways not only of African America but also of the Caribbean, specifically Haiti and Jamaica, about which she published a book in 1938. Although she is widely understood by literary historians as part of the Harlem Renaissance, she had strong ties to northeastern Florida (the setting of *Their Eyes Were Watching God*), which is far closer to the Caribbean than to New York. There was, within her conception of Blackness, a strong element of what I discussed in the introduction vis-à-vis Gary Younge's analysis of *Small Axe* and Paul Gilroy and their shared interest in "a particular, hybrid cosmopolitan Black … identity."[23] Something similar was true of Du Bois, of course, who was a delegate to the first Pan-African Congress (held in London in 1900) and a frequent attender of such events in England and France, as well as someone who made interventions at the founding of the United Nations and who died in Accra as a citizen of Ghana. Frederick Douglass voyaged to Britain and, most importantly, to Ireland, in 1845, where he encountered and shared a podium with Daniel O'Connell, the legendary crusader for Catholic emancipation known as "The Liberator." All of this was in search of a nationality that was most definitely American. That's true even in the case of Du Bois, who wound up in Ghana not because he could trace his ancestry to that part of Africa but because that country's president Kwame Nkrumah was an icon of 1960s Pan-Africanism who encouraged African-Americans to relocate to the newly independent republic. All of these writers are nationalist in the way that Gilroy is identifying, but were defined by a seriously internationalist engagement with comparable national experiences.

That search for a nationality, one that reaches outward but never loses sight of a specific national identity, was the real core of négritude, much more so than any kind of thick, essentialist understanding that it is too easy to characterize the movement as being defined by. Senghor could be prone to such conceptualizations in his later years. In 1967 he told a Cairo audience (which included Gen. Gamal Abdel Nasser), "Let us come back, as always, to the emotional power of the African – white or Black: to the intensity of their affective energy, stored like a battery"[24] (m.t.). Contrary to popular belief, this kind of broad talk isn't typical of the movement, and in order to see that, one has to go back to one of its key documents, which is Césaire's poetic masterpiece *Cahier d'un retour au pays natal*, first published in 1939 and finalized in 1947. Writing of "la calebasse d'une île et ce qui est à moi aussi, l'archipel arqué comme le désir inquiet de se nier,"[25] he goes on to say:

> My island, my non-enclosure, whose bright courage stands at the back of my Polynesia; in front, Guadeloupe split in two by its dorsal ridge and as wretched as we ourselves; Haiti where negritude rose to its feet for the first time and said it believed in its own humanity; and the comic little tale of Florida where they are just finishing strangling a Negro; and Africa gigantically caterpillaring as far as the Spanish foot of Europe: the nakedness of Africa where the scythe of Death swings wide.[26]

What Césaire is longing for is a community, a specific, nameable landscape and culture, as an undifferentiated "polynésie" gives way to a Caribbean community that crosses three different nation-states who were all products of revolution: France, Haiti, and the US. These three places are the sites of different *national* identities. They cannot be collapsed as part of what Césaire sardonically refers to in *Cahier d'un retour au pays natal* as a "les nègres-sont-tous-les-mêmes"[27] approach to belonging, something he so clearly sees as alienating. He developed this approach in his 1955 text *Discours sur le colonialisme*, wherein he writes:

> So that unless, in Africa, in the South Sea Islands, in Madagascar (that is, at the gates of South Africa), in the West Indies (that is, at the gates of America), Western Europe undertakes on its own initiative a policy of *nationalities*, a new policy founded on the respect for peoples and cultures … Europe will have deprived itself of its last chance, and with its own hands, drawn up over itself the pall of moral darkness.[28]

Césaire's imperative was for Europe to seize the moment of decolonization in a way that recognized not just the rights and the consciousness of undifferentiated Black people from South Africa to the Caribbean to the Americas but rather the rights of the *nations* that are found across that vast continuum. If that is Europe's response, then what is there to say, really? What Césaire, like so many invested in that movement known as négritude, seems to be saying in response is something like "It's nation time."

II. Amiri Baraka's "Nation Time" and Gary, Indiana

In Newark, when we greet each other on the streets, we say, "what time is it?" We always say "It's nation time!" … Nationalism is about land and nation, a way of life trying to free itself.
– Amiri Baraka, at the Congress of African People, September 1970, as reproduced on *Black Journal*, episode 56, first broadcast 1972

I do not choose that phrase lightly. Rather, I allude to a poem by Amiri Baraka, published as a pamphlet in 1970, as well as to the National Black Political Convention which unspooled in Gary, Indiana, in 1972 and was presided over by Baraka. That convention was the subject of a recently restored film by William Greaves, *Nation Time* (1972/2020), and therein lies a tale. Before his death in 2014 Greaves was a key part of Black American cinema, but his experimentalism and his internationalism have always made him something of an awkward fit. *Nation Time* is not an experimental film but it is an internationalist one, in ways that draw attention to Baraka's place in a globalized Black nationalism as well as pointing toward the longstanding internationalism of that generation of US Black nationalists who were in such a complex, if sometimes implicit, conversation with négritude.

Perhaps the way to start, then, is to introduce William Greaves. Scott MacDonald's 2021 book *William Greaves: Filmmaking as Mission* is a major contribution to the scholarship on documentary film for the way that it brings a too-long-neglected figure out of the shadows. It is also important for the way that it illuminates connections between experimental cinema and sponsored documentaries, educational television and political cinema. MacDonald has been writing about Greaves for a long time, mostly in terms of his experimental (and, ironically, best-known) film *Symbiopsychotaxiplasm: Take One* (1968). The 2021 book, on the other hand, is comprehensive, and makes it clear how broad Greaves's experience in documentary filmmaking was. Greaves was particularly adept at navigating large institutions, having made films for the United Nations and the US Information Agency, and then eventually settling down to produce *Black Journal*, which ran on the National Educational Television network from 1968 to 1970 and on PBS from 1970 to 1977. Following that experience, Greaves formed his own production company with his wife Louise Archambault (now Greaves), a Québécoise whom he had met in the late 1950s during his time in Montreal, where he was employed by the National Film Board of Canada.

For our purposes here the most relevant Greaves work is the film that was restored in 2020 as *Nationtime*[29] and whose "star" is Amiri Baraka. Baraka is an unusual figure in the world of American poetics, inasmuch as he is a bridge between Beat poets such as Allen Ginsburg or Diane di Prima and post-Beat postmodernists such as Charles Olson or Ed Dorn, all of whom he published under the imprint of Totem Press, which he founded with his then-wife Hattie Cohen. But Baraka is mostly remembered in literary circles as a key figure in the later days of the Black Arts Movement: for his 1964 play *Dutchman* and for his work as a poet. He is also an unusual figure in American poetics because he was exceptionally active in militant politics. To a certain extent this peaked in the early 1970s, when he was one of the founders of the Congress of African People (sometimes written as the Congress of Afrikan People). As was common in radical African-American circles of the time, Baraka took a lot of interest in the anticolonial struggle in Africa. He was also deeply rooted in Newark, New Jersey, where he was born LeRoy Jones in 1934 (his son, Ras Baraka, was elected mayor of Newark in 2014). Komozi Woodard has argued that the Newark context is key for understanding Black nationalism of this period, and in his 1991 dissertation on Baraka and the Modern Black Convention Movement, he recalls that "[i]n 1968 Phil Hutchins, the National Program Secretary of the Student Nonviolent Coordinating Committee (SNCC) insisted, 'Newark is the key city. ... If we can't get black power here, we can't get it anywhere.'"[30] In a 2006 chapter Woodard wrote that

> Although there were a number of Black Power leaders in Newark, over time the poet and playwright Imamu Amiri Baraka emerged as a leader of leaders in the Modern Black Convention Movement (MBCM). Baraka assumed leadership roles coordinating many of the local Black Power and Pan-Africanist groups on such key occasions as the 1970 Atlanta Congress of African People, the 1972 African Liberation Day March in Washington D.C., the 1972 San Diego International Congress

of Afrikan People, and the 1972 National Black Political Convention in Gary, Indiana … Consequently, streams of international and national figures visited Baraka and performed or lectured in Newark about African and African American art, music, dance, literature, politics, and liberation. During that period, Newark was a showcase for grassroots Black Studies and African culture and politics.[31]

Those international connections were not limited to lectures and political debates. Woodard goes on to recall how, "[f]or Baraka, one day's business at the United Nations could include as many as four diplomatic meetings";[32] gives specifics of meetings with delegations from Sudan, Guinea-Bissau, Uganda, and Tanzania; and also recounts further connections:

By the early 1970s, CAP had established relations with Maurice Bishop and the New Jewel Movement in Grenada; Amilcar Cabral of the liberation group PAIGC (Partido Africano da Independência da Guiné e Cabo Verde) in West Africa; and a number of the leaders of the liberation movements in Palestine, South Africa, Namibia, Angola, Mozambique, and Zimbabwe. Indeed, CAP was instrumental in establishing the African Liberation Support Committee (ALSC) to help end colonialism in Angola, Mozambique, Guinea-Bissau, Namibia, and Zimbabwe; the ALSC was the most important such U.S. group since W.E.B. Du Bois and Paul Robeson's Council on African Affairs in the 1930s and 40s.[33]

Robeson Taj P. Frazier also points to Sudan, Ghana, Nigeria, Congo, Sierra Leone, Algeria, Kenya, Zambia, and Gambia as being particularly important models for Baraka and his contemporaries.[34] This is an extraordinarily diverse roll call of recently independent states that the Baraka-led Congress of African People was engaging with.

Given that level of engagement, it is odd that Senegal and Léopold Senghor seem to be absent. "On l'appelle le président-poète," wrote Musanji Ngalasso-Mwatha in 2002 of Senghor.[35] Nobody was ever going to call Baraka that, but it is nevertheless hard to ignore the connections between one poet who was trying to bring his people towards nationhood and another poet, a fellow socialist (although not quasi-Maoist in the manner of Baraka), who had become the first president of one of the first independent African republics (Senghor served as president of Senegal from 1960 to 1980). But there are few signs that Senghor was on the radar screen of Baraka or his contemporaries. Greaves had actually made a film about the aforementioned Senghor-sponsored Festival des arts nègres – the film had the title *The First World Festival of Negro Arts*, was released in 1966, and was sponsored, like Greaves's arrestingly poetic exploration of freedom of expression *Wealth of a Nation*, by the United States Information Agency (USIA). One of the film's last sequences has Greaves asking, on voice-over, "What is négritude?" Over images taken of people talking and arguing during the festival's *colloque* and book fair, including a long hand-held shot that follows Senghor, he goes on: "Is négritude a positive or a negative philosophy? Is it racism or humanism? Will it help to unite the world, or divide it?" These are the kinds of questions that are sometimes asked of Black Lives Matter and its adjacent activists, and while the analogy with négritude is not perfect, that montage is a reminder that it once enjoyed the kind of global prominence that BLM now does. But by the 1970s when Baraka was coming into his own and helping to consolidate a new Black nationalism, that prominence had started to fade, as Senghor was seeming like more of an establishment figure (with his presidential administration and his tendency to use the word "nègre"), a fate that BLM will, in time, share. As the prominence of Francocentric approaches gave way to the increasingly dominant global centrality of English-language experiences centred in the US, Baraka seems to have been brought into that dynamic as the fiery young guy: more avant-garde than Senghor as a poet, admirer of figures such as the more militaristic Amilcar Cabral (whose political writings were much more widely translated into English than Senghor's), further on the left to the point of identifying with Maoism, etc.

Given the geopolitical quality of these intellectual arguments about President Senghor and the possible meanings of the literary and artistic movement he helped create, it is not a minor matter that both Greaves and Baraka had connections with the United Nations, albeit in different capacities. Greaves found work there making sponsored films upon his return to New York from Canada. Many years after that return, in 2001, he made one of his most widely seen films, *Ralph Bunche: An American Odyssey*, a portrait of the African-American political thinker who both helped to found and then worked extensively with the United Nations, being awarded the Nobel Peace Prize in 1950 for work negotiating the Arab-Israeli conflict and serving as UN Undersecretary General from 1968 to 1971. The kind of internationalism that defined both men's work was connected to the place that the UN offers small and recently independent states on the world stage. No doubt it is dominated by a small number of large states (that is to say the permanent members of the Security Council), but talk of it as some sort of singular, universal super-state misrepresents the institution's basic structure. Explaining the perspective of *Black Journal* as led by Greaves, Celeste Day Moore has written that "[t]his Black internationalist orientation, I argue, was fundamentally shaped by Greaves' own life and career, in which he had consistently looked outside of the United States to better contextualize the African-American experience and to reject the misrepresentations of Black life that persisted in the media."[36] Baraka's internationalism, as we have seen, was no less wide-ranging, and was connected to the United Nations via the role that the organization played in the decolonization processes of the 1960s and '70s. Thus the interview in the first reel of *Nationtime* with the Pan-Africanist Civil Rights veteran Owusu Sadaukai (Howard Fuller), which has him holding forth on his experiences with rebel factions in Mozambique, sets the tone for the work. Sadauki explains that he has seen how struggles for nationhood have unfolded *elsewhere*, evokes how they invariably entail the key element of *internal diversity* ("I was very impressed with their relationship to the peasants inside of Mozambique"), and offers these recollections not as an explanation of what is happening in the United States, but rather as an example of another nation whose struggle against (Portuguese) colonialism and towards sovereignty (Mozambique wouldn't become independent for another three years, in 1975) offers some lessons. In this way, Greaves is framing the African-American movement as just another national struggle, no more important or less important than other struggles around the world, echoing the way I suggested in the introduction that we should see American culture (more, not less, nation is necessary for an equitable globalism). Later in the book I will argue that this is the way that we should see English and English-Canadian culture, where more, not less, nation will be necessary for the United Kingdom to survive in any way that is at all equitable and for Canada to survive in a way that is true to its federalist roots.

The vision of nation that Baraka was developing through his political work, then, was deeply connected to the local (via Newark) as well to the global (via, among other institutions, the United Nations, about forty-five minutes down the line on NJ Transit). What was less highly developed, at least by Baraka and his circle, was the context in between. One way of seeing the problem is that this nationalist turn that Baraka was leading seemed to be missing the diversity and breadth that, following Roger Scruton's statement from the introduction, are such a key part of how the social cohesion of nation is "unlike those of tribe or religion."[37] Although I can feel some progressive readers wincing a bit at Scruton's use of the work "tribe," for our purposes here it is fortuitous. The aforementioned 1972 National Black Political Convention in Gary, Indiana, the event which Baraka helped to organize and preside over and about which William Greaves made a recently restored film, had as a key theme the creative but undeniable tension between the inherently limited view of "tribe" and the more expansive view of nation.

The restored version of *Nationtime* opens with text that includes: "The Convention adjourned without reaching consensus, and some deemed it a failure." The film's climax comes when part of the Michigan delegation walks out of the convention; Greaves cross-cuts images of the crowd with medium shots of Baraka desperately trying to maintain some control over the proceedings. But I would argue that the enunciation of the "tribe/nation" difference is a key matter in the Convention as presented by Greaves's film, and helped clarify the degree to which Black nationalism was a genuinely *nationalist* movement along the lines of what could be seen in so many other jurisdictions, and not simply a more fiery version of the Civil Rights Movement, as historians sometimes seem to present it. Key for our purposes here is when a young-looking Jesse Jackson (he was thirty-one) gives a keynote speech at the Gary convention, wherein he (as documented in Greaves's film) says:

> The tribe in Mississippi does not know the tribe in California. The tribe in New York does not know the tribe in Georgia. And now that Brother Hatcher and Baraka and Diggs have called the tribes home,[38] the challenge of our coming together is so great, until nobody has the right to rob the family of this opportunity to organise for political power …
>
> The African diaspora has trumpeted its summons to all of the tribes, with a question put forth by Brother Baraka, whose answer alone legitimises our collective existence. Brothers and Sisters, what time is it? [The crowd roars in response: "nation time!"] It's nation time. It's nation time for all of the tribes from Boston to Birmingham, Mississippi to Minnesota, San Diego to Seattle and Galveston to Gary. What time is it? [The crowd roars in response: "nation time!"]

"Tribes" in the way Jackson is using the term are indispensable building blocks of something larger, but they are not themselves what the Gary convention was seeking to defend. By the 1970s, many African-American leaders were seeking to move beyond the legacy of the Civil Rights Movement, wary of once again being subject to the limitations of coalitions with the white power structure. At one point in Jackson's speech, he says, "I don't want to be the grey shadow of the white elephant [the Republican party]; I don't want to be the grey shadow of the white donkey [the Democratic party]. I am 31, it is '72, I am a Black man, I want a Black party, I do not trust white Republicans or white Democrats!" These invocations of *time* were making clear that African-Americans were no longer living in an era of segregation-enabled insularity, where a people who shared something important (something ethnically *thick*) could content themselves with knowing only their neighbours. When Jackson intones "What time is it?" he is recalling the *modernity* of the Convention movement.

The call-and-response was an explicit acknowledgment of Baraka's ideas about the nature of Black nationalism in the United States, something that shows it to be somewhat thinner, somewhat less binary, than Paterson's analyses might suggest. In his aforementioned 2006 chapter, Woodard writes that "[b]etween the 1968 Newark Black Political Convention, the 1970 Atlanta Congress of African People, and the 1972 Gary National Black Political Convention, tens of thousands of Black leaders followed Amiri Baraka jazz-scatting 'It's Nation Time.'"[39] He is referring there to how in 1970 Baraka published (with the Chicago-based Third World Press) a pamphlet with the title *It's Nation Time*, made up of three fairly long poems. Deploying the antisemitic imagery that would plague his entire career,[40] the opening poem "The Nation Is Like Ourselves" states, "Our nation sits on stoops and watches airplanes take off / our nation is kneeling through the snow bleeding 6 layers / of jewish enterprise / our nation is standing in line ashamed in its marrow for being / our nation / a people without knowledge of itself."[41] The third and final poem, "It's Nation Time," acts as a kind of call to that people, a call to come to know one another that was phrased using vocabulary and images instantly recognizable to Black militants of the Pan-African variety, but also with a lyricism, linguistic playfulness, and tendency toward odd forms of enjambment that strongly recall his connection to Beat poetry:

> [plural n-word] come out, brothers are we
> with you and your sons your daughters are ours
> and we are the same, all the blackness from one black allah
>   when the world is clear you'll be with us
>   come out [plural n-word] come out
>   come out [plural n-word] come out

It's Nation time eye ime
   it's nation ti eye ime
      chant with bells and drum
     it's nation time

It's nation time, get up santa claus   (repeat)
  it's nation time, build it
   get up, muffet dragger
   get up rastus for real to be rasta farai
  ras jua
   get up got here bow

      It's Nation
      Time![42]

Despite the fading of Black nationalism as a part of the contemporary American political landscape, the themes of the 1972 National Black Political Convention bear out that the vision Baraka was enunciating had enormous impact, no mean feat given the explicitly avant-garde poetic diction that he was deploying. Not even Jack Kerouac could have dreamed of such *political* impact, to say nothing of Charles Olson. Part of Baraka's task, clearly, was to move his poetics out of niche experimentalism and into the realm of real coalition-building: out of Greenwich Village and up to the United Nations.

The convention's task was different but complementary. Rather than Baraka's move from The Village to the UN, thirty-eight blocks straight up First Avenue, the convention asked the people to come out, exactly as Baraka had done in "It's Nation Time," but to come out to a place where Black people held political power, where, in Jackson's words, they had a home. "We would have gone to New York, but we didn't have a home there," Jackson said. "We would have gone to California, but we didn't have a home there. Over in this little smoke-filled small city called Gary, one of our Black brothers [Gary's mayor Richard Hatcher] said, 'Tribes, come home.'" What was at issue, in Jackson's speech as in the Convention overall, was the reality of *hinterland*. A locale like Gary, Indiana, certainly serves as a repository of cultural distinctiveness, as important Black films such as Zora Neale Hurston's *Commandment Keeper Church* (1940)[43] and Julie Dash's *Daughters of the Dust* (1991), both about the Gullah communities of South Carolina's Sea Islands, have made so abundantly clear. These places – islands, mountains – are not the repository of national consciousness, but rather evidence of the diversity that is a hallmark of nationhood. Conversely, a nation with only a metropole isn't a nation; as Baraka was coming to realize, it's an avant-garde.

The National Black Political Convention was a key moment for the enunciation of African-American nationalism because it favoured neither one nor the other, and indeed sought space that sat between them. It was neither the Sea Islands nor Greenwich Village, but rather the midwestern "little smoke-filled small city" of Gary, Indiana, that served as the birthplace for a modern *nation*: a cultural group that, following Gérard Bouchard's definition that I discussed in the introduction, "[s]hares an identity, that is to say a common vision of itself and of the Other," and, through the Convention movement that Baraka helped lead, was seeking to be "endowed with any form of government, which does not necessarily need to be that of a sovereign state."[44] This convention took as its jumping-off point the recollection that, in the words of Jesse Jackson's keynote, "Brother Hatcher came up north and got a house in Gary, and said to all the scattered children in the various Black tribes across the nation 'come home. I know my home is too small, brothers and sisters, but it is home. Come home.'"

III. Looking North: George Elliott Clarke and Africadia

In truth the loyal Blacks were probably more radical in their politics than the American patriots, even though they chose not to take up arms against the British government in Nova Scotia.
– Africadian historian Frank Boyd, writing in the *The Loyalist Gazette* (1983), as quoted by George Elliott Clarke[45]

The discourse unfolded in a different way in Canada, or so it might seem at first. If the key poet of Black nationalism in the United States was Amiri Baraka, then his "opposite number" in Canada is clearly the poet and literary scholar George Elliott Clarke. I mean that literally, because the two are defined by different politics and different aesthetic approaches. If Baraka could be said to have conceptualized nation from the standpoint of the urban metropole (originally from Newark, then outward via Greenwich Village and the United Nations), Clarke has done so along exactly the opposite trajectory: originally from Windsor, Nova Scotia, then outward via Acadian communities

and Halifax. Given his emphasis on the specificity of the Nova Scotian experience of African-Canadian identity, it is tempting to make a joke about
Clarke being provincial. But in fact, the right joke to make is about Clarke
being *parochial*, because in many ways his conceptualization of nation is built
from the parish, the ecclesiastical meaning of which cannot be divorced from
his thought.

Before embarking on that "parochial" discussion, it might be useful to offer
a broad historical and terminological introduction. For the most part, George
Elliott Clarke's discussions of Black nationalism are centred in the community
variously known as African Nova Scotian, indigenous Black, or Africadian.
The last formulation is a Clarke coinage, a portmanteau of African and
Acadian that he offered in the opening words of the introduction to his two-
volume *Fire on the Water: An Anthology of Black Nova Scotian Writing* (1991).
What it refers to is the population that is (less and less) known as "indigenous
Black." That term, an excellent example of a "thin" vision of Black ethnicity
in that it is inescapably grounded in the history and culture of the Black Loyalists of the American Revolutionary War and the Black Refugees of the War
of 1812, long predates the replacement in Canada of the term "Aboriginal"
with "Indigenous," an effort that gained widespread popular acceptance
in Canada upon the election of Justin Trudeau's Liberals in 2015 and their
renaming of various government departments by way of synchronizing
with the United Nations Declaration on the Rights of Indigenous Peoples
(UNDRIP). On the rare occasions when the term "indigenous Black" is still
used in Nova Scotia, the "i" is sometimes capitalized, although following what
I wrote in the introduction, it probably shouldn't be. For in this case, "indigenous" isn't a proper noun that refers to a specific side in the specific dia-
lectic of settler-colonial state formation, but really is just an adjective, not so
different from my example in the introduction of Iceland's indigenous film
industry. That is to say, the word "indigenous" is meant to distinguish the
Black community that is rooted in Nova Scotia from people who identify as
Black but may have relocated to Nova Scotia from Fort Saskatchewan, Min-
neapolis, Montreal, Port-au-Prince, Manchester, Accra, etc. (seeing all such
people as unchangingly Black in more or less the same way as the Africadians
would be a more customarily North American "binary" view, to return to
Patterson via Wacquant). I remember that term from my days at Dalhousie
University in Halifax, where it is used less and less but whose law school does,
as I write this in the spring of 2024, define that term this way: "African Nova
Scotians (Indigenous Blacks): a distinct people who descend from free and

enslaved Black Planters, Black Loyalists, Black Refugees, Maroons, and other Black people who inhabited the original 52 land-based Black communities in that part of Mi'kma'ki known as Nova Scotia."

That invocation of "free and enslaved" Black people tells the real tale, which is of war with the United States. Most Africadians trace their roots to the American Revolutionary War, to the group known as the "Black Loyalists," some of whom were enslaved, who came north and in some cases fought alongside Crown forces rather than be part of the republic of the thirteen colonies. They were promised land and liberty, promises that were not always fulfilled in ways consistent with the Honour of the Crown. The community is thus founded via an experience of migration and dispossession, but also (as the epigraph that opens this section) has come to be defined by a simultaneous attachment to cultural difference that is connected in equal parts to a certain attachment to the British Crown and a deep suspicion of the functionaries who claimed to act on the part of that Crown, a tension that is familiar in contemporary Indigenous radicalism.[46] A similar migration occurred during the War of 1812, when British warships managed to dock at various southern ports and Admiral John Warren issued a proclamation that anyone who could make their way to those ships "will have their choice of either entering into His Majesty's sea or land forces, or of being sent as free settlers to the British possessions in North America or the West Indies where they will meet with due encouragement."[47] That group of 1812 is generally known as the "Black Refugees."

All to say that while the Africadian experience is not Indigenous in the capitalized fashion, it's not correct to link it to relatively recent patterns of immigration, as would be the case for the majority of Canada's Black population. This is partially because until well after wwii, immigration to Canada was overwhelmingly white.[48] There is thus a good chance (not 100 per cent, but far from trivial) that a Black person born in Calgary, Toronto, or Montreal will have a relative they can ring up in the "old country," have heard family stories about how unpleasant it was to deal with Canadian immigration officials, or have perhaps heard about that wonder that my own (Italian-American) father recalls from his childhood of going to a friend's house for the first time and thinking "wow, for a grandma she speaks really good English." For the indigenous Black communities of Nova Scotia, none of this is at all relevant. That community's experience is based in migration, but migration that took place during the end of the eighteenth century or the first years of the nineteenth.[49]

Clarke's anthology *Fire on the Water* is more than a simple collection of writing from people who more or less hail from that community; its opening essay is a wide-ranging attempt to frame that community in a broader Atlantic context, one that makes it clear that this Africadian community had adopted strategies of survival that were more complex than something like "the Civil Rights movement, but with better winter gear." In a 2008 essay (reprinted in Joe Pivato's 2012 anthology on Clarke's corpus), Alexander MacLeod writes, "I want to suggest that the most important work Clarke has done thus far in his career is his introduction to the first volume of *Fire on the Water* … it should be clear to anyone familiar with Clarke's writing life that the intellectual concerns, the political issues, and the recurrent themes of exile, religious faith, and violence that come back so often in the rest of his œuvre find their first full enunciation here."[50] I am in complete agreement; this introduction bears no resemblance to the usual summary and throat-clearing exercises of such anthologies, and is instead a major work of literary-focussed national history. Clarke's overall analysis is that Africadia has been historically defined by parochialism, and as I promised earlier, that really does mean something. He recalls how "Africadians adopted the socialistic evangelism of Henry Alline, the eighteenth-century divine whose New Light movement helped to prevent Nova Scotia from joining the American Revolution … The politicized faith of Africadians was also exemplified by the refusal of the ABA (and its descendent, the African United Baptist Association [AUBA]) to dissolve itself and integrate with white Baptists."[51] What they were seeking in Nova Scotia was consistent with the promises made by the Crown, which is to say settlement, not integration into a majority-white society. They were seeking their own parish, literally and figuratively.

By figuratively I mean something like "seeking their own society," one that would mark Africadians out as something like (1) in Will Kymlicka's formulation which I discussed in the introduction: that is to say a group seeking "self-government rights," which manifested itself in these struggles around church formation. I can imagine an argument that Africadians are more correctly filed under Kymlicka's (3), "special representation rights." That is more or less their contemporary place, as arguments about legislating "safe seats" in the Nova Scotia legislature for both historically Black and historically Acadian communities are a perennial issue there (and the recent creation of the office of minister of African Nova Scotian Affairs, as well as individual ministers of Acadian Affairs and of Gaelic Affairs, were widely seen as major victories for those communities). But the one thing that is clear is that

Africadians are most definitely not part of Kymlicka's (2), "polyethnic rights." They have not historically acted in the manner of the Sikh community in Montreal, or for that matter in the manner of the Congolese community in Saskatoon, which is to say that their militancy has not focussed on greater integration, but rather on the building of (to deploy a term now guaranteed to tighten the shoulders of all Canadians who have followed the news since 1987) "a distinct society." Clarke is explicit on this matter, writing in the *Fire on the Water* introduction:

> Given this history of, first, a radical commitment to the acquisition of land and liberty; secondly, the formation and maintenance of a deliberately separatist church; thirdly, the adherence to a belief in the spiritual superiority of Black worship; fourthly, the adherence to an ideology espousing the construction of a just society; and fifthly, the practice of communal democracy within the church; it is natural that Africadians should believe that they constitute a distinct society.[52]

Africadians therefore occupy a place in Canadian society that is unlike that of other immigrant groups. That is because their heritage is barely connected to immigration at all; their communities are *foundational* in Nova Scotia, not in the manner of the Mi'kmaq, but entirely comparable to the Acadians. Nobody who understands the history of either Canada or Europe would say of an Acadian boy and a young man whose mother came to Halifax from Paris in the 1980s, "ah, sure, two French guys." For exactly the same reasons, it is insufficient to think of an Africadian born and raised in Halifax's North Preston neighbourhood and a woman from Ottawa whose father emigrated from Jamaica in the 1960s simply as "two Black Canadians." In both cases the definition I give as inadequate is correct but unilluminating. In order for these conflations to make sense, it is necessary to scrub all details of heritage, locale, and, ultimately, *national* belonging. In this way, the Africadian experience is actually much closer to that of the majority of Black Americans than to that of the majority of Black Canadians, inasmuch as the matter of immigration seems distant and nearly irrelevant to the present-day contours of the nation, and that irrelevance is an important element of their distinctiveness.

Thus it is ironic that Clarke has felt it necessary to go to some lengths to distinguish the African-American and Africadian experiences. Irony or no, he has good reason to do so. Surveying the scene in a 1998 anthology of African-Canadian literature, he expresses some hostility towards critics who see this as a matter of a flourishing of Black expression throughout the Anglophone world as a whole, albeit mostly centred (purely by coincidence, mind you!) in the United States. Clarke writes that "the truth cuts deeper … Nor are there clear parallels between the U.S. Black Arts / Black Power movement of the 1960s and the *flourison* of African-Canadian writing in the 1990s."[53] It is in his 2002 collection *Odysseys Home: Mapping African-Canadian Literature* (mostly made up of previously published papers) where he sets to this task more fully. Throughout he is hard on Paul Gilroy for so studiously ignoring Canada in his trailblazing study *The Black Atlantic*. Criticizing Kwame Anthony Appiah and Henry Louis Gates Jr's *Africana: The Encyclopedia of the African and African American Experience*, he laments "the swath of vital writers [that] goes unremarked and unnoticed, while those few who garner attention have their Canadian ties either Americanized or airbrushed out of existence."[54] Later on he rails against what he calls "model Blackness," which is really just unacknowledged Americanism: "While an imperishable and ineluctable Pan-Africanism prods African Canadians, especially Anglophones, to adopt African-American role models, modes of discourse, and aesthetic agendas, this adoption is never pure, never without a degree of implicit and deforming violence."[55] Further on in the same paper he is blunter still, writing that "there is a Canadian-ness about African-Canadian culture that cannot be subsumed under the banners of an 'imperial' African Americanism."[56]

Clarke is more comfortable with nationalism because he has seen what happens when such distinctions are ignored in the name of "larger" questions: cultural distinctiveness is simply bulldozed by the more numerous and/or powerful entity, an entity that generally refuses (in the manner of liberalism, as I discussed in the introduction and to which I will return throughout this book) to acknowledge that it is an entity at all. A summary of Clarke's impatience with Yankee solipsism is his sense, offered in *Odysseys Home*, that "African-American scholars have tended to regard African Canadians as a failed version of themselves, or as a warning to others who may tumble beyond the precincts of the contiguous – and *holy* – forty-eight states."[57] He clearly saw that dynamic at work in the response to the musical *Show Boat* being staged in Toronto, a production that was met with protests about racism that played out as though this was just another American city, something Clarke discusses in an impatient tone.[58] This sense of being dismissed is also palpably present when African-Canadians more closely connected to immigration engage with Africadians, something Clarke wrote about using imperial imagery guaranteed to make the former group uncomfortable: "Intriguingly, old-line African-Canadian communities are mainly rural and African-American in derivation, while the post-1955 new black communities are urban and diverse. Significantly, too, relations between 'aboriginal' and 'naturalized' writers replace those between First Nations and mainstream Canadian writers, with tensions developing *vis-à-vis* resource allocations (arts and research grants) and appropriation of discourse."[59] As with relationships "between First Nations and mainstream Canadian writers," I am inclined to invoke Robert Frost's maxim that "good fences make good neighbors," which is more or less the philosophy that most Canadian progressives have adapted when it comes to settler-Indigenous relations (something that is, as we will see, not at all the case in New Zealand). That fence generally takes the form of nation; that is certainly the case with Clarke's sense of Africadian distinctiveness. He speaks in terms of nation when it comes to Africadians, and unlike in the United States (as we saw in the previous section of this chapter), that has not generally been true of prominent Black Canadian intellectuals.

M. NourbeSe Philip, for instance, in her most famous essay "The Absence of Writing, or How I Almost Became a Spy," writes about the degree to which Canadian modes, along with the Canadian language itself, remain foreign for her: "If possession is, in fact, nine-tenths of the law, then the one-tenth that remains is the legitimation process. It is probably the hardest part, this reclaiming of our image-making power in what has been for a long time a foreign language."[60] Clarke's position on language is altogether different, inasmuch as he does not see Africadians as speaking or writing in a foreign tongue. His introduction to *Fire on the Water* states that "[r]esearch is needed to discover the major authors who have left their imprints on Africadian literature" before offering a massive list of names that includes John Milton, Virginia Woolf, Walt Whitman, W.E.B. Du Bois, Zora Neale Hurston, Langston Hughes, Margaret Atwood, Michael Ondaatje, and, yes, M. NourbeSe Philip.[61] Philip points out, with undisguised scepticism, that other Caribbean writers have seen matters this way as well: "Some writers – Derek Walcott and Wilson Harris immediately come to mind – have publicly acknowledged their gratitude for the 'blessing' conferred on them by the imposition of the English language and have, in fact, refused to acknowledge that there even exists a dilemma."[62] That is more or less the way that Clarke sees the matter of linguistic inheritance, although it seems clear that he can see the dilemma (something that also seems clear to me chez Walcott, given his re-claiming of the *Odyssey*

as *Omeros*). In any event, this sense of inheritance as opposed to being alienated from cultural memory is consistent with the way that Clarke sees territorial belonging as well. Philip writes that this subversion of language "began
when the African in the New World through alchemical ... practices succeeded in transforming the leavings and detritus of a language and infused
it with her own remembered linguistic traditions."[63] In Africadia, such linguistic memories belong to the eighteenth century; there are no "remembered
linguistic traditions" linked to Africa. What is remembered is *place*, and that
place is the Canadian maritime region.

Hence the ongoing attachment to Africville, the majority-Black neighbourhood whose lands were expropriated and whose houses were demolished between 1964 and 1969, its residents displaced throughout the city, all by the
municipal government of Halifax. It serves to this day as a singularly powerful
symbol within the African-Nova-Scotian community, and no discussion of
Africadian belonging gets far without invoking its memory.[64] I am not trying
to imply that Africville has been around since the 1780s, rather to evoke the
degree to which Africadian belonging has indispensable connections to the
eastern coast of Canada. Once we are discussing Black communities in Toronto (which Rinaldo Walcott, in his critique of Clarke's maritime-centricity,
points out are very old indeed) or the Black communities of the prairies (most
although certainly not all of which trace their heritage to the second half of
the nineteenth century or the first years of the twentieth), we are discussing
something else: not something more or less authentic or more or less Canadian or anything like that (and that is the gist of Walcott's critique of Clarke,
that he sees Africadians as less citified and therefore more authentic), but definitely something *different*.

In terms of NourbeSe Philip's sense of language, Clarke is not interested
in taking English apart or rejecting its strictures so much as unifying disparate
elements. As I say, though, he (like Derek Walcott, I hasten to repeat) can see
that there is a dilemma there, something he has made manifest in much of
his poetry. We can see this in Clarke's "Language" (part of his 2006 collection
Black), which early on calls English "a tongue that cannibalizes all other
tongues" and which concludes this way:

A "herring choker" Negro with a breath of brine,
I gabble a *garrote* argot, guttural, by rote,
A wanton lingo, taunted and tainted by wine,
A feinting *langue* haunted by each slave boat.

My black, "Bluenose" brogue smacks lips and ears
When I bite the bitter grapes of Creole verse –
Or gripe and blab like a Protestant pope
So rum-pungent Africa mutes perfumed Europe.[65]

This vision of a mixed-up, impure English is far from being romantic about cultural mixture, given how "haunted by each slave boat" the entire proceedings are. But the violence is not overwhelming: a "'Bluenose' brogue" – that is to say a British English infused with the sounds of maritime Canada – can carry Black-inflected meaning; "rum-pungent Africa" does survive in the memory of "A 'herring choker' Negro with a breath of brine," a line that deploys a term which the *Dictionary of Canadianisms on Historical Principles* defines as "*Slang*, a Maritimer, *q.v.*, especially one from New Brunswick."[66] Colonial violence is present in these verses, but that is not *all* that is present.

Something similar can be seen in *Whylah Falls*, the experimental prose-poetry hybrid that really put Clarke on the map when it was published in 1990. There he writes:

She salts her stored, miniature sea, churns it with a walnut spoon, then lifts goodness, a kiss, to her lips while spicy, flamboyant smells green her kitchen into Eden.

Cooking is faith. Cora opens her antique cookbook, a private bible, enumerating Imperial measures, English orders, – pinches, pecks, cups, teaspoons of this or that – and intones, "I create not food but love. The table is a community. Plates are round rooves; glasses, iced trees; cutlery, silver streams."

Her Jarvis County cuisine, gumboing the salty recipes of Fundy Acadians, the starchy diets of South Shore Loyalists, and the fishy tastes of Coloured Refugees, includes rappie pie, sweet potato pie, pollen pancakes, streamed fiddleheads, baked cabbage, fried clams, dandelion beer, mackerel boiled in vinegar, and basic black-and-blue berries …[67]

That invocation of "the salty recipes of Fundy Acadians, the starchy diets of South Shore Loyalists, and the fishy tastes of Coloured Refugees" evokes a whole world of Africadia, an identity that was forged through violence but which has persisted through centuries and become something new. If that violence has not been fully redeemed, then it has at least become something *meaningful*, and thus the possibility of redemption lies off in the distance.

That is part of the faith that Clarke is evoking; Clarke writes in *Odysseys Home* that "Africadia – a particularity defined by race and religion – is a community of believers."[68] That is different from the linguistic ethics that Philip is sketching out.

Rinaldo Walcott has also taken serious issue with Clarke, spurred on by what Clarke had written about his 1997 book *Black Like Who? Writing Black Canada* in his 1998 essay "Treason of the Black Intellectuals?" (given as a lecture at the McGill Institute for the Study of Canada and reprinted in *Odysseys Home*). There Clarke criticized what he saw as confused thinking about nation, pan-Africanism, and Black Canadian writers.[69] Walcott responded in turn in the 2003 edition of the book, focussing on a 1997 essay called "Honouring African-Canadian Geography" and writing that "Clarke's mapping supposes an authentic older and rural black Canada set against an inauthentic newer and urban black Canada, as if the two have not always and cannot live side by side … Clarke's regressive localism, as Kobena Mercer would call it, fails to account for diaspora connectedness, exchanges and circulation of cultural forms and artifacts as at least one avenue through which people live their lives whether in rural or urban areas."[70] Walcott summarizes his overall position by saying that "[n]ation-centred discourse can only be a trap that prohibits black folks from sharing common feeling, especially when common actions and practices of domination seem to present themselves time and again in different spaces/places/nations."[71] That position is more or less the commonly held one in progressive circles: by definition a nation doesn't include everyone, and good things don't follow from exclusion. It is rather a broad unity among populations before whom "practices of domination seem to present themselves time and again" that should be imperative. I sense this scepticism on Walcott's part when he writes, "I understand Clarke's response as melancholic because it cannot exceed the modern category of the nation as a place to which one is born and naturally belongs. His criticism remains locked in a discourse of heritage and genealogy which it believes once revealed will both install and correct a lack of knowledge."[72] My book is offered in no small part as a challenge to this mainstream progressive understanding of the nation, a challenge that rejects the idea that "the modern category of the nation" is something that it is important to exceed. No small part of my position on that flows from Stuart Hall's statement in his posthumously published book[73] *The Fateful Triangle: Race, Ethnicity, Nation* that "'[n]ation,' like 'ethnicity,' I would argue, has in itself no necessary political belongingness."[74] He goes on to say that "nowhere … has the idea of a black nation come to fruition in the form imagined or delivered by the diaspora's principal thinkers. Yet none of this destroys the power of the nation *as a discourse* and its potent effects on the black imaginary."[75] Much of George Elliott Clarke's work – in criticism, poetry, and experimental prose – has been devoted to giving voice to the ways in which that *discourse* has affected the Black communities of Canada's Atlantic over the long haul of the last four centuries.

In any event, that widespread progressive scepticism is not Clarke's position at all, and Walcott sees it as a problem (even though that doesn't really seem to be Stuart Hall's position either). Specifically, Walcott argues that "Clarke's Red Tory position fails to account for, or in many cases reduces all black Canadian politics to, his own Red Tory desires."[76] I wouldn't say that Walcott is wrong here, and I'm not sure that Clarke would either; nor am I entirely sure that Clarke would see that as so meaningful a disagreement. He writes in *Odysseys Home*, for instance, that the critique of technological liberalism offered by George Grant (as I mentioned in the introduction, the original Red Tory) shows "[t]his implicit alliance between Canadian Red Toryism and African-American social-democratic principles."[77] What Clarke is calling towards is the communitarian ethos that has been so dominant in Black political discourse on both sides of the 49th parallel, a communitarianism that is clearly born of the community-shattering experiences of slavery specifically and racism in general. The paper in *Odysseys Home* where Clarke follows Grant's critique of technology-led liberalism (particularly important in Grant's 1969 collection *Technology and Empire* and his last published collection, 1986's *Technology and Justice*) was a comparison of the "conservative modernity" that he argues is key in recent Africadian and Acadian poetry of a nationalist bent. He is actually tentative about his conclusions along those lines, entertaining the possibility that "I am too hasty in asserting the triumph of a nationalist, quasi-religious poetic for Africadians."[78] That may be, but what it is crucial to consider here is the *nationalist* quality of the poetic voice he is tracking. His argument is that variants of *nationalism* are a key part of that tradition, just as they were in the United States, from figures such as Du Bois (so admired by the theorists of négritude) right up to Amiri Baraka and his circle. That is not the same as conflating "all Black Canadian politics" with Red Toryism.

Indeed, this seems an odd claim to make given how explicitly Clarke has discussed his Red Tory tendencies in his critical writing, which is more than can be said for Walcott's position, a mixture of radical calls for social change (and I mean this in the true sense of the word: a call to change society *at the root*) coupled with an unspoken liberalism that frames the results of those calls in mostly individualist terms. Clarke says as much in his "Treason of the Black Intellectuals" essay, that "Walcott himself obeys a shibboleth of liberalism."[79] This mixture of radicalism and liberalism is not at all unusual in academic discourse, even of the more militantly activist variety (Walcott is a highly respected scholar and activist, currently chair of SUNY-Buffalo's Department of Africana and American Studies, having also served as the director of the Women and Gender Studies Institute at the Ontario Institute for Studies in Education). The regional stakes of the game become somewhat clearer when Walcott writes that "Toronto is Canada's most densely populated black space/place with both recent and older migratory communities dating back to before Confederation. Clarke's Red Tory desire to belong to a Canada propagated on a particular narrative of black invisibility is troubling and a conceptual blind spot."[80] This isn't a blind spot at all chez Clarke; he is explicit about the degree to which his community is not part of "Canada's most densely populated black space/place," and his work (as Walcott also says) is defined by a certain melancholy he derives from that fact. Clarke writes in *Odysseys Home* of the Africadia that he knew: "There was no righteously destabilizing Black Power activism, for our provincial community of less than 30,000 souls was too small and too conservative to tolerate much more than casually militant rhetoric."[81]

The real issue, then, is that it is not at all clear that Clarke believes that Africadians belong to Canada in the manner of African-Canadian communities of Toronto, that is to say in the manner of Kymlicka's (2): "polyethnic rights." This is not to deny the Canadian-ness of Clarke or Africadian communities, any more than one can deny the American-ness of that native son of Newark who formed the core of my last section. Rather, it is to point out that like the Québécois and the Métis,[82] Africadians have historically sought to "belong to a Canada" in ways that would accommodate *national* difference; indeed, in all these cases, that has been the *primary* justification for this belonging. It is a myth brought on by an imperial liberalism (that is to say, a liberalism that does not recognize itself as simply one position among many but rather as a sort of metaphysics, outside of which it is impossible to conceptualize justice) which holds that the state's primary ethical imperative is the recognition of a minority subject's individual ethnic specificity. That is certainly the assumption that flows from Canadian multiculturalism, introduced by the federal Liberals as policy in 1971 and as part of the Pierre Trudeau–era constitution

in 1982.[83] Walcott's *Black Like Who?* has a lengthy critique of Canadian multiculturalism's inability to engage Blackness, writing at one point that "the Canadian nation-state has no way of making sense of communities founded
across and upon difference. Official multicultural policy in Canada actually
works to produce a definition of community that is about one's relationship
to another nation-state."[84] Be that as it may, Africadian nationalism is precisely
dependent on the *lack* of "another nation state," even as it is equally dependent
on an adherence to the Canadian state (although not necessarily the English-
Canadian nation). As both the Québécois and the Métis know all too well,
this is not the relationship that Canadian multiculturalism was made to enable, regardless of whether or not its proponents are or aren't living up to its
promises. So the real difference between Walcott and Clarke is that Walcott
reads Canadian multiculturalism as phony; for Clarke (as for the Québécois,
and the Métis, and First Nations groups, and the Inuit), Canadian nationalism
is more or less beside the point. Strongly influenced by George Grant and
more influenced by African-American discourse than may be immediately
apparent ("To carry the Atlantic into Montreal in epic suitcases with Harlem
accents," he writes in "Africadian Experience"),[85] Clarke's vision of Africadia
simply follows a different path. Early on in *Odysseys Home*, Clarke laments
how in some Pan-Africanist approaches, "[o]ne sees here a reductive reading
of *blackness* which cannot accommodate – or cannot hear – the *different* blackness of Nova Scotia."[86] Just as it did among the négritude poets and among
Amiri Baraka and his circle, that difference has a name: nation.

IV. Kwame Anthony Appiah and Paulin Hountondji: *Cosmopolite, nationaliste?*

My colleagues and I felt that the word "traditional" would incline the reader
to perceive this kind of knowledge as something fixed, immutable and reluctant to change over the centuries. We preferred the word "endogenous" to
dwell on the origin of a cultural product or value that comes from, or at least
is perceived by people as coming from inside their own society, as opposed
to imported or "exogeneous" products or values – though we should admit,
in a sense, that there is no absolute origin at all, and the concept of
endogeneity itself should therefore be revitalised.
– Paulin Hountondji, "Producing Knowledge in Africa Today"[87]

So far I have been offering a fairly chronological genealogy of understandings of "the nation" in Black thought: from négritude to African-Americans of the 1970s to conceptions of Africadia since the 1990s. All of these have, one way or another, wound up at "nation." At what point do Black intellectuals abandon such thinking, or at least radically revise it? The critique of these various positions of Black nationalist discourse that is the most relevant for a contemporary understanding of national identity can be found in the work of Kwame Anthony Appiah. He has emerged as one of the key liberal thinkers of the twenty-first century, and despite my desire to critique liberalism and all it hath wrought, there is a lot in his work that seems particularly urgent for our present moment. What I want to do here, though, is illustrate the degree to which his classically liberal position is not (to continue my discussion of liberalism's meaning from the introduction) as anti-left as it sometimes appears to be. His critique of mainstream concepts of identity and his defence of a broad cosmopolitanism are strongly influenced by the Beninois philosopher Paulin Hountondji.

Appiah's work is varied, but he has a longstanding interest in matters of cultural identity and pluralism; the key works of his professional philosophy are, for our purposes here, *In My Father's House* (1992) and *The Ethics of Identity* (2005). The former is actually something of a hybrid work, being both a detailed critique of arguments on Pan-African idealism and a memoir of growing up in Ghana with a father who was an important part of the opposition establishment: recalling a visit by the Queen to a hospital where he was, as a young boy, a patient, he sardonically recalls, "Throughout all this, the president [Kwame Nkrumah], who had only recently locked up my father, stared at the ceiling tapping his foot (making, as it turned out, a mental note to return my doctor to what was then still Rhodesia)."[88] The latter is a more straightforwardly academic work along the same political lines, although much more general in focus. Those lines are fundamentally liberal, and Appiah is now well-known as one of the leading liberal intellectuals of the global Anglophone world, largely because of two books written in a more popular idiom: 2006's *Cosmopolitanism: Ethics in a World of Strangers*, and 2018's *The Lies That Bind: Rethinking Identity* (which, we will see, expands the critique of *The Ethics of Identity*). *In My Father's House* is important for our purposes here because it lays out Appiah's scepticism about identity's relevance for philosophy, specifically African identity's relevance. He is clearly impatient with a lot of négritude's writers, whom he sees as too quick to give away the philosophical game. He writes at one point in *In My Father's House* that "[i]f there is white philosophy, why not also black philosophy? The origins of the argument are intelligible – and it is somehow healthier than the view of the apostles of negritude, that black men should give the intellect over to whites and explore the affective realm that is their special property."[89] But he quickly rejects that possibility of "black philosophy," going on to say:

> But black philosophy must be rejected, for its defense depends on the essentially racist presuppositions of the white philosophy whose antithesis it is. Ethnocentrism – which is an unimaginative attitude to one's own culture – is in danger of falling into racism, which is an absurd attitude to the color of someone else's skin.[90]

I recognize here the rhetoric of those non-rhetorical questions that William Greaves posed at the Festival mondial des arts nègres: "Is négritude a positive or a negative philosophy? Is it racism or humanism? Will it help to unite the world, or divide it?" Appiah's answer to that three-part query would seem, roughly, to be "negative, racism, divide."

Given this position towards négritude, it is entirely consistent that he is also sceptical of what I argued was the real quest of négritude, and that is nation. In a chapter of *In My Father's House* called "Altered States," Appiah writes that "[i]f the history of metropolitan Europe in the last century and a half has been a struggle to establish statehood for nationalities, Europe left Africa at independence with states looking for nations."[91] Part of his support for this scepticism comes from the great Nigerian novelist Chinua Achebe, whom he quotes as saying:

> For instance, take the Igbo people. In my area, historically, they did not see themselves as Igbo. They saw themselves as people from this village or that village. In fact in some place "Igbo" was a word of abuse; they were the "other" people, down in the bush. And yet, after the experience of the Biafran War, during a period of two years, it became a very powerful consciousness. But it was real all the time. They all spoke the same language, called "Igbo," even though they were not using that identity in any way. But the moment came when this identity became very powerful.[92]

I take the point; nations are artificial, and they come into being on the basis of sometimes unhappy conditions, in this case the bloody Biafran war of the late 1960s. But it does not follow from that insight that the term "nation" is therefore meaningless and shouldn't be taken seriously by pluralists. And to support that, I have a Chinua Achebe quote of my own, and about the Igbo no less. In his Harvard University lectures published in 2001 as *Home and Exile*, Achebe writes that "[t]he Igbo people of southeastern Nigeria are more than ten million strong and must be accounted one of the major peoples of Africa. Conventional practice would call them a tribe, but I no longer follow that convention. I call them a nation."[93] Achebe spends some time wrestling with the pitfalls of that term in ways that Appiah would no doubt recognize, but he never backs off from that basic change of heart. Drawing his discussion along these lines to a close, he writes that "[t]he Igbo have always lived in a world of continual struggle, motion and change – a feature conspicuous in the tautness, overreach and torsion of their art; it is like a tightrope walk, a hairbreadth brush with the boundaries of anarchy."[94] I would suggest that one way of shoring up those boundaries is the consolidation of national identity. That role for nation is a distinctly modern phenomenon, and is in keeping with Achebe's sense of the Igbo as defined by "struggle, motion and change." I do not accept that this acknowledgment of change, this willingness to move confidently into what modernity has to offer, must somehow exclude nation. To assume that is to beg the question of the nation's modernity – that is, to define it in a way that presupposes its pre-modern or anti-modern essence. That doesn't seem right to me at all, and not only because Anderson's *Imagined Communities* went to such lengths to explain its roots in modernity, specifically print culture and the sense of "simultaneity" that print culture enabled. Instead, I rely heavily on the image that George Orwell offered in the first pages of *The Lion and the Unicorn*. I hear echoing in Achebe's sense of the ever-changing Igbo nation Orwell's question: "What can the England of 1940 have in common with the England of 1840? But then, what have you in common with the child of five whose photograph your mother keeps on the mantlepiece? Nothing, except that you happen to be the same person."[95]

I can see Appiah wrestling with the definition of "the nation" over several books, but he never entirely abandons the hostile position that he staked out in *In My Father's House*. In his 2005 monograph *The Ethics of Identity*, he writes that "I want, in fact, to distinguish the nation and the state to make a point entirely opposite to Herder's; namely, that if anything is arbitrary, it is not the state but the nation."[96] He goes on to say that "[t]he nation *is* arbitrary, but not in the sense that we can discard it in our normative reflections,"[97] so perhaps not all is lost. But it is difficult to read the word "arbitrary" as anything other than pejorative. Let me make an effort to read it otherwise, because really, I don't disagree with this assessment. Having said that, I repeat that I reject the idea that nations are inherently based in ethnicity or blood lines, as we can see from the aforementioned panoply of multiethnic nations. None of these nations are arbitrary, since each has emerged from a complex series of political and historical intersections, all in some way linked to a territory. To follow Patrick Deneen (whose critique of liberalism I will discuss at greater length in the next chapter), the nation is readable as "arbitrary" only if the sole relevant locus is the individual subject. Deneen argues that liberalism posits that "[t]he place where one happens to be born and raised is as arbitrary as one's parents, one's religion, or one's customs,"[98] but this arbitrariness is a relevant consideration only within the "everywhere and nowhere" variety of liberalism that he evokes. Reading "the nation" as arbitrary because it takes so little notice of individual sovereignty is consistent with the liberalism at the core of Appiah's thought, but of course liberalism is not the only way to see the world.

When he tries to define nation in a semi-sympathetic way thirteen years later in his mass-market book *The Lies That Bind: Rethinking Identity* (2018), Appiah returns to that question-begging sense that such belonging must be about the past. He writes there that "a nation is a group of people who think of themselves as sharing ancestry and also *care* about the fact that they have that supposed ancestry in common."[99] But here we run into "the naturalization problem," wherein, as we will recall from the introduction, Benedict Anderson marvels that "from the start the nation was conceived in language, not in blood, and that one could be 'invited into' the imagined community. Thus today, even the most insular nations accept the principle of naturalization (wonderful word!), no matter how difficult in practice they may make it."[100] As I said there, I don't really accept the "conceived in language" piece, something that will become clear in every chapter that follows via Ireland (English/Irish), India (twenty-two official languages), New Zealand (English/Māori), Scotland (English/Gaelic/Scots), and the Métis (French/Michif/Cree/English). But that is comparably minor compared to my objection to Appiah's "supposed ancestry in common" piece, which I think is entirely wrong-headed (as opposed to the broad spirit of Anderson's formulation, which is consistent with assuming that nations, like other social forces, have adapted to modernity). Even though, as I said earlier, I was born in Philadelphia and raised in Colorado, I've held a Canadian passport since 2005 and describe my nationality to anyone who asks as "English Canadian." My wife, whose mother was born in Scotland and came to Canada as a young teacher recruit and whose Métis father grew up working the Cree-speaking traplines of northern Alberta, generally gives the same response (actually she usually just says "Canadian," a slippage I'll discuss in more detail in the second chapter devoted to "Federations"). My wife and I have no ancestry in common, and that is an understatement; what we share is a *national* identity. To return to the Paulin Hountondji quote that opens this section, national identity is not "something fixed, immutable and reluctant to change," but it is "endogenous," inasmuch as in the case of, say, English-Canadian identity, it comes from inside of the society to which I, my wife, and our two sons (for whatever happenstances of birth, relocation, and marriage) belong.

Appiah's work is worth dwelling on at this length because he seems to have staked out a position that might be considered "post-négritude," and which seems to take the other positions that I have dealt with in this section so far into the present day: into the realm of the post-national, into the realm of the liberal. He is near-explicit about this in *In My Father's House*, where he writes, "it is crucial that we recognize the independence, once 'Negro' nationalism is gone, of the Pan-Africanism of the diaspora and the Pan-Africanism of the continent. It is, I believe, in the exploration of these issues, these possibilities, that the future of an intellectually reinvigorated Pan-Africanism lies."[101] The Appiah texts I have dealt with here vary in their tone and their approach, but they do share that common analysis: négritude and its antecedents are over, the age of cosmopolitanism is upon us, and the search for new models is the moral imperative for people concerned with pluralism. Most of the new models he proposes, I have tried to show, are based in traditional liberalism.

But something else that these texts share is the influence of the Beninois philosopher Paulin Hountondji, someone who is clearly a touchstone for Appiah, and who is not a liberal in this traditional mode. Hountondji is one of the founding figures of modern African philosophy, and his early work is devoted to sketching out what Africa needs from philosophy, *real* philosophy as opposed to the folk wisdom that many Europeans had been passing off as "native" philosophical thought. In a 1981 article in *Présence africaine* on this problem, Hountondji talks about "the real power of philosophy. As a critique of 'ideology,' it performs a top-level clarifying function by which it contributes to clearing away, cleaning up and freeing up the field of politics in terms of its connections to productive activity, material interests and conflicts of those interests, and finally the class struggle"[102] (m.t.). That sense of philosophy as "une fonction clarificatrice de première plan" is central; that has tremendous importance in much of west-African culture, but it has nothing to do with the quasi-ethnographic studies of the continent's culture that Hountondji believed had been passing for "African philosophy." Of all Appiah's books *In My Father's House* is the most explicit about Hountondji's influence, having a full chapter devoted to this specific matter of philosophy's vocation in Africa, titled "Ethnophilosophy and Its Critics." Over the course of his career Hountondji wrote a great deal about why this "ethnophilosophy" tendency is inadequate as an approach for African philosophers. He staked that territory out fairly early, writing in a 1970 article (which would later become part of his best-known book, *African Philosophy: Myth and Reality*) that "African philosophy has, up to now, been in essence an ethnophilosophy only: imaginary research after a collective philosophy, which might be unchangeable, shared by all Africans, even if it existed in an unconscious form."[103] This was a problem for Hountondji because it was essentialist, but it was also a problem because that sort of essentialism bypassed a local readership and engaged with a touristic European who was looking to move beyond particularity and towards the universals so beloved of liberalism. He writes in that same 1970 article:

> Thus one sees that "Africanist" particularism is itself, in the abstract, part of an abstract universalism, *objectively*, since the African intellectual who is assumed by it is engaged at the same time; above the shoulders of his people in a mythical dialogue with Europeans who speak the same language, he is engaged in the constitution of a "civilisation of the universal."[104]

It feels mean to point it out, but that is not far off of the dialogue that Appiah is participating in, a dialogue that seeks to illuminate just such a "civilisation of the universal." This is most evident in his 2006 book *Cosmopolitanism: Ethics in a World of Strangers* (like *The Lies That Bind*, a mass-market paperback), where we find statements such as (defending UNESCO's 1954 *Convention for the Protection of Cultural Property in the Event of Armed Conflict*) "Framing the problem this way – as an issue for *all* mankind – should make it plain that it is the value of the cultural property to people and not to peoples that matters. It isn't peoples who experience and value art: it's men and women."[105] Again, this breeziness issues from a liberalism about which Appiah is more explicit than many critics of nationalism, but which does sometimes seem perilously close to the pseudo-metaphysical variety that I mentioned earlier. Hountondji proceeds from a position that has elements of this liberalism, but

is really defined by a more communitarian ethic. In that 1981 *Présence africaine*
article, he continued this criticism of ethnophilosophy by writing that it "is
a philosophy in the 3rd person. It consists of parsimoniously hiding behind
the thought of the group, in avoiding taking a position yourself and pro-
nouncing on problems that this ancestral thought has responded to in its own
manner"[106] (m.t.). Here it is the *self* that is at issue, since he is dressing down
philosophers who refuse to put *their own* positions on the line, so to speak.
He also defines "African-ness" (l'africanité) in a way that recalls some of Appiah's scepticism of identity but still retains a sense of sympathy for the sense
of connection that such concepts retain:

> My definition of African-ness, like the one I propose for philosophy, is
> above all polemical. It seeks to recall that in the most current sense of
> the term Africa is a continent and not a philosophy or a value system,
> and that this word designates a part of the world and nothing more, that
> this concept is geographical, empirical and contingent, not something
> that can be determined *a priori*.[107] (m.t.)

In interpreting this sense of cultural belonging (not exactly national but close
to it) as "un concept géographique, empirique et contingent," it would be
tempting to see Hountondji's position as a reaction against négritude's sense
of African-ness as something that is inherent in the entirety of Africa and its
diaspora, and therefore widely misunderstood. There certainly is that sense
in statements like this, and a lot of Hountondji's work is a critique of négritude
and its simplifications. But here, I am more inclined to focus on this sense of
l'africanité as *contingent* and *geographical*, two key elements of the approach
to nation that I am defending in this book because of the way that they leave
such identity (and identity broadly, to respond to Appiah's *The Lies That Bind*)
open to newcomers and consensual in terms of adherence, and thus are consistent with a broader progressive project of social cohesion.

That is a critique of négritude that it is important to take seriously: one
that expresses discomfort with some of the romantic essentialism that is a
perhaps-inevitable reaction to the experience of a colonialism that reduces
such a diverse group to the common status of "nègre," but which was nevertheless defined by the spirit that Senghor expressed in the last stanza of his
1945 poem "Joal": "I remember, I remember / In my head the rhythm / Of
such a weary walk across the long days of Europe where sometimes / An or-
phan jazz appears that sobs sobs sobs."[108] That plangent sense of longing for

connection across forms, across seas, had a different meaning in 1945 than it would in the twenty-first century, a difference that is as marked as the one between Senghor the Paris student and Senghor "le président-poète." Hountondji can see this, and his memoir *The Struggle for Meaning* (originally published as *Combat pour le sens*; Appiah wrote the foreword to the English edition) has a short section devoted to his encounters with both Césaire and Senghor, years after the initial dust had settled and both men were now senior statesmen (in Senghor's case literally so). Hountondji recalls how at a conference he "warned against the temptation of a reductive, unilateral and overly simplifying reading of cultures and especially, of worldviews of the African continent," a position that is not so far from the one that Rinaldo Walcott has taken on George Elliott Clarke. Indeed, Hountondji writes that he saw Senghor as "the ideologue of a négritude that I did not accept, and one of the bridgeheads of neocolonialism in Africa."[109] But upon meeting him at a conference, he asks: "Childishness on my part? I don't know, but I was charmed by the man, and secretly proud of him … I think Senghor's official functions and political choices counted heavily for the negative reception of his work by Africa's progressive youth. From the moment he demonstrated, by resigning, the extent to which he put those functions themselves in perspective, he is being read with new eyes, being rediscovered."[110] Perhaps his retrospective respect for the way Senghor handled political power was in some small part due to Hountondji's own experiences on that front, having served as Benin's minister of national education from 1990 to 1991 (that is to say, during the country's transition to democracy) and then minister of culture and communication from 1991 to 1993. In any event, that kind of rediscovery is overdue not just for négritude, but for African-American nationalism and for those invested in the defence of Africadia as well. In so doing, we can take what is valuable from Appiah (and from liberalism as a whole, it is important to concede), that is to say a concern for both openness and an ethical cosmopolitanism, at the same time insisting that we should, following Césaire, "[not] say *ethnicity* but *identity*, because that makes matters clear." And in so doing, we will also find ourselves relying on the solidity, however constructed, of that geographical, empirical, and contingent structure that is the nation.

CHAPTER 2

Republics

The words "republic" and "republican" do a lot of work in a lot of different cultural and historical contexts. In Ireland the word "republican" has, for at least four centuries (the eighteenth, nineteenth, twentieth, and twenty-first), been synonymous with "violent or violence-adjacent separatists." In contemporary France, "republican" often means "someone opposed to multiculturalism." In the Republic of Georgia, to say that it meant one thing during the Soviet period and another during the post-Soviet independence period would be a massive understatement, to say nothing of the fact that neither definition really synchronizes with what it meant during Georgia's *first* independence period, 1918–21. In India, it seems to mean just the opposite of what it means in France, given that country's dizzying cultural and linguistic diversity; most viscerally it calls to mind the fact that independence from the British crown was hard-fought and relatively recent. Globally speaking, the word "republic" generally summons simple images of "independent country, not a monarchy," and thus it's no surprise that this is the most common form of political organization among independent states (and the most common aspiration for sub-state groups seeking independence). Given that prominence, it is imperative to have some sense of the diversity of countries whose names bear the term, hopefully with the end result being a clearer sense of what these diverse formations have in common.

The key question is what is genuinely *distinctive* about a republic, as opposed to other specific forms of political organization that I'll go on to discuss: commonwealths and federations. That prominence of "republic" also imposes an imperative to explain how, exactly, it connects to the larger, meta-level structures that define this book: nations and states. What I will try to do here is look at a diverse range of cultural and political actors – a philosopher, a president who refused to call himself a president, and a group of filmmakers – by way of showing that definitions of "republic" have little holding them together save the centrality of diversity itself. I know that sounds like a hopelessly pious formulation that is also dizzyingly circular – "it's held together by the fact that nothing holds it together!" So let me try again. Republics are forms of political organization that aspire to the *universal*; the "uni" part of that is important, but perhaps not as important as the implication of the infinite.

Further to that aspiration towards universalism or hints at infinite diversity, perhaps the winner of the "most unlikely example" prize for this book can be awarded here, to Abbas Kiarostami's film *First Case, Second Case* (1979). Before his death in 2016, Kiarostami was well-established as one of the major figures of post-wwii world cinema. He began his career, however, making children's films for the Iranian governmental agency Kanoun, also known as the Institute for the Intellectual Development of Children and Young Adults (its existence spans the pre- and post-Revolutionary periods). These are charming in terms of the performance of the child actors, often graphically interesting, and sometimes offer a preview of the realist aesthetic Kiarostami would develop and then radically deconstruct in his mature work. *First Case, Second Case*, though, is different. Organized as a combination of re-enactments and then interviews with authorities, the film is a kind of symposium on an ethical question: should a child, punished as part of a group even though he didn't really do what they are all accused of, denounce the truly guilty friend to his frustrated teacher? Or should he accept unjust punishment in the name of solidarity with his fellow students? It's not so surprising that most of the adults Kiarostami interviews argue for the latter. What is a surprise is the political and cultural diversity of these moral authorities that the film presents: Islamists such as Ayatollah Sadegh Khalkhali, who was the first head of the Revolutionary Courts (his *New York Times* obituary of 29 November 2003 notes that he ordered the execution of hundreds of people; in this film he says forcing such a confession is contrary to the teachings of Islam); but also Rabbi David Shoftet, the leader of the Iranian Jewish Community (who would soon go into exile in Los Angeles); Bishop Ardok Manoukian, religious leader of Iran's Armenian community; Noureddin Kianouri, head of the Tudeh Party, more or less the Communists, banned as of 1983; and a host of artists, intellectuals, and activists, some of whom are women (none of the women wear any Islamic headgear). Begun just before the revolution, the film was finished in the earliest of the post-Shah days, and it serves as a poignant reminder both of how genuinely diverse a country Iran was (and in certain sectors struggles to remain), and how such diversity really could have been served by the transfer from a centralized monarchical system to an adjective-less republic. The country's official transformation, within months, into the very strongly adjectivized *Islamic* Republic of Iran here comes to seem wholly inconsistent with a republican idea as such. No wonder the film was shelved by the Islamic Republic's cinema authorities, unseen until global interest in Kiarostami's cinema started to lead to the organization of *complete* retrospectives. It is a fleeting glimpse of what an Iranian republic – one defined by religious, cultural, and political diversity – could have looked like, of an Iranian universalism that was not to be.

By paying closer attention to three specific examples – France, Georgia, and India – I want to show some of the different ways that "universal" part of the republican ideal as such has come to be expressed. My perspective is thus a limited one, and deliberately so. France is often used by contemporary pundits as a case study in the ways that a republican model suppresses diversity. It is very common to find, in mainstream discourse, discussion to the effect of "why is France hostile to multiculturalism? Because republicanism!" But Simone Weil's blueprint for a resurrected republic, *L'enracinement*, shows that this is not at all the case; French understandings of republic are in fact much more supple and complex than "we're all just French and nothing else" or some comparable simplification. Georgia, on the other hand, is widely understood by commentators outside of the country as being made up of, well, Georgians. Visitors to Georgia are invariably told by locals that the name in Georgian for the country is "Sakartvelo," and that this means "Land of the Georgians." In fact "Sa*kartve*lo" means "Land of the *Kartve*lians," which is Georgia's dominant ethnic group; there are many other such groups within the state's borders, only a very few of which have any sense of being something other than "Georgian." Thus Georgia is a kind of inverse of France: far more groups consider themselves Georgian than may appear to be the case at first. India comes right up the middle: a republic that has diversity as an existential fact, as the thing that makes it different from neighbours such as Pakistan or Bangladesh, both defined by Muslim majorities well into the 90 per cent range. These three examples thus provide a wide range of insights into the term "republican."

Charles Taylor's sense of republicanism is a useful way into these questions. He wrote in a 1989 essay called "Cross-Purposes: The Liberal-Communitarian Debate" that "the very definition of a republican regime as classically understood requires an ontology different from atomism, falling outside atomism-inflected common sense. It requires that we probe the relations of identity and community, and distinguish the different possibilities, in particular the possible place of we-identities as against merely convergent I-identities, and the consequent role of common as against convergent goods."[1] In this rejection of convergent individualities, Taylor is consistent with French thinkers such as Tzvetan Todorov, whose 1995 text *La vie commune* is clear on this matter. Todorov memorably writes that "a plurality of solitudes does not a society make"[2] (m.t.). Towards the end of the book he reaffirms this in more metaphysical terms that echo Taylor's 1988 *Sources of the Self*, writing that "[t]he self only exists in and by its relations with others: intensifying social exchange intensifies the self"[3] (m.t.). That sense of a society defined by an explicit opposition to atomism is key, and accounts for some of the centralizing tendencies so widely assumed to be a defining quality of French republicanism. But an equally important aspect of what Taylor is identifying and Todorov is echoing is the "consequent role of common … goods." What, exactly, are those common goods? Much of the hostility towards multicultural models in French life indicates that this can be taken as something like "the good of an uncomplicated, shared Frenchness." It should not be so difficult to see how such an identity can be seen as a good, considering the kinds of social cohesion and pluralism that "we are all just basically French" can indeed lead towards. It is thus important not to dismiss this desire for what in many Francophone countries is known as *cohésion sociale* as simply ethnocentric or chauvinist.

Furthermore, there are good historical reasons for France of all places to be the home of a certain scepticism about multiculturalism. The Crown of France was comfortable making special arrangements with various dukes and seigneurs in the name of keeping together a culturally and linguistically diverse kingdom that was held together by little more than an allegiance to that Crown. The revolution meant to wipe away all the capricious inequality of that kingdom, and in so doing impose a common and level regime defined by the famous aspirations towards freedom, equality, and brotherhood. For the state to care about someone identifying as Algerian or Muslim and ameliorating accordingly can therefore seem suspicious because it recalls the old Crown caring if someone was Breton or Protestant, given the degree to which that Crown would have made arrangements with such groups (or actively repressed them) with the goal of maintaining its own supremacy.

Having said all that, it is not at all clear that a simple identity inherently constitutes the only *common* good worth preserving. That may well be the

case for many French citizens, but it's clearly not the case *universally* (a term
I will return to shortly). Especially relevant for such considerations are groups
such as the Catalans of France, who have had to struggle mightily for linguistic
rights (such as Catalan-medium schools), but whose activists have never
shown any serious interest in separatism or irredentism with the rest of Els
Països Catalans (which I will explain in more detail in chapter 4, the first of
two devoted to "Federations"). The best-known of those activists, Llorenç
Planes, wrote in his seminal 1974 pamphlet *El petit llibre de Catalunya-Nord*
that "Catalans in the north [i.e. in France] who have always considered themselves Catalans also qualify themselves as French: 'Yes I'm Catalan, but I'm
French too!' This is a very common response. The southern Catalans, on the
other hand, often simply say that they are Catalans"[4] (m.t.). The common
good at issue here is adherence to this sense of "més també francès!" wherein
"francès" is clearly a *national* identity that distinguishes Catalans in the north
from their southern neighbours (or their Catalan-speaking counterparts in
Andorra, Valencia, the Balearic Islands, etc.). This sense of *catalanité* is an "I-
identity" but it is nevertheless enmeshed in the "we-identity" of Frenchness.
This recognition of this kind of difference is fully consistent with the ideals
of republicanism, and should not simply be read as a sop to a North American–style multiculturalism inappropriate for life in the Hexagon.[5]

Taylor expanded on these nuances of the republican tradition in a paper
he delivered in 1986 in a tentatively democratizing Chile (Pinochet was in
power until 1990), published in 2012 as *Democracia Republicana / Republican
Democracy*. He wrote there of "a view which allows for the central place of ri-
valry and struggle in a free society ... but also sees the members as united
around a central pole of identification."[6] He goes on to argue that this pole
is largely institutional: "The long-term stable democracies have been generally
those ... where the national narrative, whether mythical or veridical, has taken
the growth of democratic institutions as one of its main themes, where belonging to the nation is partly defined in terms of allegiance to these institutions."[7] I am aware that institutional loyalty is not the same as national
identity. Indeed, I am mindful of Patrick Deneen's sense that an overreliance
on liberal proceduralism "induces a zero-sum mentality that becomes natio-
nalized polarization for a citizenry that is increasingly driven by private and
largely material concerns. Similarly, the 'cure' by which individuals could be
liberated from authoritative cultures generates social anomie that requires
expansion of legal redress, police proscriptions, and expanded surveillance."[8]

Given that I have already invoked him several times, it may be worth a brief pause at this point to explain the importance of the work of Patrick Deneen for this book's overall project. His 2018 book *Why Liberalism Failed* made enormous waves in American political circles, mostly but not entirely on the right (President Obama was a sympathetic reader, saying in an 18 June 2018 Facebook post, "I don't agree with most of the author's conclusions, but the book offers cogent insights into the loss of meaning and community that many in the West feel, issues that liberal democracies ignore at their own peril").[9] I find myself sympathetic with the overall ethic of the book, which is rigorously communitarian.[10] As with the journal *First Things* (to which he occasionally contributes, including an essay on Christopher Lasch in the December 2004 issue), what the left can find *chez Deneen* is a critique of liberalism that is both impatient with constant appeals to individual autonomy (recognizing there, as some of his "opposite numbers" on the Christopher Lasch–inflected left still do, a justification of selfishness dressed up in the costume of liberation) and sharply critical of the rapaciousness of globalized capitalism. But as with *First Things*, the devil is often in the details, and it is easy for a left reader of Deneen to be drawn into culture-wars–style complaints about the dangers of too much talk about diversity. I have a lot more sympathy with the overall goals of multiculturalism than Deneen does, even though I often find myself impatient with its advocates' frequent appeal to the easy conflation of what Michael Igantieff has called blood and belonging.[11] In the examples that follow – France, Ireland, Georgia, and India – I think we will see republics which allow for a diverse set of groups to belong, without any real interest in blood, so to speak. The diversity at issue in my examples flows from language, religion, and culture, all structures into which people are born, for sure, but all structures that people do need, at some point in their lives, to make an *active* effort to belong to if belong they shall.

As I mentioned in the introduction, I am a white guy of mostly Irish and Italian heritage. This is a matter of ethnicity, and since there is really nothing I can do about it I don't expect many people outside my family to take much interest. Thus other than protection against explicit discrimination (pretty rare in my case, obviously less rare for others), there is little I expect state or national formations to engage with on that front. But I am also Anglophone, Catholic, and English Canadian, all *elective* affinities that do indeed engage state formations. In Canada that has to do with the constitutional protection of the English language in Quebec; the provision of "separate schooling," i.e.

Catholic schooling, as a result of the *Quebec Act* (1774);[12] and the protection of local cultural production via bodies such as the Canada Council for the Arts, the CBC, and the National Film Board of Canada. Bodies such as these have a complex relationship with liberalism inasmuch as they depend on *my willing* (and thus individualist) affiliation to a *group* (which makes them anti-individualist). In my personal case those groups are Anglophones, Catholics, and English Canadians. But note the groups that state formations are *not* designed to protect: people whose heritage is from England, people whose heritage is from a majority-Catholic country such as Ireland or Italy, people whose heritage is English Canadian but now live, say, in the United States. I understand the place that a state can have in supporting such affiliations, and only the most churlish would object to modest public support for an Italian Benevolent Society in Saskatoon, or a Canadian Cultural Centre in Denver, inasmuch both are part of the historical fabric of the country in question and so deserve some support. But it is difficult to imagine a political framework that flows from the fact of a lot of people of Italian descent living in a certain jurisdiction, or a country that actively legislates in the interests of a diaspora community (Canadians in Denver, say) with no legal claim to citizenship. What critics of multiculturalism are often motivated by is an impatience with a legislative framework that *does* seem to flow from facts of ethnic memory or heritage rather than of living cultures, cultures that are living because they are open to newcomers (via integration or naturalization) in a way that ethnic memory or heritage, by definition, are not.

And we can find in Deneen's arguments a defence of that kind of living rather than manufactured or sentimental culture. A lot of *Why Liberalism Failed* is devoted to defending American distinctiveness, something that has long been a part of his scholarly work in political theory (he is a well-regarded scholar of de Tocqueville, for instance). Later on in *Why Liberalism Failed*, invoking Aleksandr Solzhenitsyn's famous "Harvard address" of 1978, Deneen writes that "[l]iberal legal structures and the market system mutually reinforce the destruction of cultural variety in favor of a legal and economic monoculture – or, more correctly, a mono-anticulture. Individuals liberated and displaced from particular histories and practices, are rendered fungible within a political-economic system that requires universally replaceable parts."[13] To return to my own case, most of my affiliations are singularly inefficient from an economic or legal standpoint. The *anglophonité* of people like me necessitates (among other things) an extra school board in Quebec; my wife and I insist on educating our children in French, necessitating the creation of an extra school board in Saskatchewan, where we currently live. Our family's Catholicism continues to necessitate the creation of yet another extra school board in Alberta, Saskatchewan, and Ontario (ironically the only provinces where the specifically religious strictures of the *Quebec Act* are still observed in the structure of school boards).[14] And our English-Canadian-ness? The expense of protecting such culture via the Canada Council for the Arts, the Canadian Broadcasting Corporation, and the National Film Board of Canada easily exceeds that of these extra school boards. It would all be *a lot* easier if everyone in this country could just speak English, send their kids to the same kinds of schools, and consume whatever commercially produced literature, visual art, and mass media happens to come down the pike (and, ideally, not pay too much attention to the extraordinary coincidence – move along, nothing to see here! – that nearly all of that turns out to be American). God knows that's how global conglomerates such as Netflix, when presented with the need to support Canadian cinema in exchange for the right to operate within Canada's media architecture, have generally responded. *Geez, isn't this all a bit much? Can't you just be blander? It would make global capitalism work a lot more smoothly if you could!* When Deneen talks about "a mono-anticulture" and the liberal legal and market systems that reinforce such a culture, he is opposing that kind of blandness, pointing out that the gain in capitalist efficacy is obviously not worth the loss of distinctiveness of language, religion, or culture, and that those who benefit from globalized capitalism are going to a lot of trouble to make that seem a lot less obvious.

Playing Taylor off Deneen is thus useful here because of the degree to which we can see their common adherence to a *communitarian* ethos, one that is at the heart of modern republicanism. To return to our friend the French Catalan speaker, what she needs from her state is precisely a recognition that Frenchness can accommodate the "cultural variety" of *catalanité* as opposed to the overwhelmingly Francophone nature of the country's cultural industries or the strictly legalistic monoculture of French life, both aspects to which too many republican fundamentalists are contributing, through an idealist (and sometimes aggressive bordering on belligerent) investment in state neutrality. But what are most likely to actually enable that difference *within Frenchness* are the kinds of "democratic institutions" that Taylor invokes. No doubt there is a constant danger of the sort of state overreach that Deneen invokes, but the vacuum created by the absence of such robust institutions will doubtlessly be filled by just the kind of diversity-erasing market forces that Deneen dreads and which Taylor, good social-democrat that he is, would also view with suspicion (I have in mind corporations such as Amazon or Netflix because of the degree to which cultural blandness is obviously in their economic interests). Taylor's "Liberal-Communitarian Debate" paper is over-all much more sympathetic to liberal proceduralism than Deneen; he sees within that regime the means by which diversity can be protected in ways that that are relatively transparent.

But Taylor is clear about liberal proceduralism's inadequacies, and he points to Quebec as illustrative. He writes in that same paper that "[a] society like Quebec can't but be dedicated to the defense and promotion of French culture and language, even if this involves some restriction on individual freedoms. It can't make cultural-linguistic orientation a matter of indifference. A government that could ignore this requirement would either not be responding to the majority will or would reflect a society so deeply demoralized as to be close to dissolution."[15] Taylor points to Quebec because of its special status as an island of French in the otherwise English-speaking sea of Canada and the US. But I have long been attracted to this aspect of political thought in Quebec (let's call it "protectionist" for lack of a better term) because I do not accept that the survival of the French language and the world of that language in North America is a unique problem. English Canada and, indeed, the United States, to say nothing of the Indigenous nations of North America, have comparable kinds of distinctiveness that are in serious danger of this sort of wiping-out. This is what Deneen is seeking to defend, as George Grant had before him. Quebec was an inspiration to Grant (he was a great admirer of both Henri Bourassa and René Lévesque), and I think what he saw there would have a lot of appeal for Patrick Deneen as well. Governments that leave their citizenry to have its cultural distinctiveness swamped by a voraciously globalized capitalism are no more "responding to the majority will" than a French government determined, on the basis of "neutrality," to efface all marks of regional specificity, one of which is the Catalan culture and language.

As we can see through many such comparable examples, the problem of cultures being swamped by an American-dominated mass culture is much larger than Quebec. The degree to which Hollywood cinema, like American TV, serves as a kind of baseline for cultural production, with work produced in any other locality seeming vaguely exotic and exceptional, is part of the same system that refuses to acknowledge "American" as one nationality among others, and which acts instead in the manner of omnipresent empire. In the pre-streaming era this tension was casually visible in the way that Canadian films were, in nearly every video store in Canada, shelved either in their own section or, just as commonly, as "foreign films." The films that were shelved simply as "current releases" were, with nearly no exceptions, American. The Québécois exist in a state alongside many English Canadians who blithely assume that everyone north of Mexico more or less speaks English, in the manner of film industry executives blithely assuming that "cinema" more or less means Hollywood cinema, with both parties willing, if pressed, to acknowledge the existence of a few charmingly folkloric exceptions here and there. The alienation from your own culture, the ever-present sense that anything that's not American is a little weird and exists only with the indulgence of that larger cultural formation, that is to say the indulgence of the people responsible for the creation of a "real" (read American) culture, are just the facts of Francophone life in North America. Indeed, twenty-first-century globalization has made such alienation constitutive of most places that are not the United States. Thus we are all living in Quebec now; I am perpetually frustrated that only the Québécois (along with a few others, as this book will bear out) seem to know it.

I may be giving the impression that "republican" is a somewhat contentious term in France, but that pales in comparison with the situation in Ireland, and it is worth turning there to really sharpen our understanding of the concept. As I mentioned above, in the English spoken in Ireland, the term "republican" carries inescapable associations with the struggle for independence from the UK and that war's still-ongoing aftershocks in Northern Ireland. In the north, to use that term rather than "nationalist" is to indicate a ferocity of commitment to a unified Ireland that is not necessarily engaged in armed struggle but is in that neck of the woods, just as the term "loyalist," rather than the more moderate appellation "unionist," does for the other side. Thus Richard Kearney's attempt to redefine the term in his 1997 book *Postnationalist Ireland* was a major task. He writes at one point that "[t]here is a battle to be fought over the meaning of the term 'republican' for Irish citizens in the emerging Europe. Waging this debate means confronting the following questions: Is the term so tainted by the campaign of IRA violence in Ulster[16] as to stand unredeemed and unredeemable? Has it denigrated irreversibly into the adversarial extremes of sectarian nationalism and loyalism?"[17] Kearney's answer to both questions is, more or less, "no," and for reasons that strongly recall the thought of his old MA supervisor Charles Taylor. The core of this reasoning is quasi-classical; it is about returning republicanism to its core qualities, which involve a tension between difference and cohesion. He summarizes his task this way:

It is surely in rethinking, and redebating, the various strands of the republican heritage that a new political paradigm might emerge: one capable of transmuting the old ideologies into new visions, denouncing
aberrations in order to save the honour of the name, reconciling the particular rights of the people(s) on this island with the universal rights of
man. In this respect there is, I believe, a great need for a novel appreciation of the *universalist* dimension of republicanism, as we move toward
greater integration with the common house of Europe and the wide
world. And there is a corresponding need for a reappreciation of its *lo-
calist* dimension, if we are ever to realize the possibilities of participatory
democracy which the project for a decentralized Europe of the regions
will, if achieved, open up.[18]

The invocation of "people(s)" is the key element, really. This republicanism
Kearney is striving for is invested in the usual business of a state organized
along the lines of liberalism; thus what is at issue would be problems such as
access to abortion or to marriage for same-sex couples, to invoke the most
significant political debates in the Republic of Ireland in the twenty-first century. It has been commonplace over the last few decades to assume that such
issues constitute the "real" politics of modern Ireland, with the "national question" of whether the whole island could unite into a single state, that is to say
the question of Irish *peoples* rather than just Irish people, seemingly consigned
to a distant century now long-passed (*sure nobody cares about that sort of thing
anymore! Who do you think you are, Wolfe Tone? All anyone really cares about
is the same stuff they care about in the United States!*).

This has proven illusory. Let's leave to the side for the moment Traveller
communities or residents of Gaeltacht areas[19] (who are by virtue of that res-
idence presumed to live their lives mostly through Irish[20] rather than through
English) to focus on the unionists of Northern Ireland who consider themselves British rather than Irish. The Irish unity that they have historically
opposed has recently taken on a new urgency with the passage of Brexit.
Northern Ireland voted about 55–45 for Remain (on 24 June 2016, BBC News
put it at 55.8 per cent to 44.2 per cent), and as a result many unionists who
would have previously found the notion of applying for the citizenship in the
Republic of Ireland which is their birthright[21] totally unthinkable seem, if the
massive surge in applications for Irish passports originating from Northern
Ireland is any indication, to have suddenly found it to be acceptable as they

saw their citizenship in the European Union vanish into history. Precise statistics are not easily available, but there is a good chance that there either is
right now or will soon be a majority of residents of Northern Ireland who are
citizens of the Republic of Ireland. I'll discuss all of this in more detail in chapter 4, the first of two devoted to "Federations," where I suggest that 1970s proposals for a federal Ireland are looking more and more relevant as each day
goes by. Such a discussion will need to proceed from the kinds of republican
principles Richard Kearney was seeking to recover: that is to say, not from
those that have defined the Republican movement in Ireland since 1921 and
before, but rather from a sense that a republic depends on respecting the autonomy of the individual but nevertheless has as its main goal the pursuit of
a "we-identity," something that recognizes Todorov's sense that there is no
self except in relation to others. To some extent this has to do with balancing
the needs of people (a Muslim woman in France who wants to wear a hijab
in public; a same-sex couple seeking to get married in Ireland) and the needs
of peoples (the Catalans of France, the unionists of Northern Ireland, etc.).
But if a republican regime is to be able to make such balances between autonomy and cohesion, it must be defined by a *cohesive* culture to which citizens
will be motivated to adhere (or not). Deneen and Taylor, in their common
sense of the inadequacies of procedural liberalism, are more or less in unison
on this. So let's have a look at a few different figures who conceptualized such
a republic: Simone Weil, who imagined a reborn, *raciné* republic while working for the exiled "Free French" in London; Noe Jordania, who presided over
the briefly independent Democratic Republic of Georgia only to find himself
exiled to France, and seemed to wonder if, really, that was where all of his dif-
ficulties had begun; and finally, a trio of extraordinary Bollywood filmmakers
who gave cinematic life to Jawaharlal Nehru's early, socialist-inflected nation-
building project, and in so doing enunciated the delicate dance between pluralism and the imperatives of a nation whose majority culture had too long
been marginalized as a quaint folkloric irrelevance. What I think we'll be able
to see via these examples is that republics are nothing if they are not diverse
and outward-looking, but those progressive virtues are not enough on their
own; they are inevitably defined by some sort of political and institutional
core designed to nurture both the "we-identities" that Taylor evokes and the
universalist aspirations so important to Richard Kearney.

I. Simone Weil's Republique française

It sometimes seems that it's only a matter of time before discussion of republican politics circles back to France. Tom Nairn, in *Faces of Nationalism*, writes that "France was the most important political model for modern and contemporary statehood. Although other formative revolutions preceded that of 1789, none established such a general template."[22] Lost in most of the broad discussion are the details of how this "general template" came to exist, no doubt because of the amount of constitutional upheaval that France would go on to experience in the century following its "Liberté, Égalité, Fraternité" moment – seven different regimes in the nineteenth century alone (First Republic, First Empire, Bourbon Restoration, July Monarchy, Second Republic, Second Empire, Third Republic), to say nothing of the four different constitutional regimes of the twentieth century (Third Republic, Vichy regime, Fourth Republic, Fifth Republic). Simone Weil's only book that was written as a book,[23] *L'enracinement: Prélude à une déclaration des devoirs envers l'être humain* (1949), offers a chance to examine the French concept of a republican state, albeit in a hypothetical form.

Weil has been a widely read voice in French philosophy for a long time now, so much so that it is tempting to think of her as a kind of "cult" figure in English-language circles (although she certainly continues to attract a lot of attention in the Francophone world). She was important, for instance, to the group clustered around Dwight Macdonald's magazine *politics*, which published translations of four of her essays in 1945 and 1946; the most famous of these, "The Iliad, or, the Poem of Force," was translated by Mary McCarthy. By 1963 she had become enough of a presence that Susan Sontag thought it necessary to critique the phenomenon, opening an essay simply titled "Simone Weil" with "The culture-heroes of our liberal bourgeois civilization are anti-liberal and anti-bourgeois; they are writers who are repetitive, obsessive, and impolite, who impress by force – not simply by their tone of personal authority and by their intellectual ardor, but by the sense of acute personal and intellectual extremity."[24] The "extremity" she was referring to had mostly to do with Weil's death in 1943, which came at the age of thirty-four when despite her already-failing health (she had been diagnosed with tuberculosis) she starved herself, refusing to eat any more than the rations offered to residents of occupied France. She also cultivated a singularly intense form of Christianity (although she had been born into a prosperous Jewish family in Paris). She refused to be baptised, possibly out of hostility towards an institutional church (as I will discuss in the next section), but also as part of a lifelong program of denial and self-sacrifice. She died not in France but in England, where she had gone to join the France libre movement led by General de Gaulle, who from his London exile had taken on a near-religious quality as an icon of the eternal, undefeatable France (in contrast to the false France embodied by an Assemblée nationale that voted, on 10 July 1940, to establish the collaborationist Vichy regime). Indeed, Weil writes in *L'enracinement*, using imagery from her "Iliad" essay, that "above all General de Gaulle, surrounded by those who have followed him, is a symbol. He symbolizes France's faithfulness to herself, which for a moment was concentrated almost entirely in him, and above all everything in Man which revolts against the servile adoration of force."[25] Weil's demand for purity thus extended to the France libre movement itself, and that did not end well given the reality that the London encampment was meant to be a *government* in exile, and really thought of itself as a government in waiting. Jean-Luc Barré's entry on Weil in the *Dictionnaire de Gaulle* notes that she "disapproved of the transformation of the Free French into Fighting France,[26] which she saw as a betrayal of the essentially spiritual vocation of the Gaullist enterprise … she quit her post in June 1943, before dying alone, two months later, at the Ashford Sanitorium in Kent"[27] (m.t.).

Most of her work for the Free French was about writing an outline for a fully reconstructed, post-occupation France; in a way, then, *L'enracinement* is one of the oddest government memos ever committed to paper. It most forcefully brings us back to Sontag's sense of what readers find nourishing in Weil. Sontag wrote in that 1963 review, "I cannot believe that more than a handful of the tens of thousands of readers she has won since the posthumous publication of her books and essays really share her ideas."[28] I understand what Sontag is getting at here when it comes to the singular intensity of Weil's approach to Christianity. But I agree with Toril Moi, who writes that "Sontag underestimates the power of Weil's ideas,"[29] and there is no better example to demonstrate this than *L'enracinement*. In what follows, then, I want to take the book more or less on its own terms.

L'enracinement's vision is of a society that is highly ordered and in many ways hierarchical, and yet at the same time defined by a forceful, morally uncompromising form of both socialism and republicanism. This combination can be summarized by one of her proposals involving what she called "une triple propriété," a trinity of land, house, and machine. In the section called "Déracinement ouvrière" she explains:

The machines would not belong to the company. They would belong to the minute workshops scattered about everywhere and these would, in their turn, be the property of the workmen, either individually or collectively. Every workman would, besides, own a house and a bit of land.

This triple proprietorship comprising machine, house and land would be bestowed upon him by the State as a gift on his marriage, and provided he had successfully passed a difficult technical examination, accompanied by a test to check the level of his intelligence and general culture.

The choice of a machine would be made to depend in the first place on the individual workman's tastes and natural abilities, and secondly on general requirements from the point of view of production. It should be, of course, as far as possible, an adjustable automatic machine with a variety of uses.

This triple proprietorship could neither be transmitted by inheritance, nor sold, nor alienated in any way ... On a workman's death, this property would return to the State, which would, of course, if need be, be bound to maintain the well-being of the wife and children at the same level as before. If the wife was capable of doing the work, she could keep the property.[30]

I think this is a remarkable passage for a number of reasons, chief among them the level of detail that we can see here (something facilitated by the period in the 1930s Weil spent working at a Renault factory). More to the point, though, the socialism on display here makes due concessions to individual autonomy (it is the *worker* to whom the machine belongs, according to his "goûts et connaissances") at the same time that it is completely unambiguous about the essence of socialism: collective ownership of the *means of production*. Indeed, the individual is really only at issue here as a means by which those means of production are deployed. This "gift from the State" isn't really a gift at all inasmuch as the worker is not free to do with this material whatever he wishes (notwithstanding the "réglable et à usages multiples" quality of the machine). The prohibition on selling it or passing it on brings the "gift" fully outside of a capitalist system inasmuch as it has no real effect on the individual's capital at all. All of this flows, however, from a highly traditional sense of social organization, which is to say, it is all based in *family life*; the triple propriété comes at the moment of marriage, the state remains obligated to support that family unit in case of force majeure, etc. (this is partially why I use the "generic he" above). Questions of socialist economics aside (and such economics are certainly not prerequisites for a republican form of governance), this combination of the deeply radical (at the level of economics) and the highly conservative (at the level of social organization) cultivates that sense of a "we-identity" inasmuch as "I-identities" are nearly absent. To perfectly invert Margaret Thatcher's famous dictum,[31] in Weil's republic there is no such thing as individuals; there is a society, and there are families. The fact that part of the task here is the reconstruction of French identity should be clear enough considering the degree to which the French state had been shattered by the Vichy regime, but this comes into clearer focus with brief allusions to more contemporary situations that I will discuss in more detail later on. As I will discuss in chapter 5, the Métis Settlements of Alberta hold their territory in common. Each member of a Settlement can apply for land on that Settlement, as well as support to build a house there (along with the requisite infrastructure of electricity and water, no minor considerations in the northern Alberta landscape where they are all located). Repairs and maintenance are the responsibility of individuals, although most Settlements have schemes to support major repairs made necessary by flood, fires, etc. In turn, members cannot sell these homes nor these parcels of land; as capital, they are as useless as the machines "gifted" to Weil's citizen upon his marriage.[32] But like that citizen, if he dies neither his wife nor his dependent children can be evicted from that home, whether or not his wife is a Settlement member (the member can also will the land to family members who are eligible or who can become eligible to live on the Settlement). The degree to which this essentially socialist scheme[33] is tied to a project of nation-building among the Métis should be self-evident. That's no less true in France.

This may be worth explaining, because Weil's relationship with "the nation" is complicated. On the one hand, national identity is clearly part of the "enracinement" that the title of her most famous book refers to. But she has mixed feelings. Noting the plethora of allegiances that would have been common until recently – "villes ou ensemble de villages, province, région"[34] – she laments that "[t]he nation, single and separate, has taken the place of all that – the nation, or in other words, the State; for there is no other way of defining the word nation than as a territorial aggregate whose various parts recognize the authority of the same State. One may say that, in our age, money and the State have come to replace all other bonds of attachment."[35] I agree with the latter clause in that lament, but I don't accept the premise of the first, that is to say, the interchangeability of "nation" and "state," both of which seem, in Weil's eyes, to be as morally suspect as "money."

Indeed, I'm not totally convinced that Weil really sees the state and the nation as so interchangeable. She writes about some of the sub-state groups of France or the United Kingdom (Alsatians, Bretons, Welsh, Cornish, and Irish), largely in the context of trying to head off the Vichy regime's appeasement of autonomists such as the Bretons as part of their larger strategy of shattering the highly centralized post-revolutionary French state. But in so doing she sometimes sounds like the theorists of Els Països Catalans, the Catalan-speaking countries that I will discuss in chapter 4. That's certainly true of her question "wouldn't it be a natural thing for Brittany, Wales, Cornwall and Ireland to feel themselves, in regard to certain things, to be parts of the same environment?"[36] presumably on the basis of their shared Celtic languages as well as their rich seafaring heritages. The fact that this "same environment" would cross three states (France, the UK, the Republic of Ireland) is fully consistent with Weil's impatience at a sense of loyalty that is overly invested in a state that overwhelms any other bonds of attachment. But it does not have to be that way, as Weil makes clear when she discusses Alsace. Alluding to the year that France lost Alsace-Lorraine in the Franco-Prussian war, she writes, "The year 1871 was the last year of that particular French patriotism born in 1789 … [Frederick II] couldn't understand why the Alsatians, hardly knowing a word of French, speaking a dialect close to German, brutally conquered at a relatively recent date, refused to have anything to do with Germany. He discovered that the motive for this was the pride felt in belonging to the country which had produced the French Revolution, to the sovereign nation."[37] Her choice of the phrase "the sovereign nation" makes me think that this is all connected to what I had to say about the Catalans of France; that is to say, that these Alsatians seem to have become *French* in a way that is also true of the Catalans del nord, even as they retain some sense of difference, most (although not all) of which is linguistic. These groups are adhering to more than "the sovereign state," adhering to more than a materialistic and instrumentalist force that, to follow Weil's imagery, has no more cohesive or *enracinant* value than money.

What the denizens of Strasbourg share with those of Perpignan, Lille, and Paris is an adherence to the *republic*. Weil laments that since the Third Republic of the late nineteenth century, "[t]he ideal of the Nation, in the sense in which the men of 1789 or 1792 understood the word, which used to bring tears of joy to people's eyes – all that belonged irremediably to the past. Even the word nation had changed its meaning. In our day, it no longer denotes the sovereign people, but the sum total of peoples recognising the same State; it is the political structure created by a State and the country it controls."[38] I can see how the case of the Catalans del nord or the Alsatians could seem to fit this understanding of peoples adhering to the apparatus of control that the French state embodies, and using that apparatus for purely instrumentalist purposes. But as Weil writes of the Alsatians and as (as I note above) Llorenç Planes writes of the Catalans del nord, when confronted by those with whom they share only a language, they are keen to emphasize allegiances to that republic in a way that seems baffling to those outsiders; yes they are speakers of a Germanic language, but they are French too! This is, as Planes says, a very common response,[39] and it derives from that aspiration towards universalism that Kearney sees as central to the republican tradition. That universalism is something that different groups can choose to buy into. We can think of such groups as *peoples*, by way of designating their sub-national qualities, as distinct from sub-state *nations* such as, to return to Weil's Celtic roll call, the Welsh, the Bretons, or the Irish. These are national groups that clearly have not adhered to a larger nation, even in the cases where they may have, more or less, adhered to a larger state (as we see with the Welsh, where support for political separatism has never been high enough to make a winning a referendum imaginable but where a national consciousness is clearly a matter of near-consensus). Accommodation of that "Alsatian" or "Catalan" degree of difference is the key to the universalism that Kearney speaks of, and the recognition of that level of difference will be key to efforts to bring northern Protestants into a potentially unified Irish republic, an outcome that is more possible in our post-Brexit moment than it has been in a century. I will discuss this further in chapter 4.

II. Independent Georgia's Republican Difficulties

Although most well-informed observers know well that Georgia was one of the first Soviet republics to gain its independence as the USSR collapsed, its earlier period of independence is much less widely understood. Partially this is because of the brevity of its existence: 1918–21. As the Czarist empire fell apart, a number of new states and political formations emerged in the Caucasus mountains. The Transcaucasian Democratic Federative Republic, a federation composed of Armenia, Azerbaijan, Georgia, and a small part of what is now eastern Turkey, existed scarcely longer than the month of May 1918. When Georgia seceded, the federation could no longer hold together. That Georgian secession would prove somewhat optimistic. The period 1918–21 is the entire life of the Democratic Republic of Georgia, an independent state whose government was made up of social-democratic "Mensheviks," a term that the Bolsheviks saw as pejorative largely because of their overall moderation in terms of central control of the economy. Stephen Jones has argued in numerous venues that this government formed the blueprint of the European social democracy that seems such a familiar part of the northwestern part of the continent today, from France, the Benelux countries, and Germany up to Scandinavia. He concludes his 2005 book *Socialism in Georgian Colors* by writing that "Georgian social democracy was a movement which sought to wed socialism with European values of pluralism, individual rights, and private property. It sought a 'third way' before the term was invented."[40] Eric Lee, in the conclusion to his 2017 history of this first independence period, was more polemical and harder-left in his analysis: "The Bolsheviks in their hasty race to create a utopia created a hell on earth for millions, not only in Russia, but in China, North Korea, Cambodia and elsewhere. The Georgian Social Democrats, during their short period in power, showed that an orthodox Marxist approach – no skipping of steps, but a patient building up of a society in preparation for an eventual transition to socialism – might have worked, given time."[41]

The Democratic Republic's leader was Noe Jordania. After a period of student activism that often flirted with illegality he left to spend a few years in Warsaw. Upon returning to Tbilisi he got involved with social-democratic politics and thus faced arrest, so he left for Switzerland. He spent the last years of the twentieth century moving from European city to European city (Paris, Stuttgart, London), an experience that would have an enormous influence on his politics. Jordania served as a leader of the Social Democrats in the late-imperial Russian Duma and eventually chaired the Tbilisi soviet. In 1917 that soviet voted formally to oppose the recently victorious Bolsheviks, which led Jordania to head up a group of Caucasus nations that created, on 22 April 1918, the aforementioned Transcaucasian Democratic Federative Republic, by way of standing against what seemed to be a growing Bolshevik hegemony. About five weeks later, on 26 May 1918, Jordania declared Georgia's indepen-

dence; ethnic tensions were on the rise in this extraordinarily diverse federation, and it seemed unlikely to be able to make collective decisions going forward. What formed in its wake was the Democratic Republic of Georgia. The
republican ethos remained strong in the former members of the federation,
though, and the "Déclaration des républiques du Caucase" was issued by the
governments of Azerbaijan, Georgia, and the "République de Ciscaucasie"
(mostly known in French as La république montagnarde du Caucase du Nord
and known in English as the Mountainous Republic of the Northern Caucasus) on 20 June 1919.[42] It was not exactly an opportunity to hold forth on the
finer points of republicanism, but the communiqué speaks only of "Les Républiques caucasiennes." Another front-page Georgian-government news
story published two weeks later celebrated the unification of Armenia by noting that "Unified Armenia's form of government is that of a democratic republic [la République démocratique]."[43]

The only elections the Democratic Republic of Georgia would hold took
place in February 1919; the Social Democratic Party of Georgia led by Jordania
won an overwhelming majority. For a brief period, the country was the site
of global attention in left circles. The Second Socialist International sent a
delegation in the early fall of 1920; after a long journey by trains and boats,
they entered Georgia at Batumi (part of the region of Adjara, which then had
a Muslim majority) on 13 September. They were just in time. Beginning on
11 February 1921, the Bolshevik army invaded the country and consolidated
their control fully on 18 March. The visit of the International led to the production of two books, both of which appeared in 1921, but after the Bolshevik
invasion: Karl Kautsky's *Georgien, eine sozialdemokratische Bauernrepublik*
(translated that same year as *Georgia: A Social-Democratic Peasant Republic*)[44]
and the anonymously edited anthology *L'Internationale socialiste et la Géorgie*
(which gave the aforementioned travel details and also included articles about
the trip by figures such as Ramsay MacDonald, then the leader of the UK's
Labour Party and soon to be Labour's first prime minister, albeit only for nine
months of 1924). For a few short years, the country seemed to embody the
possibilities of democratic socialism as well as coming to serve as a tragic icon
of the totalitarian and expansionist nature of the Soviet Union. It was also a
test for the boundaries of "Europe." Although it lay well to the east of Turkey,
the builders of the Democratic Republic of Georgia had their gazes clearly
fixed westward, no doubt as a result of the time that many of them (not just
Jordania) had spent in countries such as France, Germany, Belgium, and Switzerland. In the introduction to his 2014 anthology on Georgian republics,

Jones wrote that "unlike the anti-colonial movements that populated the second half of the twentieth century, Georgia was strongly pro-European. In a speech to the Georgian Constituent Assembly in 1920, Noe Jordania made it clear: 'Our life today and our life in the future is ... indissolubly tied to the West, and no force can break this bond.'"[45]

Jordania never referred to himself as "president" but rather as "head of government."[46] This was not just a matter of stationery or how to introduce the guy at a state dinner. Rather, it spoke to the kind of republic that he was seeking to build. Malkhaz Matsaberidze describes it this way:

> Georgia's model of democracy included a unitary republic with broad self-government and autonomy for the regions, and a preponderance of power in the hands of parliament alongside institutions of direct democracy. The presidential system was rejected and the president's traditional functions were allocated to a head of government. The constitution emphasized socio-economic rights, and emphasized protections of the rights of national minorities.[47]

The imperative was clearly to build a republic, but this was a delicate dance. Matsaberidze writes that "[f]ederalism was ... associated with Georgia's history of fragmentation,"[48] and was thus something of a non-starter. But Georgia is a much more ethnically diverse nation than is generally understood, so federalism might otherwise seem like a logical choice for a post-independence government. Members of the dominant ethnic group, the Kartvelians, are generally known in languages other than Georgian as "ethnic Georgians." Other ethnicities unique to Georgian territory include the Svans and the Mingrelians. The Ossetians have traditionally lived between Russian and Georgian territory, while the Abkhaz have traditionally lived in Georgia's northwestern corner. Neither territory has ever been fully integrated into any Georgian state. Both Abkhazia and South Ossetia were belligerents both in the three-way Georgian Civil War of 1991–93 and in the war that Georgia fought with Russia for about two weeks of August 2008.[49] This is all to say nothing of the significant Armenian presence in Georgia (concentrated in the capital of Tbilisi, the city that once had the largest Armenian population anywhere), or the substantial Turkish, Greek, and Azeri communities that one finds throughout the country. Furthermore, while the majority of Georgians (including the Abkhaz and the Ossetians) adhere to the Eastern Orthodox Church, there is a significant Jewish community in Tbilisi (there are neighbourhoods in Jerusalem and Tel Aviv where Georgian is spoken),[50] as well as a Muslim population that is concentrated in the southeastern region of Adjara. All to say once again that federalism might seem a more logical model for an independent Georgian state than might at first be assumed, and so those who wanted to create a republic really had their work cut out for them.

Stephen Jones, in his 2012 book *Georgia: A Political History since Independence*, identified this as a key tension in the philosophy of Mikheil Saakashvili.[51] Recalling the early days following the "Rose Revolution," when Saakashvili led a popular uprising that ousted Eduard Shevardnadze (who had been the last foreign minister of the USSR and was widely seen as Gorbachev's right-hand man), Jones quotes a speech where the younger man said that Georgia was the "home not only for all Georgians, but also for all ethnic minorities," going on to say that "[h]e sees no opposition between national cultural sentiments of minorities and their identity within the state. He envisages what Stein Rokkan and Derek Unwin have called a 'union state,' a strong center combined with minority rights and, if necessary, national territories."[52] Early in his presidency, Saakashvili was making explicit statements about the inherent diversity of the Georgian republic, statements that had not been at all typical of Georgian leaders before or since.

Like Saakashvili, Jordania and his cabinet had been strongly influenced by the time they had spent in the west, seeing a number of European states as positive models for this kind of complexity. Many observers have noted the importance of Switzerland as an example (which is not a "union state" at all, given how weak its centre famously is). Giorgi Kandelaki, for instance, has written that, "[i]nspired by Swiss constitutional practices, the creators of the constitutional framework believed that the concentration of all power in the hands of parliament, even if elected through universal franchise, could result in an abuse of power. Thus it was important to place the 'people' above the legislature by introducing the institution of referendums on 'important issues.'"[53] This was of a piece with the refusal of a presidential system; the Swiss president is a decidedly weak figure, being elected only for a single term of one year, with duties that include chairing (or *presiding* over) the meetings of the federal council and little else. Indeed, the president traditionally maintains a cabinet portfolio in addition to presidential responsibilities; as I write this in the spring of 2024, Switerland's president Viola Amherd is also the minister responsible for the Federal Department of Defence, Civil Protection and Sport.

The Swiss have a president in a literal sense inasmuch as "elle *préside* les reunions"; so it was with Jordania as "head of government." What the Georgians seemed to be creating, in essence, was Switzerland minus the cantons: a government that was organized in such a way as to resist centralization of power in one person or even one institution, but that did not necessarily disperse it throughout the country via secondary jurisdictions such as regions or states. Indeed, Kandelaki goes on to write that "[i]n one key innovation, elected local government was seen as the exclusive representative of state power locally."[54] This was clearly a matter of logistics, inasmuch as not all state power could be executed from Tbilisi. But it needed to come from the government of *Georgia*. Matsaberidze recalls that "[a]t the 1 December 1920 session of the Constituent Assembly, Noe Jordania declared democratization could give birth to threats of particularism. To prevent this, local powers should not violate the rights of the center; there should not be states within a state."[55] That, of course, is the definition of a Swiss canton: a state within a state. In the Democratic Republic of Georgia, on the other hand, power would remain vested in a central administration, *presided* over by a head of government, diffused widely enough to prevent the abuse that follows from concentration, but not simply devolved. The Georgian model was recognizably Swiss, but amazingly not federalist; it was rather a republic that sought a kind of *universalist* address, effectively insisting on the singular identity of "Georgian" while managing difference through appeal to the local. This echoes Benjamin Barber's definition of Swiss democracy. In his history of the canton of Grisons, he contrasted this concept with that of Anglo-American liberalism, writing that "in Switzerland freedom has been understandable only within the context of community. For it [Anglo-American liberalism], autonomy has suggested a private right that defines the prepolitical individual; in Switzerland, it has been a collective right that defines the self-governing community."[56] To return to the language of Richard Kearney's definition of republicanism, the efforts of the builders of the first independent Georgian state were towards "reconciling the particular rights of the people(s) [in Georgia] with the universal rights of man."[57]

In practice matters were more complicated. For if the imperative was to prevent the creation of "states within a state," then how, exactly, was authority to be exercised? Matsaberidze recalls:

> The unitary system, however, presented the Social Democrats with a conundrum. The constitution, in Chapter Eleven, "Autonomous Governance" (Articles 107; 108), stipulated that [the Muslim-majority] Batumi

district, along with Abkhazia and Zakatala [which was the subject of a border dispute with Azerbaijan], should be granted autonomy ... Pavle Saqvarelidze argued that like the Belgian Constitution of 1831, the principle of a unitary democratic republic was compatible with autonomy, as long as autonomy did not mean state autonomy.[58]

That quest for an autonomy that did not mean state autonomy was elusive. The Tbilisi government was harsh in terms of cracking down on Abkhazia, which many believed to be a hotbed of Bolshevism and thus a threat to Georgia's independence. Cory Welt discusses the government's response to a series of Bolshevik uprisings in both Abkhazia and South Ossetia, writing that "[i]n November 1919 the Georgian government responded to the rebellion with comprehensive and brutal suppression ... In the aftermath of this suppression, the Georgian government began a process of what can only be considered selective ethnic cleansing."[59] Other regions fared better. Alexander Mikaberidze writes that following the British occupation of Adjara, "the Committee for the Liberation of the Georgian Muslims founded a *mejlis* (Parliament) in Batumi and called for incorporation into the Democratic Republic of Georgia. The British administration ceded the region to Georgia in July 1920."[60] That was, of course, mere months before the Soviet invasion began, in February 1921, so it is tempting to think of that "Adjara question" as academic in the pejorative sense. But that would be a mistake, because it illuminates certain key elements of the republic that Jordania and his government were trying to build. That republic could in fact accommodate cultural difference, serious difference in this case. Recall that it is the jurisdiction of Adjara, which then had a majority-Muslim population, that *asked* to be joined with Georgia, as opposed to the majority-Orthodox regions of Abkhazia and South Ossetia, which were rebelling against such adhesion. But that was because Adjarans considered themselves *Georgian*, unlike the Abkhaz or Ossetians. Bekir Sami Bey, a Turkish politician originally from Ossetia, described Adjarans as "Géorgiens de sang et de langue."[61] Appeals to blood always sound ethnically chauvinistic to twenty-first-century ears, but I would suggest that what is really going on there is an appeal to civic nationalism. In terms of national identity Adjarans are *Georgian*, not part of some Turkish irredentist movement nor some sort of misbegotten nation of Islam that can only be incompatible with a majority-Christian nation. That's as true of the Svans of the remote mountain valleys as it is of the Armenians who have been historically concentrated in the Old City neighbourhood of Tbilisi.

It's just that it's never really been true in the same way of the Abkhaz or the Ossetians. That was the region that saw serious ethnic cleansing of non-Abkhaz (mostly of ethnic Georgians) during the civil war of the 1990s, that is to say the first years of post-Soviet independence, when Georgia tried (and arguably failed) to establish a viable state that corresponded to its Soviet-era boundaries. During the 2008 war with Russia, that ethnic cleansing was repeated on the last of the ethnic Georgians living in that breakaway region. At that stage simply supporting Abkhazian independence would seem to justify such ethnic cleansing, which is why it has never sat right with most international observers (its independence is only recognized by Nauru, Nicaragua, Russia, Syria, and Venezuela). But some solution clearly needs to be found; the situation of a Georgian state with uncertain borders is entering its fourth decade. Reviewing copies of the old (and unpaginated) *Bulletin géorgien d'informations* it is jarring to find a short piece (in the 12 May 1919 issue) that recalls how "[t]he Abkhaz National Council, elected by universal suffrage, has voted, during its session of 18 March 1919, for the re-attachment of Abkhazia to the Georgian Republic, which will unify not only racial affinities, but also a community of economic and intellectual interests" (m.t.). Such cheerfulness is a reminder that while interesting, the *Bulletin* is at root government propaganda. Having said that, that little news blurb is also a remarkable document of how longstanding, and perhaps insoluble, a problem Abkhazia is. Stephen Jones, in his aforementioned 2012 history of Georgia, describes it this way:

> Abkhazian elites resented the incorporation of Abkhazia into the Democratic Republic of Georgia in 1918, and into Soviet Georgia as an Autonomous republic in 1931. They waged a long struggle for separation from Georgia throughout the Soviet period ... Abkhazians complained bitterly of Georgianization policies from the 1930s onwards when Lavrentii Beria headed the Georgian and Transcaucasian party organizations (1931–8). Beria ended Abkhazian language radio stations and Abkhazian language schools, Georgianized their Cyrillic alphabet and place names, fired Abkhazian teachers, and began a [process] of Georgian settlement which contributed to a decline in the Abkhazian proportion of the autonomous republic from 27.8 percent in 1926 to 17.8 percent in 1989.[62]

The real question, then, is whether the Democratic Republic of Georgia could have accommodated non-*Georgian* difference in a way that would have avoided a century of ethnic conflict. That is a genuinely open question, un-answerable given the brief life of that republic.

In the wake of the Soviet invasion, Jordania and his followers fled to Paris, where they set up a government-in-exile, one that sought to keep the struggle of Georgia in the global eye. In the decades that followed the Bolshevik in-vasion there was a vigorous exile publishing scene, including a bi-monthly magazine called *La Géorgie* that appeared during the 1930s and a trans-Caucasian monthly magazine called *Prométhée: Organe de défense nationale des peuples du Caucase, de l'Ukraine et du Turkestan*, which existed from 1926 to 1938. Exile groups regularly published French-language booklets and pam-phlets from Geneva in order to try to draw attention from the League of Nations, which was headquartered there.[63] But the seat of the Georgian exile government was in the suburbs of Paris, in Leuville-sur-Orge, where they had managed to secure a small estate.[64] Georges Mamoulia writes that "[a]ccording to French sources, some 1200 Georgian émigrés lived in the Paris region during the second half of the 1920s"[65] (m.t.). They tried to organize an uprising in Tbilisi in 1924; it failed, prompting various parts of the Soviet intelligence establishment to intensify their efforts to infiltrate the Paris com-munity. The Stalin ally and eventual head of the NKVD Lavrentiy Beria, a Georgian from Kutaisi, was a key part of such efforts, a few years before his Georgianization policies that Jones discusses.

As the Soviets consolidated their position and the restoration of Georgian independence faded from the realm of the possible, a lot of Jordania's energy seemed to be directed towards a "return to the roots." He had lost his con-nection to his national roots; he could never return to Georgia. So he turned to his political roots, reading widely in classical socialist thought, with a focus on France. In 1933 he published an odd book called *Difficultés socialistes*, which is split between discussing the roots of socialism (mostly French) and the poisoned tree of Bolshevism (entirely Russian). Part of the book is about refusing the fruit of that tree, with Jordania writing at one point that "Russia is not Europe ... capitalism, the bourgeoisie, and the Constitution are the at-tributes of the west; the obchtchina [peasant community] ... and the admin-istration of the mir [Czarist-era village], these are the attributes of Russia, and it's via these attributes that they enter into socialism"[66] (m.t.). It seemed to be a call for French socialists to take care when dealing with the Soviet Union, not to be fooled by calls for a common front against fascism (some-thing that was an important part of French left politics, culminating in the

Popular Front government of 1936). Soviet socialism may look familiar, but Jordania wanted readers to know that it was, in the Russian manner, backward and authoritarian and very much not European. This was all a call back to what Jordania had done in his younger days, which Stephen Jones describes this way: "Georgian social democracy's semilegal activities from 1907–1914, though limited, were part of an attempt to europeanize Georgia and separate it from what Georgians saw as a Russian Jacobin tradition."[67] The problem predated the formation of the USSR; this was a Russian issue, not a Soviet one. It was a *national* problem.

Much of the rest of the book is given over to detailed discussion of French socialism, with special attention paid to "founding fathers" such as Jules Guesde and Jean Jaurès. The long opening chapter on "étatisme" invokes the former figure by saying that "Statism takes the workers by the belly as well as by the collar, to use Guesde's expression"[68] (m.t.). Throughout this chapter, Jordania seems to be wrestling with the compromises that he had made by way of trying to sustain a social-democratic republic, a state. The invocation here of Guesde brings to mind Eric Lee's recollection that "Guesde savaged his rival, Jean Jaurès, among others, for 'compromising' with bourgeois parties, and was one of the French Marxists that Noe Jordania had met during his exile in France in the 1890s. Guesde's purist and fanatical politics are believed to be the cause of Karl Marx's famous outburst, 'je ne suis pas Marxiste.' If that was Marxism, Marx wanted no part of it."[69] And yet, we find Jordania seeming to castigate just those kinds of compromises, à la Guesde, when he writes: "The apparent domination of the majority of the nation in fact translates into the domination of the minority; and as the minority is today known as the bourgeoisie, democracy itself has become bourgeois … A democracy must be for the people [doit être populaire], or it is not a democracy"[70] (m.t.). As though anticipating Bob Dylan's lyrics, when Jordania looked back on the experience of state-building, he seemed so much older then; exiled in France, he was younger than that now.

What falls by the wayside in Jordania's revisiting of youthful engagements is precisely the *republic*, ironic given that he was now in France. Matters of Abkhazia or Adjara, *sang et langue*, a president vs *celui qui préside*, are absent in *Difficultés socialistes*. What we find is a morally inflected meditation on basic principles: the inherent corruption of states, the hopelessly bourgeois nature of democracy, the terminally reactionary qualities of Russian approaches ("ce socialisme slavophile").[71] I understand why collapse and exile would lead to a re-examination of basic principles. But that is a loss. Matsaberidze quotes Jordania as saying that the state over which he presided was going to be "the first case in the world of the establishment of a unitary republic on the basis of a fully democratic constitution."[72] Given Georgia's internal diversity, that would have been a great accomplishment indeed, and even the three years that the state managed to exist offer lessons for those who believe in the republican model's ability to accommodate difference while still enunciating a robust sense of nationality, one that stands in opposition to the domination of imperial models. That, in the final analysis, is a far more important contribution than a series of theoretical debates about the exact nature of socialism, and for that reason, I can only read *Difficultés socialistes* with a sense of melancholy.

III. Bollywood Republicanism in Nehru's India

Melancholy is also an important element of the "golden age" of Hindi-language popular cinema, the 1950s and '60s. That is one of two counterintuitive arguments I want to make about this period in film history. The other is that the "secret star" of the best of these films is Jawaharlal Nehru, the epoch-making first prime minister of independent India whose seventeen years in office were devoted to the crucial task of nation-building. I will not belabour Nehru's biographical details here, except to say that he is a singular figure in the history of independent India. In the decades leading to independence he was an important part of the Indian National Congress, which in the post-independence period he transformed into the Congress Party. Congress has been as dominant in independent India as the Liberals have been in twentieth-century Canada or Fianna Fáil has been in the independent Irish State. Like the latter example, Congress has also been essential in Indian history for its consolidation of a distinctive nationalism, one with tremendous democratic posiblity. Maya Tudor is especially insightful on this, writing in her 2013 comparison of Indian and Pakistani nationalism that

> Congress popularized an Indian nationalism that was not just defined negatively, or in opposition to the colonial regime, but also espoused programmatic principles that helped to create a public sphere in which traditional status distinctions were rejected, at least in principle. A sophisticated intellectual, economic, and social critique of British rule and the careful manipulation of symbolic issues, by juxtaposing the interests

of all indigenous classes against those of the colonial state, defined a pro-
grammatic Indian nationalism. Congress leaders absolutely espoused
this national movement out of self-interest, in order to create a more
unified national movement that could effectively countervail colonial
claims of Congress representing a "microscopic minority." But by insti-
tutionalizing this party-defined egalitarian nationalism, broad segments
of Indian society grew ideationally committed to Congress as a party.
As such, [by] independence, Congress had become a political and ideational end in itself, rather than simply a means to an end.[73]

The "end" that this form of nationalism embodied can be summarized by laying out Congress's basics: it is a more-or-less socialist, big-tent-nationalist,
and resolutely secular party (India's first Muslim president and first Sikh
prime minister were both from Congress). Nehru is a kind of icon of this
distinctly Indian form of secular socialism, someone deeply sceptical of partition especially along religious lines and instinctively socialist on economic
matters.[74] He was also an important leader in the non-aligned movement that
came out of the Bandung Conference and played a key role in Cold War–era
postcolonialism. Because he served as prime minister for the first seventeen
years of Indian independence, he tends to be associated with the project of
creating the post-colonial state. This was particularly tricky business in a nation as diverse as India, whose constitution recognizes twenty-two languages
(fourteen at the time of its 1949 ratification), not including English (which
serves, now as in at the moment of independence in 1947, as a lingua franca).

Into the fray stepped the film industry now known as "Bollywood." This
is a portmanteau made up of "Hollywood" and "Bombay," which has been
the historical centre of Hindi-language filmmaking. The fact that Hindi is a
minority language in the state of Maharashtra where Bombay (now Mumbai)
is located speaks to Hindi's, and the cinema's, special role in state-building.
The Indian constitution of 1949 recognized both Hindi and English as official
languages of the republic as a whole, but it put a time limit on the latter. Section 343(2) states that "for a period of fifteen years from the commencement
of this Constitution, the English language shall continue to be used for all the
official purposes of the Union for which it was being used immediately before
such commencement." The original hope was that this would allow enough
time for Hindi (which is spoken in the north-central part of India known as
the "Hindi belt") to establish itself as a genuine national language. The first
independent governments generously supported the Hindi-language film in-

dustry via subsidy and tax breaks by way of encouraging a nationwide spread. But the language that emerged on the screen wasn't Hindi as such, and it was all the more connected to this process of nation-building for it. Tejaswini Ganti summarizes the matter this way:

> There was no one Hindi, as it varied according to region. Filmmakers finally settled on a type of spoken Hindi known as Hindustani – a mixture of Hindi and Urdu – a language associated with bazaars and trading that served as a lingua franca across northern and central India. This led to a peculiarity – Bombay became the only city where the language of the film industry was not congruent with the language of the region; Gujarati and Marathi being the dominant languages of the region. The fact that cinema in the Hindi language developed in multilingual Bombay, rather than in the Hindi-speaking north, disassociated Hindi films from any regional identification, imbuing them with a more "national" character.[75]

That reference to "the only city where the film industry ..." is crucial. Although "Indian cinema" is sometimes casually taken to be synonymous with "Bollywood," this is not at all the case. Indeed, the Bollywood-based Hindi-language industry is not reliably the largest of India's film industries. The Tamil-language industry, mostly based in Chennai (Tamil Nadu), regularly makes as many and sometimes more films per year (in 2015 there were 204 Hindi-language films released and 215 Tamil-language ones). There are also significant industries making films in Bengali (based in Kolkata, 95 films in 2015) and Telugu (based in Hyderabad, 86 films in 2015). But for the most part these are *regional* industries; the films do not circulate much to other parts of India or to other countries (although that is changing). The Hindi-language industry, as Ganti makes clear, has always been different. Bollywood is now a highly globalized form of entertainment, but within India it is distinct not because of its size but because it is *national*.

Achieving the "national character" that Ganti speaks of is no small order in a country such as India. The multilingual quality of the republic is only one aspect of its diversity. Although the majority of Indians are Hindu, to say there is a significant Muslim minority would be an understatement; only Indonesia and Pakistan have more Muslims living within their borders. This is to say nothing of the other religious groups in India: Sikhs, Jains, Buddhists, Christians, etc. Furthermore, India is home to numerous "tribal peoples," whose rights are written into the constitution via "Part X: The Scheduled and Tribal Areas." The degree to which diversity is a foundational part of modern Indian national identity is what sets it apart from its historical rival Pakistan. Tudor's aforementioned book is a close examination of the differences between these two states and their dominant forms of nationalism, and she writes that "India *initially* emerged from independence with a party that was able to envelop factionalism or contain ethnic differences while another country facing similar challenges [Pakistan] did not."[76] For Tudor much of this has to do with the dynamics inherent to political parties, and she also writes how "its ideational, coalitional, and organizational weaknesses left Pakistan's governing political party unable to broker agreement between its support bases on the same contentious regime building issues [as India faced]."[77] As a political scientist her analysis of these party processes is a highly detailed and enlightening antidote to any assumptions that the conflict between India and Pakistan is a matter of being a Muslim versus a Hindu state. I, a more broad-strokes cultural studies guy, am nevertheless inclined to return to the more general analysis that the key difference here is a matter of a religiously founded state as opposed to a secular one. The official name of the republic to the east is the Islamic Republic of Pakistan, and the preamble to its constitution opens by saying: "Whereas sovereignty over the entire Universe belongs to Almighty Allah alone, and the authority to be exercised by the people of Pakistan within the limits prescribed by Him is a sacred trust ..." While it is not uncommon to hear India referred to as Hindustan, this is a term that occurs exactly zero times in its constitution. Nor is "Hindustan" somehow the proper name of the country in an Indian language; again, the Indian constitution is crystal-clear on this, with Part I(1) reading, in full, "1. Name and territory of the Union.—(1) India, that is Bharat, shall be a Union of States" ("Bharat" is derived from a word in Sanskrit). Without a doubt "Hindustan" is widely albeit casually used to refer to India, from the name of the language of Bollywood to the venerable daily newspaper *Hindustan Times*, founded a century ago. But the expression has no official weight because to use "Hindustan" as a synonym for "India" is to assume that it is a more or less Hindu country and thus to deny existential aspects of modern Indian nationhood, namely diversity and secularism.[78] Thus it is no small matter that many generations of Pakistani leadership have habitually referred to their rival, whose legitimacy as a state is far from universally accepted there, as "Hindustan."[79]

Hinduism thus plays a role in contemporary Indian identity that is comparable to the role of Catholicism in French identity. Both India and France are today rigorously secular states in a *de jure* sense. The official translation of Article 1 of France's constitution reads, "France shall be an indivisible, secular, democratic and social Republic," while India updated its constitution's preamble in 1976 (via the Forty-Second Amendment) to define the state as "a sovereign, socialist, secular, democratic republic." But it would be hard to miss the degree to which Catholicism has served as a force of social cohesion in France, despite its long history of legislation to the contrary, which famously began with the *Loi du 9 décembre 1905 concernant la séparation des Églises et de l'État*. Simone Weil had a complicated relationship with this aspect of French life. Much of what she writes in *L'enracinement* is critical of the laïcité tradition, with Weil noting that "[m]any schoolteachers evince a zeal in their attachment to this philosophy comparable to a religious fervour."[80] But her overall position on the matter is utterly rational (something that is unusual for her where religion is concerned), and useful for understanding the situation in India. She goes on to write in that same section that

> The only attitude public education can adopt, in France, with regard to Christianity, which is at once legitimate and practically realizable, consists in looking upon it as one treasury of human thought among many others. It is too absurd for words that a French university graduate should have read poetry of the Middle Ages, *Polyeucte, Athalie, Phèdre,* Pascal, Lamartine, philosophical doctrines impregnated with Christianity like those of Descartes and Kant, the *Divine Comedy* or *Paradise Lost,* and never have once opened a Bible.
>
> Future professional teachers and schoolmasters should simply be told that religion has at all times and in all countries, save quite recently in certain parts of Europe, played a dominant role in the development of human thought and civilization. An educational course in which no reference is made to religion is an absurdity.[81]

Something like this sense of things can be commonly heard in Indian culture of the Nehru era. What better place to turn for such an indication that Nehru himself, who in 1946 published *The Discovery of India,* a book that shares much with *L'enracinement* in the way that it imagines what a country will look like once it is liberated from occupation by foreigners? Weil was writing

from exile, Nehru from prison. He spoke of religion's relationship to civilization in terms that were close to Weil's sense of religion as a treasury:

> As a man grows to maturity he is not entirely engrossed in, or satisfied
> with, the external objective world. He seeks also some inner meaning,
> some psychological and physical satisfactions. So also with peoples and
> civilizations as they mature and grow adult. Every civilization and every
> people exhibit these parallel streams of an external life and an internal
> life. Where they meet or keep close to each other, there is an equilibrium
> and stability. When they diverge conflict arises and the crises that torture
> the mind and spirit.[82]

Although they were not always dealing explicitly with religious matters, the
key Bollywood filmmakers of the 1950s and '60s, when Nehru was at the peak
of his power and really was trying to build a new nation along the lines of
what he had outlined in *The Discovery of India*, were highly influenced by his
ideas about Indian identity. That's most true of the "holy trinity" of Bollywood's Golden Age: Mehboob, Raj Kapoor, and Guru Dutt.

Mother India, the 1957 epic directed by Mehboob Khan (usually known just
as Mehboob) and starring Nargis Dutt (usually known just as Nargis), has an
important place in Bollywood's "golden age." Salman Rushdie put it this way
in his program notes for the 2001 Telluride Film Festival: "Of the Indian filmmakers who consciously sought to be part of the 'nation building' project in
the 1940s and 50s, and whose films promoted a broadly socialist view of Indian
social problems, only Raj Kapoor's oeuvre had an impact comparable to
Mehboob's, and no actress came close to matching the power of Nargis's hold
over the imagination of a generation of filmgoers." The film opens with a sequence (figure 2.1) that precisely reproduces a famous press photo of Nehru
and his associates, making it explicit from literally the first moments that this
is all connected to the political climate of the moment of the film's release.
Although the opening and closing images are about the opening of a network
of irrigation canals and so about the modernization of the newly post-colonial
country, the narrative is set in the past and follows the unspeakable suffering
of one family in rural India, particularly at the hands of a ruthless moneylender. The family survives (although one of the three children dies) solely
because of their self-sacrificing mother Radha. At the climax of the film
(spoiler alert!) Radha shoots her younger son Birju, who has joined a group
of bandits (which are thinly disguised versions of India's "tribal peoples,"

She refuses! You are our mother, the mother of the whole village!

Figure 2.1
Mother India (Mehboob, India, 1957), 3:34.

rather in the manner of the proverbial "Cowboys and Indians" of Hollywood westerns). She shoots him because he has kidnapped the moneylender's daughter to take as his wife. When her son scoffs at her threat to kill him if he makes off with the young woman, he says, "You are my mother." She responds to this with "I'm first a woman." Gender solidarity firmly established, Birju replies that "I am your son." Radha smoothly moves on to a wider sense of communitarian solidarity by responding in turn that she is "the daughter of the entire village." When he ignores this and takes off on his horse with the young woman on his lap, she kills him with a shot that would be the envy of a US Marine sharp-shooter. Although none of this narrative is connected to Hinduism as such, the film is dripping with religious references. Radha is named for the consort of Krishna; their love is an important part of Sanskrit- and Bengali-language narratives. Gayatri Chatterjee notes that the sons are just as symbolically heavy: "The eldest son is called Ramu: the affectionate form of Rām, the principal protagonist of one of the two great Indian epics – *The Rāmāyan*. The second is Birju, another name for Krishna, a key dramatic persona of the other epic – *The Mahābhārat* ... So the eldest son, Ramu, is good and obedient, loving towards his younger brothers. Birju, by contrast, is mischievous and disobedient, as the young Krishna often is."[83] When Radha is asked by the moneylender to marry him (her husband has abandoned the family after losing both his arms in an accident), she mockingly addresses his statue of the goddess Lakshmi: "The goddess who carried the burdens of the world! Try and become a mother. You'll give up in two steps." All to say that while the socialist-infused modernization of the Congress party is a key aspect of the film, Hinduism is also central to the narrative.

It would be easy to read the combination of the two as a matter of Hindu chauvinism, an eerie prediction of the India that Mr Modi is currently trying to build as a challenge to the dominance of Congress and a replacement for the historical memory of Nehruism. But I do not think that is what is going on here. Rather, Mehboob is deploying this kind of imagery for reasons that are comparable to the way that a Hollywood film such as *White Christmas* (1954) deploys the images of Christianity in the service of a narrative that is about post-wwii national cohesion, being a story set between New York and rural Vermont that depends heavily on memories of wartime service. These

Figure 2.2
Press photo of Nehru at Congress Party event, 1950s. Courtesy of the Internet Archive, https://ia800308.us.archive.org/21/items/HindSwaraj-Speech-02-1/d14083c50eacab7641fba67a598851cb.jpg

films do not exactly equate national cohesion with specific religious obligations, even if the details of those obligations serve as a certain kind of short-
hand for social issues, and the film assumes the audience's knowledge of the
broad strokes of the religions in question because of their majority status.
That is the kind of national epic that *Mother India* is: one made for the audience of a republic that is just as *de jure* secular and diverse as the United States.
Mother India is no more a "Hindu film" than *White Christmas* is a "Christian
film." It is possible to see this clearly without resorting to cheap intentionality,
although I will break with my critical principles briefly just to make my point
that much more strongly. In terms of its creators *White Christmas* not only
is not a "Christian film" but is really a Jewish film: its director Michael Curtiz
was born to a Hungarian Jewish family in the late Austro-Hungarian empire,
and the writer of all its songs including its famous titular one, Irving Berlin,
came from a family that traced its history to a shtetl in Belarus. Similarly,
Mother India's renowned director Mehboob was actually named Mehboob
Khan, a Muslim originally from Gujarat; its star Nargis, who still serves as an
icon of Indian womanhood because of this film, was the Calcutta-born child
of two Muslim converts. Hinduism is undeniably central in this most nation-
building film of Nehru-era cinema, but it is also one element in a complex
cultural mixture that speaks to India's fundamental diversity.

That is what Raj Kapoor was singing about in his most famous film song.
Kapoor is sometimes compared with Charlie Chaplin because he often portrayed a wandering hobo, similar to Chaplin's "little tramp." Ashish Rajadhyaksha and Paul Willemen acknowledge this while noting that "Kapoor also
asserted his debt to [Frank] Capra (their first meeting is recorded in Capra's
autobiography) and to [Vittorio] De Sica (esp. *Miracolo a Milano*, 1950)."[84]
The latter connection is important, given the degree to which Italian neoreal-
ism (the movement of which De Sica is an undisputed giant) was implicated
in the project of rebuilding a shattered Italian society after wwii. For Kapoor,
as for the neorealists, cinema was important both for the entertainment it
provided to a society in need of comfort (*Miracolo a Milano*, like most of
Kapoor's films, is a comedy) and for the way that it visualized society in ways
that were often close to documentary. Often, not always: what many casual
observers forget about the Italian neorealists is that many of them (De Sica
for sure) were formed by experiences of working on studio-produced entertainment films at the Cinecittà studio (which was nearly destroyed during
wwii and rebuilt afterwards). Kapoor's films were mostly shot in studio set-
tings, although some did make use of location shooting.

For our purposes here the most important example is *Shree 420* (1955), whose title refers to the laws around fraud and con-men and which centres on Kapoor's "little tramp" character wandering over India, post-independence-picaresque style. The film's opening number is its most famous, when Kapoor dances soft-shoe-style (there is a close-up of his shoes, soft indeed but worn), and sings the now-famous song "Mera Joota Hai Japani," whose opening words Salman Rushdie translates this way: "Oh, my shoes are Japanese / These trousers English, if you please / On my head, red Russian hat / My heart's Indian for all that."[85] The song concludes with images of Kapoor riding a camel with a man whose beard and turban mark him as Sikh, and then riding an elephant accompanied by two men with much longer beards who wear their turbans more loosely, indicating that they are probably Muslim. Later on, Kapoor more explicitly acknowledges this religious diversity when he is on the edge of a crowd listening to a speech given by a Congress Party politician (identifiable because of his hat) who offers obsequious greetings to Bombayites. Kapoor, up on a soapbox, shouts "Hindus: Ram Ram, Muslims: Salaam, Morning to Christians and Sat Sri Akal to Sikhs." When the politician boasts that head to toe all his clothes are Indian, Kapoor delivers a spoken version of his song, eventually drifting into a shouted argument with the politician, one that he wins by virtue of the crowd that flocks to him and his increasingly ridiculous speech. This is all to say that Kapoor is riding a fine line here, at once invoking much of the idealism of Nehruism while also satirizing it as manipulative and more traditionally nationalist than it may at first appear. Either way, that diversity is *central*; as Kapoor says in that speech, "let me repeat: the one thing that's Indian is my heart!" Again, some of this is satire, given that Kapoor is playing a small-time con man, but the constant invocation of diversity is of a piece with the times. What does it mean to be Indian in these first years of independence? A seriously unequal society is part of it, and that underdog view is what many champions of Kapoor's cinema, as of Chaplin's before him, have emphasized. But it also means having diversity define the everyday. Russian hats, camels driven by Sihks, knowing that Muslims say "salaam" and Christians say "morning": this is what defined the Indian republic in 1955, and would throughout these first decades of independance.

It may seem that relatively optimistic views of Nehruite nation-building were being offered by Kapoor and Mehboob, whereas the gloomy underside is to be found in the cinema of Guru Dutt. Again, I am not so sure. The sense of Dutt as a brooding dissident derives from classic films such as *Pyaasa* (1957) and *Kaagaz ke Phool* (1959). *Pyaasa* is an indictment both of artistic temperament and an emergent philistine and materialist society. The climactic song-and-dance number has the poet-protagonist (played by Dutt, who also wrote and directed the film) storming into a concert hall where an event honouring him is taking place (everyone thinks he has killed himself out of despair at his obscurity) singing "For what shall it profit a man if he gain the world / A world where the youth is driven to crime / A world where the young are groomed for the market-place" and finally crying out "Burn this world! Tear it asunder!" as the audience, which takes him to be an imposter, tries to throw him out. *Kaagaz ke Phool* has Dutt starring as a discontented filmmaker reliving memories of times when he was famous and celebrated, as opposed to his present reality of an ex-wife, a daughter with whom he is losing touch, and a complicated new romance. In both films the cinematography is spectacular; many of the musical numbers use sweeping, complex camera movements, and both films are filled with dark and shadowy images that call to mind Orson Welles. But despite the high level of craftsmanship on display here (which is what accounts for Dutt's formidable reputation in Bollywood circles), these are deeply pessimistic views, presenting a brooding, disillusioned, and alienated vision throughout.

This vision obscures the degree to which Dutt is actually of the same mind as Mehboob and Raj Kapoor. In a dialogue on Dutt's cinema in the British film magazine *Sight and Sound*, Perviz Khan asked Ashish Rajadhyaksha, "What are the particular characteristics of Dutt's cinema?" Rajadhyaksha replied:

> In a film like *Pyaasa*, you have an extraordinary mixture. It is set in Calcutta, there are a couple of lines of dialogue in Bengali, the film deals with Urdu poetry and therefore decadent Lucknow [a city in Uttar Pradesh with a large Muslim population], and there is a corrupt businessman who is clearly from Bombay. In a sense Dutt created an all-Indian space ... Dutt's work is exceptional in that it gives a sense of all India, not the India of any defined region, but a reflection of his own experience of having lived in Bangalore, Calcutta, Almora, Pune, and Bombay.[86]

What would be apparent to a local viewer, then, is that India *as a whole* is a troubled, materialist, and decadent place, but it is *our* troubled, decadent materialism. This sense of "our," that first-person-plural pronoun, can, in post-independence India, only be evoked by difference: of language, of region, and of religion. Religious difference would be implicit in the presence of Urdu poetry, although Dutt would make that explicit later in his career. The year after *Kagaaz ke Phool* appeared Dutt produced and starred in *Chaudhvin Ka Chand* (1960), one of the few films in which he would appear without both writing and directing as well (it was directed by Mohammad Sidiq). This was a "Muslim social," a minor but well-established genre in Bollywood, that centred on a love triangle; Nasreen Munni Kabir's biography of Dutt notes that "it is ironic that although the film is the most conventional in story and in treatment, *Chaudhvin Ka Chand* became one of Guru Dutt Films' greatest financial successes."[87] Perhaps that is not so surprising. I agree that this later film is conventional, but it impressive in the way that it displaces aspects of Dutt's earlier films onto an entirely different cultural context. That's true of the way that Dutt is presented by the film's script as the idealistic young man, as well as the presence of his sidekick Johnny Walker, providing comic relief here as he had in *Pyaasa* and *Kagaaz ke Phool*. It all seemed vaguely familiar, but was now placed in a context that dispensed with the pessimism and social criticism, and also changed the religious context. What remained from the earlier films was not only the star personae of Dutt and Johnny Walker, though; what remained was the centrality of an Indian experience of diversity.

Conclusion

In appealing to notions of "diversity" as the central constituent of republicanism, I am mindful of conservative critiques of the concept as promoting a bland homogeneity and leftist critiques of it as promoting the ends of neoliberalism. What we have seen here in examples as different as France, Ireland, Georgia, and India is, I have tried to show, substantially different. Republican regimes are defined by diversity, but are equally dependent on a means by which different kinds of expression can be welcomed into what Mary McCarthy has called a *singular*. She wrote in a 1954 essay called "Settling the Colonel's Hash," about being stuck next to an antisemite on a train, that "[t]he chief moral or meaning (what I learned, in other words, from this experience) was this: you cannot be a universal unless you accept the fact that you are a singular, that is, a Jew or an artist or what-have-you."[88] Simone Weil, citizen of a republic famous for its universality, is clearly defending a *singular* that is *French*; writing in exile with the Free French, how could she do otherwise? But in so doing she acknowledges the reality of other singulars such as the

Alsatians, and by extension the Catalans, seeing that these identities must be welcomed into a French republic worthy of the name, not set aside in favour of what Deneen describes as a "globally homogenous ... cultureless and place-less [world] defined above all by liberal norms of globalized indifference to-wards shared fates of actual neighbours and communities."[89] They can be welcomed into the universalist republic only via their own singular (not to be confused with individualism), and such singulars may not always go under the name of "French," as it so clearly does for Weil. The founders of the Demo-cratic Republic of Georgia rejected both an ethnically homogenous state and one where the ethnic majority would demand that Muslims or Mingrelians leave their distinctiveness aside in order to adhere; their failure to find viable strategies of *adhesion* for Abkhazia was a problem rendered permanent by the Soviet invasion that snuffed the state out. While I understand how Mr Modi and his BJP, after ten years in power, have now consolidated a Hindu-chauvinist position that seems to have done permanent damage to Indian re-publicanism, I do maintain some faith that memories of that republic's Nehru period, and generally how Congress has historically dealt with this problem of *multiple forms of adhesion* to the *singular* identity of "Indian" much more successfully, retain significant support. That assumption of diversity – real diversity of languages, religious customs, etc. – has long permeated the country's most locally and globally popular art form, Bollywood cinema, and that fact is also a source of hope that the Modi phenomenon – a narrow, re-ligiously chauvinist form of nationalism – may in time come to seem a blip in the long-term history of post-colonial Indian democracy. All of this brings us back to Richard Kearney's fundamental republican tension between (1) the nourishment of the local and (2) the aspiration towards the universal. Con-temporary identity politics – particularly in what my Colorado-based father, when he visits us here in Canada, calls "the breakaway republic to the south" – too often fetishize the former (often in the form of ethnic distinctiveness) and dismiss the latter as oppressive because it seems to demand conformity. But I reject a facile conflation of "adhesion" and "conformity." There may be some intersection on that proverbial Venn diagram, but it is no larger than the demands that other forms of sociality make upon an individual subject. These examples from France, Georgia, and India, limited though they may seem, provide a wide variety of evidence for that position.

CHAPTER 3

Commonwealths

Two thousand twenty was a big year for the restoration of independent African-American films. I have a hunch that this is not what 2020 is going to be remembered for, but bear with me. In chapter 1, devoted to "Ethnos," I discussed William Greaves's *Nationtime – Gary* (1972), a film that until 2020 had only ever been shown semi-theatrically and in a shorter version that was meant for broadcast, a broadcast that never materialized. When Indie Collect's restoration premiered at the Museum of Modern Art on 22 January 2020 as part of MoMA's annual program of recently restored films "To Save and Project," it was the first time that Greaves's 79-minute cut had been shown to a public audience. About two weeks later and two dozen subway stops away, the Brooklyn Academy of Music offered a theatrical run to *Cane River*, another Indie Collect restoration, this one directed by Horace Jenkins in 1982 with an all-Black cast and crew but never properly released. Upon its completion it had a few small screenings in New Orleans, but it quickly receded into the realm of the rumoured-to-be-terrific. Work on the restoration began in 2016 alongside the director's son Sacha (Horace Jenkins had died just after finishing *Cane River*, at the age of forty-one). Hopes to use the BAM premiere as a platform to give the film the national release that never came almost forty years earlier were dashed by the COVID pandemic. *Cane River* did, however, enjoy a high-profile presence on the Criterion Channel; it came onto the platform in May 2020, about the time that the scrapped national release would have been gaining momentum, and it was available there for streaming until the end of April 2022 (it's now available on Amazon Prime). It's not exactly what Horace Jenkins would have imagined, but the film could have done worse.

Cane River is set in the community of Natchitoches (Louisiana), which has historically been marked by a strong Creole presence; the Cane River Creole National Historical Park is located nearby. In the United States, the term

"Creole" is not widely understood outside of the deep south, just as the term "Métis" is not well-understood outside of the Canadian prairies. In both cases it has been too easy to default to an ethnic (or more specifically blood-borne) rather than cultural understanding. As I will discuss in chapter 5, too many Canadians follow this blood-borne logic and use the term "Métis" to mean "someone who is pretty sure they have an Indigenous person somewhere in their family tree." What this usage ignores is the genesis of a nation born, at the beginning of the nineteenth century, of the cultural contact that defined the fur trade. That nation established a society at Red River, originally mostly French-speaking and defined by a distinct economy, legal framework, political relationship with neighbouring nations, etc. A desire to defend this distinct society from the encroachment of the nascent Canadian state and the settlers that were following its westward expansion is what gave rise to the epoch-making resistances led by Louis Riel at Red River in 1869–70 (which led to the creation of the province of Manitoba, originally intended to be the home of the west's Francophones) and by Riel and Gabriel Dumont at Batoche (in what is now Saskatchewan) in 1885.

Creole culture doesn't have this same history of confrontation with the dominant state formation, but it is no less distinct for that. A Creole person is not simply a Black person who is pretty sure they have a French person somewhere in their family tree. Creole culture has long had a strong Francophone quality, with a significant presence of the mixed European-African languages that linguists also call creoles, but that is a *cultural* matter, not simply a genetic one. Although the term originally designated European (mostly French) settlers who were born in North America or the Caribbean rather than in France or Spain (which is more or less the same meaning that the term "Canadien" carried until well into the nineteenth century), "Creole" eventually came to mean someone whose ancestry included elements of European, African, and North American peoples. As the nineteenth century rolled into the twentieth, it came to be a form of Blackness; that sense of Creoles as a sort of North American version of the Algerian *pieds-noirs* no longer has any resonance in the United States.

A big part of why Jenkins's film was important was that it took that matter of Creoles as Black as a given, but was also unusually blunt about the way that tensions between Creoles and the larger Black community persisted. Some of this was owing to "colorism," or a sense of difference that obtained from the perception that Creoles were lighter-skinned, something that *Cane River* deals with explicitly in a way that would be almost unheard-of in the 1980s and is still rare in American cinema.[1] But Jenkins's film is clear about the *cultural* differences that drive these tensions: Louisiana Creoles were almost entirely Catholic, many owned land and were able to earn a relatively prosperous living as farmers or ranchers, as a result horse culture was particularly significant, etc. These differences are what drive the Romeo-and-Juliet-style romance in *Cane River*: the young woman in question, Maria, is descended from slaves; her suitor, Peter, comes from a well-established Creole family that owns land including the "big house" estate of his Uncle Larocque. "You know Peter, I just can't believe Black folks own all of this!" she exclaims when he takes her out there for his cousin's birthday party. Peter is keen for her to know that Black people do indeed own such properties, and none of the tension in the film means anything like "Creoles are not Black." But there is *difference* here; this is difference at the level of Protestants in the Republic of Ireland (where a sense of *Irish* identity is near-universal across religious lines), and not of Protestants in Northern Ireland (who are generally seeking recognition of their *national* difference as British, as opposed to the northern Catholics who mostly consider themselves Irish). *Cane River* can serve as a theoretical introduction to this chapter in the manner that *First Case, Second Case* served as an introduction to the last chapter; as Kiarostami's film hints at a hypothetical and tragically unrealized "Iranian Republic," so *Cane River* presents what I have come to think of as a "commonwealth of Blackness."

That concept of "commonwealth" is a little bit of my own invention, although it is connected to the generally understood meaning of the term. In deploying it in this chapter, I am trying to evoke a sense of belonging that is closer than the federalism that I will discuss in the next two chapters devoted to "Federations," but looser than the sense of "ethnos" or "republic" that I explained in the preceding ones. The in-between-ness of groups such as Louisiana Creoles or Irish Protestants can be more clearly understood, more clearly seen, by thinking of them in different ways, however tentatively. The fact is that the American variant of Black nationalism that I discussed in chapter 1 could probably accommodate Creole distinctiveness. Integration into these national formations – formations that as I try to show throughout this book should be conceived of as composite, internally heterogeneous, etc. – is the endgame, so to speak.

"Commonwealth" is a kind of intermediate space, as it has traditionally been when the term has been used to describe geopolitical arrangements. This more familiar use, though, has often been a sort of inverse of what I am proposing here. The Commonwealth of Nations, generally known as the British

Commonwealth, was created in 1926 at first to give limited autonomy to the "white dominions" (Australia, Canada, the Irish Free State, Newfoundland, New Zealand, and the Union of South Africa) and later expanded by way of taking the sting out of the gradual dissolution of the British empire. At that stage the writing was on the wall. Ireland, or at least 26 of her 32 counties, had won more-or-less-independence as the Irish Free State. Settler states such as Canada, Australia, New Zealand, and South Africa were seeking greater autonomy, and the *Statute of Westminster* (1931), which also applied to that Free State as well as to a pre-Canadian Newfoundland, all of which were legally known as Dominions, was supposed to grant that to them while still keeping them within the proverbial fold. This set the stage for a post-wwii world in which colonies such as India, Malta, and then nations in Africa and the Caribbean gradually gained independence but mostly remained within the Commonwealth, with those aforementioned Dominions taking on a sort of "elder sibling" role in that organization as they also became more and more autonomous (with Ireland leaving the Commonwealth in 1949 after passing the *Republic of Ireland Act* [1948]). That process repeated itself sixty years later on the other side of Europe, when, in 1991, the Soviet Union collapsed and the Commonwealth of Independent States (cis) formed in its wake. Although this was originally meant as the successor state to the ussr, when the Russian Federation was created the cis became a Moscow-led coalition of former Soviet republics who were now independent states, but who nevertheless wished (or felt compelled) to retain ties to Russia for a variety of economic and geopolitical reasons. Georgia left the cis as a result of its 2008 war with Russia, Moldova is currently in the process of withdrawing with an eye to being out by the end of 2024, and Ukraine has never been a full member (following its initial war with Russia over the Donbass region it ended even its informal participation in the body, and there is obviously no question of rejoining now). Apart from that, eight member states (Armenia, Azerbaijan, Belarus, Kazahkstan, Kyrgyzstan, Romania, Tadjikistan, and Uzbekistan) and one "associate state" (Turkmenistan) have maintained close ties with the cis without much sense of an encroaching irredentism. Indeed, countries whose substantial Russian minorities do sometimes seem to dream of irredentism – Estonia and Latvia – are notably absent from the cis, having instead sought and eventually achieved membership in the EU by way of a general turn towards the west. As I write this in spring 2024, the war between Russia and Ukraine has been raging for more than two years and it is impossible to say how it will rearrange Russian efforts to reassert its neo-imperial status in eastern Europe and central Asia. But there nevertheless remains, even at this most unstable moment, a community of independent states which are not in any meaningful way "Russian," even though the Russian language remains a kind of lingua franca in the way that English remains so across the Commonwealth of Nations. In both the British and the Russian cases, then, "Commonwealth" has come to stand for a community defined by a level of difference that would disallow a shared nationality.

The way I want to use it in this chapter is exactly the opposite: to explain formations where we can see a shared national identity, but one defined by a level of difference that means they don't achieve the unity of "nation time" or of the republic, even as they are defined by the "ever closer union" that a federal arrangement would generally entail. These are in-between cases: not commonwealths of nations or of independent states, but commonwealths of belonging. The concept is worth something because of the way that it explains important but complicated national formations such as the indissolubly dualistic New Zealand or the multicultural mosaic that has always been (and certainly is today) modern Quebec.

I. A Composite New Zealand

I note that the treaty settlement process is clearly one of the most important examples in the world of an effort to address historical and ongoing grievances of indigenous peoples, and that settlements already achieved have provided significant benefits in several cases.
- James Anaya, *Statement of United Nations Special Rapporteur on the Situation of the Human Rights and Fundamental Freedoms of Indigenous Peoples, upon Conclusion of His Visit to New Zealand*, 23 July 2010[2]

New Zealand provides an important example of the ways in which national identity can befuddle attempts at republican-style unity while still stopping short of the federalism that characterizes other states born of settler colonialism such as Australia or Canada. Australia's official name is actually "the Commonwealth of Australia," but that is meant to evoke a common identity shared across its six states and ten territories. Relations between those of settler heritage and the continent's Indigenous peoples remain distant, as was visible on 14 October 2023, when the country defeated by referendum a proposal described by the National Indigenous Australians Agency as "to change the Constitution to recognise the First Peoples of Australia by establishing a body called the Aboriginal and Torres Strait Islander Voice." The story in its neighbour state is different. Although Māori culture would have been relegated to the fringes of an overall New Zealand identity for the majority of its existence as a settler-colony state, that is no longer the case, much more so than is visible in either Australia or Canada. Questions of treaties aside, Australia and Canada are federations, and in both cases the federal units are geographical rather than cultural: states, provinces, and territories rather than Anglophone, Francophone, and Indigenous. But a broader spirit of federalism defines much of the politics in both places, and consequently the national identity. There is something *separate* about Indigenous nationality in Canada as well as in Australia, even if formal political separatism is not on the table, as it has been in the case of Quebec. New Zealand, of course, is not a federation; I am arguing that we should think of it as a commonwealth. The difference in Indigenous cinema in Australia, Canada, and New Zealand may help clarify this.

The last twenty years or so have seen a serious flourishing of Indigenous cinema globally; the Cannes Film Festival has had a special role in that emergence. In 2001 the Caméra d'or, the award for best first film, went to Zacharias Kunuk's *Atanarjuat: The Fast Runner*.[3] There is not a single word of English, or of any language other than Inuktitut, in the film; it is set in a pre-contact Arctic society, based on an oral tale that likely dates to the sixteenth century. In 2009 that award went to *Samson and Delilah*, Warwick Thornton's portrayal of two Indigenous teenagers living in a remote community near Alice Springs. That film is set in the present day, but it presents white culture as violent and irredeemably hostile, something from which the protagonists are struggling to separate themselves. In between was the 2006 Special Jury Prize winner *Ten Canoes*, a collaboration between the well-known white Australian filmmaker Rolf de Heer and Peter Djigirr, whose bio on the webpage of the Bula'bula Arts Aboriginal Corporation describes him as "a Djinba man from the Arafura Swamp." Like *Atanarjuat* there is not a single word of English in the film, and while the exact historical setting is unclear there is nothing that would indicate that it is post-contact. These are not simply examples chosen at random; *Atanarjuat*, *Ten Canoes*, and *Samson and Delilah* represent the height of Indigenous cinema's global visibility (no film festival in the world has a higher profile than Cannes), essentially constituting its most internationally renowned exemplars. All three present Indigenous cultures as fundamentally separate from those of their nation-states; the Canadian state seems as absent from *Atanarjuat* as the Australian one is from *Ten Canoes*. *Samson and Delilah* is somewhat more complicated on this front as its setting is clearly recognizable as part of the Australian state, but that connection is something that not only the protagonists but also the film overall are trying to move beyond.

New Zealand's most important independent filmmaker, Merata Mita, developed a different analysis of the relationship between settler and Indigenous cultures during her long career. Mita began as a documentarian, making sometimes fiery works of activist cinema such as *Bastion Point: Day 507* (1978), which dealt with the Māori protest around land from which the police were seeking to evict them, as well as *Patu!* which examined the movement to boycott the Apartheid-era South African rugby team (rugby is an extremely popular sport in New Zealand). She continued making documentaries until her death in 2010. Her most ambitious and accomplished film is to my mind *Te Pito o Te Henua: Rapa Nui* (1999), a portrait of what is known in English as "Easter Island" that uses the site as a jumping-off point for a meditation on colonialism in the South Pacific.[4] Mita's most famous film, however, is *Mauri* (1988). This work is historically important partially because it was the first feature-length narrative to be directed by a Māori woman; the New Zealand Film Commission's fiche notes that "[t]he crew numbered 33 Māori and 20 Pākehā, including interns from Hawkes Bay wānanga [Māori college]." In *Mauri*, as with all of her films, Mita is sharply critical of the degree to which Māori people have been marginalized and impoverished by the contemporary New Zealand state, but the existence they lead is far from separate from that majority settler culture (this is also true of *Patu!* where Mita presents the anti-Apartheid movement in a sprawling way that encompasses settler culture in New Zealand, Māori culture, and global anti-racist politics). The love story that drives the narrative is between a Māori woman, Ramari, and a white guy named Steve (whose father, played by Mita's husband Geoff Murphy, is a ranting racist). The scene where the two get married has everyone dressed in pink taffeta or top hats and tails, processing towards an open-air chapel where children perform a Māori dance. The couple has a child, although his biological paternity is not entirely clear because of a one-night stand that Ramari had with the troubled young man Rawi. It's nevertheless clear from the film that Steve is the child's father, and that Steve in turn is now an integral part of Ramari's close-knit extended family. There is even some joking about him slowly learning the Māori language. This is all in contrast to a tedious, ambitious cop played by Temuera Morrison (a young Jango / Boba Fett!), who at the end of the film proclaims to his dinosaur partner that he's going places because "I've got faith in the system!"; the burned-out older man, a white New Zealander, grumbles, "after twenty years in the service, this is where I ended up in the system!" The Māori culture that Mita is evoking here is a composite one, led by Indigenous cultural norms but intertwined with settler culture simply as a matter of fact.

An inversion of that, I would propose, could stand as a summary of contemporary New Zealand identity: a composite culture, one unsurprisingly led by the norms of the majority settler culture, but intertwined with Indigenous cultural norms simply as a matter of fact. These aspects are discernably different, but it is difficult to speak of "New Zealand" as a whole without keeping *both* in sight. This sense of being intertwined is an important part of Māori political culture. In a widely cited 1999 article, Andrea Tunks writes:

> Secession is not at the forefront of Maori aspirations. The physical and spiritual connection of *tangata whenua* [the people of the land] to their ancestral lands and the independent nature of tribal groups means that the carving up of territory to permit Maori independence is not a viable option. Rather, Maori aspire to independence from the social, political and legal structures of the colonial state. In order to achieve this, the state would require a new constitutional structure on the basis of *Te Tiriti* which recognises the *mana* [presence] in respect of themselves and the Crown's law-making power in respect of non-Maori citizens. The external exercise of sovereignty would have to be negotiated by hapu [clans], iwi [bands or tribes], Maori entities, and the Crown.[5]

Te Tiriti refers to the *Treaty of Waitangi* (1840), and this is a crucial document for understanding New Zealand's contemporary national identity. When James Anaya served as the UN Special Rapporteur on the situation of the human rights and fundamental freedoms of Indigenous peoples, he visited New Zealand in 2010 and wrote a short report (a quote from which opened this section). He stated there that "[a] unique feature of New Zealand is the Treaty of Waitangi of 1840, which is understood to be one of the country's founding instruments. The principles of the Treaty provide a foundation for Maori self-determination based on a real partnership between Maori and the New Zealand state, within a framework of respect for cross-cultural understanding and the human rights of all citizens."[6] Plenty of Māori and non-Māori activists and scholars have been critical of the Treaty, and claims that

the signatories did not understand the meaning of the text are longstanding.[7]
But compare this to Canada's foundational instrument, which is not a treaty
at all but rather the *British North America Act* (1867). Treaties are obviously
important in the Canadian constitutional framework, but the document that
creates the country, so to speak, involves the Crown and the Crown alone; Indigenous peoples do not figure in the text of the *British North America Act* at
all. This is in vivid contrast to the *Treaty of Waitangi*, the opening words of
which are "Her Majesty Victoria Queen of the United Kingdom of Great Britain and Ireland regarding with Her Royal Favor the Native Chiefs and Tribes
of New Zealand and anxious to protect their just Rights and Property and to
secure to them the enjoyment of Peace and Good Order has deemed it necessary …" Indigeneity is present literally in the first words of the nation.

None of this should obscure the degree to which the Māori have been sub-
jected by the New Zealand state to a colonial regime of dispossession and
marginalization. Indeed, five years after the declaration of *Te Tiriti* marks the
beginning of the conflict now widely known as the "New Zealand Wars," a
long period of low-level military conflict between colonial forces and the
Māori (along with some settlers who sided with the Māori). Historians generally put the dates of those New Zealand Wars at 1845–72. Moana Jackson's
1994 article is a wide-ranging treatment of the colonial underpinnings of what
she calls "legal pluralism," which is the tradition that I am speaking of in such
warm terms here. She writes that the *Tiriti*-informed jurisprudence that began
to emerge in the 1990s constituted "definitions which conceded certain 'rights'
to Maori but kept them subordinate to the Crown."[8] Anaya's otherwise
relatively upbeat report for the United Nations notes, for instance, that "complaints were highlighted to me by accounts of the recent refusal of the Government to allow for the possibility of the return of land within the Urewera
National Park to the Tuho Iwi," as well as noting the high rate of incarceration
among the Māori.[9] Nevertheless, optimist that I am, I would return to the
fact that *Te Tiriti* has served, and continues to serve, as the basis of an extensive
series of land claims – thirty-one of them since 1992. More to the point I am
trying to make here, those claims are being made through a *single* document.
The *Treaty of Waitangi* is singular in a way that Mary McCarthy would recognize; it establishes the *singular* that is "New Zealand."

The fact that this singularity is composed of discrete elements – the Crown
and "the Native Chiefs and Tribes of New Zealand," in the words of the Treaty
itself – means that its national identity sits uneasily with the republican notions of unity that we discussed in the last chapter. But New Zealand has not

created the kinds of jurisdictions and governance structures that we see in Canada. There is no Kiwi equivalent of the *Indian Act* (1876) and the reserve system it created, nor do we see in New Zealand some version of the Métis Settlements of Alberta, any more than we find traditionally federal structures such as the majority-Inuit territory of Nunavut (created in 1999 by way of resolving all outstanding Inuit land claims). These Canadian systems are designed, however imperfectly, to create loci of power and control that are fundamentally separate from the federal government itself (albeit all still within the ambit of a relationship with the Crown). This is sometimes indistinguishable from "dereliction of the government's fiscal responsibility,"[10] but at least in theory, independence is the goal, even if that independence takes forms that are still within the limits of adherence to the Canadian state (I will discuss these tensions in detail in the next two chapters). Independence is not the goal of the constitutional revision process currently underway in New Zealand.[11] In 2016, the Independent Working Group on Constitutional Transformation issued a report that identified six possible constitutional frameworks, most of which had three elements: the Iwi/Hapū, the Crown, and a relational component. The first of these proposals for a new constitutional framework reads as follows: "A tricameral or three sphere model consisting of an Iwi/Hapū assembly (the rangatiratanga sphere), the Crown in Parliament (the kāwanatanga sphere), and a joint deliberative body (the relational sphere)."[12] Even the ostensibly unicameral models stress the duality I have been discussing as foundational, as we see in their fifth proposal: "A unicameral or one sphere model consisting of Iwi/Hapū and the Crown making decisions together in a constitutionally mandated assembly. This model does not have rangatiratanga or kāwanatanga spheres. It only has the relational sphere."[13] To return to Tunks's sense of the political dynamics at work here, "[s]ecession is not at the forefront of Maori aspirations." Instead, the emergent constitutional framework is focussed on the creation of a nation defined by an inseparable duality.

One of Tunks's most interesting suggestions for the path New Zealand might follow is buried in one of her endnotes. By way of explaining the basic complexity of the country, she expands on the idea that the connection between the Crown and the Māori will be the subject of constant negotiation. Deploying the Māori name of the country and echoing the concerns of the *Red Paper* (which I will discuss below), she writes that "Aotearoa would probably have a multi-layered system of citizenship. Maori would belong to their tribal nations and to a state of Aotearoa; non-Maori would be citizens of the state of New Zealand or Aotearoa and could have the choice to participate in Maori processes."[14] Tunks was writing in 1999, and this is not the exact direction that the process of constitutional reform has ended up following. But it is illustrative because what she is talking about is not so much multi-layered citizenship as a form of *dual* citizenship. Such a regime would be near-unthinkable in Canada, particularly the bit about non-Indigenous people having the choice to participate in Indigenous processes. Those aspects of political life are fenced off in Canada, and for reasons that seem to me to prove the maxim of Robert Frost's companion about good fences making good neighbours. New Zealand, however, does not fence its national identities in the same way; in Frost's words, "There where it is we do not need the wall: / He is all pine and I am apple orchard." That 1840 *Tiriti* creates a sort of commons, a common field where it is perfectly plain where the pine trees are and where the orchard sits. New Zealand is not so much an example of a "commonwealth of nations," but rather of a commonwealth *as* nation.

II. *Vive la Couronne*, or, a Commonwealth of Quebec

What has been truly decisive in the Quiet Revolution, in fact, has been cultural matters: there was educational reform, but [we] had other dreams as well, desires for new attitudes. The very formal ideologies where we had found our identity rapidly faded. Catholicism, for example, ceased to be the framework of our nationality. Many believers such as myself were delighted; we see pluralism as a happy conquest. But where are we now to find that certain unanimity without which no nation can exist? We have reached a point where we must find another collective project. Is it possible? It all comes back to that question; constitutional arrangements are meaningful only in relation to it. Time is of the essence.
– Fernand Dumont, "Y-a-t-il un avenir pour l'homme canadien-français?"[15]

Gérard Bouchard and Charles Taylor's report *Fonder l'avenir*, which synthesized the work they did together as chairs of the 2007 Commission de consultation sur les pratiques d'accommodement reliées aux différences culturelles (generally known in English as the "Reasonable Accommodation" commission), asserted that "it is precisely the great originality and merit of the neonationalism spawned by the Quiet Revolution that it succeeded in combining the identity struggle with social egalitarianism and the protection of rights."[16] I am in full agreement there, and since my aforementioned first trip to Quebec in 1993 I have been tremendously inspired by the vision put forward by Quebec nationalists of the progressive, diversity-infused variety. We can see there, I believe, a movement that has been exemplary in its emergence from a fundamentally racialist understanding (wherein the race of the French-Canadian Catholics determinedly pursued their *survivance* in opposition to the sea of Anglo-Protestantism all around them) to a civic, open-ended, and fundamentally territorial sense of belonging (wherein the Québécois were defined by a common allegiance to the space of Quebec and the language of French, both elective affinities that were chosen not only by descendants of the French-Canadian settlers but also in massive numbers by people whose heritage was Italian, Haitian, Chilean, etc.). But while I am broadly sympathetic with the goals not just of Quebec nationalism but of Quebec separatism as well, I have never been convinced by the argument that an independent Quebec should be a republic. In 2017, Éric Bédard wrote in the *Bulletin d'histoire politique* of how "a veritable 'republican school' has emerged in Quebec's social sciences, defined by the work of (among others) Stéphane Kelly, Marc Chevrier, Louis-Georges Harvey and Danic Parenteau"[17] (m.t.). To shore this up on the polemical front, in 2016 Martine Ouellet, who represented Vachon (in the Montreal suburb of Longueuil) for the Parti Québécois, produced a "Constitution initiale de la République du Québec."[18]

Throughout the remainder of this chapter I will try to show that this republican idea is not convincing, at least not in the case of Quebec. Chevrier and Parenteau are the most compelling on this front. Parenteau's 2015 book *L'indépendance par la République* is a relatively short and sharply polemical defence of a republican regime, arguing that "the dominant political tradition in Canada is Anglo-Saxon liberalism"[19] (m.t.) and lamenting "sa conception atomisée de la société."[20] There is much to agree with chez Parenteau, but I cannot get past his sense that the whole concept of "The Crown" is at its root undemocratic ("foncièrement antirépublicaine" is how he puts it at one point).[21] I will argue in this chapter that while that may be true of a country such as Ireland, the situation in Quebec is fundamentally different. Chevrier's 2012 book *La République Québécoise: Hommages à une idée suspecte* is a substantial treatment of the question, one that ranges widely over the history of Quebec and the significance of political theory in understanding that history.[22] But rather than a republic waiting to happen, in the manner of France or of Ireland, I will argue here that Quebec has become a commonwealth, in the manner of an "expanded" version of New Zealand. If it chooses the path of independence, then I believe that remaining a constitutional monarchy should be a crucial part of conceptualizing that independent state.

I am aware of how provocative this must seem, but bear with me. It is a truism that in Quebec, support for the monarchy and the British connection is not high. I don't exactly disagree with this common-sense assessment of the state of popular opinion, but this does not mean that such support is non-existent, and moreover, it can be found in some central parts of the nationalist movement. Chevrier acknowledges nearly as much in *La République québécoise*, writing early on that "[t]o put matters unambiguously, the Québécois are monarchists – and have been for a long time, in fact. But this is not a fervent monarchism, like the kind that is still expressed by Canadian families of British heritage [de souche britannique] who commune with a portrait of Her Majesty hung on the walls of austere dining rooms full of mahogany furniture"[23] (m.t.). It's not entirely clear if he has in mind here someone like the novelist and filmmaker Jacques Godbout, whose credentials as a Quebec nationalist intellectual are utterly unimpeachable. That sense of being one of the elders of the movement was what led the conservative-nationalist young upstart Mathieu Bock-Côté to publish *Le tour du jardin* (2014), a book-length interview with him. Therein Godbout explains how "[f]or my part I believe in the equality of citizens before the law, in representative democracy, in a state of laws. So I prefer the British parliamentary system, with its symbolic royalty, to a presidential republic, because I don't like the idea of an individual president who embodies an entire people"[24] (m.t.). Whether his house has any mahogany furniture in it, he doesn't say.

In any event, it probably seems more consistent with the general Québécois sensibility to recall how the 2011 visit of the Duke and Duchess of Cambridge was met in *la belle province* by protests, and to point to the fact that those were a mere shadow of the riot that transpired on 10 October 1964 when the Queen passed through Quebec City (it is known as "Samedi de la matraque" or "the Saturday of the police baton"). It would be easy to allow such shows of displeasure with the British connection to overshadow the degree to which Quebec, like the First Nations, appealed to the government of the United Kingdom to intercede in Pierre Trudeau's process of constitutional patriation, which they argued was running roughshod over their rights as nations in the name of a bold new vision of cosmopolitan multiculturalism that could only be opposed by petty autocrats or folkloric nationalists (which, for Pierre Trudeau, were barely any better). On this UK connection Frédéric Bastien's 2013 book

La Bataille de Londres is essential reading. I will not rehearse the details that Bastien presents so thoroughly, but will point out that he quotes a 13 January 1982 letter from Margaret Thatcher to René Lévesque that opens with "My dear Prime Minister" and, in reference to Lévesque's appeal for the UK government to refuse patriation in the absence of Quebec's approval, writes that "I have studied your request carefully" before saying the process is too far down the line and she must now consider this "entirely a Canadian matter."[25] It wasn't the outcome Quebec nationalists were hoping for, but such interactions were hardly the stuff of a group that considered the British connections to be nothing but a colonialist irrelevance imposed by a foreign state whose meddling is to be resisted. Indeed, *exactly the opposite was the case*; the external imposition that both Quebec and many First Nations were resisting (the latter by way of a number of visits to the UK coordinated, as Bastien recalls, by "Labour MP Bruce George ... who was their [First Nations'] champion in London")[26] was coming from a Trudeau-led Liberal government hell-bent on paring that British connection down to the minimum.

Nevertheless, the reasons for widespread anti-monarchism in *la belle province* are fairly intuitive given the fact that the early sixties were marked by the revitalization of an anti-colonially inflected Quebec nationalism in the wake of the Quiet Revolution, a milieu that is covered in a high level of detail by Sean Mills's 2010 book *The Empire Within: Postcolonial Thought and Political Activism in Sixties Montreal*, and in more polemical terms by Dalie Giroux's 2020 book *L'Œil du maître*, a lament for the anticolonial road not taken by Quebec nationalism. Neither text is sympathetic to the North American history of constitutional monarchy, something that both texts basically ignore in the most genuinely studious way imaginable (and I mean that to convey admiration for the scholarship of both). I do, though, want to explain two closely connected aspects of Quebec distinctiveness that make a constitutional monarchy a logical choice for an independent Quebec: the long history of political separation from the "spiritual home" of republicanism, France; and, much more significantly, the historical and legal realities of the relationships with Indigenous nations.

Visitors who have learned French in the classroom as opposed to the home often have awkward experiences with the language on their first visits to Quebec. A question asked in French being answered in English reads as obnoxious to most Franco-capable Anglophones, to say nothing of the citizens of the Hexagon who sometimes find that their "foreign" accent triggers this quaint Québécois custom. But the truth is that there is a linguistic distinctiveness to Quebec that can flummox interactions with even the most committed Francophone outsider. The persistence in Quebec French of words such as "piastre" (which the *Multidictionnaire de la language française* has as "Archaïsme au sens de *dollar canadien*")[27] should be taken as a reminder of the pre-revolutionary roots of the language. The Battle of the Plains of Abraham in 1759 marked the final capitulation of the Kingdom of France in the northern part of North America; in French this is known as "la Conquête." This was fully thirty years before the beginning of the French Revolution, from which Francophones in that northern part of North America were fully cut off. One key effect of that Revolution was the wholesale revision and unification of the French language, based on the Parisian dialect. Assuring that the new state would share a common tongue available to all has long been a means of encouraging *egalité* and *fraternité*, if not necessarily *liberté*.[28] The Francophones of the northern part of this continent had no contact with this experience of unification except for small waves of later migration directly from France. The language that solidified in Quebec was pre-reform, not based on the Paris dialect at all but rather the result of people sent west by the Kingdom of France needing to communicate with one another, even though they were mostly Normans (who spoke a form of French that was markedly different from that of Paris) and Bretons (many of whose mother tongue not only wasn't French but wasn't even a Romance language, Breton being part of the Celtic language family). The French of North America was a contact language, certainly not in the manner of the Creoles spoken further south into the Caribbean but just as certainly not a preview of a post-Revolutionary "unified" French. Being cut off politically from republican France and its successor empires made certain that the language would stay that way.

This "certaine tendance de la langue québécoise" has echoes in other aspects of Quebec's culture. Even Quebec's history of armed insurrection has distinctly non-revolutionary roots, something that the more radical fans of the Patriotes rebellions of 1837–38 tend to sort of whistle past. Michel Ducharme's 2010 treatment of the patriotes in a revolutionary-Atlantic context is admirably clear on this matter. He writes that "[u]ntil the beginning of the 1820s, belonging to the British Empire was not an issue for the reformists, and they situated their claims within the framework of the 1791 constitution [also known as the *Canada Act*, which created Upper and Lower Canada]. Pierre Bedard and Louis-Joseph Papineau, the speaker of the Legislative Assembly, went so far as to underline – in 1809 and 1820, respectively – that *la*

Conquête had turned out to be positive inasmuch as it had brought democratic institutions to French-Canadians"[29] (m.t.). The famous *92 Resolutions of 1834*, which outlined the Patriotes' grievances for the House of Assembly of Lower Canada, begins with the following words: "Resolved, *That* His Majesty's loyal subjects, the people of this province of Lower Canada, have shown the strongest attachment to the British Empire of which they are a portion; that they have repeatedly defended it in time of war; that at the period which preceded the Independence of the late British Colonies on this continent, they resisted the appeal made to them to join their confederation."[30] Indeed, the first five of the ninety-two resolutions are exclusively devoted to shoring up the Canadiens' place in British North America and all her institutions. Of course this loyalty was not repaid by the British regime, which crushed the rebellions in what was then Lower Canada as they did in Upper Canada the same year. What they did not do in Upper Canada, though, was commission a special report, which was written by a British aristocrat and is now known generally as the *Durham Report*. Filed in 1839, the report speaks in the dulcet tones of concerned liberalism but recommends assimilation as the only logical option for the French speakers of the northern part of the continent. Durham writes towards the end of the report that "I should be indeed surprised if the more reflecting part of the French Canadians entertained at present any hope of continuing to preserve their nationality. Much as they struggle against it, it is obvious that the process of assimilation to English habits is already commencing."[31] But French-speaking Canadians did indeed continue to struggle against assimilation, although they did not turn towards a more revolutionary mode. In his 2000 survey *Genèse des nations et cultures du Nouveau Monde*, Gérard Bouchard writes at some length about what he calls "le paradigme de la survivance." He recalls there how "[a]fter 1860 ... the sociocultural elites (especially literary figures [les littéraires surtout[32]]) spoke as much about creating a national culture as about preserving old traditions"[33] and that "it is thought that the Church was the only institution sufficiently powerful and broadly enough deployed to claim to be able to claim speak for the whole nation and to take charge of its destiny."[34] Furthermore, he recalls how "[t]he nation's fragility spawns an enormous fear of the foreigner. It also generates exclusionary social and cultural behaviour towards ethnic minorities who have settled in Quebec or wish to settle there. Difference threatens the nation in some way."[35] This sense of *survivance* as inwardly nationalist, xenophobic, culturally insecure, backward-looking, and Church-bound can set the parameters for an understanding of the significant differences between the culture of France and the culture of Quebec (or, before 1867, of Lower Canada and Canada East).

After 1867 until the 1960s, that is. The 1960s, and more specifically the period after the Liberal Party defeated the long-reigning (and deeply conservative) Union nationale in 1960, is now known as the *Révolution tranquille* or the "Quiet Revolution." This is when Quebec society secularized its culture and modernized its economy, a process that reached a kind of fever pitch at the 1967 Montreal Expo,[36] and which was embodied economically by the nationalization of Hydro-Québec. This is also the period when the term "Canadien français" disappears from use in Quebec, replaced by the less *survivance*-weighted and more clearly territorial and inclusive appellation "Québécois." This modernization is certainly a work in progress, and it is reasonable to disagree about how much Quebec has really emerged from the cultural insecurity that defined *survivance*, or how well it has really resisted the temptation towards xenophobia. But the difference between the Church-bound, fundamentally racialist vision of the period that Bouchard pegs at 1840–1940 (and arguably continuing through the long reign of Duplessis's Union nationale, 1936–60, with a brief period out of power during WWII)[37] and the Quebec culture of today is stark.

Having said that, I also note that the question of whether or not the Quiet Revolution represents a fresh start for Quebec is a longstanding controversy among historians. I am strongly in agreement with Ronald Rudin's 1997 book *Making History in 20th Century Quebec*, which argues that Quebec history is indeed marked by a specific set of tensions and ruptures, mostly around colonialism and nationalism, that set it aside from other "normal" countries. Rudin writes in the preface to that book that it "began with my efforts to become an Irish historian,"[38] recalling how Irish "revisionist" historians sought to downplay the nationalist and colonialist elements of Irish history in favour of a more "professional" approach. Revisionists in Quebec were similarly motivated, although on the other side of the fence politically; whereas nothing makes a nationalist historian in Ireland madder than encountering a "revisionist" (someone who, in downplaying the sometimes-violent and definitely exceptional aspects of Irish history such as the centuries-long struggle against their fellow Europeans the British, must surely be a neo-colonialist dupe), nationalist historians in Quebec found the concept of "normality" in terms of historical development to be a key part of putting their field of study (and their *pays*) on an equal footing with Canadian history, French history, German history, etc. Thus, I can recognize the degree to which downplaying the importance of the Quiet Revolution may seem too simple. I can see what a revisionist historian such as Claude Couture is getting at when he expresses impatience with how Pierre Trudeau and Lucien Bouchard both "accept the paradigm of the folk society before the Quiet Revolution and describe Quebec as a non-modern society before 1960." He goes on to write in his 1996 book *La loyauté d'un laïc: Pierre Elliot Trudeau et le libéralisme canadien*:

> Like Bouchard ... Trudeau has a teleological concept of the history of
> Quebec, including a moment of salvation and purification that allowed
> the society to start from scratch, throwing out wholesale its past – a past
> symbolized in particular by Duplessis. But as Bourque, Duchastel, and
> Beauchemin have pointed out, Duplessism constituted a form of politi-
> cal discourse in which tradition and modernity were so tangled up that
> it was impossible to create an opposition between them.[39]

In his original work, Couture also notes how "[a]vec Lucien Bouchard, Trudeau partage cette vision métaphysique du Québec."[40] His language is not irrelevant there, for it does give a sense of the deep philosophical commitment that this sort of liberalism often imposes. Less than a politics, it can sometimes seem like a metaphysics, in a manner that I critiqued in the introduction (and which has become a central part of many critiques of liberalism, from both the left and the right). For Couture, a tendency to fetishize the Quiet Revolution is consistent with a certain kind of Trudeau-led, chauvinistically anti-national Canadian nationalism, one that is at the heart of his ongoing project to redefine Canadian culture *selon* his understanding of the liberal tradition.

As far as impatience with this sort of Trudeauvian imperiousness goes, more sympathetic I could not be. But I find less convincing the idea that Duplessiste discourse is one "in which tradition and modernity were so tangled up that it was impossible to create an opposition between them." Rather, I see it as what the English might call the fag-end of *survivance* – that is to say, consistent with a distinctly Quebec experience of insular nationalism, an insularity brought about by the failure of a nineteenth-century reform project which transformed into an armed insurrection that wound up being utterly crushed, only to have its radical ideologies lie dormant for about a century.

That is not "typical" at all (and certainly bears little resemblance to anything
going on in that spiritual home of republicanism, France), and it is hard to
imagine the story being fully told without that sense of radical difference between the pre-1960s and post-1960s, between the Quebec of Maurice Duplessis and the Quebec of René Lévesque.

Ah yes, René Lévesque: founder of the Parti Québécois,[41] premier of Quebec during its 1980 referendum on "Souveraineté-Association," salty and
chain-smoking social democrat. Lévesque is unusual among Quebec separatist leaders for being remembered in relatively fond terms by a wide range
of Quebeckers, Anglophones included. John Walker's 2016 essay film *Quebec
My Country Mon Pays* is a sympathetic portrayal of the appeal that Lévesque's
social-democratic vision of a sovereign Quebec held for young and idealistic
Anglophones (among whom the monolingual, Montreal-born, and now Hali-
fax-based Walker counts himself) during the 1960s and '70s.

One of the most important Quebec nationalist intellectuals, Fernand Dumont, wrote of this exact phenomenon in his 1971 book *La vigile du Québec*.
He asserted there that "[f]or a small people like ours, the duty of welcome
and assembly is a hard one. But it must be undertaken in terms of our lives'
justification as the highest proof that liberty is turned towards others. We
must look patiently for interlocutors." He seems to find such an interlocutor
in a veritable facsimile of a young John Walker:

> I think of a young Anglais who went campaigning from door to door
> among his compatriots for the Parti québécois. I had a long talk with him
> during the campaign: anything but assimilated, Anglo-Saxon to his fin-
> gertips and prodigiously proud of the fact, anxious as well to share our
> values, to help construct a common home here for us all. He is certainly
> not unique. We must try particularly to reach the young people in our
> English-language colleges and universities. Not to persuade them to be-
> come faithful copies of ourselves, but to invite them to take part in our
> project, leaving it to them to bring their own colours and intentions.[42]

That vision has relatively little to do with France, which hardly qualifies as
"une petite nation." Furthermore, Dumont's explicit interdiction of "per-
suader de devenir notre fidèle copie" and his call for this Anglo-idealist "d'y
apporter ses couleurs et ses intentions"[43] makes for an interesting comparison
with Simone Weil's republican vision, which I discussed in the last chapter,

devoted to "Republics." Recall there that when the state makes a wedding present of some land, a home, and a machine, "[t]he choice of a machine would be made to depend in the first place on the individual workman's tastes and natural abilities, and secondly on very general requirements from the point of view of production."[44] Dumont is as quick to move away from any sense of stifling individuality as Weil is to temper any recognition of the individual with an invocation of the needs of the state. What we are seeing here, I think, is the difference between a republic and a commonwealth. Dumont's thinking is typical of the latter in the importance that it attaches to "le devoir d'accueillir et de rassembler." Obviously this is a factor in republican regimes, as we saw in the last chapter via how the Georgian Democratic Republic sought to accommodate Muslims, Armenians, etc. (or the century of bloody problems that followed when they couldn't do the same for the Abkhaz). But in terms of a unified national identity, Noe Jordania's lost Georgia is clearly closer to France than to New Zealand. The opposite is true of Quebec, home to minorities that are well-described as "rien de moins qu'un assimilé," not exactly in the manner of the Māori, but perhaps not far off either.

Just as I do not want to downplay the historical debate around the importance of the Quiet Revolution, I am not trying to say that "the French connection" means nothing for contemporary Quebec nationalism. French models of *laïcité* are obviously the inspiration behind the political discourse that led to the passage of Quebec's *Loi sur la laïcité de l'État* (2019), which banned the wearing of conspicuous religious symbols on the part of any civil servant who exercises coercive authority over the public (as well as the wearing of face coverings on the part of anyone who gives or receives any public service). It's in the name, after all, *laïcité*, a term which has formed the basis of French secularism since 1905[45] (that is, since the passage of *Loi du 9 décembre 1905 concernant la séparation des Églises et de l'État*) right on up to more or less the present day (that is, since the passage of *Loi n⁰ 2004-228 du 15 mars 2004 encadrant, en application du principe de laïcité, le port de signes ou de tenues manifestant une appartenance religieuse dans les écoles, collèges et lycées publics*). But it is worth recalling that the Quebec secularism law was first mooted by a *very* conservative manifestation of the PQ in 2012 before being passed by the Coalition Avenir Québec (CAQ), a centre-right party of recent origin (2011) which is in some ways a return to the ideology of the Union nationale (minus all the persecution of communists and Jehovah's Witnesses). Neither party can claim to be part of the legacy of René Lévesque, evidenced by the simple fact that neither's platform bears the slightest resemblance to the detailed blueprint for a new country that he authored, titled *Option Québec*, in 1968.

That document does not speak of a "republic." The titles of its concluding sections are "Un Québec souverain"[46] followed by "... et une nouvelle Union canadienne."[47] What Lévesque had imagined was a complex form of association between a remade Canadian state and a sovereign Quebec, speaking of "examples provided by countries whose size is comparable to our own – Benelux or Scandinavia[48] – in which cooperation is highly advanced and has favoured the progress of each party more than ever before, even as we can see that none are prevented from living in ways consistent with their own traditions and preferences"[49] (m.t.). This is a system with the ring of federalism about it, but it is the federalism of the European Union or the Nordic League, not that of the Canadian state: that is to say, a federal union of sovereign states, some of which are monarchies (Belgium, Luxembourg, Denmark, Sweden), some of which are republics (Ireland, Finland), some of which are federations (also Belgium, Germany). Differences in political regime do not at all hinder confederal association of this EU or Nordic League type, any more than a Quebec of whatever political regime (republic, federation, or, as I am arguing is the best reflection of reality, commonwealth) would be hindered by forming a union with a federal country such as Canada; it could be Finland and Sweden all over again, so to speak. That seems to be the line that Lévesque's thought followed, as can be traced throughout *Option Québec*. The main critique I want to offer of this vision is not of its desire for Quebec to pursue this kind of Union canadienne; I will argue in the next chapter that this sort of arrangement would also serve English Canada and Indigenous nations well, and was already proposed in a slightly less extreme form by the political scientist Philip Resnick as far back as 1990.

Rather, what I wish to critique is Lévesque's somewhat evasive description of what kind of country he is really trying to build. Lévesque's portion of *Option Québec* opens with the words "Nous sommes des Québécois."[50] Elsewhere he describes the situation of Canada and Quebec this way: "il s'agit de *deux majorités*, de deux 'sociétés complètes'"[51] (italics his). I can see what he is getting at here, and I do not think this should be read as some form of French-Canadian chauvinism. "Nous sommes des Québécois" accommodates someone who traces her ancestry back to "la Conquête" as well as someone born in Montreal to two recent Haitian immigrants, and I confess to an impatience with assumptions that the term is somehow only meant to refer to the *pure laine*. It is extremely difficult to find a post–Quiet-Revolution nationalist of any note who has actually argued such a position, and an insistence that despite that fact this is how such nationalists really think is to me indistinguishable from mind-reading and thus unconvincing. The large-scale integration of immigrant communities has been a major priority for Quebec nationalists for decades now, and the non-ethnocentric quality of this integrative impulse is not a recent development. Mills's 2016 book *A Place in the Sun: Haiti, Haitians and the Remaking of Quebec* is illuminating reading on this front, as it opens by arguing that "Haiti was said to be tied to Quebec by a special bond, one that French-Canadian intellectuals conceptualised in familial terms."[52] He goes on to point out how "Haitian migrants of the 1960s were generally sympathetic to the Quebec nationalism of the period, although this relationship was always complex and multifaceted. Because of the shared intellectual influences of anti-colonialism and a common language of contestation, Haitian writers had a great deal of sympathy for developments in Quebec."[53] None of this should be taken to indicate that Quebec has only sought to integrate ostensibly Francophone immigrants.[54] Consider that the most controversial elements of Quebec's *Charte de la langue française* (1977), popularly known in English as Bill 101, have to do with compelling immigrants to educate their children *in French*. If Quebec nationalists were determined to exclude the non–*pure laine*, then insisting on their children learning French thoroughly seems like a singularly ineffective way to do that.

All of this is consistent with Gérard Bouchard's definition of interculturalism, which was an important part of the *Fonder l'avenir* report he wrote with Charles Taylor and which he later expanded on in a 2012 book titled *L'Interculturalisme. Un point de vue québécois.* He explains there how his formulation of interculturalism is opposed to multiculturalism because it holds that "the special attention given to the Francophone majority culture"[55] must be held in balance with the rights of minorities, not simply ignored on the assumption that this majority culture is so powerful that it will be fine on its own. This is to my mind a deeply erroneous attitude that many proponents of Canadian multiculturalism take towards Canadian culture as a whole, and I will expand on this critique of Canadian multiculturalism in more detail in chapter 5. For Bouchard, interculturalism is defined by "[a]n emphasis on integration, in accordance with a moral contract that binds all Quebecers ["ensemble des Québécois"[56]] and demands a principle of reciprocity in the harmonization of cultural difference."[57] I make no secret of my overwhelming preference for this kind of interculturalism as opposed to the multicultural models long dominant in English Canada, and I will argue in that fifth chapter that the only real problem with Bouchard's formulation is the degree to which it seems to assume that it isn't also well-suited for the nationality that I claim as my own. In any event, I hold that "Québécois" is an inclusive, post-ethnic identity, and while obviously xenophobic legislation such as the CAQ's *Loi sur la laïcité de l'État* (2019) is worrying, Bouchard himself was one of many nationalists who gave testimony arguing against the passage of that bill.

The tricky issue here is not cultural minorities who want to be Québécois but are denied adherence to that identity by a bunch of *survivance*-obsessed racists. That is a straw-man figure with no meaningful connection to the reality of present-day Quebec. The tricky issue has to do with cultural minorities who *do not* wish to be Québécois: the majority of Quebec Anglophones (Dumont's idealistic young friend notwithstanding) and Indigenous nations. In both cases, accommodations are clearly necessary. Lévesque could see this with Anglophones, and always insisted that the Anglophone community would maintain its own school system in a sovereign Quebec. Discussing the formation of the PQ, Daniel Poliquin's biography 2009 of Lévesque (part of Penguin's "Extraordinary Canadians" series) recalls how a radical wing "had moved that, in an independent Quebec, 'public funding would be limited strictly to French-language schools.' No more subsidies for English schools, Jewish schools, private schools, nothing. Lévesque immediately said no. 'The Quebec I want,' he said, 'will be pluralist, tolerant, respectful of minorities.'"[58] Lévesque is somewhat harder to pin down about the place of Indigenous peoples in such a country, although he spent plenty of time in the north and was well-known as being sympathetic to the national claims of First Nations and Inuit. Poliquin also recalls that during Lévesque's days as part of the Liberal government of Quebec, "[h]e petitioned cabinet to allow Aboriginals to vote at the provincial level, and he proposed opening schools where the language of instruction would be Cree or Inuktitut. In short, what Lévesque wanted for the Québécois, he wanted for Aboriginals in the province, too."[59] Perhaps most famously, at a 1982 First Minister's conference devoted to the patriation of the constitution he ceded his time to Mary Simon, at that time the head of the Société Makivik (the legal representative of the Inuit of Quebec) and now the thirtieth governor general of Canada. The solution to the problems of integration represented by both groups – Quebec Anglophones and Indigenous nations – is clear: an independent Quebec that also remains a constitutional monarchy.

For the Anglophone minority, the case is largely sentimental. Retaining ostensibly British symbols and political structures could help the community maintain a connection to the original Anglophone country (that is to say the United Kingdom), and remind all of the new country's inhabitants that these connections go back far indeed in Quebec's history – back at least to 1759. Furthermore, just as Irish citizens born before independence could maintain British citizenship and all people born on the island of Ireland – including Northern Ireland – are still today entitled to Irish citizenship (as long as they have at least one Irish parent), Canada should continue to extend citizenship to anyone who was Canadian at the time of Quebec's independence, and Quebec should recognize that citizenship with voting rights, just as British citizens living in Ireland have, since independence, had the right to vote there, and vice versa (I will discuss this practice's basis in the Common Travel Area in the next chapter). In terms of the English-speaking minority, retaining the monarchy would, hopefully, be read as a signal to the effect of "we are making a new country, but we recognize that the old one will always be with us." In terms of the Anglophone minority, these would all be symbolic gestures, but hopefully meaningful ones that would lead to a somewhat more peaceful coexistence.

In term of Indigenous nations, that's not the case at all; the need to retain the monarchy is a legal and moral imperative. Indigenous nations are *nations* and none have indicated, through their leadership, any desire whatsoever to fuse their nationality with that of the Québécois. That's true of their relationship with Canada as well; the leaders of Indigenous nations are not, as a rule, looking to help their people become Canadians, but rather to have their own nationality fully recognized by the Canadian state and integrated into those state formations in a way that will be of benefit to *their* citizens (benefits that may include issuing a passport, if the citizen of the Indigenous nation in question wants it).[60] As I mentioned in the earlier section of this chapter, there are fences between Canada as a nation and the Indigenous nations of this continent, and good fences make good neighbours. Legally speaking those fences are the treaties, and treaties are made with one and only one party: the Crown. The governing principle of all Indigenous-settler political negotiation has long been "nation to nation," and for the whole of the treaty-making process, the settler nation in question has been represented by the Crown. Note that

I did not say "Canada has been represented by the Crown." Some treaties pre-date the creation of the Canadian state; those that followed were still invariably made in the name of the Crown, partially as means to knit everything pre- and post-Canada together into a common legal framework.

Quebec is somewhat unusual in this framework. Most significant here is that none of the province is covered by a numbered treaty; indeed, only its easternmost fringe is covered by the Peace and Friendship Treaties made between the Crown and the Mi'kmaq. Nevertheless, the Royal Proclamation of 1763 very much does cover Quebec, having been passed in no small part to consolidate the proto-Canadian state in the wake of the end of the Seven Years War. It hardly seems a minor matter that this is a *royal* proclamation that derives much of its contemporary political force from its four centuries (the eighteenth, nineteenth, twentieth, and twenty-first) of *continuous* ob-ligation. Getting rid of the "Royal" also gets rid of the "continuous," and puts details of the future relationship between settlers and Indigenous nations in question in a way that the latter would seem highly unlikely to accept. Furthermore, the *Paix des braves* (2002),[61] an agreement intended to repair the political and environmental damage done by the long history of devel-opment in the northern region of James Bay, is between Quebec and the Cree, but even there, buried deep within the agreement, we find a call to recognize the legal implications of "the treaty relationship between the James Bay Crees and the federal Crown."[62]

This is why *La République québécoise* has a strange relationship with the case I am making not only here but throughout this book. Chevrier's chapter on the monarchy, "Le monarchisme québécois ou la politique de l'irréel," is of special importance. Here he follows the course of so much discussion of the Canadian monarchy – both in favour and opposed. That is to say, the chapter is preoccupied with questions of whether a monarchical form of gov-ernment does or does not secure fundamental liberties, whether Canadian institutions and the Canadian constitution are or are not so intertwined with the monarchy as to make them unimaginable without it, etc. Chevrier rejects these contentions, in the opposite manner of how Canadian monarchists argue for their importance. I cannot help but be nonplussed either way; these are arguments that I have always found to be hopelessly abstract. I'm sure this reflects my own ignorance of the finer points of constitutional theory, but if the only real question is one based in procedural liberalism – that is to say, does a constitutional monarchy lead to institutions that more justly or effi-ciently govern individuals – then I can certainly see how it seems like "common sense" to do away with it. That is more or less the position Chevrier proceeds from as he impatiently and sarcastically works his way through several centuries of French-Canadian and later Québécois acquiescence to monarchical structures.

It is thus startling to read in the same chapter sharp critiques of Quebec's political culture of the last fifty years or so, which he sees as defined by a Trudeau-led atomizing liberalism, one that leads to widespread self-absorption on the part of Quebec's political and cultural élites, even of the nationalist variety. Following a section where he strongly critiques the facile anti-nationalism of both Trudeau and Michael Ignatieff, he writes of "[t]he citizen who exists by himself, in sum a 'sovereign' citizen. The corollary of this sentiment is the idea, very widespread in Quebec, that the state is a reality that is exterior to us; at its best it is useful if we know how to put it at our service, and at worst it is disastrous, because it is greedy and invasive, violating our most treasured freedoms"[63] (m.t.). That is a critique of liberalism's casual and often unacknowledged tendency towards atomization and consumerism, something particularly prevalent in the imperialist manifestation of liberalism that refuses to acknowledge that it is an ideology at all. This is all fully consistent with the robustly progressive understanding of nation I have been arguing for throughout this book. It is thus strange that the Indigenous context only barely comes up in this framework, given the degree to which the communitarian quality of much Indigenous political discourse serves as a powerful opposition to an imperialist English-Canadian liberalism. We saw this communitarian opposition to atomizing, de-nationalizing liberalism in the way that Indigenous forces, *clearly aligned with the forces of Quebec nationalism*, sought to obstruct the unilateral moves of the Trudeau government to strong-arm the 1982 constitution through the British parliament.

There is also a widespread sense among many anti-monarchists (sometimes explicit, sometimes implicit as a matter of a failure to address the issue, as is the case with Chevrier) that the legal framework of the treaties, universally based in an unambiguously permanent relationship with *the Crown* (and not necessarily with Canada), could somehow be rewritten on the fly, that surely we could figure that all out once we finally get rid of that old and silly British stuff. I think this attitude is dismissive in the extreme, and generally born of a less-than-precise sense of the depth of Canada's tradition of treaty-making.[64] Perhaps the most extreme example of this kind of cluelessness was Pierre Trudeau's *White Paper* of 1969. Implementing the recommendations of that document would have required repealing the *Indian Act* and thus eliminating any distinct status for "Treaty Indians," as well as converting reserve land to private property, all of which would mean effectively abrogating all treaties. Such abrogation would be unthinkable to most Canadians (and Québécois) today, but it shouldn't be. It is completely consistent with the assumptions of contemporary liberalism, invested in individuals as the locus of sovereignty as it is. It was also part and parcel of Trudeau's quest to create a "post-British" Canadian identity, one that would allow us to leave our colonial past behind and go boldly forward into a brave new cosmopolitan and multicultural world. It is thus not at all surprising that the *White Paper* was fiercely resisted by Indigenous political actors. The key text for that resistance is informally known as the *Red Paper*, which was put up by the Indian Chiefs of Alberta in 1970. That paper's official title was *Citizens Plus* and argued that "[i]n addition to the rights and duties of citizenship, Indians possess certain additional rights as charter members of the Canadian community."[65]

On the surface it may seem that creating this sort of "post-British" identity is consistent with a support for Indigenous rights, but in legal terms it would cut off these nations from the legal and political tradition that they have built up, often at great cost, across centuries. This is why serious Indigenous political actors do not indulge in glib or self-righteous commentary about how old-timey and embarrassing all things British and monarchical are. Such political actors do not dance pirouettes behind the back of the Queen. For instance, Perry Bellegarde (head of the Assembly of First Nations from 2014 to 2021) has written that "[w]hat we have done through ceremony, we cannot break. And that is why there is a sacredness to this treaty [number 4]. That is why we have songs about the Queen, and about the Crown."[66] And in terms of casual assurances that in a post-British North American state we can surely just "figure it out," I would point to Bellegarde's statement that "[o]ur treaties are covenants with God, Creator, and all of creation. That is why these treaties are so special. That is why the covenant cannot be broken by mankind. That is why this relationship with the Crown is so important."[67] In terms of a concise and detailed explanation of more or less the same position, I know of no better example than a piece by Doug Cuthand, long-time Indigenous affairs columnist for the *Saskatoon Star-Phoenix*, on the occasion of the Queen's platinum jubilee. He wrote in mid-June 2022 that "I can see the rationale for dropping the monarchy in the Caribbean nations. The African population immigrated against their will and when they became independent nations, the British Empire left them with nothing."[68] But he also wrote that "First Nations have a very positive relationship with the monarchy ... the Crown holds moral authority and constitutional influence among Canada and the First Nations." He concluded that column bluntly, writing that "[o]ur connection to the Crown remains in place, and First Nations will never support Canada removing the Queen as head of state and becoming a republic."[69]

James Tully has also explained this relationship in several contexts. In a 1994 paper about how complex the recognition of cultural difference is in Canada (one that was strongly connected to the work Charles Taylor was then publishing on identification, such as 1992's *Multiculturalism and "The Politics of Recognition"*), Tully wrote that "[t]he Aboriginal conventions of recognition, continuity and consent are embodied in these treaty relations (in so far as they have been respected) and are best expressed in the practice of treaty federalism developed by the Haudenosaunee (Iroquois) confederation in its diplomacy with the Dutch, French, British, and (later) U.S. and Canadian governments."[70] Then, in the first volume of his *Public Philosophy in a New Key*, in language that is closer to the work he had himself done on the political philosophy of nationalism and constitutionality, he described the treaty relationship this way:

> In it, Aboriginal peoples and newcomer Canadians recognise each other as equal, coexisting and self-governing nations and govern those relations with each other by negotiations, based on procedures of reciprocity and consent, that lead to agreements that are then recorded in treaty or treaty-like accords of various kinds, to which both parties are subject ... Treaty relations were surrounded by a sea of strategic relations of pressure, force and fraud, and the treaty system itself was constantly abused. Nevertheless, from the first recorded treaties in the seventeenth century to the land-base and off-land-base agreements of the Métis from 1870 to the present,[71] the Nunavut Agreement with the Inuit of the eastern Arctic in 1993[72] and treaty negotiation with the Nisga'a nation of the Pacific Northwest today, the treaty relationship has survived and evolved, comprising over five hundred treaties and other treaty-like agreements. For most Aboriginal peoples, including those who live off Aboriginal reserves, it provides the normative prototype of the just relationship they aim to achieve by their struggles.[73]

Tearing First Nations, Métis, and Inuit away from that kind of relationship because of a sense that it has outlived its usefulness and seems embarrassingly out of place in a modern world strikes me, at the very best, as morally frivolous. If one can see both Cuthand and Bellegarde as more or less consistent with the mainstream of First Nations opinion in Canada (both are Cree men from Saskatchewan, but I am nevertheless inclined to see them in just this way), then tearing away that relationship is actually something much worse.

This need not be the path of a modern Quebec separatism, and Scotland shows that to be the case. Comparisons between Quebec, Scotland, and Catalonia have been a real growth industry in the twenty-first century.[74] As separatist movements have declined in the first but surged in the latter two (Scotland's referendum on independence was held in 2014; Catalonia held referenda in 2014 and 2017), the comparison has come to seem illuminating. But there are crucial aspects of both European movements that should be anathema to modern Quebec separatism. In the case of Catalonia, that is federalism; Quebec separatists are forever trying to escape from federalism, whereas Catalan nationalists have, since the first decades of the twentieth century, been trying to *achieve* federalism. I will discuss all of this in more detail in the next chapter, where I will also address recent thinking on federalism on the part of Quebec scholars such as Guy Laforest and Alain-G. Gagnon, both of whom, as I will discuss there, have a fully fleshed-out and ultimately radical view of the nation-federalism nexus. In the discourse of Quebec nationalism, perhaps the only greater bugbear than federalism is the monarchy, and that aspect of Scottish nationalism has, *en revanche*, received no attention at all from the Scots' *confrères Québécois*. My general experience has been that many sympathetic outside observers respond with unshakable incredulity when told that had the 2014 referendum succeeded, an independent Scotland would have retained the British monarchy. This is because Scottish nationalism has been widely (and I believe correctly) understood as being civic rather than ethnic and as being defined largely by a progressive, social-democratic political position. How could such right-thinking folks possibly have anything to do with such a backward institution? Surely the properly modern Scottish National Party would never adopt such a position! Of course, that is not correct at all, and the SNP's 2013 document *Scotland's Future: Your Guide to an Independent Scotland* is unambiguous on this matter. Therein one finds a section titled "The Monarchy and the Crown," which opens by saying, "On independence Scotland will be a constitutional monarchy, continuing the Union of the Crowns that dates back to 1603, pre-dating the Union of the Parliaments by over one hundred years. On independence in 2016, Her Majesty The Queen will be head of state."[75] Just a few days after this document was released (on 4 December 2013), Scotland's then education secretary Michael Russell spoke at Dalhousie University in Halifax, Nova Scotia. He made the case in a talk he gave to the university's EU research centre that Scotland was linked to the United Kingdom by many unions – the Union of the Crown, the political union wherein the Westminster parliament is ultimately sovereign (as part of "the Crown in Parliament"),[76] the European Union (this was about six months before the Brexit vote), and a currency union – and that the referendum sought to undo only one of those unions, the second one. He had found the perfect audience to explain this to: Nova Scotia, as its name indicates, is a place with a tremendous sense of connection to and sympathy with Scotland; it is also (along with Victoria, British Columbia) well-known as the most British part of Canada, a place where royalist symbols abound and explicit anti-monarchical sentiment is relatively uncommon (as in Victoria, that is changing).

Although it attracted little discussion, the retention of the monarchy in an independent Scotland did not come with a lot of clear justification. In all likelihood it was meant to soften the blow of independence, to assure some sense of continuity for people who were sceptical of radical breaks with the status quo. That was certainly what Russell was trying to communicate in his talk at Dalhousie. So: an independent Scotland would keep the monarchy, and for no particular reason; from what I can tell, few in Scotland seemed bothered by this, Scottish separatists very much included. Political writers in Quebec, in turn, continued to offer analogies with their situation; the Parti Québécois, as well as the more left-wing parties Québec Solidaire and Option nationale, were all part of delegations to observe the referendum and offer support, and their presence in Scotland had been of long standing.[77]

The matter of retaining the monarchy in Quebec, on the other hand, is not at all nebulous in this Scottish fashion. There is a *particular reason* for Quebec to keep the monarchy: it is a country born of colonization, and the monarchy provides a tangible, binding connection to that fact of colonization as well as serving as the custodian of the legal framework (via the Royal Proclamation as well as via the concept of "the honour of the Crown") that was supposed to protect the colonized parties. If the Crown was ok for an independent Scotland, as the silence of Quebec nationalist intellectuals on the matter would indicate, I honestly cannot understand why it would not also be OK for a new country built on territory that is still occupied and in most of Quebec remains formally unceded by the nations that are Indigenous to it.

That independent Commonwealth of Quebec, then, would emerge from the experience of Canadian federalism to become a new kind of country on the North American continent, one made up of Québécois (a multicultural blend that is in no way limited to "old stock" French Canadians), Quebec Anglophones, and Indigenous nations. Rather than some sort of new-world imitation of France, Quebec could become a Francophone companion of New Zealand. Returning to New Zealand's Independent Working Group on Constitutional Transformation one can easily imagine an independent Quebec defined by "[a] tricameral or three sphere model consisting of an [Indigenous] assembly [with delegates from each of the First Nations within the borders of Quebec as well as from the Inuit], the Crown in Parliament [with a special "carve-out" for issues of concern to Anglophone communities, such as schooling], and a joint deliberative body (the relational sphere)."[78] To return to Andrea Tunks's formulations, "[Quebec] would probably have a multi-layered system of citizenship. [Indigenous citizens] would belong to their tribal nations and to a state of [the Commonwealth of Quebec]; non-[Indigenous] would be citizens of [Quebec] or [the Commonwealth of Quebec] and could have the choice to participate in [Indigenous] processes."[79] I acknowledge that in practice the correspondence is unlikely to be this tidy, but I think my substitution of a few key words gives a sense of how closely related the situations of Quebec and New Zealand really are, as though the recent and unspeakably heavy-handed attempts to ape the most exclusionary elements of France's laïcité were not already evidence enough that the province ought to be looking elsewhere for global models. Quebec's history is not defined by a republican tradition of social cohesion but rather by the tentative, sometimes wary, but ultimately successful coexistence of distinct groups. That fundamental tension also defines New Zealand. Commonwealths are defined by that combination of "coexistence" and "distinct," as the Commonwealth of Nations makes amply clear. It is time to expand that understanding beyond its current associations with the remnants of dead empires, be they British or Soviet. As an English Canadian I am a happy member of the Commonwealth of Nations. As someone who wants to see national identity redefined in ways that take greater account of internal diversity without abandoning the possibility of a shared identity, I would be happier still to see a wider recognition of the commonwealth *as* nation.

CHAPTER 4

Federations I: Western Europe

When I wrote a 2017 article about Catalan and Scottish nationalist discourse, I opened with the quip "a spectre is indeed haunting Europe – the spectre of federalism." It was a forced joke, I suppose, legible only to the most earnest readers of Marx, but I meant it. Contemporary Europe is marked by a plethora of experiences (in the French and the English meanings of the word) of federalism: the European Union and the Russian Federation are only the largest of these. But what is striking about contemporary western Europe is the presence of countries that *should* be federations but, constitutionally or legally, aren't. The clearest example of such "federations in denial" are the United Kingdom and Spain, both multinational monarchies that are clearly nearing the limits of what such a regime can accommodate. This is not a judgment of the regime itself; another multinational western European constitutional monarchy, Denmark, seems to be doing all right in comparison (an overly casual dismissal, I suppose, and one I will somewhat undo in chapter 6, when I discuss Greenland). Rather, Spain and the UK are defined by specific historical and political tensions that would clearly be ameliorated by a robust federal approach; their recent history has been equally defined by a concerted effort to ignore such tensions, an effort that includes sidelining the sometimes-significant history of federalist thought in both places. Federalist thought is not unknown in UK politics but it has been marginalized by many political commentators and actors; I would suggest that this is by and large because of what I will call "the England problem." One way out of this deadlock may be a return to the federalist proposals that the Irish political thinker Desmond Fennell had been offering from the 1970s until his death in 2021. In Catalonia, the federalist tradition is a long and vigorous one, but it was thoroughly suppressed by the Franco-era state because of the way it challenged that fascist regime's relentless Hispanophilia. It is undergoing something of

a renaissance today, and from many of the leftist sectors from which it originally emerged, offering a potential bridge between Catalonia's nationalist *esquerra* and its historically unionist socialist party.

I noted in the last chapter that comparisons between Quebec, Scotland,
and Catalonia have been a real growth industry in the twenty-first century.
This is not surprising given that these three are probably the most globally
prominent examples of "first world nationalisms," to follow the title of Katherine O'Sullivan See's 1986 book on Quebec and Northern Ireland. What
might at first seem more surprising is that much of this work has focussed
on the various problems and possibilities of federalism generally and multinational federations specifically. But perhaps this is only surprising for a
Canadian readership. As I alluded to in the last chapter, historically the tension
between those who favour independence for Quebec and those who do not
has been between "separatists and federalists," or perhaps "sovereigntists and
federalists." Most Canadian citizens of whatever linguistic or political persua-
sion would by and large recognize "federalist" as the antonym of "nationalist."
But, as will also become clear in this chapter's section on Catalonia, there is
no inherent reason for this assumption. The work of two Quebec political
scientists in particular, Guy Laforest and Alain-G. Gagnon, calls this easy
equation between "federalism" and "anti-nationalism" into question. Laforest
is the co-editor of a number of anthologies about minority nations, such as
2011's *Le fédéralisme multinational* (with Michel Seymour), 2016's *The Parliaments of Autonomous Nations* (with André Lecours), and 2021's *Constitutional
Politics in Multinational Democracies* (with Lecours and Nikola Brassard-
Dion). These anthologies are heavily invested in a number of the nations I
will discuss in this chapter, such as Scotland, Catalonia, and Quebec, although
the Métis and Northern Ireland also come up in this work. Gagnon has edited
a number of anthologies on similar topics, that is to say the ways in which
"small nations" do or don't function well within federal frameworks. These
include 2021's *Federalism and Secession* (with J. Conde), which was a translation of the 2019 anthology *Fédéralisme et secession*; 2011's *Nations en quête de
reconnaissance: regards croisés Québec-Catalogne* (with Ferran Requejo-Coll);
2011's *Contemporary Majority Nationalism* (with Lecours and Geneviève
Nootens), itself a follow-up to their 2007 anthology *Les nationalismes majoritaires contemporains: identité, mémoire, pouvoir*; and 2001's *Multinational Democracies* (with James Tully).[1] All to say that Gagnon and Laforest have played
a central role in the reconsideration of the meaning of federalism for smaller
nations, and have done so in a massive body of scholarship in both English

and French. No doubt because of this shared interest in the complexities of federal systems, they have also co-authored a few publications. Most relevant for our purposes here is a 2012 chapter in an anthology devoted to multinational democracies edited by the Catalan political scientist Ferran Requejo-Coll, which concludes by stating that "asymmetrical federalism belongs to the category of strategies of democratic empowerment of minority nations in the vocabulary of contemporary comparative sociology"[2] and that "[t]he democratic risk of secession … remains on balance worth taking in the context of the democratic consequences of a systematic opposition to asymmetrical federalism on the axis of justice."[3] But by way of synthesizing this *bête lumineuse*[4] of a federalism that would genuinely rise to this vocabulary of "democratic empowerment of minority nations," I will mainly focus on monographs by these two, monographs that take the form of essays, that is to say, *attempts* to stake out positions, ones that each author knows will be contentious in a political framework where "federalists" and "nationalists" seem to be natural adversaries.

Laforest's 2014 *Un Québec exilé dans la fédération* is explicitly a book-length essay (its subtitle is *Essai d'histoire inellectuelle*) which argues that what Quebec needs is not to escape from federalism, but for so-called federalists to walk their talk. Like so many Quebec nationalist intellectuals he is sharply critical of the most famous Canadian federalist of them all, Pierre Trudeau, and the details of his critique are instructive. In his essai's concluding section, Laforest writes that "[f]ederalism occupied an important place in Trudeau's life. Except that an examination of his writings and actions of the 1980s … reveals in him a nationalist and sovereigntist *Canadian*, much more so than a federalist … In the twilight of his career, Trudeau dreamed of establishing, once and for all, the sovereignty of the Canadian nation and of the central government"[5] (m.t., my italics). It is something of an old chestnut among Catalan nationalists to say that if they had been part of a federation like Canada's, they would never have become separatists. Laforest, though, is clearly showing that what appeals to such nationalists is not Canada herself, but rather a general sense of what Canada is supposed to be like given how central federalism is to the political identity of the country. For Laforest as for many Quebec political intellectuals, this sense that Canadian federalism is supple and accommodating is illusory, in no small part because of the domination of the Liberal Party that was built by Pierre Trudeau.

Trudeau *père*'s most historically significant accomplishment was the 1982 patriation of the Canadian constitution via the *Constitution Act* and the

Charter of Rights and Freedoms. While polls often place the *Charter* as one of the most popular examples of something that binds Canadians together as a whole (not that this list is ever very long), its legacy is at best mixed in Quebec. This is, of course, partially because it was brought into the country's constitutional framework as part of a process led by Trudeau that ended up excluding Quebec, a province that has still never formally signed on to the 1982 constitution and which waged a fierce battle to keep it from coming into force because of a sense that it would compromise Quebec's ability to control its own destiny as a nation. This battle included extensive back-and-forth with the government in London by way of trying to bypass the federal government's relentless cheeriness on the topic and remind Westminster of its own constitutional duties toward the eight million Commonwealth citizens who resided in Quebec. As I mentioned in the last chapter, Frédéric Bastien's 2013 book *La Bataille de Londres* offers much detail on the Quebec government's attempts to get the British government to exert some control over what was going on in Ottawa.[6] Bastien's book is also admirable for the way it discusses how many provincial governments such as Alberta's tried to intervene, devoting an entire chapter to "The Wrath of the West." He also recalls how, "[i]n 1978, the National Indian Brotherhood (NIB), an organization representing the First Nations people who felt excluded from constitutional discussions, decided to call on the British government, sending a delegation to London of some three hundred chiefs, a visit put together by Labour MP Bruce George,"[7] whom (as I also mentioned in last chapter) Bastien identifies as the "champion" at Westminster of Indigenous peoples and their concerns about patriation. The English translation of Bastien's book (which is what I am drawing on here) has two chapters titled "The Empire Strikes Back" and "The Feds Strike Back," but what was really going on here was that the *federation* was striking back. That is to say, national formations such as Quebec and the First Nations (themselves a federation of hundreds of different national groups) were reminding everyone that in a federation, it is not only the central government that has a voice.

For Laforest as for so many Québécois, the most egregious example of this centralism is the *Charter of Rights and Freedoms.* Referring to its opening statement that its provisions are "subject only to such reasonable limits prescribed by law as can be demonstrably justified in a free and democratic society," Laforest writes in *Un Québec exilé dans la fédération* that "I would argue that the *Charter* begins with a clause defined by a 'defederalizing' logic, one that provokes effects that go in the same direction"[8] (m.t.). This is because the opening clause seems to make it extremely difficult for any parliament, and certainly any provincial legislature, to defy any of the *Charter*'s provisions, provisions that were put in place not by the constituent elements of the federation (that is to say, by a coalition of provinces, territories, and Indigenous nations all negotiating the details of such a charter) but rather solely by the members of the federal government of the day with occasional gestures towards consultation (whose results were, Basiten makes clear, generally treated as problems to be shoved aside, gently if possible but forcefully if not). As I write this, my home government of Saskatchewan has recently invoked the "notwithstanding clause" to override a court injunction that declared its "Use of Preferred First Name and Pronouns by Students" policy to be a *Charter* violation, which is not far behind the Ontario government's use of the clause to keep in place its 2022 amendments to the *Election Finances Act* or the Quebec government's pre-emptive use of the clause when passing its *Loi sur la laïcité de l'État* (2019). Though this clause was historically understood to be a sort of "nuclear option," recent Canadian politics have seen a lot more use of it (officially known as Section 33, it opens with the words "Parliament or the legislature of a province may expressly declare in an Act of Parliament or of the legislature, as the case may be, that the Act or a provision thereof shall operate notwithstanding a provision included in section 2 or sections 7 to 15 of this Charter," and must be renewed every five years by the parliament or legislative assembly that invoked it). But discussion of the clause's roots in a desire to check the influence of the central government and thus create a federalism worthy of the name has not been particularly visible in media discourse around these laws. It retains a vague sense of illegitimacy, as though a government that uses it is somehow engaging in dirty pool. Thus the sense in Quebec, however unfair in its own way, that the *Charter* is the ultimate realization of what Laforest decries as "la souveraineté de la nation canadienne et celle du gouvernement central."[9]

Gagnon makes a similar argument about the *Charter* in his 2008 book *La Raison du plus fort*. He writes there:

> The federal government's clearest act in terms of pan-Canadian nationalism was probably the constitutional entrenching of a *Charter of Rights and Freedoms*, which is widely considered to be the key element of the 1982 repatriation. In the first instance, the entrenching of rights was a

rupturing of the Canadian legal and constitutional order. In the second instance, the imposition of the *Charter* struck a blow against the supremacy of the provincial and federal legislatures. In effect, the insertion of the *Charter* in the Constitution – to which Quebec has still not given its consent – constitutes not only a modification of power-sharing in Canada, but even more so a reordering of the federal practice. It is, to this day, the federal government's least-disguised effort at nationalization.[10] (m.t.)

The subtitle of his book is "Plaidoyer pour le fédéralisme multinational," and that is the kind of federalism for which Laforest also fruitlessly searches in his book. That is to say, Gagnon is invested in a conception of federalism that places well-defined national communities together in ways that allow them to fruitfully work together without obscuring the plural pronoun there; *they* should be able to work together rather than combining into an ultimately homogenized single-nation whole. Gagnon argues that it is precisely Canadian multiculturalism, that other historical legacy of the first Trudeau era, that obscures such collectivity by recognizing only individual rights and those of the central government. He argues that the liberal benevolence of such policies is merely a cynical stab at Quebec nationalism, writing that "Prime Minister Trudeau, in power in Ottawa from 1968–79 and 1980–84, made himself the defender of individual rights by way of putting multiculturalism in place, in order to attenuate to the maximum every request for national recognition formulated by Quebec"[11] (m.t.). Federalism exists precisely between these two poles: a regime defined neither by atomizing individualism nor a centralism that can too quickly turn overbearing and authoritarian (but always in the name of benevolence!). If I was really feeling flippant, I might suggest that this latter regime has a different name, "liberalism," and that it is typical of Trudeau-led liberalism to obscure the difference between its tenets and those of "peace, order, and good government."

A slightly less flippant way of explaining my, and I believe Gagnon's, discomfort with Canadian approaches to multiculturalism would be to invoke Ronald Beiner's critique of Foucault as the ultimate hyper-liberal by writing that a Foucauldian approach "yields the outcome that the whole of morality is reduced to a single moral injunction, namely, 'Let a thousand flowers bloom!'"[12] Federalism has a hard time with those kinds of numbers. Let a baker's dozen flowers bloom: that would capture Canada's ten provinces and three territories. Let a half-dozen flowers bloom: that would capture English

Canada, Quebec, the Métis, the Inuit, and the collectivity of First Nations, with the culture led by the Ottawa government left in for good measure. These are smaller numbers, the likes of which political programs aimed at achieving concrete goals could actually succeed in influencing, as opposed to the more obviously fanciful invocations of the infinite diversity that a centre-less Canadian identity seems to promise. In his *Plaidoyer pour le fédéralisme multinational*, Alain-G. Gagnon writes that "[i]t is improbable that the Québécois will be satisfied with another political programme inspired by procedural liberalism, one that would, moreover, be insensitive to societal cultures and the underlying values of communitarian liberalism"[13] (m.t.). Several generations of Catalan political theorists have been good at articulating a conceptual framework for a Spanish (or sometimes Iberian-Peninsular) federalism that avoids this trap and rather empowers distinct, self-governing nations to act as the basic units of federal arrangements. This sense of the solidity of nations as federal units extends to conceptualizations of a possibly independent *Catalan* state as well, as we will see in discussions of Els Països Catalans. As I will also show, the Métis have a long history of comparable political thought about the solidity of the Métis nation as a constituent element of Canadian federalism and a comparable hostility towards the liberal variety of fuzzy-headedness, something we will clearly see in Harry Daniels's refusal to be folded into a then-emerging framework of multiculturalism. Why English Canadians seem to have accepted such a vague and ultimately incoherent view of themselves is more complicated than it may at first appear. It is strongly connected to the reasons that it has been so difficult to speak simply and plainly about a nation called "England."

I. Who's Afraid of an English Parliament?

Devolved government has territorialised UK politics, made England more apparent as a polity and created anomalies. In essence, devolution may have resolved matters of legitimacy elsewhere in the UK but this has occurred only by shifting the problem elsewhere.[14]
– James Mitchell, *Devolution in the UK*

He has always described himself as English, rather than British, he told me on Hampstead Heath. He loves England's countryside, its folk music, its language ... "I hope I don't sound patriotic," he said, moments after talking about his

claim on Englishness. "Patriotism is a betrayal of that attachment. Because
it reduces it to some sort of formula."
– Yohann Koshy, from his profile of Paul Gilroy, in *The Guardian*, 5 August 2021

English nationalism is the great unspeakable in respectable progressive debate
in the United Kingdom, carrying with it the seemingly irredeemable baggage
of far-right figures such as the British National Party, skinhead soccer hooli-
gans, and the dreaded spectre of working-class guys in white vans. I will state
my basic position as plainly as I can by saying that there is no reason for this.
Englishness is no more inherently ethnocentric than Scottishness, Catalanitat,
or Québécitude, to name the three best-known cases of nationalisms that have
become far more civic than ethnic over the past half-century or so. Nevertheless, the block persists; Alisa Henderson and Richard Wyn Jones write in their
2021 study *Englishness: The Political Force Transforming Britain* that "[t]here
is a considerable body of work on national identity and race that has demonstrated that visible minorities and immigrants are more likely to describe
themselves as British and less likely to describe themselves as English."[15] When
the Runnymede Trust published, in 2000, its report *The Future of Multi-Ethnic
Britain*, its author Bhikhu (now Baron) Parekh included the assertion that
"[w]hiteness nowhere features as an explicit condition of being British, but
it is largely understood that Englishness, and therefore by extension Britishness, is racially coded. 'There ain't no black in the Union Jack,' it has been
said."[16] I reject literally everything about this formulation, from its casual conflation of Britishness and Englishness, right down to its multiple uses of the
passive voice. Largely understood *by whom*? And *who* said "There ain't no
black in the Union Jack"? None other than Paul Gilroy, of course; that is the
title of his famous 1987 book. As the quote that opens this section indicates
unambiguously, Gilroy considers himself to be both Black and *English*, and
as my discussions in chapter 2 and later on in this chapter show, he has far
more nuanced understandings of these matters than the report would imply.

The pop-folk musician Billy Bragg offered a more anecdotal example of
this phenomenon of assuming that Englishness must refer to whiteness in his
2006 book *The Progressive Patriot*, and his plain-language commitment to a
twenty-first-century vision of Englishness has been a strong influence on this
section. Bragg writes of a conversation he had with his friend and roadie Paul,
"born in England to Jamaican parents," during the World Cup:

C'mon Paul, I'd said to him, you were born in England, you speak English; admit it – you're English. No, he replied, I'm not. What are you, then? His response amazed me: I'm a Londoner and I'm a European. Me too, I said, but what about the bit in the middle? No. He shook his head. I'm not English and I'm not British. It puzzled me that he could make such a distinction. He explained it simply enough: in London, I'm accepted. Nobody questions my right to be there. But what about Europe? I asked. I'm glad to be a citizen of the EU, that's something that was given to me. I didn't have to kick down any doors to get it. So it's about acceptance, then? That's right.[17]

Of course I take the point made both by Lord Parekh and by Billy Bragg's roadie that Englishness has, until relatively recently, seemed to be at root an ethnic identity; both are indeed speaking to a widely felt sense of the national identity of that sceptred Isle. I do not doubt that many non-white people have a hard time seeing Englishness as anything that could include acceptance for someone whose parents were, for example, born in Jamaica. But that is true of many identities which have, since the 1960s, clearly transformed themselves from racial-ethnic into civic-national forms, the transformation of the French Canadians of Quebec into Québécois being only one of countless examples. I would thus argue that both Bragg's friend Paul and Lord Parekh are describing a widespread social phenomenon that has to do with pervasive racism (something that is hardly a phenomenon unique to England) rather than anything inherent to Englishness itself. That is because I cannot help but observe a certain kind of circular logic at work here. Why doesn't Englishness include Black people? Because Paul is Black, and he's not English. Why is Paul not English? Because Englishness doesn't include Black people. In contemporary discourse on British politics there are no comparable round-and-round-we-go arguments about Scottishness. Rather, a tendency to point out that Humza Yousaf (as I write this in the spring of 2024) serves as leader of the Scottish National Party and thus also the first minister of Scotland and Anas Sarwar currently serves as leader of Scottish Labour, and that both are Muslims of South Asian heritage, is what usually follows inquiries about whether Scottishness is ethnically or religiously limited. I genuinely do not understand why the presence of a London-born Hindu whose parents immigrated from Uganda such as the Right Honourable Dame Priti Patel in the Conservative cabinets of Theresa May and Boris Johnson (for whom she served as home secretary), or the London-born Suella Braverman (who succeeded her as home secretary and whose parents are of South Asian heritage from Mauritius and Kenya), to say nothing of the rise to prime minister of Rishi Sunak (whose parents were Indians born in what are now Kenya and Tanzania), or the election of a Muslim of Pakistani heritage such as Sadiq Khan as the Labour Party mayor of his birthplace of London, do not attract comparable assessments of the post-ethnic state of Englishness. It can't simply be up to political prejudice; Khan the social democrat doesn't seem to make much more of a difference than neo-Thatcherites such as Sunak, Patel, and Braverman in terms of convincing a wide swath of the population that all manner of people who don't trace all of their ancestry solely to the middle part of the island of Great Britain are just as English as those who do.

Part of it may have to do with a casual and pervasive sense of London as a place apart, somehow separate from Englishness, but like many people I cannot accept that. In 2019 John Cleese was roundly and more or less rightly pilloried for saying that London no longer felt like an English city. Like those who criticized him (including Sadiq Khan, whom the *Guardian* quoted as saying that "[t]hese comments make John Cleese sound like he's in character as Basil Fawlty ... We are proudly the English capital, a European city and a global hub"), I think Cleese was fundamentally wrong, even if the Twitter-fuelled ferocity of those attacks sometimes seemed a little over the top, however typically so.[18] Anyway, the bias appears to be genuinely *national*: Humza Yousaf and Anas Sanwar embody a new Scottish national identity; Rishi Sunak, Priti Patel, and Sadiq Khan never seem to figure into discussions of Englishness, drearily backward-looking and irredeemably ethnocentric as it seems to be. What I long for in these circular non-discussions about the inherent whiteness of Englishness is the clear-eyed and also deeply felt sensibility that Paul Gilroy (not exactly a member of the Enoch Powell brigade) expressed to *The Guardian* in the quote that opens this section. Not only does he unambiguously claim Englishness, but he feels so strongly about that *attachment* that he doesn't want to sully it with what he sees as tired formulae such as "patriotic." This is nothing new for him. He wrote, for instance, in a 1990 essay expanded for his 1993 book *Small Acts* that "the idea that 'race' is something that enters English culture from the outside during the post-war period ... shrinks before the wider obligation to adapt and transform understanding of English culture as a whole so that being black and English is no longer either a curiosity or an outrage."[19] That is precisely the sense of Englishness I am trying to identify here, like Billy Bragg before me. Gilroy also said in that 2021 *Guardian* interview, upon reflecting on his period living in the US and teaching at Yale, that "I have a weird love of England. *And London in particular* ... This is my home. God, it is. And I didn't know it was until I went somewhere else." Those italics are mine. London, as both Gilroy and her mayor Sadiq Khan remind us, is an *English* city. Narrow nostalgists such as John Cleese look no more or less foolish than faux-internationalist, *bien-pensant* liberals when they try to claim otherwise.

It may seem like I am about to make a case for England as the perpetually put-upon member of the United Kingdom, but I certainly believe that the opposite is actually the case. Henderson and Wyn Jones make a crucial point in the opening pages of *Englishness* when they write of the period marked by devolution in the UK, "To the extent that nationalism was considered at all, it was as a feature of political life in the state's periphery – that is, in Scotland, Wales, and Northern Ireland. England and the English were different."[20] They were different precisely because they were not *peripheral*. It may be that the widespread reluctance to speak of Englishness as a national identity has to do with being aware of England's more powerful and central status as opposed to the peripheral nations of Scotland and Wales. It is difficult to see why this sort of self-effacing, slightly squeamish approach has become so common among progressives who would otherwise be allergic to such gently patronizing evasiveness. It calls to mind Orwell's acidic remark that "England is perhaps the only great country whose intellectuals are ashamed of their own nationality."[21]

There is also a less charitable analysis of this situation. In the manner of dismissals of ideology as being what *other* people trade in, poor souls (as opposed to a benevolent class defined by "common sense," "reason," and so forth), nationalism has, by figures on the left and the right alike, been widely seen as something for those folks not blessed enough to be modestly but confidently in command of everything that is actually important. We come to the logic for this later on in *Englishness*, when Henderson and Wyn Jones write that "if we were to define English nationalism solely in terms of support for the establishment of a distinct national legislature, that is an English parliament, then it is clear from our results that this remains a minority preference, even among English identifiers."[22] Yeah, I bet. The establishment of an English parliament would entail an explicit acknowledgment that England is a *nation*, and that probably seems in vaguely poor taste to nationalism-averse liberals, given that England is so much larger and so much more powerful than scrappy little Scotland or Wales, among whom (mostly) liberals can, benevolently, indulge such feelings that they would never dare to claim for themselves. But what this benevolence conceals is the reality, likely well-known to the more boisterous nationalists whom these liberals seem to be in conflict with, that acknowledging England as a nation would mean that it would be one of three, maximum four, full members of the United Kingdom: that is to say *equal* with Scotland, Wales, and (at least until Irish reunification, an outcome I both favour and consider inevitable) Northern Ireland.

It is understandable (however wrong-headed) that boisterous nationalists might bristle at a diminution in English power; it's more flagrantly hypocritical for anti-nationalist liberals or progressives, a political grouping that should, really, be happy about such diminution, force for regressive backwardness as all things connected to Englishness have so long been. But of course, nobody would be happy about such a thing at all, nobody resident in England, anyway. Thus we had the odd spectacle of the Blair government's 2004 referendum on setting up an assembly for the northeast, officially known as *North East England Devolution Referendum* (2004). This would have created a legislative assembly that, while being strongly influenced by the 1999 creation of devolved parliaments in Wales and Scotland, would only have represented a handful of English *counties*. The casual conflation of a few English counties with Wales, or of Northumberland with Scotland, seems fundamentally wrong-headed to me, and I cannot imagine Scottish or Welsh nationalists finding such a conflation anything other than insulting. Unsurprisingly the referendum went down in a blazing defeat, 78 to 22 per cent.

But its aftermath remains visible among a certain strain of regionalist thought on the English left. I have in mind Alex Niven's short 2019 book *New Model Island: How to Build a Radical Culture beyond the Idea of England*. The subtitle says it all, really; his arguments finally come down to the imperative to move "beyond" England, something that doesn't seem necessary in the same way at all for Scotland, Wales, or Ireland, whose nationalists Niven seems vaguely sympathetic towards. This is no doubt because all are on the left, at least at the level of electoral politics; before Brexit the SNP and Plaid Cymru sat in the EU parliament with the left-regionalist European Free Alliance; Sinn Féin sits with the group known as The Left in the European Parliament. Niven revisits that referendum in a chapter called "Dream Archipelagoes and Regionalism 2.0," wherein he suggests that the British Isles could be governed by a series of devolved parliaments. He presents it this way:

East of England – 5,846,965
East Midlands – 4,533,222
London – 8,173,941
North East – 2,596,886
North West – 7,052,177
South East – 8,634,750
South West – 5,288,935
West Midlands – 5,601,847
Yorkshire and the Humber – 5,283,733

Ireland (united) – 6,742,400
Scotland – 5,424,800
Wales – 3,125,000[23]

As part of his larger argument that "the infrastructure of England is already organised along regional lines in numerous instances,"[24] Niven concludes his presentation of this chart by saying that "[b]oth rationally and metaphysically, then, the devolution of the nine main regions makes good common sense."[25] The fact that such common sense would also hold that there is a meaningful difference between a region (such as "South West") and a nation (such as "Scotland") isn't something that Niven addresses directly. The fact that both have more or less equal populations (around five million) seems to be enough to warrant their being politically represented in the same way. But the real problem with this formula, apart from the neurotically stubborn refusal to recognize that England is a nation, is one of redundancy. If representation is to be given out on the basis of population, as we have here (in the absence of any national designation for nine of these twelve divisions), then it does seem necessary to point out that the UK already has a legislature that does this. It's called the House of Commons.

The serious disparity in population between England (56 million) and any of the other constituent countries of the UK (Scotland is the largest at about 5.5 million, almost exactly a tenth the size) is no doubt part of the reason that Martin Laffin and Alys Thomas note that "[n]otions of a federal United Kingdom have traditionally been derided in official circles."[26] They go on to recall how "[t]he 1973 Kilbrandon Report on the Constitution dismissed any federal solution to the UK's constitutional question [to which one chapter of the final report was devoted] as 'a strange and artificial system.'"[27] At the risk of again seeming flippant, I would say that this is quite a statement from the subject of a realm that ostensibly includes such jurisdictional oddities as the Isle of Man (pop. 84,263) and the bailiwicks of Guernsey (pop. 67,642) and Jersey (pop. 103,200), none of which are technically part of the United Kingdom but all three of which, in addition to having linguistic histories entirely separate from that of English (Manx Gaelic on the Isle of Man and the variants of Channel Island French, properly called Jèrriais and Guernésiais, on Jersey and Guernsey), currently have the somewhat contradictory status of "self-governing dependencies" of that Kingdom.[28] I think we need to proceed from the assumption that the United Kingdom itself could be fairly categorized as "strange and artificial," much more so than is generally acknowledged. The strangeness of the Isle of Man / Channel Islands' jurisdictional status is absolutely of a piece with the artificiality of the situation in Northern Ireland (which, in addition to a civil war that has been going in one way or another since at least the 1960s, is also a place where nearly half and possibly soon more than half the population holds *only* the passport of a different nation-state, the Republic of Ireland) as well as the unusual situation of a community of four countries where the largest literally has ten times the population of the second-largest.

Laffin and Thomas's invocation of the Kilbrandon-led Royal Commission on the Constitution (which met between 1969 and 1973, originally under the leadership of Lord Crowther) is important, because that arguably represented the last and best chance to come to terms with England's place in the overall UK state, a chance that passed that state by. That is James Mitchell's contention, anyway; he writes in his 2009 book *Devolution in the UK* that "[t]his was an opportunity to view matters across the UK as a whole and to consider England's position within the UK."[29] But the commission seems to have missed this opportunity, quickly bogging down in unworkably complex proposals whose only goal seemed to be avoiding the recognition of England as a nation along the lines of Scotland or Wales. Mitchell writes that "Kilbrandon was divided on its recommendations for England. The commissioners agreed that neither England nor the English regions should have legislative devolution. There was more support for regional co-ordinating and advisory councils: eight Commissioners favoured such councils with about sixty members, partly nominated by central government, partly elected by local government."[30] Mitchell summarizes by saying that "[w]hat was clear is that the logic behind regional government in England was markedly different from the logic behind devolution for Wales and Scotland. Kilbrandon's recommendations for England were overshadowed by those for Scotland and Wales but were just as much part of the story of the evolution of territorial politics in the UK."[31] But as the Mitchell quote that opens this section indicates, a big part of that story has to do with England becoming visible as a polity in a way it had not been before, and the problems that this caused becoming just as significant as the parallel solutions provided by devolution for Scotland and Wales. That problem Mitchell alludes to is one of *nation*; once the UK ceases to act as a unitary state with a single parliament that is sovereign on all matters within that state, it cannot pick and choose willy-nilly which of those nations it will recognize. Either the UK is a unitary state (in which case Scottish and Welsh nationalism is as ephemeral and sentimental as English and so should not be recognized by the presence of devolved legislatures) or it is not (in which case the Scottish and Welsh nations need to be represented by such a legislature for exactly the same reason as the English one does). The problem that Mitchell alludes to, though, is also one of *change*. The United Kingdom becoming less of a unitary state is a radical change to its constitution, far more radical than Brexit or even the loss of its empire. Many prominent commentators have seen this difficulty with a changing state identity as a core part of the UK experience, and well before Brexit. Concluding the 2012 edition of her monumental study *Britons*, Linda Colley writes that "British people have long had anxieties about the connections with continental Europe, but their apparent insularity is to be explained also by their growing doubts about who they are in the present. Consciously or unconsciously, many of them fear assuming a new identity in case it obliterates entirely the already insecure identity they current[ly] possess."[32]

Furthermore, it is important to recognize how much political actors in the United Kingdom, and England specifically, have historically been averse not just to radical change but also to systematic solutions. Both cut against the grain of Common Law, so important to the English legal and the UK political system. Common Law is in many ways an extraordinarily supple form of legal reasoning as well as being a powerful defence against the excesses of tyrannical idealists. Roger Scruton, in his uncharacteristically sentimental 2000 book *England: An Elegy*, explains this aversion to systematic solutions by saying that "[t]he English did not reject mystery; they rejected the desire to explain it, to rationalise it, to replace it with abstract principles ... The reasonable person does not solve the problems of morality, religion, politics or gardening by consulting a priori rules, but by consultation, negotiation and compromise with those who seem to disagree with him but who might nevertheless be right."[33] I can see what Scruton is getting at, but the gentle invocation of how it is OK to be irrational plays right into the hands of an anti-nationalist seeking to claim the mantle of "rule-based solutions" to highly contentious positions. For instance, Perry Anderson, in his 1992 collection *English Questions* (which is a kind of mirror-image of Scruton's book-length *essai*), ascribes this aversion to the systematic to an Oxford-led Wittgensteinianism that he describes as "a purely technical philosophy, entirely dissociated from the ordinary concerns of social life," which, he goes on to say, "has thus necessarily also enjoined philistinism."[34] I also understand the complaint here, and can certainly see that tendency at play in a Kilbrandon commission which, rather than really engage the degree to which England is or is not a nation in the manner of Scotland and Wales, chose to bog itself down in the technical fineries of regional and local governance, technical fineries that sometimes look very close indeed to the language-games so central to Wittgenstein and his followers, in Oxford and elsewhere. I'm even happy enough to call all of that philistine. But seeing a safely and ultimately regressive technical Wittgensteinianism at the heart of English culture is just as reductive as Scruton's appeal to the way people solve gardening problems, or as Tom Nairn's relentless tendency to reduce English nationalism to "Powellism" (a reference to Enoch Powell, he of the infamous 1968 "Rivers of blood" speech) which he does across two chapters of his otherwise invaluable 1977 treatise *The Break-Up of Britain*. Nairn does, however, open that book's concluding chapter by writing that "[t]he theory of nationalism represents Marxism's great historical failure. It may have had others as well ... Yet none of these is as important, as fundamental, as the problem of nationalism, either in theory or in political practice."[35] I couldn't agree more.[36] But I think this has been as true for England as it has been for Scotland, Wales, and Ireland.

It may well be that the current situation, one where this lumbering beast of a state muddles through via various kinds of devolution and peace agreements (such as the Good Friday Agreement of 1998 and the St Andrews Agreement of 2006), is the best arrangement possible *dans ce meilleur des mondes possibles*. That is certainly consistent with the common-law tradition that so defines the legal systems of England, Wales, and Northern Ireland (although that is less true of Scotland). Furthermore, that is more or less the situation that J.H. Elliot evokes in his dual history *Scots and Catalans: Union and Disunion*, which I mentioned in the last chapter. One important aspect of this book, however implicit, is that it serves as a spirited defence of constitutional monarchy, which he presents as an institution that has allowed both Scotland and Catalonia to flourish. Writing of the notion of "the Spains" (a concept

that was, as we will see, also important to Catalan nationalists of the late nineteenth and early twentieth centuries) as opposed to a unitary Spanish state,
he says of the kingdom's monarchs that "theirs was a plural political entity, a
composite monarchy similar to those found elsewhere in the Europe of their
day."[37] He goes on to recall how, when such composites are formed, "the newly
acquired territory enjoyed at least nominal parity of status with the political
unit to which it now found itself joined. It thus preserved its own distinctive
identity, along with the laws, customs and institutions it possessed at the time
of its incorporation."[38] Overall Elliot sees such a composite formulation as
more flexible and less provocatively separatist than federalist approaches
would become in the nineteenth and twentieth centuries. In the previous
chapter I alluded to a similar quality of constitutional monarchy via the cases
of New Zealand and Quebec, so I really am sympathetic to a certain amount
of what Elliot presents in his book. But the devil is in the specifics. Nobody
has any difficulty defining Spain as a nation; indeed, a certain zealotry on that
front is, as we will see in the Catalan section of this chapter, a big part of the
problem with finding a solution to the present Catalan crisis. England, on the
other hand, remains a "hard case." Everyone seems to know it is a nation, but
there are few formal institutions based on that simple fact, and certainly none
that rise to the level of a parliament or legislative assembly.

Such a "muddle-through" solution to the governance of the UK may also
seem attractive because of the degree to which fully-thought-out federal proposals have been fairly thin on the ground, and those that we have seem terribly anachronistic. John Kendle's 1997 book *Federal Britain: A History* is a
survey of such proposals and experiments (one that begins with the Union
of the Crowns), but the book's recurring theme is the degree to which genuine
federal proposals have been unusual. Echoing the tendency of the Kilbrandon
commission to bog down in unwieldy institutions, he writes of Joseph Chamberlain's proposals for "a scheme of boards at the county level (County
Boards) and councils for each of the four countries of England, Scotland,
Wales and Ireland (National Councils)." He concludes, though, that this is
not federalism because in the end, the Westminister parliament remains
supreme: "This was not federalism but it was not unlike numerous home-
rule-all-round proposals that surfaced in the late [eighteen-]eighties and
throughout the nineties."[39] Isaac Butt (who served as an MP for either Lim-
erick or Cork between 1852 and 1879) and his interest in federalism is what
Chamberlain is referring to here, and the Irishman's interests along these lines
were inseparable from his status as a member of the Home Rule Party (he is

widely credited by Irish historians with having coined the term "Home Rule").
Equally inseparable, it is important to note, was Butt's status as a staunchly
conservative unionist who was deeply suspicious of Catholic emancipation,
seeing it as opening the doors to the extremism to which such folks were
prone, such as republicanism and other forms of anti-monarchism. Lawrence
T. McCaffrey's 1960 article notes that "[i]n his book *Irish Federalism*, published
in 1870, Butt guaranteed Irish and English conservatives that Home Rule
would prevent rather than encourage radical excesses in Ireland. He maintained that once Irishmen came to enjoy the benefits of self-government, they
would cease rebellious activities and become the most loyal supporters of the
Crown and Constitution in the Empire."[40]

Probably the most fully developed of these proposals, that is to say explicitly
unionist visions of an imperial federation, was the 1910 book *Federalism and
Home Rule*, published pseudonymously by "Pacificus" and based on letters
the author had written to the *Times*. The argument here is inseparable from the
imperial context, with Pacificus writing that

> The ardent and visionary federalist would like, no doubt, to see his own
> oak-tree growing tomorrow in full shapeliness and symmetry. He would
> like to see a truly Imperial Parliament supreme and sovereign over the
> whole Empire, representative of the whole Empire, and capable of speak-
> ing for the whole Empire. This would be the strong trunk of his oak.
> Then he would like to see the co-ordinate parliaments of the United
> Kingdom and the Dominions overseas – each of them sovereign and su-
> preme in their own sphere – spreading out from this trunk their mighty
> limbs of varying thickness.[41]

The book gets somewhat cooler and more rational as it moves forward, but
its proposals are still inseparable from the historical context of the early twentieth century. Home Rule is a recurring topic; the book was published just before those proposals for Ireland passed the House of Commons three times
in 1912, 1913, and 1914, only to be defeated in the Lords each time, forced into
Royal Assent via the *Parliament Act* (1911), and then finally suspended later
in 1914, never to be properly implemented. Canada is also a recurring topic
in *Federalism and Home Rule*, a country that was much closer to the UK in
those pre–*Statute of Westminster* days than it is now, and which in 1910 must
have seemed like an excellent model of a polity that was totally British without
being English in any substantive way other than linguistic. Pacificus's overall

goal was to link a series of different polities by way of preserving a unity that was starting to come undone as a result of an Irish independence movement which would, in the coming decades, serve as an example to much of the decolonizing world. Whatever imperialist shortcomings may doom this vision to contemporary irrelevance (and I am genuinely not trying to ignore those shortcomings), it has the virtue of even-handedness. Pacificus's constant refrain is that it is the *imperial* assembly that would have ultimate sovereignty, and that this sovereignty would derive from the fact that an imperial parliament is the place to which all of the nations and provinces (a distinction he fudges throughout) would send representatives. As long as the powers of that body to which everyone sends representatives are rigorously limited to issues that affect *only the Union as a whole*, this is indeed federalism, not simply home-rule-all-round. Pacificus does not suggest that England's parliament should be supreme on the basis of its greater population, any more than he suggests that England shouldn't be the one nation that doesn't get its own parliament because it is somehow different.

In terms of its status as a nation, England is *not* different from Scotland or Wales, and I am suspicious of analyses of UK politics which proceed from the assumption that it is. Despite my admiration for it, I must acknowledge that Nairn's *Break-Up of Britain* is one example of this kind of analysis. Recalling a conference on "Region or Nation" at Weston Park, a grand house near Sussex owned by the Foreign Office, Nairn writes how during the presentations on Englishness, "[t]he identity on display – one might say offensively, often obsessionally on display – in England *is* somehow different from the standards of modern nationalism."[42] Nairn is somewhat cagey on the reasons for this, writing that "it is no answer to the puzzle … to point at England's racism"[43] and considering again the matter of Enoch Powell (to whom he had already devoted a chapter), before finally saying:

> Historically, the inward lack corresponded to an outward presence: it can be explained by the fortunate place England occupied in the world's political economy after 1688. The fact is that its role was so prominent and imperial for so long, that bourgeois society required no farther drastic transformations for over two centuries.[44]

What is driving Nairn's sense that England is somehow different is based in his Marxist sense of the class-bound nature of revolutionary impulses, but he is coming down in more or less the same places as those squeamish liberals I mentioned earlier: England is so dominant, why would we want to speak of it as a nation? Coming so close to this English-liberal position is deeply strange for a radical Scottish separatist such as Nairn. This near-intersection of positions is also odd given that one of the real contributions of *The Break-Up of Britain* is to point out that "[t]he dominant progressive myth of anti-imperialism is focussed overwhelmingly upon nationalism as a justified struggle of the repressed poor against the wealthy oppressors"[45] and that this is not really useful as a definition of the concept. Nairn goes on to speak more or less favourably of Belgium, Israel, Scotland, and "the Ulster Protestant territories."[46] He goes on to argue that Catalonia also belongs in this grouping. He describes this group of nations by saying that "[t]here have also been a number of what could be called 'counter currents' – examples of societies which have claimed national self-determination from a different, more advanced point in the development spectrum."[47] I do not think that recognition of England's nationality is imperative because it needs to seek self-determination or is being kept from fully living out its "different, more advanced point in the development spectrum." Very much the opposite is in fact the case. I think it is imperative to recognize England's nationality as part of a larger project of dislodging it from its status as an invisibly imperialist hyper-power. Once we can see England as a nation, not as something larger or airier but as something on par with Scotland and Wales ("the Ulster Protestant territories" are a different story), that project is going to get a lot easier to imagine.

More recently, progressive nationalists in other parts of the United Kingdom have started to see matters more or less in this way. Éric Bélanger et al.'s 2018 book *The National Question and Electoral Politics in Quebec and Scotland* quotes an unnamed Scottish Labour M S P saying, "in the long run [devolution] starts to become difficult when you have one part of the country [England] that's not devolved in any way … That's why I'm kind of attracted to federalism"[48] (ellipsis in the original). In addition to co-authoring the aforementioned *Englishness*, Richard Wyn Jones is also the co-author with Jac Larner of a study titled "Progressive Home Rule: What Progressives Can Learn from Two Decades of Welsh Devolution." They echo the general sense of the UK's "smaller nationalisms" being forces for political good when they write that "with remarkably few exceptions, advocates of home rule have tended to be progressives who have all envisaged the establishment of a Welsh parliament and government as a means to progressive political ends."[49] It should be no surprise that they also express impatience with "the continuing (and in our view politically disastrous) tendency of progressive supporters of devolution in England to view the establishment of a regional level of government as a prophylactic against assertions of English political identity. In other words, the Welsh experience offers cold comfort to those progressives who would try to ignore Englishness."[50] The difficulty in enunciating national identity, the tendency "to try to ignore Englishness," is an *English* hang-up; it doesn't persist at the behest of anyone north or west of the border. This aversion to directly addressing English nationhood is a prime example of what Timothy Brennan, in his aforementioned 1990 essay, observed about progressive dismissal of national sentiments: "The terms of nationalism have from the European perspective apparently reversed. Not freedom from tyranny, but the embodiment of tyranny. The question is: how much is this new perspective a result of owning, rather than suffering, an empire?"[51] England's effective ownership not only of the former British Empire but also (by virtue of its greater population) the contemporary United Kingdom forces an answer to this question. I believe the short answer is "quite a bit."

None of this has anything to do with the dreaded "West Lothian Question," that is to say the spectre of English MPs not being able to vote on Scottish, Welsh, or Northern Irish affairs (which have been devolved to the Scottish Parliament, the Welsh Senedd, or the Northern Ireland Assembly) while Scottish/Welsh/Northern Irish MPs get to vote on specifically English affairs (which, lacking an English parliament, have nowhere else but Westminster to be legislated). I think this is at best a distraction, and one that tends to fuel petty jealousies and distract from the heart of the matter, which has to do with the tremendous power of the largest group. Any "West Lothian question" is going to be met in the current Westminster Parliament with an utterly overwhelming English majority; the idea that Scottish and Welsh MPs could gang up and dictate terms to poor little England is so absurd that I find it somewhat amazing that it remains an issue at all. I understand the claim that in a tight vote on a matter having to do only with England, Scottish/Welsh/Northern Irish MPs might make a decisive difference. But such MPs – English, Scottish, and Welsh alike – would presumably be voting along *party* lines. That seems undeniably true of the famously well-whipped UK party system. Thus one would need to imagine a situation where *English* MPs vote along the usual party lines but *Scottish and Welsh* MPs are somehow whipped into voting along national lines instead. Such an outcome is unimaginable in any Westminster parliament of the last three decades, and it is difficult to imagine how the situation would change radically enough to make this a real possibility (even given the reality of regionally specific parties: the DUP would never support a Labour government, nor would the SNP ever support a Conservative government). The "West Lothian Question" is, to my mind, little more than a grievance-driven and thus unenlightening thought experiment.

Moreover, it's a thought experiment that hides the fact that a prevailing non-nationalism suits England just fine. It allows liberals to pretend to be above all that grubby, backward-looking group identity stuff while enjoying the benefits of a system whose liberalism-driven assumption that individuals are the basic repository of sovereignty means (purely by coincidence, mind you!) that MPs from England will always dominate a Westminster parliament through constituting a truly massive majority of its seats. Unapologetically conservative English partisans (the Enoch Powell brigade, I suppose, although that crowd also includes Priti Patel, the architect of some of the most restrictive and brutalizing anti-immigration measures in UK history) may complain about the situation in public forums, but they also know that the state is being run on their terms and thus their permanent victory on all but a small number of cultural disputes is assured by the aforementioned massive majority. The chauvinistic nationalists strike me as less hypocritical on this front; wouldn't you expect them to be happy that they are running the show? As I have been discussing throughout this book, it's the liberals that are more concerning. I certainly think that liberalism's general tendency towards denial in terms of national identity has been, in the words of my Welsh colleagues, politically disastrous. Seeing progressives adopt this tendency has indeed been worrisome.

That is because a flight from nationalism is absolutely of a piece with the liberal flight from ideology that I discussed in the introduction, and this is not something progressives should embrace as part of a long-term, Yankee-domination-led trend towards blurring the boundaries between liberalism and progressivism. To return to those formulations, resistance to the idea that England has a *national* culture and so should have the same institutions as other nations with whom it shares a state, also means acquiescence in the arguably clueless, definitely denial-based, "aren't we all just the same" approach that is so common in contemporary liberalism. Apart from the fact that everyone has a national identity (just as they have a racial identity, a class identity, a gender identity, etc.), we are not all the same. National identity is part of human diversity, which is why recognizing the distinctiveness of the culture of Northern Ireland (as opposed to relying only on homogenizing and distorting although not exactly inaccurate phrases such as "the British Isles" or "the mainland") or Welsh culture (by refusing to see it as anything other than

"British") is imperative for most UK progressives, and for good reasons. It is long past time for such progressives to walk that talk, and, where necessary, accept that even if they are English they too have a national identity (just as, even though they may be liberals, they also have an ideological position), and that this aspect of their existence ought to be treated as equal to those with whom they share a political space. The fact that they will have to give up the dominance that comes with being *by far* the largest in terms of population simply doesn't figure in. For progressives keen to stamp out such dominance wherever it may be, the case for a loud and clear recognition of England as a nation should be an imperative. A federal United Kingdom, where parliaments in England, Scotland, and Wales would make decisions for their own countries and then each send a fixed number of representatives to a Westminster parliament (say, 75 each, which would make it a parliament about as third as large as the current House of Commons), an assembly that would legislate on the relatively few questions that genuinely affect the Union as a whole, is most effective way I can imagine to live out that imperative. Brexit probably would have played out differently.

II. A Brief Digression into Irish Federalism

The quaint English usage of "federal" originated in the 1870s, when Isaac Butt proposed Home-Rule-all-round (i.e. for Ireland, Scotland, England and Wales) in the British parliament. People knew that this meant devolution-all-around but somebody or other called it "federal devolution" and, because federalism was a political system which the English knew nothing about, the name was allowed to stick.
– Desmond Fennell, "'Unity by Consent' Requires a Federal Irish Constitution," *Irish Times*, 27 February 1978

I cannot invoke that term "the British Isles" in the context of federalism without referring to Desmond Fennell, who died at the age of ninety-two in 2021. Although his work is, as I will try to briefly show here, widely varying, in today's Ireland the invocation of his name is most likely to conjure images of a grouchy right-winger preoccupied with what have become known in North America as "culture war" topics. I reject this assessment, for reasons that Fennell himself has laid out eloquently. In an essay called "Left, Right in the New

Europe," he wrote that "[i]n Ireland periodically, people call for a realignment of Irish politics on a 'left/right' basis. It would make things so much clearer, they say. I very much doubt it."[52] Rather than locating Fennell on a left-right axis, it makes far more sense to see him as someone who bridges the divide between Fianna Fáil and Sinn Féin, both of whom he has advised in various unofficial capacities, again, mostly in the 1970s and '80s.[53]

Before that period, though, Fennell came to prominence both as a journalist for the *Irish Times* and the *Irish Press*, and then as one of the leaders of Gluaiseacht Chearta Sibhialta na Gaeltachta, the Gaeltacht Civil Rights Movement (I also discussed the Gaeltacht in chapter 2). At more or less the same time that Fennell was involved in formulating such an intellectual schema for Gluaiseacht,[54] he was also trying to arrive at new ways of theorizing what would have seemed like a more urgent problem of difference, which is Northern Ireland. In 1973 he published two pamphlets, *Sketches of the New Ireland* and *Towards a Greater Ulster*, both of which were devoted to the proposition that Ireland needed to decentralize, in part by way of achieving a United Ireland that would be able to democratically accommodate the distinctiveness of the community that Fennell habitually called the "Ulster British." In *Sketches of the New Ireland*, he proposed that the island should be broken into fifteen regions in total. Belfast and Dublin would each be a region unto themselves, as would the Gaeltacht. The key difference with the Gaeltacht, of course, is that it is not a geographically contiguous area; Fennell's proposal assumes that it would be connected via a series of federated agreements all joined by the Comhairle na Gaeltachta, which he refers to as "the regional council" (this literally means "the Gaeltacht Council"). It is just such regional councils that would become important building-blocks of Irish governance, regions that he saw as more or less based in the historical four provinces of the island of Ireland, provinces that Fennell also imagined having their own assemblies. What this self-governance approach was supposed to preserve was *difference*, in this case a difference primarily although not entirely defined by language.

That respect for difference in the Gaeltacht was the guiding principle of Fennell's sense of how to deal with the North, as he makes explicit in *Towards a Greater Ulster*. He opens that by writing (in language that was a strong influence on the previous chapter), "I want a pluralist Irish commonwealth." He goes on to say:

Consequently, I believe that the ultimate political solution to the troubles of Ulster is that which Comhairle Uladh[55] proposes: a self-governing province of Ulster, uniting the Six Counties with the Three counties, and north Louth, under an all-Ireland parliament. An essential part of this scheme is its three-tier administrative structure: strong district and regional councils under the provincial parliament, Dáil Uladh. This structure would give ample scope for the expression of local particularity, and for the building of an Ulster community of communities within a new Irish nation.[56]

Fennell's interest is not only in the fate of the "Ulster British" as a whole, but rather in the degree to which a specificity that is regional (and not solely national, nor solely religious) can thrive within a single state, a state that is able to hold the universalist sense of Irishness in balance with its *local* particularities: Gaeltacht people, Ulster British, and in more contemporary terms also Travellers, recent immigrants from Africa, etc. It is just this attention to "local particularity" that is key throughout Fennell's thought about Irish identity, and which was central to a lot of the rethinking of that identity which led up to the Good Friday Agreement.

Fennell's desire to take seriously the needs of Northern Protestants calls to mind the polemics of the great Irish-language novelist (and former IRA member) Máirtín Ó Cadhain. His *Tone: Inné agus Inniu*, the published version of a lecture he gave in 1963 to Cumann Wolfe Tone (the Wolfe Tone Association), moves freely between the eighteenth-century world of Tone's United Irishmen rising of 1798 and the world of 1963, where the conflict in Northern Ireland was yet to heat up to the violent conflict zone it would become after 1969 but tensions about the language rights of Irish-speakers in the Republic were becoming more and more of an issue. "There is a border between Irish and English," Ó Cadhain says at one point in the lecture (m.t.),[57] framing the language issue in Ireland in the terms of the more recognizable "national question" of the north. He takes this frame to a level that would be guaranteed to make an audience in the Republic of Ireland intensely uncomfortable, asking about a potentially unified Ireland: "Would you expect that the Protestant minority would be able to believe that they would get a right in the Constitution when that right hasn't yet been given to their own minority, the people of the Irish language?"[58] (m.t.). The support of the Irish language has long been widely understood as synonymous with a broader Irish-nationalist position; that's most true in the north, where the Irish language has always been sharply politicized. Thus to hear it compared with the fate of Northern Protestants, a minority on the island overall but a domineering majority in Northern

Ireland (a statelet whose boundaries were drawn in order to ensure that majority), would have been startling to most listeners capable of understanding a lecture given in Irish.

What Ó Cadhain is doing here is imagining a republic in a way that anticipates both Fennell's federal proposals and Richard Kearney's aforementioned *Postnationalist Ireland* and its passages about the meaning of republicanism. I remind readers that Kearney wrote there of the importance of "reconciling the particular rights of the people(s) on this island with the universal rights of man"[59] by way of pointing out that the slippage between "people" and "peoples" is important. Kearney's invocation of *both* echoes Ó Cadhain and Fennell in recognizing the degree to which the island of Ireland is the home of many different kinds of affiliation that make varying demands on individuals' loyalties. None of these should be irreconcilable with the universalism that Kearney ascribes to the republican tradition (which I discussed in chapter 2), and which should be able to fit within a national belonging called "Irish" more or less as comfortably as that of the people of the Gaeltacht, bound to the State by a similar degree of self-governance as the Protestant-majority regions of East Ulster, Belfast, and South Ulster.

Fennell's interest in a federal form of Irish unity gradually moved outward towards a series of proposals for the entire region (that is to say the "British Isles," which I will henceforth refer to as "These Islands"). This took form in a long, two-part article published in the opinion pages of the *Irish Times* on 23 and 25 March 1974, and a second two-part article more focussed on resolving the situation in Northern Ireland published in the *Times* on 23 and 24 February 1978, as well as a long letter to the editor of that newspaper which ran with the title "A Federal Ireland" on 8 May 1978. He synthesized these proposals in part of his 1985 book *Beyond Nationalism: The Struggle against Provinciality in the Modern World*.[60]

I can summarize by saying that Fennell first proposed a "Federation of Man," by which he meant the Isle of Man. He argued that that all of the nations of These Islands should be represented, albeit asymmetrically, in a bicameral parliament located in Douglas, the capital of the Isle of Man, "which would be a federal territory (our 'District of Columbia')."[61] He writes that "[t]he parliament would have two chambers: one, for Ireland, Scotland and Wales; the other, for England. The federal government would be drawn from both chambers equally."[62] One of the second article's subsections is titled "Would England Agree?" The question strikes me as somewhat curious, given how much less influence England would have in the four-nation federation that I have proposed above. Fennell seems to take it as a given that London dominates the political situation of These Islands, and would object to being ruled from Douglas. I generally use "London" as a metonym for the UK's national government (on the assumption that it is, following Sadiq Khan's aforementioned tweet, the English capital), but Fennell doesn't, at least not in this proposal, and that is key to why he thinks England would be forced to agree to this kind of arrangement. He writes that "[a]long with pressure from its outer periphery, London will increasingly have to cope with pressure from its inner or English periphery: the English north, midlands, west and south-west. It would suit these English regions much better if London … were made into a separate federal state of England and had to bargain with them jointly in internal English affairs."[63] What he is proposing here is a mirror of his Irish regionalization plans, where Dublin and Belfast would be regions unto themselves, sitting alongside the much less densely populated regions of Ireland. Despite the outward influence given to England by virtue of its far larger population, there is thus a certain symmetry at work across his proposals. Each nation has regions, and those regions have legislative assemblies that deal with local affairs. Each nation has a parliament to deal with all issues specific to that nation. And each nation has a place in a federal government, which deals with the relatively few issues that affect the federation *as a whole*, and nothing else.

I can sense readers starting to lose patience with some of this discussion, given that these proposals are forty to fifty years old and nothing even vaguely resembling them has ever come into force. Their time may just about be upon us, though. As I write in spring 2024 there is still considerable debate about the legitimacy of a second referendum on independence for the strongly pro-EU Scotland, given the way that Brexit has changed the situation of the United Kingdom. There are parallel discussions, no less vigorous (actually perhaps a bit more so), about the inevitability and perhaps imminence of Irish unification, given the fact that Northern Ireland was also a majority-remain territory (although by a narrower margin than in Scotland); whether the Windsor Framework that was unveiled in February 2023 makes any real difference to this restlessness remains to be seen. Over these debates about various kinds of separation from UK, though, hangs the reality of the strong economic interdependence of These Islands, something brought about in part by the ways that their citizens can freely live and work in any of them owing to the Common Travel Area (CTA) that was created in the wake of Irish independence (established in 1923, it allows citizens of the UK, Ireland, the Isle of Man, and the Channel Islands to live in any of these places with all the rights of citizenship, including voting in all elections). The CTA came up frequently in post-Brexit political discourse, largely via assurances from the UK government that it would be respected and maintained. Fennell's federal proposals (which were influenced by and in turn influential on proposals offered by Sinn Féin in the 1970s)[64] now more than ever need to be dusted off by way of also *expanding* the CTA and thus creating a new political framework that takes full account of the post-Brexit world, and all of the separation that it may entail.

The most urgent of those separations, I believe, has to do with Northern Ireland. I make no secret in this book of my sympathy with the broad strokes of Irish republicanism, nor of my belief that Irish unification is both desirable and inevitable. But I also understand that there is a substantial unionist community in the north-eastern part of the island of Ireland, that their unionism does not flow from some sort of "false consciousness" or the like, and that they have the right to have their national distinctiveness recognized and protected. Fennell was always a staunch republican and a relentless critic of British imperialism (with special impatience with the cultural variety), but he also respected the national difference that is a real part of life in Northern Ireland. He wrote in *The Revision of Irish Nationalism* that "[w]ith regard to the Northern communities, it had seemed to me that they deserved names not merely *qua* political groups ('nationalists,' 'unionists') but also *qua* people, and that unionists, moreover, deserved a name which could endure even when, or if, sometime in the future, there were no more Union. So I had called the communities the Six-County Irish and the Ulster British, respectively."[65] In the second part of his article, arguing that the strife in Northern Ireland could potentially be overcome by a federal solution, he wrote that "our aim is to make a federation which will put a lasting end to lethal conflict, work reasonably well, and make its citizens feel at home in it."[66] The first and last of those clearly entailed recognizing that there were two different peoples in Northern Ireland, but the middle one, for Fennell, proscribed a federation between the Republic and Northern Ireland. He waved such an arrangement away as ridiculous, saying that "[i]t is like Canada, as a single unit, being federated with the French-speaking province of Quebec,"[67] a proposal that actually was made by Philip Resnick in 1990 and which I will argue in the next chapter could serve as a stepping-stone to a Canadian federalism worthy of the name. In any event, Fennell favours, building on his regionalist proposals of the late 1960s and early 1970s, what he called a "four-province proposal," wherein each of Ireland's historical provinces (Leinster in the east, Munster in the south, Connacht in the west, and Ulster in the north) would have a legislature and the "Ulster British" would enjoy a majority in the Ulster assembly of roughly 55–45.[68] Fennell, always a bit grumpy about his ideas being ignored by Ireland's Dublin-led liberal elite,[69] seemed unusually bothered by the degree to which his ideas about Irish federalism never gained much traction. In an 8 May 1978 letter to the editor of the *Irish Times*, responding to an England-based northern Protestant who took an interest in his federal proposals, he lamented the fact that they had generated little discussion closer to home: "Only Provisional Sinn Féin contacted me and asked me to give some lectures on the topic," he wrote. He didn't give up; on 6 October 1983 he made a submission to the New Ireland Forum (which is collected in their *Report of Proceedings*). The New Ireland Forum was a series of public hearings convened at Dublin Castle by Ireland's mainstream nationalist parties and aimed at finding a nationalist solution to the northern troubles (that is to say, one that did away with any formal union with the United Kingdom). The Forum's report, published on 2 May 1984, contained a chapter titled "Federal/Confederal State," although its sketch of this possibility bore little resemblance to Fennell's proposals, indicated by its opening formulation: "A two state federal/confederal Ireland based on the existing identities, North and South, would reflect the political and administrative realities of the past 60 years and would entrench a measure of autonomy for both parts of Ireland within an all-Ireland framework."[70] The report also states that "[i]n a federal/confederal arrangement, each state would have its own parliament and executive."[71] Fennell, as I mentioned above, saw this sort of arrangement as being as absurd as the "Canada-Quebec union" that I will discuss in the next chapter; his vision of federalism was based in an Ireland whose historical four provinces would *each* have its own parliament, not in the duality of an independent twenty-six-county republic and a six-county statelet created in 1921 suddenly coexisting on equal terms. A dozen years later Fennell synthesized these "federal Ireland" proposals into an article for the *Canadian Journal of Irish Studies*, wherein he summarized the argument by emphasizing that more than Northern Ireland was at issue: "The division of the country into several federal units would give the greater part of Ireland, which is now the Republic, a more serviceable system of government than it now has."[72] Note he says "*several* federal units," and not two.

Fennell's ongoing goal has always been greater regionalization, and therefore greater recognition of *difference*, in Ireland; that is what connects proposals about local government, about the Gaeltacht, about Northern Ireland,

and about These Islands as a whole. There is a dizzying array of linguistic, regional, and national experience in that roll call I just rattled off. As Ireland
faces the real possibility of unification in the wake of Brexit, there is a clear
need to re-examine what it means to have a united Ireland. A single-culture,
unitary Irish republic that tries to simply swallow up the Ulster British is
bound to be a disaster.

In fairness, there is a fair bit of discourse in Irish political circles along these
lines; people are clearly starting to think about some new models. But it is
somewhat disappointing that one of the most ambitious recent attempts at
such thinking, Brendan O'Leary's 2022 book *Making Sense of a United Ireland*,
explains a confederation of Ireland and Northern Ireland as part of a chapter
called "What Won't Happen" and offers a mostly technical explanation for
that ("For there to be an Irish confederation, Northern Ireland would first
have to become a sovereign and independent state")[73] as opposed to Fennell's
more expansive examination; has only one chapter devoted to federalism that
opens by saying that "[a]n Irish federation is improbable rather than impossible";[74] and mentions Fennell only once, and that in the caption of a graphic
that presents Sinn Féin's 1972 Éire Nua proposal. Although I strongly disagree
with its overall position and the positions of nearly all of its twenty-one con-
tributors, I think that the newly-updated-in-2021 edition of the anthology
The Idea of the Union: Great Britain and Northern Ireland, co-edited by John
Wilson Foster and William Beattie Smith, is a more fulsome and open-minded
discussion of what might be the next steps and how those steps might be influenced by the complexity of unionism in the North. Graham Walker writes
that "[g]iven the security of the Union, many Protestants in Ulster might start
to rediscover the radical dissenting tradition of some of their ancestors and
put them to work in a politically dynamic fashion."[75] Former Irish ambassador
to Canada Ray Bassett (who had attracted attention for his *Globe and Mail*
opinion piece of 2 March 2017 suggesting that Ireland needed to at least consider following the UK out of the EU, and put up a June 2017 positition paper
along the same lines)[76] writes that "[a]nother institution which needs to be
energized is the British-Irish Council (BIC). This brings together the Irish and
British Governments; the devolved administrations in Edinburgh, Belfast,
and Cardiff; the Crown dependency of the Isle of Man; and the Bailiwicks of
Jersey and Guernsey ... The concept of a Council was suggested by the Ulster
Unionists during the Good Friday talks as a counterweight to the North/South
Ministerial Council."[77] William J.V. Neill writes, "On a personal note, return-

ing recently to Ireland from a foreign trip, I presented my British passport to a border official at Dublin Airport. He took a perfunctory look and said 'Welcome home, sir.' Those three kind words did more to waken in me my Irish roots than three decades of armed IRA struggle."[78] This is the sort of thinking that picks up where Fennell left off, and in his spirit: wide-ranging, respectful of *national* identity in all its varieties, and open to a historically informed rethink of conceptual frameworks whose times are clearly at an end. *The Idea of the Union* is radical, but to my mind mistaken in the end. *Making Sense of a United Ireland* is defined by a cool, detached expertise that sometimes evinces a bit too much confidence that its author knows that his preferred outcome of this wild historical moment is inevitable. As I indicated earlier, it is an outcome that I also favour, and that I will admit to also considering inevitable. But I cannot deny that as a model for thinking through the complexity of "the national question" in Northern Ireland, I far prefer *The Idea of the Union*.

To follow the quote from Alain-G. Gagnon earlier in this chapter, "It is improbable that the [Ulster British] will be satisfied with another political programme inspired by procedural liberalism"[79] (m.t.). A united Ireland that genuinely moves beyond the sectarian conflict that has defined Northern Ireland for the entirety of its more than a hundred years of existence[80] is going to need to be defined by more than facile proceduralism, that is to say by more than vague, liberal-inflected assurances that everyone will get to be Irish in their own individual way. Some variety of federalism is the strategy most likely to offer long-term success. Fennell's proposals for such a political regime, mostly forged in the heat of late-sixties and early-seventies politics, have never been more relevant.

III. La república federal dels Països Catalans

In terms of building the Catalan Countries, we could consider federalism as a model for the state itself (these days, because of our internal diversity, it's difficult to conceive of a form of the "Catalan Countries" that's not based in a federal or even confederal model), as well as a model for the whole of Europe (the model of a Europe of the nations, versus more homogenizing and unitary models, like that of the American melting pot).

– Bernat Joan i Marí, *Els Països Catalans: Un projecte articulable*[81] (m.t.)

Although this proposal for a federation of These Islands may seem eccentric
to contemporary eyes, it is important to consider that they have strong echoes
in nearby political situations. I have in mind specifically the Iberian Peninsula
in the 1930s. That is the period of the Second Spanish Republic, which lasted
from 1931 to 1939, and whose constitution granted autonomy to Catalonia,
the Basque Country, and Galicia. Of course this ended with the bloodshed
of the Spanish Civil War, when Catalan nationalist leaders were well-known
for being staunchly socialist defenders of the Republic; the fascist victory in
the Civil War led to a massive refugee crisis on Catalonia's border with France.
Catalonia has been in the news a bit over the last few years because of the ongoing crises surrounding the aftermath of the 2017 referendum on independence. Spain's supreme court declared the referendum unconstitutional, but
the Catalan government, led by a nationalist coalition, staged it anyway; this
led to a massive crackdown that ended with seven Catalan lawmakers and two
civil society leaders being sent to prison, as well as former Catalan president
Carles Puigdemont fleeing into exile in Belgium. The nationalist leaders were
pardoned and released from prison on 22 June 2021. Puigdemont remains in
Belgium, and as recently as 23 September 2021 was arrested on a Spanish warrant in the historically Catalan-speaking Italian city of Alghero,[82] although
he was released after spending one night in jail. In the autumn of 2023 Catalan
nationalist parties made amnesty for all of the leaders of the 2017 referendum
(in addition to the ones who had already been jailed and then pardoned) a
condition for their support of a coalition that would allow the Spanish Socialists to form a government; they got what they wanted on that, although
as I write this in spring 2024 the coalition remains somewhat unsteady.

Given this emotive history and present-day situation, perhaps it is understandable that the Catalan connection to European federalism sometimes
seems to have been forgotten. This is a shame, because it is there that we can
see many of Fennell's ideas in action, even if "actually existing federalism"
was snuffed out by the Spanish Civil War and has been prevented from revival
by the overly centralizing tendencies of the Franco-era and post-Franco Spanish state, the likes of which led to the aforementioned crackdown. In all of
Fennell's writing about Irish federalism, his most provocative statement may
come when he says that moving forward from nationalist and sectarian conflict "means, among other things, taking a critical look at the bourgeois
nationalist cult of separation as the *sine qua non* of national existence."[83]
That would sound shocking indeed to contemporary Irish ears formed by a
hundred years of independence from the UK, a period defined in part by

a serious lack of radical-socialist discourse of the "taking a critical look at the bourgeois-what-have-you" variety, at least in Ireland's mainstream political discussions. But Catalan nationalism of the nineteenth, twentieth, and twenty-first centuries has been one long critical look at just this problem of whether or not a nation's independent destiny has as its *sine qua non* the creation of a fully separate state. This debate takes the form that is still recognizable today in turn-of-the-(twentieth-)century texts by Francisco Pi y Margall and Enric Prat de la Riba.

Pi y Margall (born in Barcelona in 1824 and sometimes known as Francesc Pi i Margall) is better known in Spanish history as a politician than as a theorist, having served as president of the First Spanish Republic for one month of its troubled not-quite-two-year existence. But for students of Catalan nationalism, it is Pi y Margall the political theorist who is more important, his 1877 book *Las Nacionalidades* serving as a blueprint for a decentralized Spanish state that was not uniquely, or even primarily, Castilian. He was at his most idealistic and, I believe, his most prescient when he wrote, "Federation, and only federation, can resolve the political problem of today"[84] (m.t.). The political problem to which he was referring was the collapse of both the Spanish monarchy in 1873 and the republic, which was undone by a series of military coups in 1874. What emerged in the wake of those collapses was known as "el sistema de la Restauración," which saw the restoration of the Bourbon dynasty presiding over a decidedly unstable country. Simon Barton writes that "[t]he perennial problem was how to prevent those excluded from power from seeking to regain it via a military *pronunciamento* or a popular revolution. Cánova's solution to this conundrum was to devise the *turno pacífico* (literally 'peaceful alternation'), a two-party system, inspired by the British model, in which the main political groupings who were not opposed to the monarchy … alternated in power."[85]

This system offered shades of things to come. When Spain emerged from Francoism in the late 1970s, its new democratic constitution was marked by a compromise between Hispanophilic "one-nation" approaches (some of which were led by a left-wing antinationalism) and the demands of the constituent nations of that part of the Iberian Peninsula, such as the Galicians, the Basques, the Valencians, and the Catalans. That compromise emerged in the form of the 1978 constitution's Section Two, which reads: "The Constitution is based on the indissoluble unity of the Spanish nation, the common and indivisible country of all Spaniards; it recognises and guarantees the right to autonomy of the nationalities and regions of which it is composed, and the solidarity amongst them all."[86] That set up a tension between "la Nación española" and "las nacionalidades" which remains unresolved today. The supreme court ruling of 2010 on Catalonia's 2006 *Statute of Autonomy* (officially known as *Sentencia 31/2010, de 28 de junio de 2010*) is unambiguous about the singular quality of the word "nación," stating that "from the constitutional point of view there is no other nation than the Spanish one" (m.t.). In fairness, what the ruling says is "no hay más nación que *la española*." In Spain there is a strong distinction between the term "española," which refers to the state as a whole and almost nothing else, and the term "castellaña," which refers to both the language and the nationality that most English speakers would simply call "Spanish." The Tribunal constitucional is clearly speaking of what we discussed in the introduction as a "state-nation," along the lines of what Alfred Stepan, Juan J. Linz, and Yogendra Yadav argue is "a political-institutional approach that respects and protects multiple but complementary sociocultural identities."[87] In any event, what Spanish unionists of all stripes have hoped would take the place of a series of irresolvable national tensions was a Spain ("una nación *española*") that would be defined by conflicts that are both political and *pacífico*, that is to say defined by Simon Barton's formulation of "a two-party system, inspired by the British model … [led by] the main political groupings who were not opposed to the monarchy." Since the death of Franco this has meant the Partido Popular (popularly known as the PP) on the right and the Partido Socialista Obrero Español (popularly known as the PSOE or the Spanish Socialists) on the centre-left.

That *turno* held until the Spanish elections of 2015, which saw the rise of parties such as the left-wing Podemos (which won as many seats in the first election it contested as the Partido Popular lost in the same election) and the right-liberal Ciudadanos, which was not far behind with forty seats, also in its first national election. This meant that the larger parties needed to rely on cooperation from smaller regional parties, many of whom were Basque or Catalan nationalist (the former tended to support the PP, the latter the PSOE), rather than focusing on one another in the two-party reality that had predominated in the post-Franco era. To bring this all back to Pi y Margall, in Spain the political problem of the day is the fragmented cross-Spain political landscape that emerged at the same time as the consolidation of nationalist coalitions in the Catalan parliament and the referenda on independence that they, wholly unsurprisingly, chose to stage in both 2014 and 2017. These two events combined to signal that the 1978 constitution, despite having led Spain out of the darkness of the Franco era, may be nearing the limits of what it can do for the modern state. Federal solutions, so long in the background of Spanish politics as a whole (for a survey see Luis Moreno's 2001 book *The Federalization of Spain*), seemed to have finally found their day.

One major contribution that this Catalan thought about federalism has made, in spite of the efforts of an overly centralizing Spanish state, is to divorce nationalism from separatism. This difference is key in the thought of Enric Prat de la Riba, who wrote in his 1906 text *La nacionalitat catalana*, "Catalan nationalism – which has never been separatist and which has always intensely desired to unify the Iberian nationalities in a brotherly, federative organization – is the aspiration proclaimed by a people who, conscious of their rights and their strength, stride confidently down the road of the great progressive ideals of humanity"[88] (m.t.). Prat de la Riba, like Pi y Margall, had a career as a politician, serving as the first president of a devolved Catalonia (known in Catalan as La Mancomunitat de Catalunya) from 1914 until his death in 1917. But also like that former president of the First Spanish Republic, he is better remembered by Catalans as a regionalist thinker and political philosopher. *La nacionalitat catalana* is a book-length explanation of a Catalan identity that was emerging from two centuries in the shadow of the Spanish state. What the re-emergence of that identity led to was not the creation of a straightforward separatist movement, but rather a complex set of political discourses that were regionalist, nationalist, and internationalist in roughly equal measure.

The crucible for this combination was Cuba. Readers are likely to know that the island's war of independence from Spain ended in 1898 and the Republic of Cuba was declared in 1902, after a brief American occupation. What is less widely understood is the important role played by Catalans in Cuba of the late nineteenth and early twentieth centuries. In his history of Cuba's influence on a burgeoning *Catalanisme*, Lluis Costa writes that "I insist on the hypothesis that the Cuban experience influenced the structure of Catalan regionalism, as much on the strategic level as on the conceptual one"[89] (m.t.). What he sees there was "the type of regionalism that was defended by the Catalan bourgeoisie, and which did not at all question ... the integration of Catalonia into the Spanish project"[90] (m.t.). Prat de la Riba was writing just a few years after the establishment of that República de Cuba, and it is difficult to separate his sensibilities from this "in-between" conceptualization of what it meant to be an independent nation. His work is an investigation of "la *nacionalitat* catalana," the Catalan *nationality*, not "l'*estat* català" (or the Catalan

State, the name of a pro-independence party founded by Col. Francesc Macià in 1922). He writes at the beginning of a chapter called "El nacionalisme polítich[91]" that "[e]ach nationality must have its own state,"[92] but he spends the rest of the chapter explaining how much the concept of "l'estat" needs to be expanded if it is to accommodate smaller nations. Prat de la Riba saw Catalonia as a nation that needed to be integrated into the Spanish project *as a nation*, and was thus opposed to the unitary states that "el sistema de Restauración" and its successor democracies, however well-intentioned, seemed to lead to. The fault line in a state, for Prat de la Riba and his contemporaries, was *national*, not political; if political fault lines could be kept from actually splitting a country via a common commitment to the crown or the state, then there was no reason that splits of nations couldn't be accommodated in a parallel manner. It was in Cuba that this problem of accommodation seemed to come to a head. The Catalan-speaking merchant class of the nineteenth century was an important part of the Spanish imperial project, and Catalans were to be found all over South America and the Caribbean. In Cuba, though, they were important because of the degree to which they were so present in Spain's tobacco trade. As this became an increasingly important aspect of the Spanish economy, Catalans were uniquely positioned between two poles: those who had an interest in seeing the Spanish state prosper economically partially by exploiting emergent global networks, and those who saw the outermost parts of that state (as Catalonia in Spain's north was, or Cuba overseas was) as potential loci of sovereignty and the key to new arrangements of that state. Thus there were some Catalans who supported Cuban independence because of its connections with a burgeoning Catalan nationalism, and some who opposed that independence movement and were part of the struggle to keep Cuba within Spain, something that would synch up with both federalist and more strictly unionist analyses of Catalonia's future. The indispensable survey of these connections is Oriol Junqueras's *Els catalans i Cuba* (1998), which recalls "the experiences of many Catalans, living on that Caribbean island, who dreamed that their home country would achieve the independence that their adopted country had won. These hopes would stay alive until the 1930s"[93] (m.t.). Junqueras himself is also in the news a lot these days, not because of his work as a historian, but because as vice-president of the Catalan parliament during the 2017 referendum, he was the highest-ranking politician to be tried for and convicted of both sedition and the misuse of public funds. In October 2019 he was sentenced to thirteen years in prison, although he and eight other separatist leaders (two of whom were civil society figures) were released in June 2021 as part of the Spanish government's pardon.

Even as a modern Catalan separatism along the lines of what led to the 2014 and 2017 referenda on independence began to emerge, an interest in federalism remained. Here the key figure is Antoni Rovira i Virgili. As with Pi y Margall and Prat de la Riba, Rovira i Virgili had a career both as a politician and as a theorist of nationalism and federalism. In the former capacity he helped found two small political parties, first Acció Catalana, and then Acció Republicana de Catalunya; the latter was one of the many small parties that were, between 1931 and 1932, folded into Esquerra Republicana de Catalunya, known in English as Republican Left of Catalonia (Junqueras is, as I write this in spring 2024, their president, having served in that role since 2011). After forming part of four governing coalitions of the Catalan parliament (known as the Generalitat), Esquerra was reduced to third place in the 2024 elections (the socialist PSOE, who are historically unionist, won the most seats but fell short of a majority). [94] Esquerra is also the oldest political party in the country, historically occupying a left- to centre-left position on the nationalist end of Catalan politics (with the far-left currently being occupied by the Candidatura d'Unitat Popular or CUP, a party that first ran candidates in 2012 but which, ideologically speaking, traces its roots back to the anarchist brigades of the Spanish Civil War). [95] It was as leader of Esquerra that Oriol Junqueras served as the vice-president of the Catalan parliament; he was part of a long line of politician-intellectuals on the Catalan nationalist left. When Esquerra presided over a devolved Catalonia from 1932 to 1934 and again from 1936 until the fascist victory in 1939, it followed a socialist platform of a recognizable "popular front" variety; indeed, its rise to power roughly coincides with the Front populaire government in France from 1936 to 1938. Rovira i Virgili became the Generalitat's vice-president in 1938, just as the Spanish Republic was nearing collapse. In the wake of the fascist victory he escaped into French exile first in Montpellier and then in Perpignan, and he served as the president of the Catalan parliament-in-exile from 1940 until his death in 1949. His career as a politician, then, always had the sense of being cut a bit short; his work as a political theorist, though, is widely regarded in Catalonia as towering.

And again as with Pi y Margall and Prat de la Riba, the key theme of his writing was federalism. His 1917 book *Nacionalisme i Federalisme* was a collection of essays on this topic, one that opened with a long meditation on the legacy of Pi y Margall. The book's overall argument, though, is for a form of federalism that can sustain *autonomous* nations in close connection with each other. In a chapter called "Institucions autònomes" he writes that "[a] nation needs, as an indispensable instrument of its existence, a parliament or legislature, a judiciary, and an executive. That is to say: freedom to make laws, freedom to apply them and freedom to execute them"[96] (m.t.). He concludes by squaring this belief in strong nations with his belief in federalism: "Thus, a strong nationalism, perfectly defined by the right ideas, does not need to be at all limited in its autonomy as far as the form of government and political freedoms. Such limitations are neither obligatory nor essential in federalist doctrine; very much to the contrary"[97] (m.t.). Rovira i Virgili understood the reality of "mixed nationality," writing in *Nacionalisme i Federalisme* of peoples whom he called "nacionalment mixt," saying that "such is the case with Finland, or of the Irish province of Ulster"[98] (m.t.). He also understood the existence of mononational federations such as Switzerland, a country he wrote about often. But he was more drawn to federal arrangements that were defined by an ethic dear to the hearts of English Canadians, that of the mosaic. He deployed that term in an essay called "Catalunya i el federalisme espanyol," which he wrote in exile in 1945 and published in the Montpellier-based newspaper *La Humanitat*: "what interest would anyone, Castillians or Catalans, have in making these states into a federation, constitutionally converting a single and unified 'Castille' into a mosaic, patching together Andalucía, Murcia, Extremadura, the two 'Castilles' *stricto sensu*, Aragon, the Canaries, all of it? If the greater Castille – that is to say Spain – wants to do this, we Catalans would accept it, since this respects our freedoms"[99] (m.t.). Thus it is hardly surprising that a socialist such as Rovira i Virgili was a keen observer of the Soviet Union, travelling there in 1938 and filing a number of long dispatches to Catalan newspapers (these were published in 1968 as a collection called *Viatge a la URSS*). He admired a certain amount of what he saw there, but he chafed at what he saw as the Leninist-Stalinist sense of "the working class as the only organ for the will of the nation"[100] (m.t.) and concluded by saying that "we could say that the Soviet Union of 1939 is like the United States, but without capitalism or individual freedom"[101] (m.t.).

Part of the reason that federalism holds such appeal for Catalan nationalists is that the territory of the Catalan language is something of a federation itself. The concept of "Els Països Catalans," or the Catalan countries, is a crucial element in Catalan culture. These "Catalan countries" are made up of Catalonia (sometimes known as "El Principat"), the southern part of France which borders it and is more or less coterminous with the French department of Roussillon, La Franja de Ponent, Valencia, the Balearic Islands, the city of Alguer on the island of Sardinia (its Italian name is Alghero), and the microstate of Andorra (which is a fully independent country, a UN member since 1993, and approximately the size of the city of Montreal, with about 4 per cent of its population). These are all places where Catalan has historically been spoken and remains alive in one way or another, sometimes weakly so (as in France's *pays catalan*), sometimes securely (Andorra's only official language is Catalan). Whatever linguistic unity may attain to Els Països Catalans, that's a pretty diverse roll call: regions large and small, a city, and a fully independent although tiny country. It is a challenge to conventional notions of national identity. Rovira i Virgili struggled with this reality; in another text written in exile, 1947's *L'Estat Català: Estudi de dret públic*, he offered a contrast between "the Spains" and "the Catalonias," writing that "[t]he Spains do not make a single Spain. The four Spains – Castille, Catalonia, Portugal and the Basque Country – are four nations. The three Catalonias – Principat, Valencia, and the [Balearic] Islands – are three regions of a single nation"[102] (m.t.). A few lines later he acknowledges the reality of Catalan in Roussillon (southern France), La Franja (just to the west of the Principat), and what he calls "the little Catalonia that is the co-principality of Andorra" (a description that is virtually guaranteed to irritate Andorrans), using the terms "strict and greater" ("l'estricte i l'ampli") as modifiers for the noun "Catalonia." Even then, he doesn't know what to do with Alguer, saying that "we shouldn't call this Italian Catalonia, nor Catalan Italy."[103] Since then, the Balearic writer Bernart Joan i Marí has tackled this issue in a more thorough and theoretically nuanced way in his 2004 book *Els Països Catalans: Un projecte articulable*. There he makes the case for a *Catalan* state that is federal, opposing it to both centralist and federalist approaches that keep Catalan-speaking territories within Spain. He writes that "Catalan separatism [L'independentisme català] ... on the other hand, is working to build a Catalan state (one that is federal, which is what practically everyone in our country who is *independentista* says), a state that is both independent and inserted with its own personality and without any intermediary into the European Union"[104] (m.t.). This is a vision that dispenses with the real dangers of Catalan nationalists becoming what it is that they have so long disliked in their opposite numbers in Castille: centralizing, chauvinistic nationalists. The French-Catalan activist Llorenç Planes was always railing against what he called "[e]l jacobinisme barceloní," that is to say a view that all Catalan culture is basically that of Barcelona, in the manner of French revolutionaries reconstructing their nation along the linguistic and cultural norms of Paris. Even though a sense of a distinct identity is real in the historically French-Catalan area of Roussillon, support for Catalan unification, federal or not, is low to nonexistent there or anywhere else in France (the CUP, for instance, runs candidates in elections in Roussillon as part of their support for an independent republic of Els Països Catalans, but they have never won a seat at any level). I discussed this briefly in chapter 2 via Simone Weil and explored it at much greater length in the introduction to a special section of *Dalhousie French Studies* I edited in 2019 on the Catalan parts of France, so I am loathe to rehash the details here. Suffice it to say that Roussillon, probably Alguer, and without a doubt Andorra are homes of a linguistic distinctiveness to be sure, but also the homes of *national* differences (French, Italian, Andorran) within that language group. Such difference makes it difficult to imagine any of the Catalan-speakers of these places wanting to be part of an independent Catalan republic, federal or not. For the other parts of Els Països Catalans, which have shared a sometimes-unhappy relationship with the Spanish state, federation within an independent Catalonia is more of an imaginable possibility. Even here, one should not overstate the case; support for Catalan separatism has never been high in Valencia, whereas in the Balearic Islands it is a bit more of a live issue. Joan i Marí, for instance, served three years as the vice-president of Esquerra Republicana's national council, and was also elected as an Esquerra MEP from the islands from 2004 to 2007. His vision of federalism goes out from Catalonia, towards Els Països Catalans, and, as the quote from his book that opens this section indicates, outwards towards Europe itself.

The possible confusion surrounding who is and isn't Catalan may be solved (or perhaps increased) by recalling Margaret Canovan's formulations in her 2005 book *The People*. She writes there that "[a]lthough the two are often treated as equivalent, there are some grounds for conceiving of 'a people' as a political community that is neither a nation nor an ethnic group."[105] That is exactly what is going on in Els Països Catalans. The distinctiveness of Andorrans, like the French-ness of the Catalans of Roussillon or the Italian-ness of those of Alguer, all share the mark of *language*, and this is not to be confused with nation. Language is of course the bearer of a certain amount of common culture. But it is not an automatic badge of *national* difference; as the Irish speakers of remote areas such as Donegal and Connemara make abundantly clear, sometimes the exact opposite is in fact the case. Following Canovan,

Catalans are a *people*, whose shared homeland is Els Països Catalans; we find there numerous *national* formulations, and the fact that one of those is also confusingly called "Catalan" should not lead anyone to see those countries as a single undifferentiated nation or ethnicity.

The larger point to be made here is that federalism has long been a key element of Catalan nationalism, but this has been a certain kind of federalism. For Francisco Pi y Margall, a federation can "[e]stablish unity without destroying variety, and can work to unify humanity in one body, without undermining the independence or altering the character of nations, provinces or peoples"[106] (m.t.). That last clause is important; the purpose of a federal agreement is to *preserve* national distinctiveness, not to obscure or neutralize it via a de facto subservience to a central authority. That is what Joan i Marí is talking about in the quote that opens this section, that concept of a "federation of nations" which would be a state that kept true to the internal diversity of Els Països Catalans as well as a "Europe of the nations," that is to say an EU that held to the same ethic (an ethic that is not at all different from Charles de Gaulle's vision of a "Europe des patries"). By the same token, then, the purpose of *nationalist* movements is not simply to achieve a state formation; the purpose of such movements is to defend the *nation* in question via whatever political arrangement is going to be best. In some cases this will indeed be a separate state; I think Quebec provides a good example there, as did Ireland before her. In other cases, the best strategy for national survival will proceed along different lines, along the lines of a federation which (in a way that Rovira i Virgili explained in *Nacionalisme i Federalisme*, among other places) recognizes distinct nations as self-governing while providing those nations with the protection that will be required to keeping them from being swallowed whole by larger, more unitary state formations that they may border. I can think of no clearer examples of this principle than the Métis and the English Canadians, and those are the nations that will form the basis of the next chapter.

CHAPTER 5

Federations II: Towards a Union

The Catalan situation, with its fertile, nationally inflected history of federalist thought, offers a vivid contrast to the politics of my home of Canada. This is deeply strange given that federalism is (along with constitutional monarchy) the basic fact of our political regime. In fact, though, the country has been defined by a sclerotic constitutional tradition that seems to hold federalism to be something that involves the federal (that is to say central) government acting benevolently in everyone's interests. As in the UK, Ireland, and Catalonia, this obscures the history of a more fully-thought-through understanding of the federal idea, a history that has long been present in English Canada as within Indigenous nations. This is certainly the case with the Métis, something that the politician and thinker Harry Daniels sought to bring to the fore in the period leading up to Canada's patriation of her constitution. That these are all different concepts of federalism does not mean that I am comparing apples with oranges; rather, laying them beside one another can help us see that, really, we all need a little more fruit in our diet, and that both apples and oranges are awfully good for us.

I. Toward a Métis Republic?

Metis nationalism is Canadian nationalism.
– Harry Daniels, *We Are the New Nation: The Metis and National Native Policy*[1]

The term "Métis" has got to be one of most misunderstood in contemporary Canadian politics. It is the French word for "mixed." In France that term still carries decidedly pejorative connotations, being perilously close to how "mulatto" sounds in contemporary English. In Canada, though, the word "Métis" is (like federalism or constitutional monarchy) a basic fact of our constitutional framework, with section 35(2) of Canada's constitution reading, in full, "In this Act, 'aboriginal peoples of Canada' includes the Indian, Inuit and Métis peoples of Canada." Most Canadian schoolchildren are taught this at some point, and are also taught about the two "Riel Resistances" ("Rebellion" would have been the common term until about ten years ago, something I will explain in more detail momentarily) at Red River in 1869–70 and Batoche in 1885, and about the ways in which the former led to the creation of the province of Manitoba. Once liberated from the classroom, though, matters turn remarkably fuzzy remarkably fast, with far too many Canadians leaning on the literal meaning of the word "métis" and assuming it means something akin to "a person who has some Indigenous ancestry, but probably isn't a 'pure blood' Indigenous person." Darryl Leroux has pointed out (on Twitter among other places) that such a definition would add around 8–10 million people to the population considered "Indigenous" in Canada. This is bothersome enough in casual conversation with one's neighbours and so forth, but when someone as prominent as the political philosopher John Ralston Saul can open his 2008 examination of Canadian culture *A Fair Country* with the assertion that "we are a métis civilisation,"[2] I think we have a problem. What the Saul formulation indicates is that the term "métis" (note that he writes it in lowercase) has become synonymous with being kind of Indigenous, but not necessarily in a "pure" way, something that also evinces a cluelessness about the degree to which Indigenous nations, *like all other nations*, are always *composite* forms. I explained this in the introduction via the ruling of the Cherokee Supreme Court on the citizenship rights of Black people descended from those who were enslaved in the 1800s by Cherokee people; the court's distinction between "the Cherokees" (an ethnic group) and "the Cherokee Nation" (a nation with sovereignty over its territory, exercised in part by a supreme court) is key for my considerations in this section on the Métis. If there is no more misunderstood word than "Métis" in Canadian politics, then in terms of Canadian understandings of Indigenous politics, there is no myth more pernicious than that of the "pure blood."

This literal misunderstanding of the word "Métis" has led to an ethnic or blood-borne as opposed to national conceptualization of Indigenous identity, something that has had serious repercussions lately in terms of the "pretendian" phenomenon[3] but which speaks overall to the inability of most

Canadians to see anything outside of the framework of liberal individualism. This inability has also led to a simple-minded and ultimately inflexible view of federalism, one that has disempowered the Métis Nation in ways that are utterly inconsistent with the historical promises around the foundation of Manitoba, the 1982 patriation of the Canadian constitution, the 1990 creation of the Métis Settlements of Alberta, and the efforts made by the Metis National Council in the twenty-first century to consolidate the place of the Métis *as a nation*. I will explain each one in turn.

In her 2003 (more or less classical-liberal) polemic *The Once and Future Canadian Democracy*, Janet Ajzenstat gives a brief history of the emergence of Canadian confederation via the Quebec and Charlottetown conferences of 1864, dutifully going through the votes and negotiations in Canada West, Canada East, British Columbia, New Brunswick, Prince Edward Island, Nova Scotia, and even Newfoundland (which at the time decided against joining) before stating that "Red River is decidedly an exception. The Dominion of Canada more or less ignored the lively debate on Confederation in the councils of Red River and, in outright violation of the principle of popular sovereignty, simply annexed the population."[4] This annexation is what the inhabitants of the Red River settlement, led by Louis Riel, were resisting. The degree to which the incursion by the Dominion authorities into the affairs of the settlement were, just as Ajzenstat says, an "outright violation of the principle of popular sovereignty" accounts for why Métis nationalists, among others, bristle at the term "rebellion" to describe the ensuing military conflict between those authorities and the forces of the Métis-majority provisional government who raised arms against them. Although it might seem that the vocabulary has changed in the last few years as part of a wholesale linguistic revision when it comes to Indigenous issues, this one has an older pedigree. Auguste-Henri de Trémaudan's 1936 *Histoire de la nation métisse dans l'ouest canadienne*[5] states that "it is evident that the Métis weren't rebels and revolutionaries, as they have been and continue to be called"[6] (m.t.). De Trémaudan also recalls how the *orangiste* J.C. Schultz, a newspaperman (and future lieutenant governor of Manitoba) who promoted the idea that the inhabitants of Red River were dangerous extremists in need of suppression, "knew that the epithet *rebels*, applied to the Métis, was nonsensical, but he also knew that the people would complacently go along without a great fuss. He found it advantageous for the Métis to be considered rebels, even if they were the only ones to support the established authority [à soutenir le pouvoir établi]: the Hudson Bay Company"[7] (his italics, m.t.). De Trémaudan debunks this use of the term "rebellion" in even greater detail on pp. 272–5. The larger point, though, is exactly the one that Ajzenstat is making; as the Canadian state consolidated in the period after the 1864 conferences and the 1867 *British North America Act*, Red River remained an exception in terms of consultation or integration into anything even vaguely resembling a democratic process.

This "democratic deficit" is, once the gunfire stopped, what led to the creation of the province of Manitoba. In today's Canada this seems to be one of the least conspicuous parts of confederation; it does not flirt with various kinds of separation in the manner of Quebec or Alberta (or even Saskatchewan or Newfoundland), is not plagued by the poverty and alienation of the Maritime provinces, and is not defined by a physical separation from the majority of the Canadian population in the manner of the territories. But it was not so inconspicuous in the nineteenth century. Manitoba was at first home to a French-speaking majority, and its entry into confederation via a settling of the grievances of the Red River settlement is inseparable from this linguistic reality. Even taking into account the role of Indigenous languages such as Cree, Michif, or Saulteaux, in that period Métis identity was primarily Francophone; people identifying as "half-breeds" would have been English-speakers mostly of Scottish and Cree heritage, and while they gradually integrated into the Métis community, a sense of separateness would have persisted until well into the early twentieth century (for a nuanced reflection on this duality, see Gregg Dahl's 2013 chapter "A Half-Breed's Perspective on Being Métis"). The "French fact" is something that contemporary Canadians, at least outside of specialist political or historical venues, only hear about in the context of Quebec or, occasionally, Acadie, rather than Manitoba. Janique Dubois's chapter in the aforementioned anthology *Constitutional Politics in Multinational Democracies* is one such venue, and drawing on Alexander Begg's history of Manitoba, she writes there of "the Métis-led provisional government organized to negotiate the conditions under which the local population would agree to enter into confederation. Presented in the form of a List of Rights, the provisional government demanded full provincehood; guarantees for the French language and for Roman Catholic schools; the protection of settled and related common lands; the distribution of land to Métis children; and amnesty for those who had participated in the resistance efforts against Canada."[8] De Trémaudan's history, on the other hand, was written for a general readership, but one much closer to the Métis culture of 1870 and 1885. Thus he speaks casually about the Francophone reality of that culture, writing early in his text how, "[f]rom any point of view, the creation of a French province in the west would have been a good thing"[9] and later wonders "if this province, as law and logic seemed to demand, would become a second Quebec."[10] I realize that there is a Francophone bias in de Trémaudan's history, a bias that a newer generation of Métis scholars has sought to undo. For instance, Jacinthe Duval argues in a 2001 article that "[u]nderstanding the Métis as part of La Francophonie, the global French speaking civilization, the church defended them against Anglophone chauvinism and Canadian state aggression while simultaneously trying to excise the Native cultural traits it found so alien to its European worldview."[11] But being reminded of the "French fact" of Manitoba is to be reminded that its creation was meant to preserve difference. It was not simply about creating another province to allow a more ordered and uniform governance from west to east. Very much the opposite was in fact the case. Manitoba was created to place the Métis as a nation, and the French language that most members of that nation spoke, at the heart of confederation. In the long run this was not entirely successful, either in terms of the French language (according to the 2016 census almost sixty times as many Manitobans reported that they mostly spoke English rather than French at home: 1,035,475 to 16,865) or Métis identity (89,355 reported identifying as Métis, about 6 per cent of the province's population). Manitoba nevertheless remains an important part of Métis life, simply because it is the historical site of the Red River colony. This is the reason that the Manitoba Métis Federation has long been a highly influential constituent part of the Metis National Council, and its departure from that body in 2021 (out of anger over the MNC's reluctance to crack down on people from central and eastern Ontario claiming citizenship in the Métis Nation of Ontario) seems to me calamitous. But historically speaking, in terms of its founders' original vision of having a majority-Francophone province that would also be the seat of the Métis Nation, Manitoba's contemporary reality is utterly different.

The process of patriating the Canadian constitution seemed to offer a chance to rectify this situation. The key figure here is Harry Daniels.[12] A Métis man originally from Saskatchewan, Daniels was the head of the Native Council of Canada from 1976 to 1981. The NCC was a body that spoke on behalf of "Non-Status Indians" and Métis people; that is to say, it represented Indigenous people (and, in the case of the Métis, Indigenous *peoples*) who seemed to fall "between the cracks," who were neither Inuit nor members of a band with treaty rights. This period when Daniels ran the NCC was a turning point in Canadian history, for it is marked by the run-up to Pierre Trudeau's 1982

Constitution Act, which both introduced the *Charter of Rights and Freedoms* and severed the last of Canada's constitutional ties to the Westminster parliament (while retaining the UK monarch as the head of state). During this "run-up" period Daniels was extremely active as a speaker, intervenor at conferences, and negotiator on behalf of the Métis. A number of his key contributions were collected in his 1979 book *We Are the New Nation*. Two themes he comes back to over and over in that collection are the real meaning of federalism and the unsuitability of multiculturalism for the Métis people. In a paper titled "The Metis: Cornerstone of Canadian Confederation," he pressed the position that federalism was key to Canadian identity, and that true federalism demanded the recognition of *national* units. "Today, there is an opportunity once again to recognize that one of the cornerstones of federation is represented in Canada's native history," he wrote. "To ignore this reality is to undermine the essential concept of federation and distort the development of a nation which has the potential to become truly Canadian."[13] The essential concept of federalism that he was referring to there was close to Antoni Rovira i Virgili's aforementioned sense that a nation "does not need to be at all limited in its autonomy as far as the form of government and political freedoms. Such limitations are neither obligatory nor essential in federalist doctrine; very much to the contrary"[14] (m.t.). Daniels could see that what was at stake at Red River was precisely these distinct forms of government and political freedoms. American annexation of the area would obviously threaten such distinctiveness, as plenty of Indigenous nations were finding out as the nineteenth century wore on. In that same paper Daniels is clear on this matter, recalling how "[i]t was the Metis who insisted on federation with Canada and resisted American annexation policies. Two Metis wars of resistance were fought to protect their land rights and to gain such other democratic freedoms as representation in parliament, language rights for both French and English, etc."[15] This is what federalism meant for the Métis: not the possibility of being good Canadian citizens like everyone else, but rather the ability to preserve distinct ways of life, linguistic difference, and autonomous political institutions. They were seeking to preserve their *nationhood*, and thus Daniels was showing Canadians that they were a good example of the sort of real nationalist movement I discussed before. As opposed to a separatist movement, Métis activists were seeking whatever political arrangement was going to be best for their nation. If that would be within a Canadian federation, then that was fine. It was the continuation of a distinct *national* life that was the priority.

Because he saw a quest for a robust federalism as key to the Métis's political future in Canada, Daniels was unequivocally hostile towards multicultural approaches, which were becoming a key part of the Trudeau program. He was blunt about this in a paper called "Towards Co-equality: Integration vs. Assimilation." He clearly saw multiculturalism as a means towards the latter. Taking strong exception to a speech by Trudeau as well as an early form of the *Constitution Act*, he wrote that "[t]hese documents assume we are part of Canadian society, that we are like ethnic or immigrant minorities ... We are a historic national minority with rights which go beyond the right to equality of opportunity."[16] He summarized the problems facing the Métis under the emerging constitutional regime this way:

> There are basically three options opened to us concerning how we should relate to your society. The first is to accept assimilation as being inevitable and become full participants in your society, thereby forsaking our history and distinct identity. The second is to exercise our right of self-determination and establish ourselves as a separate political entity in Canada. The third is to work out a political formula whereby we become integrated into your society but with guarantees which allow us to retain our identity. We favour the third. However, we do not believe this can be accomplished through multi-culturalism. It can only be accomplished through opportunities to represent ourselves in legislatures.[17]

In the book's final paper, "The Metis and Multiculturalism," he tried to temper this opposition while still being sympathetic in terms of the ethic of pluralism: "It should be stressed that while the Metis political leadership must vigorously oppose the federal government's policy of multiculturalism which relegates a native and national minority such as the Metis to ethnic status within the so-called Canadian mosaic, the Metis are not opposed to multiculturalism in principle. In fact the Metis are pioneers of multiculturalism!"[18] I can hear in this statement some of the reasons that contemporary scholars in Métis studies are sometimes uneasy with Daniels, that is to say his overall sense of "Métis as mixed" that Chris Andersen invests so much effort in debunking in his 2014 book *"Métis": Race, Recognition, and the Struggle for Indigenous Peoplehood*. Andersen argues vigorously there against the belief in literal *métissage* as constitutive of Métis identity on the basis that such a blood-borne understanding is defined by a racialist logic that is colonialist to the core and works to suppress the *political agency* of a Métis *people*. Jennifer Adese expresses this kind of unease with Daniels in her 2016 article on the *Daniels* decision when she writes, "Daniels and the organization he presided over represented both Métis and non-status Indians in the very early stages of constitutional talks, and as outlined by [Richard] Dalon, supported the view of Métis identity as deriving from bloodlines."[19] But Daniels goes on explain the ethnic heterogeneity of the Red River settlement, the importance of jigs in Métis culture, etc., and thus I think is making a larger point, one that is close to what I have been discussing throughout this book: nations, including Indigenous nations, are hybrid and composite structures, not at all the tools of reactionary homogenization that anti-national liberals often portray them as. To return to Roger Scruton's 2006 booklet *England and the Need for Nations* which I quoted in the introduction, it is the nation that is the best guarantor of *difference*, as opposed to religious or tribal affiliations (recall from chapter 1 Jesse Jackson's lament about the African-American nation: "The tribe in New York does not know the tribe in Georgia"). Thus the Métis Nation, like most nations, is itself multicultural; it is marked by linguistic difference (French, English, Cree, Michif, etc.), by cultural difference since its ethnogenesis in the Great Lakes region of the early nineteenth century (integrating people who would have identified as French, Irish, and Scottish, as well as a wide variety of Indigenous groups, mostly from the Algonquin language family),[20] by clear distinctions in terms of cultural geography (there are worlds of difference between the member-residents of the Métis Settlements of Alberta, descendants of the Red River settlement still resident in Winnipeg, and tribal citizens of the Turtle Mountain Chippewa reservation in North Dakota, all key parts of the Métis Nation), and so on.

Offering multiculturalism as a solution to the aspirations of Indigenous peoples was clearly part of Trudeau's long-term strategy to undercut Quebec nationalism. Marc Leman's 1999 online government document outlining Canadian multiculturalism's broad contours says nearly as much; he writes that "[p]ressures for change stemmed from the growing assertiveness of Canada's aboriginal peoples, the force of Québécois nationalism, and the increased resentment of ethnic minorities towards their place in society."[21] Indeed, for many observers in Quebec (and, as we are seeing, elsewhere), the policy seemed aimed at effectively making all non-Anglophone-heritage citizens (and a few Anglophones too, such as the Irish) just one of many "cultural communities" in Canada, each no more or less important than any other, and thus none being terribly likely to threaten secession or demand a place in confederation that would be equal to that of the Anglo-settler majority. Multiculturalism preferred to "assist cultural groups to overcome barriers to their full participation in Canadian society," in the words of Trudeau's speech of 8 October 1971 announcing his government's new multicultural policies.[22] It cannot accommodate groups – that is to say *nations* – who wish to exist *alongside* Canadian society, not within it. As I have mentioned earlier, Alain-G. Gagnon has written of Stephen Harper–era reforms to the federal relationship with Quebec that "[i]t is improbable that the Québécois will be satisfied with another political programme inspired by procedural liberalism, one that would, moreover, be insensitive to societal cultures and the underlying values of communitarian liberalism"[23] (m.t.). Likewise, it was always improbable that the Métis would be satisfied with this sort of political program, based in procedural liberalism, however pseudo-communitarian it might have sometimes seemed.

The Métis clearly did not figure into Trudeau's liberal and anti-nationalist conception of multiculturalism, but the effect was more or less the same: the neutralization of concrete political demands on the part of *nations* and their replacement with assurances that everyone would be able to live their best lives by having their individual ethnic makeup recognized by the Canadian state, a state that assumed everyone's shared desire to be as closely integrated into it as possible. Pierre Trudeau made this individualist quality of multicultural explicit in that address to the House of Commons on 8 October 1971:

> A policy of multiculturalism within a bilingual framework commends itself to the Government as the most suitable means of assuring the cultural freedom of Canadians. Such a policy should help to break down discriminatory attitudes and cultural jealousies. National unity, if it is to mean anything in the deeply personal sense, must be founded on confidence in one's own individual identity; out of this can grow respect for that of others and a willingness to share ideas, attitudes, and assumptions. A vigorous policy of multiculturalism will help create this initial confidence.

The forward-looking pretense of these policies only hides what they really depend on, which is an appeal to a confidence in expressing one's "individual identity," something that clearly derives from the *ethnic*. The give-and-take inherent in these composite groupings, the slow and unpredictable evolution of national identity to which this give-and-take leads: none of this is constituent of *ethnicity*, which is based in an appeal to essential, genealogically borne characteristics. As I mentioned in chapter 1, George Orwell lyrically captured this aspect of Englishness in *The Lion and the Unicorn* when he asked, "What can England of 1940 have in common with the England of 1840? But then, what have you in common with the child of five whose photograph your mother keeps on the mantlepiece? Nothing, except that you happen to be the same person."[24] It is difficult to imagine a comparable conception of ethnicity.

What Métis political actors wanted, as did their Québécois counterparts, was the modern, flexible, and forward-looking concept of nation to be recognized in the constitution. Having multiculturalism encased in the *Charter of Rights and Freedoms* (section 27 reads, in full, "This Charter shall be interpreted in a manner consistent with the preservation and enhancement of the multicultural heritage of Canadians") has been seen by Quebec nationalists as something of an affront, a way of saying that the country will be run according to the assumptions of Canada's central government, and everyone else will just have to deal with that. The Métis, at least, got section 35(2), which calls them by name.

Whatever *de jure* assumptions may seem to flow from that section, the *de facto* situation has been that the federal government has mostly refused to consider the Métis as anything other than a provincial responsibility. One bit of immediately post–*Constitution Act* activism that tried to ameliorate this situation centred on the creation of a Métis parliament. Reporting on a meeting of 22 January 1983 that established the Métis Constitutional Council, John Weinstein recalls in his 2007 book *Quiet Revolution West: The Rebirth of Métis Nationalism*:

A "nationalist" wing of delegates called for the establishment of a third Métis provisional government with a mandate transcending provincial boundaries and, in effect, replacing provincial Métis associations. The concept was sweeping: a directly elected national legislature or Métis Parliament located in Batoche (close to Saskatoon), Saskatchewan; an executive branch initially responsible for intergovernmental negotiations leading to a land base and self-government and then applying the legislation of the Métis Parliament; an administration to absorb the self-delivery apparatus of the provincial bodies and Métis institutions such as the Dumont Institute; and a judicial branch to adjudicate disputes over matters within the jurisdiction of the Métis government ... Its fore-most proponents were Elmer Ghostkeeper, who believed that the [Al-berta] Métis settlements would constitute a natural electoral district for the representation in this national legislature, [Métis Nation of Saskat-chewan president] Clément Chartier, and the Manitoba Métis.[25]

The leadership of this "nationalist wing," at least as Weinstein recalls it, makes a third provisional government sound like a federation itself, and one whose "asymmetrical" qualities recall Els Països Catalans. But these proposals went nowhere, and the jurisdictional gaps only seemed poised to get worse. The Métis, although now inscribed in the constitution, had no treaty relationship with the Crown like the First Nations; they also had no history of extensive land claims in a contiguous territory in the manner of the Inuit. Thus there seemed to be no basis for engagement with the federal government. The only province with any history of stepping into this breach has been Alberta. I allude there to the *Metis Population Betterment Act* (1938), which, following the recommendations of the Royal Commission on the Condition of the Half-breed Population of the Province of Alberta (sometimes known as the Ewing Commission)[26] led to the setting up of twelve Métis "colonies," later reduced to eight and renamed "Métis Settlements." These communities existed in a sort of political limbo for six decades, each one electing a settlement council but executive authority on each actually being held in the person of a prov-incially appointed commissioner. The *Alberta-Metis Settlements Accord* (1989) and the *Metis Settlements Act* (1990) transformed this situation, replacing the commissioners with an executive branch based in Edmonton called the Gen-eral Council, made up of an elected president, vice-president, secretary, and treasurer, along with every member of the settlement councils.[27] The *Accord* also guaranteed that Settlements could benefit from subsurface rights in their territory by vesting fee simple title in General Council. This led to the creation of Resco, a General-Council–owned company which manages the funds that each Settlement with oil activity contributes to a general pool.[28] This legisla-tion also set up the Métis Settlements Appeals Tribunal (MSAT), an admin-istrative tribunal that rules on disputes involving land access (mostly matters between individual Settlements and oil companies) and membership (Ca-therine Bell's *Contemporary Metis Justice: The Settlement Way* is a compre-hensive treatment). The Métis Settlements seem to me the best example of a "Métis Republic,"[29] much like the devolved Catalan Republic of Civil War–

era Spain (which lasted only a few days of April 1931 before being recreated as the Regió autònoma de Catalunya, within the Second Spanish Republic). I think that in some ways the Settlements should be thought of as being part of a "Pays Métis" along the lines of Els Països Catalans that I discussed in the last section of this chapter.[30] That is to say: they make up a discernible (although non-contiguous) territory, over which directly elected members have decision-making powers and in turn relate to other governments with which they coexist in a federal network. It's just that so far, those "other governments" have mostly been the Albertan one.

It wasn't supposed to be that way. The late 1980s and early 1990s are well-known to most Canadians as an era of frustrated constitutional upheaval. That is to say, this was the era of the Meech Lake and Charlottetown Accords, both attempts to get Quebec, who refused to sign on to the aforementioned 1982 patriation, into the constitutional fold. Meech Lake began working its way through the provinces in 1987 but collapsed in 1990 because it could not make it through the Newfoundland or Manitoba legislatures in time. In fact its death knell was when the Manitoba MLA Elijah Harper refused to yield the floor on the basis that Indigenous nations had not been sufficiently included in discussions. This denied the accord the unanimous consent that was necessary for it to pass by the deadline. The Manitoba legislature thus adjourned, and the accord officially collapsed (on 22 June 1990). Charlottetown was meant to do somewhat better on this front; it was still focussed on Quebec (which it would have formally recognized as a "distinct society"), but it also included provisions for Indigenous government. Former Canadian prime minister Joe Clark was named the special liaison on this aspect, a job to which he took with gusto.[31] The final text of that *Charlottetown Accord* included two provisions dealing with the Métis. Article 55 read in full: "The Constitution should be amended to safeguard the legislative authority of the government of Alberta for the Metis and Metis Settlement lands. There was agreement to a proposed amendment to the *Alberta Act* that would constitutionally protect the status of the land held in fee simple by the Metis Settlements General Council under letters patent from Alberta." Article 56, titled "Metis Nation Accord," made official that "the provinces of Ontario, Manitoba, Saskatchewan, Alberta, British Columbia and Metis National Council have agreed to enter into a legally binding, justiciable and enforceable accord on Metis Nation issues," but specific territory was not part of the article. This inscription of the Settlements into the constitution, on the other hand, would have been a major step for Métis governance, representing a *territory* over which the Métis would have constitutionally protected sovereignty, albeit through the government of Alberta. On 26 October 1992, the accord failed by a nationwide vote of 54.3 per cent to 45.7 per cent.

Since that period of constitutional turmoil, the main inflection points for the Métis have involved court cases: *R. v. Powley* (2003) and *Daniels v. Canada* (2016). *Powley* centred on hunting rights around Sault Ste Marie in Ontario, and hinged on the matter of whether a historical, rights-bearing Métis community really existed there. Spoiler alert: one did, and the Powleys (Steve and Roddy, father and son), who were cited for hunting on Crown land without a licence, were victorious. *Daniels* (which was litigated by both Harry Daniels and his son Gabriel, along with Leah Gardner, Terry Joudrey, and the Congress of Aboriginal Peoples) was largely about the question of whether the Métis were "Indians" for the purposes of the federal government having fiduciary responsibility for them. Spoiler alert again: they are, and it does. *Daniels*, since it was promulgated, has caused considerable discussion in Métis political circles. The court's ruling that the federal government did indeed have as much responsibility for the Métis as for First Nations is going to be important for making progress in ongoing struggles for greater sovereignty. But the court's analysis in *Daniels v. Canada* (2016) also posited that Métis identity was an ethnic matter, holding that "'Métis' can refer to the historic Métis community in Manitoba's Red River Settlement or it can be used as a general term for anyone with mixed European and Aboriginal heritage." This goes against an important current in Métis studies, initiated in academic discourse by Jacqueline Peterson and continued today by scholars such as Adam Gaudry and Chris Andersen. Peterson's aforementioned 1985 chapter laid down these terms precisely: "The 'new people' of Red River – not merely biracial, multilingual and bicultural, but the proud owners of a new language; of a syncretic cosmology and religious repertoire; of distinctive modes of dress, cuisine, architecture, vehicles of transport, music and dance; and after 1815 of a quasi-military political organization, a flag, a bardic tradition, a rich folklore and a national history – sprang only metaphorically from the soil."[32] For Peterson and for most of the serious scholars that followed her, the Métis are a *people*, in the manner of the Catalans or the Irish or the English, not simply "anyone with mixed European and Aboriginal heritage." As I mention above, Chris Andersen's book *"Métis": Race, Recognition, and the Struggle for Indigenous Peoplehood* threw down that gauntlet in more contemporary terms, after *Powley* and anticipating *Daniels*. He argues vigorously against what he calls the

"Métis as mixed" understanding, which he sees as defined by a racialist logic that is colonialist to the core and which works to supress the political agency of a Métis *people*. His book is also strongly invested in the position that the Métis are defined as a people not simply by ethnic mixture but rather by the experience of Red River and its aftermath, their borders delineated by the migrations that followed the aforementioned resistance movements of 1867 and 1885. He is as blunt about this as it is possible to be, writing that "when I am asked why 'other Métis,' not linked to Red River, shouldn't be able to make political claims to Métis peoplehood, I reply 'Because there are none.'"[33]

All of this should be seen in the light of the Métis National Council's recent efforts to limit who the Métis are. Understanding them as "anyone with mixed European and Aboriginal heritage" would seem to open the door to the "eastern Métis," that is to say to groups outside of the northwest who have encouraged people to join and then claim section 35(2) rights on the basis of finding an Indigenous person in their genealogy (in the Atlantic region usually Mi'kmaw; in Quebec usually "Algonquin"). This understanding has become widespread in Quebec and the Maritimes, with many "eastern Métis" organizations springing up in the last few years, basing their claims not on the existence of a longstanding political community seeking to assert its historical sovereignty over a specific territory, but rather on individual genealogical research that often reaches back to the seventeenth century. Darrell Leroux's 2019 book *Distorted Descent: White Claims to Indigenous Identity* is a thorough survey of that phenomenon in Quebec; his contribution to the anthology *Daniels vs. Canada: In and Beyond the Courts*, edited in 2021 by Andersen and Nathalie Kermoal, surveys Quebec as well as the Maritimes, and explains the Acadian connections to these claims of Indigeneity. The MNC took two steps to combat this phenomenon. In 2018 they issued, with the Assembly of Nova Scotia Mi'kmaq Chiefs, a joint Memorandum of Understanding making their shared position on the matter of an "eastern Métis" people derived from the Mi'kmaq clear. The MOU states, "The Parties are concerned about individuals claiming Métis identity and declaring the presence of Métis Nations in the Province of Nova Scotia" and "The Parties agree to cooperate as follows: To recognize each other's Nationhood within their respective traditional and current territories; To work collaboratively on the issue of individuals misrepresenting themselves as Métis in Nova Scotia ..."[34] That same year, the MNC issued a map that illustrated the boundaries of the Métis nation: the whole of the provinces of Alberta, Saskatchewan, and Manitoba; as far north as a bit of Northwest Territories; as far south as the northern bits of Montana,

North Dakota, and Minnesota; as far east as the western edge of the Great
Lakes Region; and with a western border formed by the Rocky Mountains.
Those boundaries were well-known to all Métis people, and were enunciated
in poetic language by de Trémaudan in his *Histoire de la nation métisse dans
l'ouest canadien:* "The Métis, as I've already observed, had as their homeland
the immense territories of the Canadian west, a gigantic country that stretches
from the Great Lakes and the Rocky Mountains, a country covered by forests,
spotted with lakes as vast as seas, streaked with majestic rivers which meander
through horizonless prairies where game that is as varied as it is abundant
fruitfully multiplies, while in these crisscrossing waters all manner of fish are
swarming"[35] (m.t.). The specific borders attracted some criticism from Indigenous groups with overlapping claims to sovereignty in some parts of that
same territory. But rather than a basis for a full-on land claim, the MNC map
was clearly meant to show the ways in which Métis identity was *limited*, just
as that of any nation is. Like the statement they made with the Assembly of
Nova Scotia Mi'kmaq Chiefs, this was all part of a larger strategy to return
the discourse around the Métis to an argument about a *nation*.

That is why federalism is so important, and why liberal multiculturalism
is so inadequate, for the future of the Métis. A multiculturalism that is based
in accommodation of individual ethnic difference makes few real demands
on a larger state: general assurances of non-discrimination enshrined in law,
some affirmative initiatives often in the form of relatively modest subsidies
to benevolent societies and the like, and perhaps some specific accommodations on matters such as, to follow the discussion of Will Kymlicka in the introduction, allowing Sikh men to both wear a turban and serve in the RCMP.
The Métis have more wide-ranging demands than Kymlicka's "Polyethnic
rights" or "Special representation rights." Rather, they are a clear example of
a group in search of "Self-government rights," the likes of which can only be
achieved by full inclusion in a federal system. The rise of ethnic understandings of "Métis" – someone is Métis because they have mixed European and
Indigenous ancestry – badly undercuts the push for such inclusion because
it is impossible to accommodate countless *individuals* in a federal system. To
return to Beiner's critique of Foucault as hyper-liberal, it is impossible to *actually* allow a thousand flowers to bloom. Federalism, and the powers that
federalism can lead to, tends to be about broad issues such as sovereignty over
both cultural and economic matters in a specific territory. It is a political regime that can only help a few flowers to bloom, to really bloom: a few hardy,
substantial flowers that each have different colours and forms but can still

share the same garden, which we call a federation. Following thinkers as such as Harry Daniels, Jacqueline Peterson, and Chris Andersen, I have tried to show in this section that the Métis Nation is a highly diverse but nevertheless discrete organism that needs to be allowed to bloom freely, rather in the manner of England, Ireland, or Catalonia. By way of conclusion, I will try to explain how this is just as true for English Canada.

II. Speaking of the Rest (of Canada)

I am as much touched by English Canadian nationalism and our own struggle for a distinct identity as any Quebecois nationalist may be touched by that of Quebec.
– Philip Resnick and Daniel Latouche, *Letters to a Québécois Friend*[36]

I identified the myth of the "pure blood" as one of the most pernicious in understandings of Indigenous identity; the myth of "Canada as postnational" occupies a comparable place in contemporary understandings of life above the 49th parallel. The most well-known and widely quoted perpetuators of that myth are the father-son prime ministerial duo of Pierre and Justin Trudeau. Trudeau *fils* attracted widespread attention in 2015 when he told the *New York Times*'s Guy Lawson, who was profiling him for the newspaper's Sunday magazine,[37] that Canada was "the first postnational state" because "[t]here is no core identity, no mainstream in Canada." The *Times* presented this as a welcome return to the chic sophistication of the period when his father was running the government. What this kind of talk sounds like to me, though, is a sentimentalized twenty-first-century version of Trudeau *père*'s books such as *Le Fédéralisme et la société canadienne-française* (1967) where he presents nationalism and the sovereignty that makes its expression possible as the preoccupation of the undemocratically backward and drearily unmodern (the section of that book titled "La nouvelle trahison des clercs" opens with the assertion that "[c]e n'est pas l'idée de nation qui est rétrograde, c'est l'idée que la nation doive nécessairement être souveraine").[38] For this kind of high-handed condescension the elder Trudeau remains even in death strongly disliked among Quebec intellectuals, and not exclusively nationalist ones. This sense that Canada's sophistication is to be found primarily in its rejection of national passions has been received differently in English Canada, having emerged as a kind of truism among most liberal-progressive Anglos, just as it has in England.

As I discussed in the English case, it is possible to read this as a sort of self-effacing desire to accommodate. Sure, Indigenous people speak openly in terms of "nation," but isn't that OK, given how rough a time they've had as far as cultural identity goes? It's been a rougher time even than the Welsh have had! Isn't it thus a little unbecoming of the strongest party in the Canadian mosaic to speak in nationalist terms? I think the best we can say about such a tendency to think nationhood is OK for others but a bit gauche for English Canadians is that it is defined by the kind of upper-class evasiveness that I discussed in the case of the English tendency to avoid speaking of nation as religiously as they avoid talk of, ahem, *what you earn*. And as with the English case, I find this nearly indistinguishable from simple, typically upper-class liberal squeamishness about national affiliation, or about anything else which departs from the gospel truth that the basic repository of sovereignty is the individual.

As in the English case, there is a less charitable analysis of this situation as well. I argued above that in the manner of huffily imperialist dismissals of ideology as being what *other* people trade in, poor souls (as opposed to a benevolent class defined by "common sense," "reason" and so forth), nationalism has been seen by English-Canadian liberals and progressives as something for those folks not blessed enough to be self-effacingly but confidently in command of everything that is actually important. For someone possessed of such casual confidence in their own supremacy, it might seem like you hardly need nationalism when the constitution you support (recalling that affection for the *Charter of Rights and Freedoms* regularly tops poll results as something Canadians see as core to their identity) is so completely out of touch with the sensibilities of the second-largest national group that they have not signed on to it more than forty years after it was patriated over their vigorous objections, and show no sign of doing so anytime soon (when Quebec's Liberal premier Phillipe Couillard speculated that this might be a nice thing to try to do before the Canada 150 celebrations in 2017, he was roundly pilloried from all sides of the Quebec media, and the idea has not been even casually broached since). I know of no better explanation of the problems of this sort of anti-nationalism than the one offered by Gérard Bouchard in *Les nations savent-elles encore rêver?* which I discussed in the introduction. That work has a chapter devoted to Canada (as distinct from the chapter devoted to Quebec) called "Le Canada: le rêve contre la réalité?" wherein Bouchard explains, with discernible impatience, the degree to which English Canadians have developed a form of nationalism that is, at its core, anti-nationalist. The imperiousness with which this non-nationalism is deployed by English-Canadian elites makes it, in comparison with the older, explicitly imperialist, and now so widely and vigorously derided version, something of a lateral move. After tracing that older imperial model, Bouchard opens the section called "Le nouveau nationalisme canadien" by saying that "[a]gainst this background of doubt, uncertainty and timidity, one is amazed to observe numerous expressions of a vibrant nationalism bordering on vanity, and sometimes even a certain arrogance."[39] What he is identifying there is the arrogance of a liberal position that will not acknowledge itself as a *position*, but rather as the simplest and most just way of doing things. I'm not sure I'd agree that this is evidence of "un vibrant nationalisme," but it is definitely "confinant à la vanité." That is to say, Canadian multiculturalist discourse tends to present it not as a culturally determined way of organizing a society, but rather as a near-law-of-physics that Canadians have, in their quiet genius, had the good fortune to integrate into their constitution, that document which they had to ram through the British parliament over the objections of both the Québécois and the First Nations (recall Bastien's discussion of the National Indian Brotherhood's "delegation to London of some three hundred chiefs").[40]

Bouchard, along with Charles Taylor, has been the chief theorizer of what many Québécois intellectuals have posited as the alternative to multiculturalism, which is "interculturalism." Although it is not uncommon to hear jokes to the effect that nobody knows what interculturalism means apart from "definitely not multiculturalism," Bouchard has gone to considerable lengths to define it, and Charles Taylor has also written in precise terms about the concept, for instance in a 2012 article titled "Interculturalism or Multiculturalism?"[41] Their shared engagement on the topic came to the forefront of public discussion in the aforementioned *Fonder l'avenir*, the 2008 report of the Commission de consultation sur les pratiques d'accommodement reliées aux différences culturelles (generally known in English as the "Reasonable Accommodation" commission), which Bouchard chaired with Taylor. Their basic position in that report (which I see as a major work of political theory) is that "the integrative dimension is a key component of Quebec interculturalism. According to the descriptions provided in scientific documentation, interculturalism seeks to reconcile ethnocultural diversity with the continuity of the French-speaking core and the preservation of the social link."[42] The principal differences from multiculturalism have to do with an explicit recognition of a "core" culture, as well as an explicit desire to preserve a *collective*, that is to say a "social link." Both principles are inconsistent with multiculturalism as it is generally practised in Canada, where the role of *Canadian* culture is generally absent from the discourse. Bouchard's 2012 book *L'Interculturalisme: Un point de vue québécois*,[43] spins out that definition at much greater length and in much greater detail, but the basic principle remains: interculturalism seeks to balance the needs of immigrant cultures with those of the host culture, as opposed to multiculturalism, which tends towards indifference to the latter. He offers a chart giving interculturalism's seven basic elements early in the text,[44] and throughout makes an effort to be as precise as possible, hopefully heading off further complaints that nobody really knows what "interculturalism" means.[45] Christian Joppke's would be one such critique; of the difference between "inter-" and "multi-" he writes that, "[i]n the end, one amorphous term competes with another amorphous term, and it may be preferable to use neither, or just use the concept of 'integration,' which does most of the work that 'interculturalism' and 'liberal multiculturalism' do."[46] But I don't accept that "liberal multiculturalism" does the work of "integration" at all, given that such integration into a collective is an inherent infringement on the sovereignty of the individual. Nor do I accept that "interculturalism" does the same work, inasmuch as it also seeks to accommodate, in the words of Bouchard's book, "mutual recognition of the legitimate desire of each of these components to ensure its future in terms of identity and sense of belonging."[47] If that were the case, only one of these components, the host society to be integrated into, would be at issue.

For Bouchard and Taylor, Canadian-style multiculturalism is a problem to which interculturalism is the solution because Quebec is a scrappy underdog, along the lines of what we have seen in this book so far in Senegal, Georgia, Scotland, Wales, Ireland, Catalonia, and the northwest. They write in their "Reasonable Accommodation" report: "For a small nation such as Québec, constantly concerned about its future as a cultural minority, integration also represents a condition for its development, and perhaps for its survival."[48] Taylor echoed this definition in his 2012 "Interculturalism or Multiculturalism?" article, wherein he echoed these basic contours around the imperatives of integration. He also wrote:

> The intercultural story is not simply made for Quebec. It also suits better the situation of many European countries. The features which make it applicable to Quebec also often apply in Europe. There: (1) many coun-

tries have a long-standing historic identity which is still shared by the great majority of their citizens; (2) this identity frequently centres around a language which is not spoken elsewhere, and is under pressure from larger, "globalized" languages; and (3) the same kind of not-fully-structured fears for the future of its culture and way of life may arise there as I noted in Quebec. Points (1) and (2) make the intercultural story a better fit than the multicultural one.[49]

I agree completely; interculturalism is not only made for Quebec. I believe it is made for English Canada as well.[50] Obviously Taylor's second point about a language not spoken elsewhere doesn't hold for English Canada, although given the global vibrancy of la Francophonie, I'm not sure how well it really applies to Quebec either (I understand that in the strictly North American context this matter of linguistic fragility does apply to Quebec in a way it does not to English Canada). The first and the third points, in any event, are live issues up here. English Canada certainly has a longstanding historical identity still shared by most citizens, one that has to do with the adaptation of British parliamentary institutions, a search for coexistence with Francophone and Indigenous peoples, an experience of a sometimes-harsh northern climate (even in the southernmost parts of the country in BC or the Great Lakes region), an experience of having a land border with only one country (if one can agree that the sea-ice border with Greenland is primarily part of Inuit as opposed to English-Canadian culture), a regionalist sensibility robust enough that it is impossible to ignore what province one lives in, etc. And there *is* the possibility in English-Canadian life that the distinct ways of living out this identity are in danger because of the colossal influence exercised by the aforementioned single country with which we share a non-frozen land border. I don't want to spend a lot more time on the degree to which American culture is wiping out Canadian culture (as readers will recall, I have already offered my own lament along these lines in the introduction), and so will only observe two things: (1) In the first-year English class I taught this morning on the subject of Glenn Gould's 1967 radio documentary *The Idea of North*, when I asked how many of the fifty eighteen-year-olds in the room had listened to CBC radio or watched CBC television at all in the last six months *one* student raised her hand; and (2) as I sit writing this in the city of Saskatoon (population approximately 250,000), there is not a single Canadian film playing in any of the city's movie theatres (unless one counts Denis Villeneuve's *Dune: Part 2*, which, love his films though I do, I don't). Taylor's points (1) and (3) make the interculturalist approach, and the shoring-up of a network of clearly threatened institutions that support a core identity in English Canada, a far better fit than the multicultural one.

The real problem with multiculturalism as it is deployed in this country, though, is the degree to which successive Liberal governments have presented its Canadian version as a universal and timeless model rather than one that is inseparable from a specific place (Canada) at a specific time (the late sixties to the late eighties). This is the most egregious example to my knowledge of modern English-Canadian liberalism's cluelessness about its own assumptions. I don't doubt that this specific model of multiculturalism has come to represent a consensus position in English Canada, one that transcends divisions between Liberals (the party that introduced the policy-based version in 1971 and the constitutional version in 1982) and Conservatives (who were the party to actually inscribe multiculturalism into law, in 1988). If pressed I would even admit to having a certain amount of sympathy for it myself, good English Canadian that I am. But it is just that: a specifically English-Canadian vision of social organization. Calls to "move beyond" such un-hip concepts as "English-Canadian," so central to the ideology of post-national Trudeauism in its *père* as well as its *fils* forms, only obscure that kind of specificity, giving the impression that such historically, politically, and nationally inscribed concepts "belong to the world." This is what Bouchard means by "une certaine arrogance": a tendency to think that nationalism is just for other folks, people who we, in our infinite, multiculturally inflected patience, are confident will one day arrive *chez nous*.

Thus we come to the nub of my concluding discussion, which has to do with English-Canadian identity itself. As I joked in the introduction, the least English-Canadian thing about me is my whole-hearted and serious embrace of an English-Canadian identity. I'd thus like to propose a term, the linguistic clunkiness of which means it will have no chance of ever catching on: "The EngCan Paradox." My embrace of this paradox marks me as an outsider in nearly every social interaction in which I take part; few native-born Canadians who I hang around with talk about Canadian identity the way I do, or at all for that matter. That Trudeauvian sense that Canada is somehow "post-national," that Canadians don't really have a national culture, is remarkably widespread throughout my cohort (English-speaking Canadians born after 1970 who are educated, politically progressive, self-consciously cosmopolitan, middle- to upper-middle-class, etc.: if not the proverbial 1% then probably something like "the 5–10%").

For me this is, not to put too fine a point on it, vexing as Hell. I am an immigrant to this country, and that's because I wanted to be part of a society that I had admired from afar. I was not drawn here by the lack of a core identity; I was drawn here from the United States by the vigour of a common culture that stressed the kind of pluralism that only a genuinely robust federalism can bring, by a different (by no means perfect but inarguably dissimilar) relationship with this continent's Indigenous peoples, by the possibilities of bilingualism, by a really odd and interesting and potentially fertile relationship with the United Kingdom (the Clinton/Lewinsky scandal made a monarchist of me; no way would that guy have been able to bear a single audience with a sovereign or a viceregal representative at the height of his mess), by the colder-than-cold winters, and by my hopelessly romantic sense of the CCF (by a cruel twist of fate, I wound up first settling, as I mentioned in the introduction, in Alberta, just a few kilometres too far west). These are the sorts of elements of a common culture that are needed for what Bouchard and Taylor call "the preservation of the social link," and I long for a robust interculturalist approach that will help protect them. To return to and just slightly revise the language of *Building the Future*, "For a small nation such as [English Canada], constantly concerned about its future as a cultural minority, integration also represents a condition for its development, and perhaps for its survival."[51] Despite the widespread outward squeamishness I complained about in this book's introduction, I in fact believe that most English Canadians, my self-consciously cosmopolitan cohort notwithstanding (so let's call that, roughly, "the 90–95%"), *are* concerned for their culture's survival. And I believe that most of them, formed by the broad spirit of pluralism that multiculturalism has indeed had laudable success in fostering, also understand that the integration of newcomers will be crucial if that culture is to survive into the future. But those newcomers must have something to integrate *into* if these acts of arrival and then belonging are to have any meaning. That sort of balanced approach would suit English Canada, scrappy underdog that it is in an Anglophone world so totally dominated by the cultural industries of the United States, just fine.

To a certain extent, I am calling back to the Canadian nationalism of the 1960s and '70s. The key text there was George Grant's 1965 *Lament for a Nation*, a work that was extremely influential on the growing movement to get Canada out from under the shadow of the United States. Despite Grant's avowed conservatism (or perhaps because of it), his text was influential on figures of the movement who spoke in vaguely anti-imperialist and socialist terms. Margaret Atwood's 1972 book-length study of Canadian literature, *Survival*, is a good example there, with her casual evocation of "English Canada now while the Americans are taking over,"[52] or her invitation to the thought experiment "Let us suppose in short that Canada is a colony"[53] by way of introducing what she calls "Basic Victim Positions" (there are four, the first of which is "To deny the fact that you are a victim"). I understand that this kind of talk seems dated today. I suppose my continuing affection for it is the reason that one of my closest friends in the Film Studies Association of Canada jokingly refers to me as "The Last Canadian Nationalist" (sort of like The Littlest Hobo, although distinctly unable to "just keep movin' on"). I also take Janet Ajzenstat's point about Grant (and, I think she implies, about most of the nationalism he inspired, including Atwood's): "the nation he describes is not immediately recognisable. It does not appear to include the provinces of the west, for example ... [I]t is impossible to escape the conclusion that the work as a whole centres on the 'heartland,' Ontario and Quebec, with an occasional glance at the Maritimes."[54] The other glaring exclusion from this vision of the nation is Indigeneity, hardly surprising given that we are talking about the 1960s, although perhaps not so casually excusable given that a document such as the rightly celebrated "Symons Report" on Canadian studies (officially known as *To Know Ourselves: The Report of the Commission on Canadian Studies*, presided over by Thomas Symons), put up in 1975 by the Association of Universities and Colleges of Canada, has an entire section (in volume IV) devoted to "Native Studies in Canadian Post-Secondary Education." In any event, I identify strongly with the polemical fire of works such as *Lament for a Nation* and *Survival*. Explaining the title of her book in terms of *survivance*, Atwood writes that "[f]or French Canada after the English took over it became cultural survival, hanging on as a people, retaining a religion and a language under an alien government. And in English Canada now while the Americans are taking over it is acquiring a similar meaning."[55] As I write this in the spring of 2024, I continue to lament that in an English Canada where the Americans, at least in terms of the mediascape and the political discourse that mediascape so strongly influences, have definitely taken over, we have failed to transform that concept of *survivance* in the manner that the Québécois have as the most substantial and lasting accomplishment of the Quiet Revolution.[56] But I also accept that history has, to some extent, moved on.

In fact, my overall view of such matters is more contemporary, but just barely. During the politically fecund period between the beginning of the

Meech Lake process and the second referendum on Quebec sovereignty, the UBC political scientist Philip Resnick sketched out a series of analyses of English-Canadian identity that, like Fennell's federalism proposals, I believe remain sturdy and ought to be dusted off.

This began in 1990, when he published, at the height of the Meech Lake fiasco, *Letters to a Québécois Friend*, written by Resnick as a letter to an imaginary resident of Quebec but published with a response from the McGill political scientist Daniel Latouche, an important figure in separatist circles (this was simultaneously published in French as Latouche's *Réponse à un ami canadien*).[57] Resnick was clear that he had, like many English-Canadian intellectuals on the nationalist left, been greatly inspired by Quebec nationalism of the 1960s and '70s, but now felt betrayed by the way that the movement had turned neo-liberal and insular. In this way he is strongly influenced by George Grant's anti-American nationalism, something that he explicitly acknowledges in this letter to his imaginary correspondent.[58] In a tone that would define the book, he wrote to Latouche that "I am tempted to ... voice my rage at your wilful ignoring of our deepest sentiments on free trade, at your total selfishness where Meech Lake is concerned, at the posturing that has come to characterize your claim to some monopoly on nationalist sentiment."[59] He was referring there to the negotiations around what would become NAFTA, which was seen in some sectors of Quebec, including nationalist ones, as a fabulous way to modernize the economy and move into a brave new world of *américanité*, a continental existence where borders between nation states maybe wouldn't mean so much, and so Quebec could, in any variety of ways, just be Quebec. A push towards free trade with the United States was the defining issue of the 1988 election that Brian Mulroney's Progressive Conservatives had won so decisively. That included winning the overwhelming majority of seats in Quebec, and Resnick proceeds from the assumption that this gave the undeniable impression that even "soft nationalists" were on board with their right-liberal economic policies. Free trade also seemed to be just fine with the centre-right, sometimes-nationalist-sometimes-not Quebec Liberal Party of Robert Bourassa, which had been elected in November 1985. Resnick saw in Quebec of the late '80s an openness to continental integration and a corresponding indifference to how this would impact an English Canada whose cultural distinctiveness was now in serious danger of being swallowed up by a pitiless Anglophone Leviathan to the south. For him, this was a terrible betrayal. "We have been through a moment of collective consciousness-raising with respect to free trade," he writes to this imaginary

Québécois. "Yet many in English Canada, myself included, feel profoundly hurt by your lack of concern when what we took to be our future as a nation was at stake."[60] Latouche's furious response, published in the same volume, presented this as silly and neurotic: "I will grant you that at the outset the free trade debate passed almost unnoticed in Quebec. Most Québécois know nothing of the anguish this has caused in English Canada."[61] Most of what he writes back to Resnick gives the impression that he takes deep offence at being told how to be a good nationalist, although there are occasional, sardonic gestures of respect for what the westerner has written. "If dialogue is never easy, as you say, you make it especially difficult by resorting to rhetorical stratagems which I could undoubtedly consider offensive and insulting were it not for the fact that we Québécois have made considerable use of them in the past. It is ironic to be served one's favourite medicine."[62]

What Resnick was raging against in *Letters to a Québécois Friend* was the passing of a historical moment. Latouche can see this, and responds harshly: "You are getting old, my friend. You, the Canadian Left, the NDP, the Canadian Labour Congress, and *This Magazine* are getting incredibly old."[63] What he was referring to was a romantic sense of what revolutions were supposed to be, and a sense of exhaustion at the toll state-building actually takes, particularly when that state won't, even over the course of many decades, actually come into being. English Canada was still pretty new at this ("Remember that you are the new kids on the nationalist block," Latouche tells Resnick at one point), and so it is really more tempting to believe that the McGill political scientist was, in caricaturing his BC counterpart and indeed the entire Canadian left as too old for this sort of thing, thinking of the Fool's words to King Lear: "Thou shouldst not have been old before thou hadst been wise" (act I, scene V). But the source of Resnick's sense of betrayal was that Quebec nationalism seemed no longer to be part of a global flowering of "small nations," some of which were postcolonial (Senegal under the leadership of Senghor, which I discussed in chapter 1), some of which weren't (Portugal now shorn of its empire and, thanks to a revolution led by alienated soldiers who had fought in those colonies, of its fascist government), and some of which were in-between (the Czechoslovakia of the Prague Spring). English Canada seemed to fit into that middle spot: small and scrappy, although clearly not postcolonial; sort of like Portugal, maybe, but without the military coup that dislodged a dictator? Anyway, as that period of the sixties and seventies gave way to the eighties, the animating ideology behind a new, vaguely progressive form of nationalism shifted from the solidarity-oriented communitarianism animated by the idealism of postcolonialism to a more insular, individualistic sense of national destiny animated by the equally globalizing force of an emergent neo-liberalism. By the late eighties, the period of Mulroney and Bourassa, it seemed to be every nation for herself. Latouche objects to this too, writing in the last section of his essay that "[i]f I look around me at the structural forces that are pushing Québec towards greater sovereignty and more interdependence with other nations, I feel confident."[64] But for Resnick, those networks of interdependence were obviously looking towards the United States rather than to smaller, embattled formations that might also include that new kid on the block. Latouche's vague indifference towards the matter of free trade, a policy whose broader ethic is the unfettered spread of global (read Yank-dominated) capitalism, does indeed seem to me to border on the unforgiveable, given that it has left the linguistically distinct Quebec close to unscathed in terms of culture but has utterly devastated Canadian sovereignty on culture-industry matters.

This is on my mind, because I had my first-year class again today. I again asked them simple questions about their relationship with the CBC, and they were even more clear and detailed about having no idea *at all* what I was talking about. You see, they cheerfully informed me, they simply get their news exclusively through various social media platforms whose feeds they have curated to suit their own interests. These social media platforms are, *hmm, now that you mention that I guess it's true*, mostly owned by American corporations. Just a coincidence, I'm sure. In any event, the comparative approach that I have taken throughout this book has been a way of showing that even though a neo-liberal, *sauve-qui-peut* approach to national identity has won out (and that's true even in much of the post-colonial world, despite its status during the 1960s and '70s as a veritable crucible of national identity formation), other more genuinely internationalist and communitarian understandings of nation remain possible. Resnick's 1990 missive may seem dated in its political details, but as a *cri du cœur* for that lost spirit of internationalist communitarianism, it feels contemporary.

The year after the publication of those letters, as Meech Lake really was collapsing, Resnick published a somewhat more traditional study called *Toward a Canada-Quebec Union*. He opens that work by capturing the moment this way: "It is the summer of 1990 – sun-drenched days and cool evening breezes, out here on the country's western periphery, far from the Atlantic seaboard and first colonial outposts where it all began. Like many other English-speaking Canadians, I would like to forget about Meech Lake, the constitutional squabbles we have just been through, the intellectual and moral bankruptcy of what passes for a government in Ottawa and in a good number of provinces."[65] His basic argument is that the Canadian state is dominated by "two sociological nations" – English Canada and Quebec. His sense of the former is defined by the kind of composite complexity that I have been trying to draw to the fore in my discussion of nations throughout this book. He writes that "[i]n truth, English Canada is sociologically a remarkably diverse grouping of people, which should allow us to avoid the excessively homogenizing (and intolerant) side of ethnic nationalism."[66] He goes on to say:

> The English Canada I am interested in seeing as a sociological nation, living side by side with Quebec, is an open one, where citizenship is based on common institutions and political loyalties rather than on ethnic pasts. This open English Canada is also one with a significant French Canadian minority, especially in Ontario, Manitoba, and New Brunswick. These minorities, wherever numbers warrant, will continue to have claims to educational and other governmental services in their own language, even if official bilingualism and biculturalism within English Canada becomes a thing of the past.[67]

In challenging this appeal to "ethnic pasts," Resnick would predict one of the major critiques that interculturalism makes of multiculturalism. Richard Zapata-Barrero writes of interculturalism (in his chapter in the aforementioned anthology 2016 anthology *Multiculturalism and Interculturalism*) that "[f]rom its starting premise, it criticises, then, the ethnically-based and rights-based approaches of multicultural citizenship. From this perspective, intercultural citizenship's main concerns are to do with ensuring the basis of contact, communications and interaction. That is why it is much more exclusively concerned with anti-discriminatory programmes and anti-racist practices than MC [multiculturalism]."[68] What this emphasis on *contact* logically leads to is a community that *joins* various groups into a common national core, rather than excluding such relative newcomers (via an indifference to contact with the national core) in favour of supporting their independent development. Given such proto-interculturalist faith in the ultimate cohesion of "sociological nations" – nations that are, as matter of course, diverse and composite structures whose specific qualities are always in flux – what Resnick finally proposes is a country called "The Canada-Quebec Union," which looks something like this:

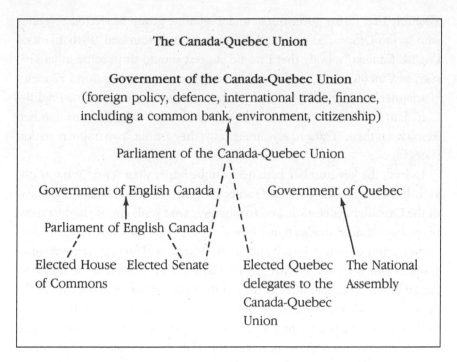

The Canada-Quebec Union

Government of the Canada-Quebec Union
(foreign policy, defence, international trade, finance,
including a common bank, environment, citizenship)

Parliament of the Canada-Quebec Union

Government of English Canada   Government of Quebec

Parliament of English Canada

Elected House   Elected Senate   Elected Quebec   The National
of Commons   delegates to the   Assembly
                                      Canada-Quebec
                                      Union

Figure 5.1
The Canada-Quebec Union. Resnick, *Toward a Canada-Quebec Union*, 117.

In reproducing this chart and advocating for its general usefulness, I am mindful of James Tully's contention in his aforementioned 1994 paper "The Crisis of Identification" that "[t]he separation of Canada into two uniform nation states would also fail to solve the crisis of political identification. Each new state would face the same problems of cultural diversity within their new borders."[69] This broad sense of a "Canada-Quebec," I would nevertheless suggest, is in keeping with the spirit of the work of figures such as Alain-G. Gagnon and Guy Laforest, specifically their interest in asymmetrical federalism as a means for minority nations (which like all nations, as I have tried to argue throughout this book, are defined by, rather than opposed to, diversity) to achieve democracy. Because it is consistent with this vision of self-governing nations working together, it represents a viable way forward for a renewed understanding of federalism. That is to say, what Resnick proposes is a multi-national federation, *une vraie*. It is a system that recognizes the existence of distinct nations, each with its own sovereign and distinct governing system. Note that the Quebec arrangement, with its combination of the national assembly that forms government and a separate group of elected delegates who "go to Ottawa," is not at all the same as the bicameral "Parliament of English Canada," a body that I would suggest should sit in some other city, such as Vancouver, St John's, or, following the spirit of Desmond Fennell's "Parliament of Man," Yellowknife. More to the point: note that the English-Canadian and Quebec governments are not mirror images of one another. Resnick has them arranged asymmetrically; they are not "two uniform nation states" at all.

Indeed, the key number here needs to be larger than "two." What is obviously missing in the Canada-Quebec Union is the Indigenous component of the Canadian federation, and so whatever wise souls choose to dust these proposals off need to also figure how the peoples of the Canadian constitution's section 35 – Inuit, First Nations, and Métis – will form their governance systems, which would, as with English Canada and Quebec, (1) be fully sovereign in all affairs that directly impact their nations or, as in the case of the First Nations, their federation of nations; (2) send delegates to the Parliament of the Canadian Union, which would, in the manner of the federated United Kingdom I discussed above, deal with the relatively few issues that genuinely concern the Union as a whole; and (3) have no obligation whatsoever to be arranged in a way that is symmetrical with the dominant (in this case English-Canadian) nation. The Inuit Tapiriit Kanatami (with its four constituent governments in the NWT, Nunavut, Labrador, and northern Quebec), along with the proposed Métis parliament that I discussed in the previous section of this chapter, would be good models there. The Assembly of First Nations also provides a tentative model for such a constituent element of a revivified confederation, although some shifting of its present form would likely be necessary (the AFN currently has representation for 634 separate bands and nations, many Indigenous people see it as a "chiefs' organization" and thus too closely linked to the *Indian Act*, etc.).

The shortcomings of Resnick's original 1990 specifics notwithstanding, this kind of model is what would put the nations of Canada on a truly equal footing. It is precisely that lack of equality at the level of governance that has been the longest-standing, and is currently the most urgent, threat to Canadian unity. My discussion in chapter 3 indicated that I more-or-less believe that Quebec would be better off as an independent country, as a Commonwealth of Quebec. In the next chapter, I will make similar arguments about both the Mohawk and, to a limited extent, the Inuit. I realize, though, that these views are eccentric, and to a certain extent I am offering them in the form of thought experiments that illuminate the future of national identity, specifically the substantial flexibility that accrues to the concept in an age of globalization. And anyway, the first one there is marked by the fact that support for actual Quebec separatism is at an all-time low, and the second is marked by the fact that almost nobody is advocating that the Mohawk secede from both the US and Canada to form an independent country except for one lone white guy from Saskatoon. Only the third enjoys any relationship with political reality, given the ongoing arguments about whether Greenland should make a full break with Denmark and become an independent nation-state. But even that one is a long shot; as I will discuss in the next chapter, plenty of people in Greenland (and some Inuit outside of Greenland) are sceptical, inasmuch as an independent Greenlandic economy is likely to be based on an offshore oil and gas industry. Similarly, it seems likely that despite widespread discontent in Quebec, in Indigenous communities, and elsewhere (Alberta, for instance), we will have the basic form of the Canadian state with us for the foreseeable future. Part of my purpose in making those formulations (the "Common-wealth of Quebec" discussion probably as much of a thought experiment as that of Mohawk or Greenlandic independence) is to make the fissures at the heart of that state more visible, hopefully prompting some reconsideration about one particular fissure, which takes the form of national identity. This is hardly a minor consideration in a state defined by federalism as the Canadian one is. Overall, I am reminded of Benjamin Franklin's famous (and probably apocryphal, which seems OK since I am about to rewrite it) answer to the question "Doctor, what have we got?" A federation, if you can keep it.

Keeping it is going to necessitate acknowledging that yes indeed, English Canada is one of the constituent nations of that federation, with all of the rights and responsibilities that obtain to that status. Four years after publishing *Toward a Canada-Quebec Union*, and the year before Quebec's second referendum on sovereignty, Resnick published a more popular-idiom book that dealt entirely with this matter: *Thinking English Canada*. One of the matters he addresses there is the Indigenous component of this revitalized Canadian government, writing of the possibility "to make provision for separate representation by aboriginal nations in legislatures and Parliament. Aboriginal people living on aboriginal lands would have voting rights in matters where aboriginal nations were subject to provincial or federal jurisdiction; they would have no such rights where aboriginal governments, were, in fact, autonomous."[70] Rather than a proposal to roll back enfranchisement, what I hear here is an echo of some Indigenous people's refusal to vote in Canadian elections of any kind on the basis that to do so is to participate in the political process of a foreign nation. But most of *Thinking English Canada* is devoted to the proposition that English Canada is a nation, and that English Canadians need to become more comfortable with that basic fact if Canada as a whole is to have any viable future. In his chapter on multiculturalism he anticipates my argument about the suitability of interculturalism when he writes that "English Canadians must be careful not to deny the ability to think of themselves as a nation."[71] He hits the nail called "nationhood" right on the head towards the end of the book, writing:

> It is almost as though English Canadians are allergic to that moment of recognition that comes from calling themselves a people, content at most with the symbolic trappings of centenaries or flags rather than with deeper existential commitments. Indeed, it is often the newest Canadians, freshly minted in their allegiance, who bring the greatest passion to this cause.[72]

Throughout this book I have been devoted to the proposition that the progressive left is comparably allergic, and that this is not helping any of the causes that this left has historically sought to support. In English Canada, as in England, this has given the game away to ethnocentric reactionaries. To return to Richard Wyn Jones and Jac Larner's sense of the self-conscious ignoring of English identity, this has certainly been politically disastrous, because so few people want to ignore their national identity or enjoy being told that it means nothing, especially when the other nationalities that surround them do not seem to suffer from these self-worth issues. Matthew Rose has spoken in similar albeit more general terms, writing in his 2021 collection of portaits of radical-right philosophers *A World After Liberalism* that "[o]ur loyalties to a nation, culture, or people can, of course, become dangerous when severed from truths that transcend them. But they are not parochial loyalties that need to be exchanged for more cosmopolitan ones. They are essential aspects of every human life, and to ask people to apologize for what they are right to value, and to be ashamed for what they are right to need, is to tempt political catastrophe."[73] When progressive forces make such a show of doing just that, of ignoring and dismissing feelings of national belonging, they make it easy for a large number of people to believe that their loyalties logically belong elsewhere. I thus want to end this chapter by quoting Billy

Bragg's "Take Down the Union Jack," and propose that it's time for both the English and the English Canadians to pay more attention to those nations – Quebec, Scotland, Ireland, Catalonia, the Métis, among others – whose citizens "just might understand / How to take an abstract notion of personal identity / And turn it into nationhood."

CHAPTER 6

Two Visions of the Future

What stands out the most among national identities missing from the preceding chapters are two of the three groups that the Canadian constitution identifies as "aboriginal." Just to be explicit once again, s. 35(2) of the *Constitution Act* (1982) reads, in full, "In this Act, 'aboriginal peoples of Canada' includes the Indian, Inuit and Métis peoples of Canada."[1] The last chapter discussed the Métis at some length; First Nations and Inuit, though, never seemed to make it into the mix in terms of my discussion of federalism. There is a good reason for that. Both groups – specifically the Mohawk and the Inuit of the eastern Arctic – represent the future of the idea of nation. We can see in both places radical shifts in the politics of national belonging, shifts that are going to transform the way that the nation is widely understood, I believe for the better.

I. A New Microstate: The Mohawk

The Akwesasne Mohawk Territory is one of the most complicated geopolitical landscapes that one can find in North America, if not in the world.
– Ian Kalman, *Framing Borders: Principle and Practicality in the Akwesasne Mohawk Territory*[2]

Now we will discuss a strange country, one that hasn't known any wars or suffered any invasions or sackings, one which has neither lost nor conquered a single bit of territory, which has not won battles nor known defeat and, as a result, has no national heroes, no collection of trophies, no *Arcs de triomphe*, no commemorative monuments, no sarcophagi and eternal flames behind

any tombs. Andorra's trajectory has been different from that of other
countries.
– Josep M. Guilera, *Una història d'Andorra*[3] (m.t.)

Now, after so many years after my interview with him [Richard, a Brooklynite
who may or may not have Mohawk ancestry, it's hard to tell], I think back to
him as I continue to meet people who claim Indian identities in similar, very
abstract, culturalist or behaviourist ways, in ways that are actually not about
political recognition or refusal but individualist self-fashioning.
– Audra Simpson, *Mohawk Interruptus: Political Life Across the Borders
of Settler States*[4]

In the history of Canadian press photography, there are few images so iconic
as the one known as "Face to Face." Taken by Shaney Komulainen during the
Oka Crisis of July–September 1990, it is a medium close-up of Private Patrick
Cloutier staring at a masked and armed Brad Larocque, an Ojibwe man who
had come from Saskatoon (where he was an economics student at the University of Saskatchewan, where I am currently writing this book) to support
the Mohawk defence of a traditional burial ground from the expansion of a
golf course.[5] Following the failure of the Sûreté du Québec[6] to contain the
situation (indeed, it degenerated badly, and one of their men, Cpl Marcel
Lemay, was killed in a shootout with members of the Mohawk Warrior Society), the army was called out by Quebec premier Robert Bourassa, the same
leader who had requested the help of the army almost exactly twenty years
earlier during the period known as the "October Crisis." Although it dominated the domestic media for many months and its recent thirtieth anniversary provoked a Canada-wide return to those events (including the release of
Tracey Deer's fictional film based on them, *Beans*), the crisis, I believe, remains
illegible to most Canadians.

I have been led to this assumption by my experience teaching two seemingly
different films about Mohawk political struggles: Mike Mitchell's *You Are on
Indian Land* (1969) and the great Abenaki filmmaker Alanis Obomsawin's
Kanehsatake: 270 Years of Resistance (1992). I've taught both at three different
Canadian universities – Alberta, Dalhousie (in Halifax, Nova Scotia), and
Saskatchewan – over the course of four decades (the 1990s, 2000s, 2010s, and
2020s). The response from students has been stable across time and place.

They know they are supposed to like *You Are on Indian Land* but find it extremely confusing and mostly hope it never comes up again. And they absolutely love *Kanehsatake: 270 Years of Resistance.*

I am aware that I am running the risk of seeming uncharitable towards undergraduate students, which is genuinely not acceptable for a guy in my line of work, but I have long felt that they love the Obomsawin film literally for all the wrong reasons. The most significant of these is because it is in some ways a war film. Obomsawin and her crew were fearless in a way that never ceases to amaze, even after repeated viewings. Perhaps more important than that, she had foresight. Obomsawin shot material from the beginning of the crisis, when a few activists were sitting on a dirt road, and she stayed until the end, when the army arrested the remaining Mohawk militants[7] in a chaotic …. words fail me. The Irish would call it a donnybrook. As a viewing experience her film is incredibly visceral, in no small part because Obomsawin's cameras are always in immediate proximity to the action, some of which is violent (one sequence where a battered and bloodied Randy Horne, a.k.a. Spudwrench, is brought by his comrades in arms into the house where militants are hunkered down, is powerful). There is an intense, "you are there" quality to the filmmaking, and students identify with this in a way which seems perilously close to the way that my elementary-school comrades and I identified with the rebel heroes of *Star Wars*. This bothers me because of the other basic fact about *Kanehsatake: 270 Years of Resistance,* which is that it assumes a viewer who really does understand details of the situation at Oka, not one who is simply looking to vicariously live an experience of righteous rebellion against a monolithic Canadian state. There is a historical digression about half an hour into the film that goes on a real deep-dive; as a helicopter lands behind a Sulpician church ("where the trouble all began, 270 years ago," the voice-over says), Obomsawin takes us back to the earliest days of contact between European and Indigenous nations. That's the sort of didacticism she engages in: disruptive to the linear flow of the film, highly detailed in terms of historical facts going back centuries, and polemical. But as far as the details of the Oka Crisis itself, she assumes that her viewer understands. Perhaps this is because when the film was released, in 1993, Oka was still a fresh memory for everyone, as it really had overtaken the national consciousness for the better part of 1990. Viewers could be expected to know the basics. That, in my experience, is far less true today.

Take the title, for instance; in my experience very few students indeed can explain the meaning of its first word in terms of geography or politics.

"Kanehsatake" doesn't refer to the well-known reserve from which many of the militants who initiated the blockade of the Mercier Bridge hailed. That is Kahnawake (sometimes spelled Kahnawá:ke), a First Nations reserve that sits just outside Montreal. Rather, the placename "Kanehsatake"[8] refers to a territory that the Mohawk claim as part of their traditional lands (which is the reason that it has a history as a burial site), but which was never made part of a formally constituted reserve. The territory was the subject of land claims in the 1970s and '80s, but none of these resulted in it being affixed to a reserve community under the *Indian Act*. As a result, the part of the land in question, where Mohawk were buried, was from the standpoint of Canadian law just another part of the town of Oka, Quebec. That's why municipal officials were so completely convinced of their right to stage a development project on it, in this case the expansion of a golf course. Obomsawin's voice-over explains all of this in the first moments of the film, where she briefly deploys a map and offers a quick twentieth-century history of the dispute, one that is full of placenames. The context-setting does not even take up ninety seconds of this 119-minute film. And why should it? She assumes that her viewer understands, and that all she's doing in this opening minute or two is jogging people's memories. Furthermore, it's logical to assume that Mohawk viewers *will* understand, because these issues are far from marginal to their politics. That's still the case, since some of these disputes are ongoing, including the status of Kanesatake, which the federal government purchased in the wake of the crisis and has subsequently sought (with mixed success) to legislate into more or less the status of a reserve, including via the *Kanesatake Interim Land Base Governance Act* (2001). All to say that the struggle to regularize the Mohawk land base is complex, a complexity that underwrites *Kanehsatake: 270 Years of Resistance* without really being an explicit part of the film itself. When you take out that complex if implicit superstructure of territorial politics, what is left is a story of plucky rebels fighting a larger, more formally organized, and thus coldly impersonal military force. That is what students take away from the experience of watching *Kanehsatake: 270 Years of Resistance*, and I think that is not far off of what the Canadian public generally understands about the Oka Crisis. The pleasures of righteous outrage that the film generates are significant, and seem not to be at all compromised by a general fuzziness about what exactly is going on. All that just seems too complicated, best left to specialists, or insiders, or anyway to *somebody else*.

   And *Kanehsatake: 270 Years of Resistance* deals only with the eastern portion of that land base; the film that students won't admit that they don't like, *You*

Are on Indian Land, deals with the western part, which is where matters get *really* complicated. They get more complicated, as the quote from Ian Kalman that opens this section argues, than almost anywhere else in the world. Mike Mitchell's film is ostensibly a documentary about a protest organized by activists on both sides of the Akwesasne Mohawk Territory against the infringement of their rights under the *Jay Treaty* (1794), which they argue allows them to move across the US-Canadian border without a passport and perhaps more to the point without customs officials charging duties or insisting on inspections, both of which would be an issue if someone living on one side of the border buys groceries on the other.[9] The *Jay Treaty* reads, in part, "It is agreed, that it shall at all times be free to His Majesty's subjects, and to the citizens of the United States, and also to the Indians dwelling on either side of the said boundary line, freely to pass and repass, by land or inland navigation into the respective territories and countries of the two parties on the continent of America." The key element there is not so much "freely to pass and repass," but rather the clear separation between "His Majesty's subjects, and … the citizens of the United States, and also … the Indians dwelling on either side of the said boundary line." Those are unambiguously being enunciated by the *Jay Treaty* as distinct groups, distinct *national* groups. Thus the expectation that someone needs to formally adhere to either US or Canadian nationality (by, say, accepting a passport from one of those countries) in order "freely to pass and repass" simply ignores the third category that this document explicitly enunciates. Such casual disregard obviously violates the treaty's spirit as well as its letter. This is an issue for the Mohawk of Akwesasne because part of their community sits on the Canadian side of the border (near Cornwall, Ontario, and Dundee, Quebec) and part of it on the American side (near Hogansburg, New York). Recognition of their rights under the *Jay Treaty* is about preserving their right to move freely *within their own territory*. That is what the protest in *You Are on Indian Land* was about; the assembled activists were asking whether they were part of a unified community or not. To return to the Mary McCarthy–inflected terminology of my discussion of Simone Weil, they were reminding the authorities in both Canada and the US that they were not "American and Mohawk" or "Canadian and Mohawk." They were *a singular*, and in this case one that was not seeking entry into either a universalist republic or a federation, however *vraie* either might promise to be. In the opening moments of the film Mitchell makes this explicit in a press conference that the cameras record him giving: "We don't want to be a Canadian citizen. We don't want to be an American citizen. They told us a long time ago that we were North American Indians. And today we feel this way too." They, the Akwesasronon, were *Mohawk*, and figuring out the details of how that simple fact would affect tax collection at the border of two different states really was not their problem to solve. As with Obomsawin twenty-five years later, Mitchell clearly assumes that his viewer knows this.

Here the justification has less to do with an Oka-esque sense that this was in the media all the time for a while, but rather with the details of its production. This was a project of the Indian Film Crew, which was part of the National Film Board of Canada. The Indian Film Crew was actually part of the NFB program known as Challenge for Change, which attempted to bring filmmakers closer to the communities they were making films about.[10] One of the project's principles was that its films were primarily being made *for* these communities, not simply about them and for general consumption. Indeed, George Stoney, who served as *You Are on Indian Land*'s executive producer, has recalled how "we said 'All right, now we want to show this to the Royal Canadian Mounted Police and to the other white officials who were involved.' The Indians were quite angry about this. They said 'We thought this was *our* film!' I said, 'Well, what good is it if you aren't using it with these other people?' So with their cooperation we set up a series of screenings with the RCMP, the local police, and other government officials."[11] Compromises could be made, but one thing was always clear: *You Are on Indian Land* was *the Mohawks'* film, and *they* sure understood these political details. Given that kind of production context, why should the film bother explaining matters to the uninitiated? Like so many of the films of Challenge for Change, this wasn't *for* them; it was for the communities that the films were about, and for those who might impact the lives of those communities.

What I am trying to do via a discussion of these films is illustrate the degree to which the Mohawk have enunciated a national consciousness that is inseparably linked to territory, and have also engaged in difficult and occasionally violent struggle to defend and consolidate that territory. The work is incomplete and ongoing, but *that* has been the work: the reclaiming of political control over some portion of their traditional territory in a way that will allow them to move forward *as a nation*. The Mohawk philosopher Taiaiake Alfred has been critical of Indigenous politicians who lose sight of this, most centrally in his watershed work 1999 work *Peace, Power, Righteousness: An Indigenous Manifesto*.[12] In a section called "Sovereignty: An Inappropriate Concept," he writes that "[i]nstead of treating nationhood as a value rooted in traditional indigenous philosophy, many Native politicians seem to regard it as a lever to get a better bargaining position … For such politicians there is a dichotomy between philosophical principle and politics. They don't believe in a sovereign right for indigenous peoples; it is simply a bargaining chip, a lever for concession within the established constitutional framework."[13] The key word here is *peoples*, which really must not be confused with *people*. Alfred is proceeding not from the liberal-inflected standpoint that individuals are fundamentally autonomous and thus the goal of reconciliation should be to recognize the ethnic specificity of various *persons* (which seems to be the assumption of Audra Simpson's Brooklynite interviewee, on whom more momentarily), but rather from a communitarian standpoint which holds that it is communities, and in his formulation *peoples*, whose exercise of power must be reconciled with that of the Canadian state. If that means steady withdrawal from the life of that state, so be it; in the interview section of the book he argues that "[s]overeignty today, unfortunately, is conceived as a wholly political-legal concept. I would prefer that social processes determined how the people feel about things and whether they are willing to act as a single unit. If they could just be content with a more closed society, people would have to pay attention to them."[14] But Alfred is deliberate about stopping short of independence, short of statehood. Of the latter he writes that "[t]raditional indigenous nationhood stands in sharp contrast to the dominant understanding of 'the state': There is no absolute authority, no coercive enforcement of decisions, no hierarchy and no separate ruling entity."[15] Of the latter, he states in the interview section of the book that "independence is wrong. In our situation, it's a Two-Row wampum concept. I think we can be an independent people without using the word 'independence.' We can agree with Canada not to raise our own army, if they promise not to use an army against us."[16] We can see here shades of some of the discussion of Catalonia in chapter 4, the first devoted to "Federations," wherein the matter of what will or won't be good for the nation is paramount, and if it turns out that continued inclusion within a larger state is what will be good for that nation then that's fine. Thus we have the phenomenon of the non-separatist nationalism that (as I discussed in the last three chapters) until recently has been dominant in Catalonia and has long been a part of the politics of Métis belonging to Canada, and which is represented in Quebec by the currently governing Coalition Avenir Québec. That seems to be more or less where Alfred sits in terms of the national movements that we have seen so far in this book.

This is not the only tendency within Mohawk politics. Ian Kalman's 2021 book *Framing Borders* is the result of extensive fieldwork within Akwesasne, on both sides of the Canada-US border, and he excavates a wide variety of political opinion about the future of the territory, almost all of which could reasonably be filed under "separatist." Indeed, reading the book made me wonder if this quasi-consensus within Akwesasne is part of what Alfred is writing against in *Peace, Power, Righteousness*. Kalman traces a recognizably modern form of this politics to the immediate post-WWI period, recalling "the mission of Cayuga[17] Chief Levi General ('Deskaheh') to the League of Nations on a Haudenosaunee passport in 1923 – an early precursor to the international movement of Indigenous peoples."[18] Problems crossing the border with a Haudenosaunee passport (which is issued by the Haudenosaunee Development Institute in Ohsweken, Ontario) are a recurring theme in Kalman's and Simpson's books. Such problems crop up in the media every once in a while, most recently in 2018 when the team representing the Haudenosaunee Confederation at the World Lacrosse Championships, held that year in Israel, managed to travel there on that document; they had made a similar but unsuccessful effort for the 2010 championships in the UK.[19] What this speaks to is the degree to which, in Kalman's formulation, "[f]or many in Akwesasne, the Canadian and American states work best when they are illegitimate and impotent."[20] This may be consistent with Alfred's general scepticism towards state formations, his sense that they are inherently inconsistent with Indigenous approaches to governance. But I am not so sure. What Kalman documents among the Akwesasronon is a deep and entirely justifiable unhappiness with *Canadian* and *US* state apparatuses. It doesn't necessarily follow from this that these are the only models of statehood. It could be possible to follow a trajectory that is different from that of other countries.

I allude there to Andorra, a quote from Josep M. Guilera's 1960 history of which opens this section. I am aware that this may seem like a ridiculous place to take this discussion, but I'm not the first scholar to move in that direction. Lawrence Rosen, in a 1997 critique of Will Kymlicka's *Multicultural Citizenship* (which I discussed in the introduction), has written that "[j]ust as nation-states like Sikkim, Monaco, and the Vatican have agreements by which their defense or foreign policy is contractually assigned to another state, so, too, encouragement could be given through international agencies to apportionment of some sovereign powers among indigenous groups and surrounding states."[21] Andorra could be added to that list of sovereign microstates who benefit from formal agreements with their larger neighbours. Until its admission to the United Nations in 1993, Andorra had existed as a sort of condominium of Spain and France, between which it sits (as I mentioned earlier,

in total it is about the size of Montreal with about 4 per cent of its population).
Even following that full emergence into statehood, traces of this earlier history
remain. Andorra issues its own stamps, but has no postal service; such matters
are handled jointly by Spain's Correos and France's La Poste. It has no standing
army; its police force provides some border security (tourist agencies often
warn hikers to watch out for plainclothes officers trying to intercept drug
smugglers in the mountains), but serious defence matters have historically
been and still remain the joint responsibility of Spain and France. This somewhat but not entirely symbolic connection to these larger countries is given
form by Andorra's heads of state (whose roles are indeed entirely ceremonial).
The country's official name is the Principality of Andorra, and its "co-princes"
are, on an ex-officio basis, the president of France and the bishop of Urgell.
The latter is important because Urgell is the part of Catalonia that Andorra
borders; bishops from this area are reliably fluent in Catalan and this helps
keep the linguistic specificity of Andorra central to its public profile. Catalan
is the Principality's only official language, which means that it, as opposed to
Catalonia, is the Catalan language's only representative among the community
of states. If you want to communicate in Catalan with the United Nations, as
I have indeed done, literally the only way this is possible is through their ambassador from Andorra.

This is the vision that I would, as part of a no doubt too-bold thought experiment, like to put forward: the creation of a fully independent Mohawk
state, along the lines of Andorra. Rather than representing the Catalan language on the global stage, the worldwide Indigenous community would finally
have a presence there. This would be done by a country that would be made
up of the Mohawk territories of Kahnawake, Kanesatake, and Akwesasne.
Consider by way of comparison the microstate of San Marino, known officially as the Most Serene Republic of San Marino (in Italian la Serenissima
Repubblica di San Marin). San Marino is surrounded entirely by Italy but is
a completely independent state with a seat at the United Nations (to which
it was admitted the year before Andorra). Its population of 33,000 is not far
off of the total number of people in both the US and Canada who identify as
Mohawk, which is about 29,000 in total. That figure includes people living
off-reserve; the combined total population of Kahnawake, Kanesatake, and
Akwesasne is just over 15,000, which is on the small end of microstates but
not outrageously so: Monaco and Lichtenstein (the latter of which depends
entirely on both the army and the currency of Switzerland, and like that larger
neighbour has stayed out of the EU) each have about 38,000 inhabitants;

Vatican City, on the other hand, has about 800. In any event, like Andorra, a Mohawk state would be a newly independent country with a long history of previous joint governance by two much larger powers, but which had nevertheless more or less managed to forge its own path politically. The still slightly ambiguous, "more or less" quality that Andorrans know so well could be represented, Andorra-style, by a purely ceremonial joint head of state for the Longhouse. I would propose that this take the ex-officio form of Canada's governor general (to represent that history of colonization by the British Crown and their enduring responsibility to make good on promises made during that period) and the chief justice of the Supreme Court of the United States (to represent the framework of laws that have theoretically, albeit imperfectly, defined the relationship between two sovereign nations since 1776).

I believe this form of a state would be entirely consistent with the political vision so thoroughly laid out in Audra Simpson's 2014 book *Mohawk Interruptus*. Throughout that text, one can sense her writing against the sense that the Mohawk are particularly invested in blood-borne understandings of nationhood, an understanding that has been encouraged by a steady stream of media reports since 2010 of Kahnawake forcing residents to leave if they have "married out."[22] She, like so many scholars in Indigenous studies, is keen to complicate simplistic notions of "blood quantum" as the basis for Indigenous identity, in no small part because it is something easily used by colonial forces to politically disempower successive generations of Indigenous people as they steadily fail to meet colonially imposed standards of racial purity because of the sort of intermarriage that, in other national contexts, would just be a fact of life. In recent years this ethnic conception of Indigeneity has had what seems to be the opposite effect, but one likely to have a similarly disempowering outcome: the enabling of "pretendians" who claim to be Indigenous on the basis of a sense that there is an Indigenous person somewhere in their family tree, and thus dilute the consideration given to members of Indigenous *communities* that have long histories of cultural marginalization and economic disempowerment and who are seeking the redress of such inequity, seeking such redress *as collectives*. The Indigenous nation that most severely faces this problem with individualist, blood-borne ethnicity being confused for national belonging is the Métis, something that I discussed in the last chapter via the work of Chris Andersen and Darryl Leroux. Problems with people claiming Cherokee heritage on the basis of the proverbial "one drop of Indian blood" are more numerous in the United States, something I discussed in the introduction. This is an issue for Indigenous nations throughout North

America, though, and Simpson's book faces this head-on. Her discomfort with that interviewee from Brooklyn, his sense that he is somehow Mohawk (far from surprising, given the long tradition of Mohawk steelworkers building the skyscrapers of Manhattan) but mostly in "very abstract, culturalist or behaviourist ways, in ways that are actually not about political recognition or refusal *but individualist self-fashioning*,"[23] is completely consistent with my ongoing critique of the domination of liberalism in contemporary political discourse. That's why I have added the italics to Simpson's recollection. In a regime dominated by the assumptions of liberalism, claims to political power will inevitably be based on individualist concerns. When such regimes simultaneously seek to redress the *communal* inequality that they have inflicted over centuries, partially via attempts to force assimilation into that regime of individualist liberalism through institutions such as the Residential Schools system (where the destruction of communal identity was a top priority), problems will unsurprisingly abound.

That is the contradiction that defines many of Canada's struggles to come to grips with reconciliation. Canada's government and civil-society institutions, both dominated by liberalism at least since WWII if not for the whole of the twentieth and twenty-first centuries, have been accustomed, as a result of their decades-long embrace of multiculturalism, to addressing inequality by recognizing individual ethnic difference within a singularly Canadian legal framework. This sensibility is much more widespread than many will admit. I am struck by Kalman's interviews with Canadian border guards about the way they applied Canadian law about border-crossing; "border guard" is not a profession, I can confidently say, that is typically thought of as a locus of liberal sentiment. And yet, he summarizes these by saying that, "[f]or some, the special status afforded to Akwesasronon challenged their sense of liberalism and the feeling that all Canadian citizens should be equal under the law. Others recognized the need to treat Akwesasronon distinctly, but lamented the lack of formal legal support for doing so."[24] Even when the guards didn't want to conform to liberalism, the Canadian regime of citizenship compelled them to do so anyway, and it was precisely that compliance, willful or not, which led to serious problems for Akwesasronon trying to lead their lives (say, shopping for groceries without being hassled about paying duty) in their own community. Canada's government and civil-society institutions have been trained by a comparably longstanding (and probably more intense) hostility to Quebec separatism to reject any hint of discrete or distinct national sensibilities. Thus Canada, as with much of the Anglophone world (with the possible exception of New Zealand), lacks a conceptual framework that can accommodate the claims that Indigenous *nations* are making, claims they are advancing *collectively*. Those claims are, more or less without exception, *political*, in the manner of Quebec separatists who have been the bane of Canadian liberal existence for so long. Land-claim disputes, arguments about the jurisdiction of customs officials, arguments about whether band councils or hereditary leaders are the legitimate voice of a people: none of these are about the recognition of individual ethnic difference on the part of the state. That, however, is the only claim that the Canadian state really seems capable of addressing; much the same has been true of the US as well.

That is not the kind of claim that *Mohawk Interruptus* is defending. Explaining the origins of Mohawk concepts of national belonging, Simpson writes:

> The heterogeneous composition of the historical community may be viewed as the setup for the conditions of the contemporary crisis over membership. "Premodern" (and later modern) Mohawks were open to those who at this time might be considered outsiders, to people of different nations and races. The clan structure that was in place made it possible for all those people to become Mohawk. Thus identity was not a problematic, an ethical issue, a matter to be confused by. It was not to be confused with political membership; it was political membership.[25]

Much of Simpson's book is defined by a certain melancholy that this fundamentally political vision has been obscured by a recent focus on racial mixing, which she argues has served in turn to obscure larger and likely insoluble problems stemming from large-scale territorial dispossession. But such dispossession does not mean that the Mohawk nation whose *political* membership exerts sovereignty over a *specific territory* has been extinguished. These narratives of extinguishment are not identical to an apology for the Canadian state's history of trying to destroy non-Canadian nationalities that sit within its borders, but the defeatism that defines it means that the final outcome is more or less the same: the Mohawks aren't a real nation anymore, it's all just been pared back too much, so we may as well recognize the "individualist self-fashioning" that some folks will engage in, because at least that will remind Canadians (English Canadians, anyway) of how morally upright we are by being committed to multiculturalism. None of that, of course, is true. The Mohawk *have* hung on to some territory; they *have* created at great expense some of the apparatus of international statehood, such as passports; they *have* put into place serious language revitalization schemes. The latter one makes me recall Ireland at the end of the twentieth century, which saw the revival of Irish as inseparable from the revival of Irish nationality, in no small part because it opened the door for people who lived there, considered themselves Irish, but did not belong to the ethno-cultural majority, people such as Douglas Hyde, a Protestant and key early member of Conradh na Gaeilge (the Gaelic League), who would go on to be the first president of the independent Irish State. The Mohawk land base is not geographically contiguous in the manner of Ireland, and while I'm sure that would create some logistical problems for an independent state, it seems equally reasonable to think of that as an extreme but near-perfect inversion of the situation with the geographically noncontiguous United States from which it would break away. Nobody should doubt that Kahnawake, Kanesatake, and Akwesasne could all be part of a unified Mohawk state any more than anyone currently doubts that Alaska, Hawai'i, and the "lower 48" are all part of the American state, that most famous republic of them all. By showing that Indigenous nations can emerge from colonialism and struggle towards recognition on the international stage, the Mohawk have done enormous amounts to revitalize understandings of "nation" just as they have provided a radical challenge to conventional notions of Canadian citizenship, and like the Métis, to Canadian confederation itself. But unlike the Métis, or as we will see in the next section the Inuit, Mohawk political leaders clearly do not wish for their nation to be part of the Canadian state, however much that state may manage to transform itself into a real federation along the lines of what I discussed in the last chapter. And so I am again drawn to the Emerald Isle, by way of recalling the words of the famous "patriot song" by Thomas Davis: "And Ireland, long a province, be / A nation once again!"

II. The First Macrostate: The Inuit

"The foundation, protection and enjoyment of Arctic sovereignty and sovereign rights all require healthy and sustainable communities in the Arctic. In this sense, "sovereignty begins at home."
- *Circumpolar Inuit Declaration on Sovereignty in the Arctic*, adopted by the Inuit Circumpolar Council in April 2009 (3.12)[26]

What I am proposing for the Mohawk could well be called "The Greenland Option." This is not a simple matter; a separatist strategy, wherein an Indigenous nation emerges fully into the world of sovereign nation-states along the Westphalian model, has proven contentious in Greenland's case. The reasons for this illuminate much about the future of sovereignty and its relationship to the concept of "nation." The sense that the future is to be found in the Arctic should not be surprising. For the most part Inuit territories exist in the popular imagination of the south either as timeless places where tradition is strong and modernity in folkloristically short supply, or as barren hellscapes of poverty and isolation that reflect southerners' worst views of themselves. In fact the Arctic has long been a key locus for global transformations. This has certainly been the case in cinema. Our all-digital cinematic present was visible in fully realized form as far back as 2001, when Zack Kunuk's film *Atanarjuat: The Fast Runner* won the Caméra d'or (the award for best first film) at the Cannes Film Festival, then as now undisputed as the most prestigious such event in the world. Kunuk's film, shot entirely on HD video, was the product of a cinema that had been formed not by film but by broadcast. In the case of the group of Arctic communities Kunuk hailed from, this broadcast was enabled by satellite technology, specifically the launch of Anik B in 1978, which allowed television signals to reach the high Arctic and led to the creation of the Inuit Broadcasting Corporation by way of dealing with the snowstorm of English that followed.

On a different matter, as I wrote the first draft of this chapter, one of the most painful issues in Indigenous politics was leaking out into the Canadian daily press: the place of oil and gas in Indigenous economic development. In the same week of December 2021 both the centre-right *National Post* and the centre-left *Globe and Mail* published op-eds from Indigenous political figures that tried to make sense of the protests on Wet'suwet'en territory (in British Columbia) over logging and oil activity. Both argued, in admirably polite tones, that non-Wet'suwet'en should mind their own goddamned business.[27] No issue causes more strife within Indigenous communities, and thus the spectacle of Canadian progressives casually presuming to take what seems to be the obviously righteous side of those opposed to such extraction makes them look as clueless as those in the corporate sector who talk in chirpy optimistic tones about all the terrific job-creation that the petroleum and forestry industries always leave in their wake. Both look like outsiders keenly trying to take sides in a messy and acrimonious marital dispute: that is to say, insufferably insensitive buttinskies. This struggle has been on display in

Greenland for the whole of the twenty-first century and for a few decades before that, as generations of her leaders have fought bitterly over whether political independence from Danish colonial power is worth participating in oil and gas development, the only industry likely to lead to enough economic activity to sustain it as a state unto itself.

What that argument speaks to has implications that go beyond the specific matter of oil and gas, and into the realm of state formation and the meaning of "sovereignty." As I mention above, some Indigenous scholars, Taiaiake Alfred among them, have questioned the applicability of the term "sovereignty" for Indigenous political practice, inasmuch as it relies on Euro-American ontologies that are foreign to the intellectual frameworks that belong specifically to the North American continent.[28] I certainly take the point there, but it's not clear to me that this is a consensus position. I am led to that sense because of the way that Inuit governmental bodies have deployed that term to explain their political aspirations. The key document is *A Circumpolar Inuit Declaration on Sovereignty in the Arctic*, issued by the Inuit Circumpolar Council in April 2009. The quotation from this document that opens this section, to the effect that "sovereignty begins at home," should give some sense of the degree to which the term is resonant within Inuit political discourse. What is more of an issue in Inuit politics, consistent with some of Alfred's critique of "sovereignty"-led discourse, is the role that state formations should play.

This is such an issue among the Inuit because of the success of the aforementioned Inuit Circumpolar Council. The ICC traces its roots to 1977; Thierry Rodon explains it this way:

> The first pan-Inuit meeting organized by Inuit was held in Barrow, Alaska in 1977, at the invitation of Eben Hopson, a visionary Inuit leader who used money from oil development to assemble Inuit living throughout the circumpolar region. Inuit from Alaska, Canada and Greenland were present, as well as Saami representatives invited as observers. The decision to create a transnational organization was made during this seminal event. The Inuit Circumpolar Conference (ICC) was officially incorporated in 1980 at the Nuuk General Assembly.[29]

This was the moment when the term "Eskimo" fell out of general usage in Canada and was replaced by "Inuit."[30] It was also the moment when the unquestioned centrality of the Westphalian state started to recede a bit, at least in the Arctic. Over the last six decades, the ICC has gradually incorporated itself into the decision-making processes of the states whose territory encompasses some part of the area north of the Arctic Circle. John English summarizes matters by writing of "the ICC, which emerged as an important international actor in the 1980s, producing an environmental strategy and taking part in constitutional talks on Canada and Denmark."[31] The connection between these two states is perhaps mostly vividly embodied in the figure of Mary Simon, born to an Inuk mother and a white father in the northern Quebec community of Kangiqsualujjuaq, head of the ICC from 1986 to 1992 (and so encompassing the full period of the Meech Lake and Charlottetown Accords), Canadian ambassador to Denmark from 1999 to 2002, and, since 26 July 2021, the thirtieth governor general of Canada. This influence that the ICC has gained since this period of the 1980s has perhaps culminated in its achieving permanent "observer" status at the Arctic Council, the group of those eight states (Canada, Denmark, Finland, Iceland, Norway, Russia, Sweden, and the US) who collectively make decisions about the region. The ICC's aforementioned *Declaration on Sovereignty* is clear about this, stating that "[t]he development of international institutions in the Arctic, such as multi-level governance systems and indigenous peoples' organizations, must transcend Arctic states' agendas on sovereignty and sovereign rights and the traditional monopoly claimed by states in the area of foreign affairs" (4.2). This desire to transcend the state is a key theme in Inuit political discourse, and is strongly connected to the critiques of state formations that often crop up in Indigenous political discourse further south.

One particularly valuable aspect of the Inuit critique of statehood is the degree to which it is based in a pragmatic desire for more, not a willingness to accept less, sovereignty. Shadian's 2010 article adopts the term "Inuit polity" by way of indicating the degree to which political control is at issue although the term "state" isn't the right one: "Combined, the varying parts of this Inuit polity – either through the ICC or through local governance arrangements – create something greater than their separate pieces may afford for analytical purposes."[32] That is because this Inuit polity is made up of different constituent parts, all of which come together in groups such as the ICC, which also exercises political influences but which is also not a state. This is what has led scholars such as Barry Scott Zellen to argue (in a 2022 article) for a kind of "co-management" approach to sovereignty, which he defines as a "triangular relationship between domestic, international and transnational entities."[33] This, he argues in this article (as well as in his 2009 book *On Thin Ice: The Inuit, the State and the Challenge of Arctic Sovereignty*), will bridge the gap between contemporary Indigenous governance models and the global system of states: "co-management has become so widely and reciprocally embraced by tribal peoples and states alike that it now presents us with a viable and scalable foundation for bridging the Indigenous, transnational world with the Westphalian world of states and statecraft across the entirety of the circumpolar arctic."[34] What we can see in this co-management-based Inuit polity should seem familiar from the last chapter, devoted to "Federations," in terms of Els Països Catalans. Readers will recall that as I rattled off the combination of Catalonia, the southern part of France that borders it, La Franja de Ponent, Valencia, the Balearic Islands, the Sardinian community of L'Alguer, and the microstate of Andorra, I wrote, "that's a pretty diverse roll call: regions large and small, a city, and a fully independent although very small country." You could also say that they would benefit a great deal from a "triangular relationship between domestic, international and transnational entities." Perhaps I was also channelling Gary N. Wilson and Heather A. Smith, who write that "we have today de facto states, subnational governments, and national organisations all linked in various ways to the ICC, which often represents these organizations and governments internationally."[35]

By "de facto states" they clearly mean Greenland, which is the part of the "Inuit polity" that is the closest to independence, due in some part to the *Lov om Grønlands Selvstyre* (2009), known in English as the 2009 Self Government Act.[36] This devolved all powers pertaining to Greenland to the Greenlandic parliament; in practice this was nearly everything except for monetary policy and defence. The next logical step would seem to be full independence, and there is certainly a significant part of Greenlandic society pushing for this. Hannes Gerhardt's 2011 article recalls his interviews with government officials a few years after the passage of that law to the effect that "it is the Greenlandic government ... that must strive to achieve greater sovereignty for the Inuit of Greenland through the establishment of an independent Greenlandic nation-state. This view was often repeated in various forms of my interviews."[37]

But Greenland, although it is the largest part of the Inuit polity both in terms of geographical size (2.166 million km^2 as opposed to Nunavut's 2.093 million km^2) and of population (about 56,000, in contrast to Nunavut's ~39,000), is far from being an economic powerhouse. Gerhardt is unblinkingly pessimistic about this reality, noting that much Greenlandic separatist rhetoric is based on the island's ability to exploit offshore oil and gas resources; he is far from alone. He concludes by stating that "an 'Inuit' petrostate and the transformation needed to bring it about would in all likelyhood lead very far away from the cultural integrity that is largely at the root of the aims of the ICC and its conception of the Inuit position with regard to sovereignty."[38] In framing the issue he was echoing a lot of recent work about "petrostates" and the problems that flow from that single-resource status. Terry Lynn Karl's 1999 article laid out the issue in stark terms: "What distinguishes oil states from other states, above all else, is their addiction to oil rents. Where this oil addiction takes hold, a skewed sense of both political and market incentives so penetrate all aspects of life that almost everything is eventually up for sale. Actors in oil states do not behave the same as they do elsewhere; they simply don't have to."[39] Greenland has long had a modest fishery but that was never enough to sustain it as a fully sovereign state; as with its sister realm within the Kingdom of Denmark, the Faroe Islands, it is only when the possibility of offshore oil activity comes into the picture that the modern separatist program really gains momentum (and in the Faroes, the lack of sustained activity of this kind has kept that program in a sort of suspended animation).

Having offered that cautionary tale about oil being a unique kind of natural resource, Gerhardt's overall tone is fairly tentative and descriptive. He also writes of the degree to which "[i]t is possible that the process of establishing a Greenlandic state will, as a consequence, work to obstruct more counter-hegemonic Inuit strategies inspired by a non-Western [sic], indigenous political ontology."[40] He is more or less taking a position, but not one that will exactly inspire non-Inuit to chain themselves to any pipelines. Rather, his aspiration here is clearly to draw greater attention to the degree to which the situation of the Inuit is not identical to that of an earlier generation of decolonizing nations. It may be that the path of independent statehood is the right one for Greenland; I suppose that I am on the opposite end of the "flirting with the 'unforgiveable buttinsky' tendency," inasmuch as I am as vaguely in favour of such an outcome as Gerhardt is vaguely opposed. Even if Greenland never opts to blaze this particular path, though, we are both basically pointing to the importance of the ICC and the degree to which it has already laid down a unique trail. Its 2009 declaration unambiguously states that "[t]hough Inuit live across a far-reaching circumpolar region, we are united as a single people" (1.2). That is to say, the Inuit are moving away from conventional understandings of the state, but also towards the nation.

Conclusion

The "Conclusion" that every doctoral advisor urges on his students
as a professional obligation has always seemed to my notoriously
inconclusive temperament to be so much wishful thinking.
– Simon Schama, *Dead Certainties: Unwarranted Speculations*[1]

Upon reaching the end of a book-length study, it's only natural to think about all the material that you should have covered, different ways that each chapter might have been organized, and how the whole thing should have just been *more*.

Chapter 1, devoted to "Ethnos," could have just as well been devoted to the Jewish people and modern conceptions of nation that draw upon Biblical narrative but rewrite this in significant ways across many languages, most significantly Hebrew and Yiddish. I admit that the second chapter, devoted to "Republics," is a bit odd inasmuch as it does not have a section devoted to the United States (although that country doesn't exactly suffer from a lack of discussion in other venues, so its exclusion on my part is something of a "sorry not sorry" sort of issue). In terms of chapter 3, devoted to "Commonwealths," the example that could have also been part of the discussion is the officially trilingual Grand Duchy of Luxembourg, where differences between those more comfortable in French and those more comfortable in German mean basically nothing because (1) both languages are near-universally spoken there, and (2) Lëtzebuergesch (which is not mutually intelligible with German) is the dominant mother tongue of the overwhelming majority of the population (including children of immigrants; see Joel Fetzer's book for a sustained treatment) and is spoken nowhere else except for the Grand Duchy. This linguistic mix has led to what Luxembourgers have long called "Mischkultur" as the defining quality of their national identity (see Matias Gardin et al.'s 2015 article for details), something that has strong connections to New Zealanders' shared adherence to *Te Tiriti*. In terms of the chapters on federalism, there are few countries which take federalism more seriously than Switzerland, and that could have just as well been the subject of the chapter as Catalonia. The strongest tension in these chapters overall is between "Commonwealths" and "Federations," and as I write this, that tension is on display in the war between Russia and Ukraine. Is Ukraine's rightful place as part of the Russian Federation, to invoke the official name of the USSR's successor state? Is that federation really closer to a "commonwealth," the nations it is made up of just as inseparable as the Māori and settler elements of New Zealand culture? Vladimir Putin certainly seems to think so, and he is following a long line of Russian nationalist thought on this matter. No less a figure than Aleksandr Solzhenitsyn, for instance, wrote in the earliest post-Soviet days (in his short 1990 book *Rebuilding Russia*) that "[a]ll the talk of a separate Ukrainian people existing since something like the ninth century and possessing its own non-Russian language is a recently invented falsehood."[2] Is the Russian invasion thus basically a war on Ukrainian national identity, something that is as multifaceted (think, for instance, of the Ukrainian Tatars, the majority of whom [1] are Muslim and [2] have since the collapse of the USSR mostly identified as Ukrainian) as Russian identity itself (think again of the ethnic Koreans of Russia's far east, most of whom identify primarily as Russian and have little connection to the neighbouring North Korea[3])? If the answer to that question is indeed "yes, the Russians are waging war on Ukrainian national identity," that would take an entirely separate book to debate properly, one that drew on both Russian- and Ukrainian-language sources on that identity.

The book has gaps and occlusions like this for good reason. What I have tried to do throughout it, rather than provide a sort of encyclopedic or linear-historical view of national distinctiveness, is use a very few specific examples (small essays in their way) to try (*essayer*) and tease out some of the key aspects of the concept of "nation" that have been, and continue to be, or should be, defended by the left. My argument for the continued validity of this concept have emerged across a few key lines: a challenge to liberalism, a haven for diversity, and a means of solidarity.

I. Liberalism

When I sent an earlier draft of this book to a friend, he responded with a characteristically generous memo that summarized the argument this way: "Votre ennemi: l'individualisme libéral bien-pensant, au cœur de la mondialisation, faussement universel." It was gratifying to read that. That "faussement universel" aspect of contemporary liberalism, particularly of the Anglo-American variety, is something that the left should oppose for exactly the same reason that it has opposed capitalism, or imperialism: these are all ideologies that refuse to acknowledge themselves as such, pretending instead to be a sort of "common sense" or "natural way of doing things." This sense of contemporary liberalism is one way in which I am in strong agreement with, and one way this book has been strongly if implicitly influenced by, the overall framework of Yoram Hazony's *The Virtue of Nationalism*. He writes at one point that "the empire, which claims to give law to all mankind, necessarily concerns itself with abstract categories of human need and obligation, categories that are, in its eyes, 'universal.'"[4] He argues throughout that book this is how institutionalized liberalism proceeds, and my sense of the nation has been defined by a critique that is not so far from that. As I mentioned earlier, Hazony is coming from a neo-conservative and now a national-conservative position (he currently serves as chair of the Edmund Burke Foundation in Washington, DC),[5] but his critique of liberalism is useful for a progressive seeking a way out of the circular logic that so dominates discussion of that political position (something that is also true of Burke's critique of revolutionary idealism in his famous 1790 missive on the troubles in France). Indeed, the position is very close to Adrian Pabst's, whose 2016 article and 2021 book-length version of more or less the same argument *Postliberal Politics: The Coming Era of Renewal* I drew upon earlier.

I did all of this in the service of my insistence, pressed throughout this book, that liberalism is one position among many, as opposed to simply synonymous with "just" or "open" or other question-begging caricatures of opposing positions. So even though Hazony spends a lot of time (including in the passage I am about to quote) critiquing institutions that I support, such as the United Nations and the European Union, I cannot help but agree with his statement that "[a]ll these things are pursued by university-trained Lockeans, hardly aware that there might be intelligent and decent persons whose estimation of the worth of such enterprises is very different from their own."[6] It should hardly be controversial in progressive circles to say that this level of

cluelessness about other views of the world has a name: imperialist. That is
the core of Hazony's argument, and of Pabst's as well. Hazony summarizes by
saying that "'[l]iberal internationalism' is not merely a positive agenda for the
erasure of national boundaries and the dismantling of the national states of
Europe and elsewhere. It is an imperialist ideology that incites against nationalism and nationalists, seeking their delegitimization wherever they appear
in Europe, or among nations such as America and Israel that are regarded as
having emerged from European civilization."[7] Again, there is a lot to disagree
with here, such as the tacit indictment of the European Union (which I reject
given how important it has been for sub-state nations in search of the recognition that their states would deny them, such as Scotland and Catalonia,
which I discussed at length in the first chapter on "Federations"), or the tacit
assumption that Israel somehow "emerged from European civilization"
(something that I reject out of a sympathy for Zionism, which depends on
the historical connection of the Jewish people not to Europe but to *the Middle
East* and thus insists that Israel must be seen as a *Middle Eastern country*).

But I think it is important to take seriously Hazony's tendency to speak of
an imperialist liberalism. This is not simply because of the far-too-often-
forgotten fact that most colonial projects (most especially British and French)
were launched in the name of bringing "uncivilized" populations into liberal
enlightenment and which found their highest-level sceptics on the *conservative* end of the political spectrum (this was true of Charles de Gaulle,[8] to
whom we could add Disraeli, who once referred to "accursed colonies which
are like an albatross around our neck"[9]). This sense of an imperialist liberalism is also connected to what I have said about the anti-nationalism so key
to the liberalism of English Canada, among other places: a refusal to acknowledge one's political or national standpoint does not constitute modesty or
something like it, but is rather the highest form of arrogance, in essence assuming that lesser mortals are limited by *their* national identity or *their* ideological standpoints, something that the benevolent liberal globalizer has
"moved beyond."

Furthermore, Hazony's critique of liberalism is not at all far off from the
long haul of a left critique of liberalism, especially of neo-liberalism. I understand that liberalism and neo-liberalism are not exactly synonymous, but the
latter does grow out of the former. What is liberal about neo-liberalism? What
is new about it? Precisely the insight (to its defenders) or the presumption (to
its detractors) that the basic principles of liberalism – the autonomy of the
individual; the scepticism that limitations on that autonomy can be ethically

imposed by larger, collective structures; etc. – can also be applied to far larger structures, such as corporations. To borrow a phrase from Pierre Trudeau, the phrase that is often taken as *the* seminal statement of modern Canadian liberalism, if there can be no place for the state in the bedrooms of the nation, then what place could the state possibly have in its boardrooms?[10] William Davies's 2016 contribution to *New Left Review* is a concise but comprehensive history of neo-liberalism, which he breaks into three phases: combative (1979–89), normative (1989–2008), and punitive (2008 and ongoing). None of these, of course, are consistent with left understandings of economic justice, but nor are any of them inconsistent with the classical liberal understanding of the state's ethical imperative to preserve what Isaiah Berlin famously termed "negative freedom," that is to say the freedom from restraints or pre-determined behaviours. Once the state can simply get out of the way, individual economic actors (be they the sovereign individual of classical liberalism or the sovereign corporation of neo-liberalism) are more "free" to live out their liberty as fully autonomous liberal subjects. This is in vivid contrast to what Berlin described as "positive liberty," of which he wrote in "Two Concepts of Liberty" that "the real self may be conceived as something wider than the individual (as the term is normally understood), as a social 'whole' of which the individual is an element or aspect: a tribe, a race, a church, a state, the great society of the living and the dead and the yet unborn. This entity is then identified as being the 'true' self which, by imposing its collective, or 'organic,' single will upon its recalcitrant 'members,' achieves its own, and therefore their, 'higher' freedom."[11] As the scare quotes indicate, he saw this as a slippery slope towards tyranny. But it is something closer to this sort of "positive liberty" that the left has historically defended, not simply because a few well-placed members of artificially created collectives impose their will on the recalcitrant by trading in illusions of higher or truer ways of being by way of justifying their sinister stratagems. Rather, left political actors have favoured that vision of liberty because they see it as the most likely to offer effective resistance against large forces that wipe out diversity and complexity, often in the service of nothing more meaningful than colonially or imperially inflected economic exploitation. This very much includes political actors and cultural figures this book has dealt with, such as Léopold Senghor, Paulin Hountondji, Noe Jordania, Jawaharlal Nehru, Paul Gilroy, Harry Daniels, or Alanis Obomsawin, all of whom have resisted colonial or imperial forms of domination. It also includes some figures from this book who are closer to the political right, such as Simone Weil, Desmond Fennell, and Roger Scruton; actually, it's those three who have been even more explicit about the need to draw upon the structures of the nation and the "positive freedom" it enables, by way of making a meaningful life in the shadow of rapacious capitalism.

II. Diversity

Having just discussed Yoram Hazony's *The Virtue of Nationalism*, I want to in turn acknowledge the degree to which this book has also been strongly, if again for the most part implicitly, influenced by his "opposite number." I refer there to Yael Tamir, specifically to her 2019 book *Why Nationalism?* released the year after Hazony's work, which I briefly discussed in the introduction. As I explained there, Tamir sits on the other side of Israeli politics from Hazony. She is a former peace-movement activist and has served in different Labour cabinets (she was minister of immigration from 1999 to 2001 and then minister of education from 2006 to 2009). Her sense of nationality centralizes complexity and openness in ways that give the lie to the old chestnut that nations are about nothing more than, to invoke Michael Ignatieff's most famous book, *Blood and Belonging*. The same year that work of Ignatieff's appeared, Tamir wrote in her 1993 study *Liberal Nationalism* of the structure she wished to defend that "[i]t is pluralistic and open, sees national groups as not only a product of history, but also of human will, and broadly follows humanistic tradition."[12] She offered a similar formulation twenty-six years later, writing in *Why Nationalism?* that, "[i]n its prime, nationalism was 'the great equalizer'; it turned subjects into citizens, motivated the construction of an inclusive public sphere, and inspired the creation of a comprehensive education system and a shared language that promoted a fusion of high and low cultures into one national culture to be enjoyed by all members."[13]

The importance of openness and pluralism is too easy to forget when considering nation. This is due in part to the widespread tendency to conflate "nation" with "ethnicity," and resisting that conflation has been a key concern of this book. That is because ethnicity, by its very nature, is not defined by openness at all, but by the basically biological facts of descent. Nations can welcome newcomers and thus change and evolve across time; that is not true of ethnicity, which is no small part of why Paul Gilroy's writings on race (another key influence on this book, again often implicitly) are so hostile towards the concept. I discussed this in the introduction, how he acidly dismissed race's "specious ontologies," writing that "[i]t knits together science and superstition."[14] Nation works differently. A product of modernity, nation is fluid and complex in the manner of so many modern structures, print culture among many others. This, of course, is the real subject of Benedict Anderson's *Imagined Communities*.

Recall that I earlier quoted that book to the effect that "such choruses are joinable in time. If I am a Lett [a Latvian], my daughter may be an Australian."[15] I see exactly what Anderson is getting at, I think it is fundamentally correct, and I acknowledge that it cuts both ways. Midway through the writing of this book, a beloved former student, part of a small group of such *camarades* who had been reading chapters as I completed them, told me that he thought the real subject of this work was whether or not my sons were Métis. I brushed him off at the time, saying that I didn't need a whole book to simply say "no." About a year later, my mother asked a similar question. For her I recounted the conversation my wife and I have had with the boys, which went something like this. They are exactly as Métis as they are Scottish, having one grandparent born and raised in each nationality. Nobody thinks that this makes them Scottish so there's really no reason that it would make them Métis. To follow Anderson, if their grandmother is a Scot, then they are English Canadians. If, when they grow up, one or both decide that they want to live as a Scottish person, their mother and I can, by virtue of their grandmother's British passport and her extensive family network in Scotland, help them out with that: they can move to the UK, settle in Scotland, and after a few years, apply for UK citizenship on their own. People there wouldn't accept them as Scottish at first, but in time, after they'd really made a commitment to that life, for the most part they would. Fundamentally the choice is theirs, but it must be made in a slow and complicated negotiation with the people they wish to live among as compatriots. Either way, it has relatively little to do with ethnicity; Scottish identity, as with all modern nations, is more diverse than that. It is important to my wife and me that the boys understand that for the Métis *exactly the same applies*: if their grandfather, their uncle, and their cousins (all of whom live on Fishing Lake Métis Settlement and have really never lived in any culture other than that one) are Métis, then they are English Canadians. If, when they grow up, one or both decide that they want to live as a Métis person, their mother and I, by virtue of their grandfather's Métis Nation of Alberta card or his nearly lifelong Settlement membership and residency, can help them out with that. People wouldn't accept them as Métis at first, but in time, after they'd really made a commitment to that life, for the most part they would. Fundamentally the choice is theirs, but it must be made in a slow and complicated negotiation with the people they wish to live among as compatriots. Either way, it has relatively little to do with ethnicity; Métis identity, as with all modern nations, is more diverse than that.

My mother, correctly much bolder on such matters than my former student, pushed back at this; surely, she said, one can be African-American without living in Harlem? I didn't really realize it at the time, but she was cutting to the heart of the matter. It has to do with the difference between *race* and *nation*. Most Canadians have the same sense as my mother does, seeing "Métis" basically as a matter of race, in a way that they would not see as true of "Scottish." My wife and I do not; neither, really, do any of the Métis people she grew up with or worked with in the early years of her career when she was a civil servant for the Settlements' government.[16] For them as for us, "Métis" is about *nation*. For my mother the American, whose only substantial experience of Canada is the time she has spent with us over the years, this is totally fine. The Métis are not on the radar screen of Indigenous politics in the United States, so a certain fuzziness about who exactly they are is reasonable.[17] For English Canadians and Québécois this is less fine. The Red River Settlement is a formative part of Canadian history, Louis Riel a key figure in the history of Francophones in North America, and Batoche a turning point for both. Thus for someone born, raised, and/or holding citizenship north of the 49th, being a little fuzzy on whether someone with some/any Indigenous heritage is or isn't Métis is sort of like a person from England wondering if the New Model Army refers to gays and lesbians being allowed to serve in the military.[18]

We have seen this tension between "race" and "nation" throughout this book, very much including chapter 1, devoted to "Ethnos." I argued there for the importance of recognizing a national consciousness in African-diaspora communities, but I think it became quickly evident that this was more than a matter of race or ethnicity. To return to my mother's query about Harlem, George Elliott Clarke clearly believes that yes indeed, you do need to have some connection to *Nova Scotia* in order to really be Africadian (or African Nova Scotian, to use the more widely deployed term). Maybe you don't have to be from Africville or North Preston, but being Africadian is not the same as being a Black person who happens to be resident on Canada's east coast. The Gary conference that *Nationtime* so closely documents was clearly about bringing together African-*Americans* as a nation. Maybe you didn't need to live in Harlem, but Jackson was calling together "the tribes" from California, New York, and Georgia, not from Cameroon, Nigeria, and Ghana. Recent immigrants from those places were certainly includable in that African-American nation, but *primarily* as people who had integrated into *those tribes,* that is to say as people coming from Birmingham, Boston, Minnesota, Mississippi, San Diego, Seattle, Galveston, Gary, or some other part of that federal republic in which they held a citizenship that did not seem able to accommodate their distinct nationality. In this way, Sujatha Gilda and Alan Horn were correct; African-Americans are indeed "archetypically American," *but so is their distinct nationality.* Race certainly figured into Clarke's or Jackson's sense of identity, but *national* identity is what they were defending. Rather than being defined by the insular, backward-looking, and exclusionary conception that Rinaldo Walcott accused Clarke of evincing (and which I discussed in some detail in chapter 1), Clarke's writings on Africadia are a defence of *diversity.* Africadian identity survives being swamped by a homogenizing American Blackness (something that, as I discussed in chapter 1, is a preoccupation of Clarke's, and for very good reasons) in a similar manner to how the Catalan-speaking Andorran identity (population ~80,000) survives being swamped by the stateless but still far more massive culture of Catalonia (population 7.5 million). That kind of diversity, I have tried to argue throughout this book, is protected by *nation.*

III. Solidarity

One figure that the earlier draft of this book I mentioned engaged more with was Máirtín Ó Cadhain. I managed to preserve passing mention of this greatest of Irish-language writers in chapter 4, when I discussed Irish approaches to federalism. But Ó Cadhain is a major literary figure in Irish-language circles and deserves to be more widely known in Anglophone circles. Regularly compared to James Joyce, he is probably most famous for his 1949 novel *Cré na Cille,*[19] something of a *Ulysses* for Irish Gaelic. Where he differed radically from Joyce was in his militancy. A member of the IRA but resident in the Republic (either in the western Irish-speaking villages of Connemara or in Dublin), he spent most of WWII interned in a prison camp in Co. Kildare (which in an address to the Merriman Winter School published as *Páipéir Bhána agus Páipéir Bhreacha* he called "Sibeir na hÉireann," or Ireland's Siberia; Ireland was neutral, and anyone deemed a "combatant" on Irish soil was rounded up).[20] Because he had been active in Irish-language activism since the 1930s, he was also a sort of senior statesman for the aforementioned Gluaiseacht Chearta Sibhialta na Gaeltachta (Gaeltacht Civil Rights Movement) of the late 1960s and '70s (he died in 1970, giving fiery speeches in the rain until almost the very end). Throughout the 1960s he had also been an avid writer of polemics and pamphlets, sometimes in English, sometimes in Irish. Gluaiseacht was not a separatist movement; it was not seeking an independent territory, or a separate nationality for Irish-speakers. It was a movement that sought their full integration into a national culture that claimed to centralize their mother tongue (Article 8.1 of the Irish constitution states, in full, "The Irish language as the national language is the first official language") but in fact marginalized it because, for the most part, the independent State functioned in English. In a word, the movement was seeking to make post-independence Ireland make good on its promises of *solidarity*.

In chapter 4, the first devoted to "Federations," I briefly discussed one key piece of Ó Cadhain quasi-ephemera, a long speech he gave that was posthumously published as the book *Tone: Inné agus Inniu* (Tone: Yesterday and today). That work was a call for a new, renewed understanding of the non-sectarian idealism of Wolfe Tone, son of a Prominent protestant family and himself a deist who was one of the founders and key leaders of the United Irishmen, they of the celebrated rising of 1798 (Tone had spent time in both Paris and Philadelphia). The United Irishmen were devoted to finding a form of Irish solidarity that went beyond Catholic nationalism, although as we will see for Ó Cadhain as for Simone Weil, one did have to go *through* that majority position. By way of synthesizing some of what I want to say about the kinds of solidarity the nation supports, I want to briefly discuss two other ephemeral pieces, works that demonstrate my (no doubt eccentric) belief that Máirtín Ó Cadhain is, intellectually speaking, the Irish cousin that the solidarity-obsessed Simone Weil never knew she had.

The logical starting place for establishing this "family tie" is *L'enracinement* (which, as we saw in chapter 2, is a careful and provocative discussion of what forms of solidarity would define a France reborn after Nazi occupation) and Ó Cadhain's pamphlet *Gluaiseacht na Gaeilge: Gluaiseacht ar Strae?* (which, as we will see here, is about sharpening that form of national identity defined by cross-linguistic solidarity that Gluaiseacht was agitating for). Ó Cadhain's pamphlet was based on a lecture that he gave in Donegal in 1969, a response to the direction of the Irish-language movement; he argued that this had been born as part of the rise of radical republicanism at the end of the nineteenth century but had, over the previous century, lost much of its political edge, much of its quest for a real *solidarity* across the languages of Ireland. The pamphlet is most famous for its declaration that "[t]he Irish language is the recapture of Ireland and the recapture of Ireland is the salvation of Irish. The people's language will save the people"[21] (m.t.). This became a rallying cry for the more radical elements of the language movement, a precise and fiery way to connect the language with the broader strains of Irish Republicanism. Ó Cadhain's semi-religious tone here, his talk of "slánú na Gaeilge" (the salvation of Irish) and the desire to "a shlánós an mhuintir" (save the people) recalls how, as I mention above, Weil saw the Free French movement in spiritual rather than geopolitical terms. She is explicit about this in *L'enracinement*, writing that "[t]he true mission of the French movement in London is, by reason even of the military and political circumstances, a spiritual mission before being a military and political one."[22] In both instances we can see the political imperatives being justified by something that lay beyond the realm of the procedural. The rhetoric on the part of Weil and Ó Cadhain is not exactly messianic, although it contains remnants of the religious sensibilities that would be powerful influences in both France and Ireland. But in both cases, this is complicated. Ó Cadhain shares with Weil an uncompromising form of socialism, one that sees adherence to such principles as a matter of duty. That's exactly how he put it in the *Gluaiseacht ar Strae?* pamphlet, where he writes that "Irish-speaking people have a duty to be socialist"[23] (m.t.). That sense of "dualgas lucht na Gaeilge," the duty of those people of the Irish language, sounds a lot like Weil's assessment (in her 1933 text "Allons-nous vers la révolution prolétarienne?") of the brief to reconcile workers to their work and to their state: "C'est la tache propre de notre generation."[24]

Ó Cadhain was widely known for his anticlerical sensibilities, sensibilities that flowed naturally from a form of Irish socialism that would have as a key part of its analyses the argument that priests had long served as a counter-revolutionary form of authority. But his sensibilities on this front are complicated; in a lecture that he gave in November 1962 to the Irish Soviet Society about his trip to Kyrgyzstan, he opened by saying, "I don't belong to any association nor political party. I am not now nor never was in the Communist party. I am a Christian, a Catholic."[25] The Catholic Church was omnipresent in Irish life because it was a symbol of Irishness (given the Protestant nature of the British Crown), and thus when co-opted it (and of course its priests) served as a singularly effective tool for social control. This sort of co-opted distinctiveness was a big part of what the United Irishmen stood against, and that stance is in turn a big part of the reason for Tone's importance to Ó Cadhain. But as late as 1962 he would still define himself, almost insistently, as a Catholic. Weil would seem to be a study in contrast given the intensity of her religious commitment and the breadth of her religious writings. But as I mentioned above, she never accepted baptism, and there is much in her writing about remaining distant from the institutional church. As late as January 1942 (about a year and a half before she died), she wrote to her father in a letter titled "Hésitations devant le baptême" that "I have not the slightest love for the Church in the strict sense of the word, apart from its relation to all these things that I do love," which she cites as God, Christ, the saints, "the liturgy, hymns, architecture, rites, and ceremonies,"[26] along with the "six or seven Catholics of genuine spirituality whom chance has led me to meet in the course of my life."[27] Really, she is a sort of mirror image of Ó Cadhain: both reluctant to engage the institutional Church as well as unwilling to let go of a sense of somehow belonging to the faith. This is all to say that Ó Cadhain's recourse to images of salvation by way of describing an Irish republic that he sees as worthy of the name is less about the sectarian nationalism so familiar from the northern conflict and more about a desire to imagine a kind of country that is consistent with the revitalized, *reraciné* republic that Weil was sketching out from her London exile. They both saw republics in terms that go beyond matters such as "native rule" and moved instead towards concepts such as "dualgas lucht na Gaeilge" and "taches propres de notre generation." Their goals had little to do with finding better forms of liberal proceduralism; what they were interested in was duty and obligation, not all of which they were entirely comfortable with (especially when it came to Catholicism), as the gateway to solidarity. The fact that both were hostile towards political parties should come as no surprise.

Ó Cadhain's 1964 pamphlet *Irish above Politics* is as radical in spirit as *Gluaiseacht ar Strae?* but the bulk of the pamphlet is given over to more pragmatic concerns of manipulating the party system for the good of the language. Midway through he writes that "I personally could not tie myself to any party machine. As such, I think this is a course that can be acceptable to the most extreme Republican as well as to [the] most extreme Fine Gael person believing in a Gaelic Ireland. The important thing is the priority of belief, of the definiteness if the consequent action."[28] Clearly part of the hostility towards parties here derives from a widespread indifference to the fate of Irish-speakers, especially in the Gaeltacht. But this hostility towards political parties is especially significant in the Republic of Ireland, where, as I mentioned in

chapter 4, politics do not shake out tidily along a "left/right" basis. Party affiliation in Ireland is primarily about *nation* (being based in divisions that go
back to the Irish Civil War, that is to say divisions between those who accepted
the treaty with the UK and those who did not), and at best secondarily about
politics (although this is changing with the recent southern successes of Sinn
Féin, by far the most republican of all Irish parties, which as I mentioned earlier sits with The Left in the European Parliament group). For Ó Cadhain to
reject political parties is also to reject the divisions of the Civil War, basically
in favour of centralizing the language, a position that, as he would argue five
years later in the *Gluaiseacht ar Strae?* pamphlet, is what would lead to a proper
republic. The rejection of parties was thus not only pragmatic but it was, in
an Irish context, *republican* inasmuch as it sought to move beyond the legacy
of the Civil War, that conflict which did *not* create a republic, by centralizing
an issue specific to Ireland herself, in this case the language.

In so doing Ó Cadhain strongly recalls Weil's hostility towards the party
system. She writes in *L'enracinement* in terms that lamented its corrosive effects on solidarity in France's always-unstable but somehow longest-lived
Third Republic. We find there: "Party strife, as it existed under the Third Republic, is intolerable. The single party, which is, moreover, its inevitable outcome, is the worst evil of all. The only remaining possibility is a public life
without parties."[29] Weil had already discussed this matter at length in a 1943
essay called "Note sur la suppression générale des partis politiques." She writes
there, in terms that seem entirely consistent with Ó Cadhain's situation in an
Ireland where parties were important but left/right meant almost nothing,
that "[o]ur republican ideal was entirely developed from a notion originally
expressed by Rousseau: the notion of the 'general will.'"[30] Ó Cadhain was hoping for a "volonté générale" that would support the Irish language and from
that a proper Irish republic; everything else is mere orthodoxy. Indeed, Ó Cadhain's trademark anti-clericism is on display in *Irish above Politics* when he
dismisses the usefulness of voting for any Dublin-based candidate at all: "I
have heard certain clerics say – I forget whether under the pain of mortal sin
or not – that it is the duty of everybody to exercise the vote. Intelligent abstention is also exercising the vote!"[31] Weil, as she is really getting up a head
of steam to denounce political parties, writes that "[w]e must acknowledge
that the mechanism of spiritual and intellectual oppression which character-
ises political parties was historically introduced by the Catholic Church in its
fight against heresy."[32] The imperative for universalism and pluralism means
that republics cannot be controlled literally by a specific church. Although

the Republic of Ireland sometimes seemed to challenge that basic tenet, it was *de jure* the case even there (Article 44.2.2 of the Constitution of Ireland reads, in full, "The State guarantees not to endow any religion"). Ó Cadhain, in rejecting allegiance to political parties, is seeking to expunge the last of that Churchly sensibility, to finally put paid to what Weil describes as "[la] lutte contre l'hérésie,"[33] and move towards a republic that would be, in all senses of the word, Irish, as she wanted one that was more fully French.

That desire to be more fully Irish, more completely French, is what animated both of these great republican writers. Their task was one that was shared by so many of the figures in this book, "les littéraires surtout," to again invoke Gérard Bouchard, but also politicians: Amiri Baraka's mix of Gary (Indiana), the United Nations, and avant-garde poetics; George Elliott Clarke's invocation of "A 'herring choker' Negro with a breath of brine"; Raj Kapoor's Japanese shoes, English trousers, red Russian hat, and Indian heart; Antoni Roviri i Virgili's passionate commitment to federalism, inside or outside of Spain, including from his presidential seat in France; and Eben Hopson's vision of a circumpolar continuity of Indigeneity. All of this leads us back to Charles Taylor, with his emphasis on "we-identities as against merely convergent I-identities, and the consequent role of common as against convergent goods." That sort of solidarity has been what those on the left who have defended the notion of nation have been after.

IV. *Quelle heure est-il?*

Since I began this chapter with topics this book should have covered, I'll end it with titles it could have been given. "Away from the state, towards the nation," which in the last chapter I used to summarize the path of the forward-thinking Inuit, might not have been a bad one. Across as wide a variety of examples of national groups as I can summon – Black people, the French, the Irish, the Georgians, the Indians, New Zealanders, Québécois, the Catalans, the English, the Scottish, the "Ulster British," the Métis, English Canadians, the Mohawk, and the Inuit – I have tried to illustrate the degree to which national consciousness is both highly multifarious and yet also visible in reasonably stable forms, even in our supposedly "postnational" era. As I think has been clear throughout this book's discussion, belief in such an era requires no small amount of faith in liberalism as the defining quality of our globalized politics. I think such faith is an error; my discussion in the introduction of the Anglo-specificity of this tendency puts me in mind of the old joke about the genius of Jerry Lewis: 50 million Frenchmen can't be wrong! What I really mean is that France's political culture is one of many which do not hold much truck with casual use of "liberal" as a synonym for "just." That kind of conflation is an error for a global left which has historically placed its faith in collective action and has been suspicious of the degree to which individualist empowerment has enabled and supported a rapacious capitalism.

"The nation" is certainly not the only collective formation that can serve as a bulwark against this relentless form of globalized neoliberalism: of course we think also of the cohesion that is provided by other elective identities such as religious, professional, and so on. But among such elective affinities, few are both as large and tolerant of diversity as the nation; "religion" scores high marks on the former but low on the latter, with "profession" basically reversing that tally. But "nation," as we see, is both all-encompassing in terms of a near-universal affiliation with it (even stateless people usually have some *national* identity from which they are cut off, usually owing to a lack of documents) and tolerant of diversity (as I hope that my discussions of groups as various as Georgian Muslims, Irish Protestants, and Québécois of Haitian origin have demonstrated).

Part of the reluctance on the part of progressives to embrace "nation" has to do with a lingering suspicion that it is basically an ethnic category, a misconception that liberals worldwide have been keen to encourage. Justin Trudeau's aforementioned talk of Canada as "the first postnational state" is only the most famous recent example of such misrepresentation. For me one of the most moving and simple (and moving because simple) explanation of what a nation is comes from Numa Denis Fustel de Coulanges's pamphlet *L'Alsace est-elle allemande ou française?* (dated 27 October 1870, it is reprinted in his posthumously published 1916 collection *Questions contemporaines*). Defending the French nationality of the people of Alsace[34] from simplemindedly racialist understandings of the people of that place as basically Germanic (and in a way that strongly anticipates Simone Weil's sense of their Frenchness that I discussed in chapter 2), he writes that "[w]hat distinguishes nations is neither race nor language. Men feel in their hearts they are one people when they have a community of ideas, of interests, of affections, of memories, and of hopes. This is what makes a homeland … It may be that Alsace is German by race and by language, but by nationality and affection for her homeland [le sentiment de la patrie], she is French"[35] (m.t.).[36] That shared "present tense" of ideas and affection, joined with a "past tense" of memories and a "future tense" of hopes: this is a language in full, the language of nation. It is a language that allows us to make all manner of statements to all manner of people, in a way that other languages of collectivity – to follow Roger Scruton, in a way that those pronouns of tribe or religion – do not.

While chapter 1, devoted to "Ethnos," acknowledges that there is some crossover between ethnicity and nation, these are basically different categories. Even within that first chapter, partially by way of confirming Paul Gilroy's thorough critique of that "specious ontology" which "knits together science and superstition," I think within that "ethnos" we saw serious kinds of internal diversity, best illustrated by Jesse Jackson's moving lament that "[t]he tribe in Mississippi does not know the tribe in California. The tribe in New York does not know the tribe in Georgia." Readers will recall that he goes on to say that "[t]he African diaspora has trumpeted its summons to all of the tribes, with a question put forth by Brother Baraka, whose answer alone legitimises our collective existence." That sort of collective existence, made up of many "tribes" in the sense that Jackson deploys the term, has a name: nation. For a global left that seeks to oppose the atomizing individualism of an imperialist liberalism that refuses even to acknowledge itself as one path among many, let alone to consider that maybe it's not the best way to move through the world, and for the international community of progressives in search of a means to oppose the pitiless forces of a homogenizing capitalism that fuels what (as I discussed in the introduction) G.K. Chesterton called "the brute powers of modernity,"[37] I hope that I have been able to show what time it is. It's nation time.

Notes

INTRODUCTION

1 Tilly, "Citizenship, Identity, and Social History," 5.

2 Orwell, *The Lion and the Unicorn*, 64.

3 Orwell, *Notes on Nationalism*, 1.

4 Ibid., 2.

5 Ibid.

6 Fennell, *The Changing Face of Catholic Ireland*, 40.

7 Edgerton, *The Rise and Fall of the British Nation*, 221.

8 Ibid., 334.

9 Ibid., 386.

10 Two years after Edgerton's book came out, Brian Russell Graham published a much shorter and more polemical call for what he called a "shared national culture." His book suffers from the same problem as Edgerton's inasmuch as it reads "national" as "British," something that is in terms of geography deeply confusing (Northern Ireland, which is simply not part of the island of Great Britain, gets only a handful of words from Graham) and in terms of vocabulary rather obfuscating (like so much of the left in the UK, Graham sort of whistles past the question of whether England, Scotland, and Wales are nations).

11 Brennan, "The National Longing for Form," 45.

12 Nehru, *The Discovery of India*, 565.

13 Miley, *Self-Determination Struggles*, 22.

14 Ibid., 154.

15 Ibid., 115.

16 *Twilight of Democracy*'s most egregious example of this is when Applebaum recalls an interview with the political scientist Karen Stenner: "Over a crackly

video link between Australia and Poland, she reminded me that the 'authoritarian predisposition' she has identified is not exactly the same thing as close-mindedness. It is better described as simple-mindedness: people are often attracted to authoritarian ideas because they are bothered by complexity" (106). That is pretty rich coming from someone who published, in the November 2021 issue of *The Atlantic*, an article about right-wing eastern European governments titled "The Bad Guys Are Winning."

17 Horowitz, "Conservatism, Liberalism, and Socialism in Canada: An Interpretation," 158.

18 Chesterton, *The Napoleon of Notting Hill*, 17.

19 He is particularly instructive as a case study in the danger of assuming that "conservative" is basically synonymous with "whatever the US Republican party is up to right now." He wrote in a *New York Times* op-ed dated 18 July 2018 that Donald Trump "is a product of the cultural decline that is rapidly consigning our artistic and philosophical inheritance to oblivion. And perhaps the principal reason for doubting Mr. Trump's conservative credentials is that being a creation of social media, he has lost the sense that there is a civilization out there that stands above his deals and his tweets in a posture of disinterested judgement."

20 Applebaum, *Twilight of Democracy*, 8.

21 Nehru, *Discovery of India*, 515.

22 Scruton, *Philosopher on Dover Beach*, 325.

23 Scruton, *England and the Need for Nations*, 16–17.

24 Tilly, "National Self-Determination as a Problem for All of Us," 32.

25 Tilly, "States and Nationalism in Europe 1492–1992," 137.

26 Tilly, "Time of States," 279.

27 Nairn, *Faces of Nationalism*, 26.

28 Crenshaw, "Mapping the Margins," 1297.

29 Nairn, *Faces of Nationalism*, 181.

30 Pelletier, *Au Québec, c'est comme ça qu'on vit*, 40.

31 This is the brother of Thomas Symons, whose watershed report on Canadian Studies I will also discuss in chapter 5.

32 Symons, *Combat Journal for Place d'Armes*, 99.

33 Morton, *The Canadian Identity*, 131.

34 Such critique has also been prominent in a lot of recent UK political writing. On that front, see especially Adrian Pabst's 2021 book *Postliberal Politics: The Coming Age of Renewal* and his more precise 2016 article in *Political Quarterly*. In the latter he writes that "[a] new oligarchy seeks to centralise power, concentrate wealth and manipulate public opinion by using media spin, closing down

debate and ironing out plurality. Their aim is to entrench a system to which there is no alternative" (91).

35 Locke, *Political Writings*, 178.

36 Ibid., 183.

37 Tilly, "Political Identities in Changing Polities," 619.

38 Antoine Schwartz's recent survey in *Le Monde Diplomatique* of young liberal polemicists in France is especially clear on this matter. Recalling the reflexively defensive position of most French liberals, he mentions, in a casual tone which reveals the degree to which he is following what he sees as a broad consensus, that "for its followers, liberal doctrine suffers from unpopularity, what with its image as a bourgeois ideology that is keen to mask the brutal interests of the world of business, all of which has led to it being vigorously attacked, as much from the left as the right" (20).

39 Applebaum, *Twilight of Democracy*, 160.

40 Jean-Numa Ducange's recent book *Quand la gauche pensait la nation* is a more focussed historical study of the nineteenth-century German-speaking *belle époque*, and so makes for an enlightening companion to Benner's analyses. His overall argument is that "[t]he German-language workers' movement … offers particularly interesting cases which trace a path for a grass-roots and progressive version of the nation" (13, m.t.). Writing of his work's contemporary resonance, Ducange concludes by saying that "[b]uried in the archives, press and journals of another time, as well as in scattered longer works, these debates and propositions have been forgotten. It is time to rediscover these traditions and experiences" (280, m.t.). I am strongly in agreement there.

41 Benner, *Really Existing Nationalisms*, 245.

42 Ibid., 253–4.

43 Having said that, the way that the liberal American press has recently dealt with the American right's interest in Viktor Orbán's Hungary has been distinctively patronizing, and largely serves as an unwitting confirmation of Benner's critique. The key examples are Elizabeth Zerofsky's article in the 24 October 2021 issue of the *New York Times Magazine* and Andrew Marantz's in the 4 July 2022 issue of the *New Yorker*.

44 Macpherson, *Democratic Theory: Essays in Retrieval*, 184.

45 Ibid., 87.

46 Taylor, *Varieties of Secularism in a Secular Age*, 319.

47 Macpherson, *Democratic Theory*, 201.

48 Ibid., 172.

49 Moyn, *Liberalism against Itself*, 176.

50 Jessop, *The State*, 27.

51 Ibid., 241.

52 Stepan, Linz, and Yadav, "The Rise of 'State-Nations,'" 52.

53 Ibid., 53.

54 Anderson, *Imagined Communities*, 6.

55 Aquin, *Blocs erratiques*, 81 / *Writing Quebec*, 29, translation modified slightly.

56 Gilroy, *Against Race*, 53.

57 The title is clearly an allusion to the Bob Marley song of that name, which has the lyrics "If you are the big tree / We are the small axe / Sharpened to cut you down." It is also clearly an allusion to Paul Gilroy's 1993 book *Small Acts*, itself something of an homage to the Marley song. McQueen was a student of Gilroy's at Goldsmith's in London, and Gilroy has a consultant credit on each of the *Small Axe* films. I will discuss the anti-racist conceptualization of Englishness that Gilroy offers in *Small Acts* in chapter 5.

58 Younge, "What the Hell Can I Call Myself Except British?," 10.

59 Kimberlé Crenshaw explained this more concisely as far back as 1991. Citing Catherine MacKinnon's *Feminism, Marxism and the State*, she writes, "I capitalize 'Black' because 'Blacks, like Asians, Latinos, and other 'minorities,' constitute a specific cultural group, and as such, require denotation as a proper noun' ... By the same token, I do not capitalize 'white,' which is not a proper noun, since whites do not constitute a specific cultural group. For the same reason I do not capitalise 'women of color" (1244n6, italics hers). For reasons that are less clear, she also capitalizes "Brown": "They were concerned, apparently, that the data would unfairly represent Black and Brown communities" (1253); "After all, it has always been someone's wife, mother, sister, or daughter that has been abused, even when the violence was stereotypically Black or Brown, and poor" (1260).

60 Tall Bear, "The Political Economy of Tribal Citizenship," 74.

61 For a more traditionally academic discussion also see ibid.

62 Baker, *Effect of Cherokee Nation v. Nash and Van v. Zinke*, 3.

63 Anderson, *Imagined Communities*, 145.

64 Bouchard, *Les nations savent-elles encore rêver?*, 26.

65 Kymlicka, *Multicultural Citizenship*, 29–33.

66 Ibid., 177.

67 Ibid., 32.

68 Bouchard, *Les nations savent-elles encore rêver?*, 363.

69 Tamir, *Why Nationalism*, 166.

70 I feel similarly about the title of James Kennedy's 2013 study *Liberal National-*

isms: *Empire, State, and Civil Society in Scotland and Quebec.* I wrote about this book at length in the *Literary Review of Canada* (June 2013), so I will not repeat my arguments here. Suffice to say that this is a highly focussed historical study (it covers the end of the nineteenth to the beginning of the twentieth centuries) that admirably traces the emergence of more-or-less progressive (Scotland) but also more-or-less communitarian (Quebec) forms of nationalism. I'm not at all convinced that this is consistent with the ideals of liberalism, but I certainly agree with the main argument, which is that these earlier movements served as models for the civic nationalism that would emerge in the post-wwii period.

CHAPTER ONE

1   Willemen, *Looks and Frictions*, 209.

2   Berger and Bostock, *Return to My Native Land*, 45, *inter alia.*

3   Ibid., 47, 73, *inter alia.*

4   Fanon, *Peau noir, masques blanques*, 88.

5   Fanon, *Black Skin, White Masks*, 89.

6   For admirably sceptical French-language coverage of the blow-up around this issue of "le mot en n" prompted by the CRTC's cautioning of Radio-Canada, see Étienne Paré's front-page, above-the-fold story in the 10 July 2022 issue of *Le Devoir.*

7   For linguistic discussion of both of the words I have in mind, see Marie Treps's 2005 article in *Communications*, 225. She also discusses the word "nègre" on pp. 218–19 in ways that are far more nuanced than anything one will find in Quebec or Canadian media or academic discourse. Also see her more popular-idiom 2020 book *Maudits mots: La fabrique des insultes racistes.*

8   Wacquant, "Resolving the Trouble with 'Race,'" 76–7.

9   Patterson, "Four Modes of Ethno-Somatic Stratification," 76.

10 Ibid., 79.

11 Gilda and Horn, "Caste, Race – And Class," 16.

12 Gilroy, *The Black Atlantic*, 31.

13 Brière, "Black Soul," 126.

14 Césaire, *Discours sur le colonialisme*, 89. This passage is in the "Discours sur la Négritude" part of the text, which is not included in Joan Pinkham's 1972 translation *Discourse on Colonialism.*

15 This version of the "tigritude" quip is from an unsigned review in *Time Magazine*, 17 November 1967, of two of his recent plays: "Soyinka, 33, has no complexes

of self-consciousness about being an African. While fond and proud of his Nigerian heritage, he has small use for such concepts as 'negritude.' 'Does a tiger feel his tigritude?' he asks" (52).

16 Having said this, it is important to note that *Présence africaine* maintained an English edition for many years, and that Soyinka himself published a great deal in the journal, both in that edition and in French translation.

17 Gilroy, *The Black Atlantic*, 211.

18 Ibid., 33–4.

19 Gilroy, *Against Race*, 92.

20 On 27 February 2023, the American online magazine *Slate* published "The New Black Film Canon." This was a list made up of 75 films in total. Can you guess which country no fewer than 63 of these films came from?

21 Senghor, *Ce que je crois*, 138–9.

22 Césaire, *Discours sur la Négritude*, 88.

23 Younge, "What the Hell Can I Call Myself Except British?," 10.

24 Senghor, *Les fondements de l'africanité*, 54.

25 Césaire, *Cahier d'un retour au pays natal*, 24.

26 Césaire, *Return to My Native Land*, 29.

27 Césaire, *Cahier d'un retour au pays natal*, 35.

28 Césaire, *Disourse on Colonialism*, 77–8.

29 *Nationtime – Gary* is the title that comes up in the first moments of the film. That is also the title under which MOMA premiered the restored version of the film on 22 January 2020 as part of its "To Save and Project" festival of preserved films. The film's US distributor has released it both on DVD and via streaming platforms under the title *Nationtime*.

30 Woodard, "Imamu Amiri Baraka (LeRoi Jones)," 11. The ellipses are Woodard's. The source for the quote is the *Newark Evening News*, 24 June 1968, p. 8.

31 Woodard, "Imamu Baraka," 47–8.

32 Ibid., 48.

33 Ibid.

34 Frazier, "The Congress of African People," 145.

35 Senghor, *Poésie complète*, 1165.

36 Moore, "William Greaves," 272.

37 Scruton, *England and the Need for Nations*, 17.

38 The introduction to the *Indiana Historical Society's National Black Political Convention Collection, 1972–1973* (collection # SC 2643) notes that "[t]he steering committee consisted of Gary mayor, Richard G. Hatcher, U.S. representative Charles C. Diggs, and Imamu Baraka (also known as poet LeRoi Jones)" (2).

39 Woodard, "Imamu Baraka," 50.

40 For a summary, see Benjamin Ivry, "Setting the Record Straight on Amiri Baraka," *The Forward*, 20 January 2014, https://forward.com/culture/191239/setting-the-record-straight-on-amiri-baraka/.

41 Baraka, *It's Nation Time*, 7.

42 Ibid., 23–4.

43 This is something of a post-facto work, edited by Bret Wood out of footage shot by Hurston and audio taken by Norman Chalfin, both of which are now held in the Margaret Mead / South Pacific Ethnographic Archives Collection. Hurston was a classic example of an ethnographer who used the film camera as a kind of notebook, shooting massive amounts of footage over the years. She was not a filmmaker, though; her footage really exists only as raw images. Since the 1990s it has "popped up" at semi-regular intervals in various scholarly and cinephile milieux, and is also scattered across a number of compilation DVDs (these include Kino-Lorber's *Pioneers of African-American Cinema* and *Pioneers: First Women Filmmakers*, where *Commandment Keeper Church* can be found). A properly comprehensive collection of her fieldwork footage is a real "sujet à approfondir" for film studies.

44 Bouchard, *Les nations savent-elles encore rêver?*, 26.

45 Clarke, *Fire on the Water*, 13.

46 In his *Fire on the Water* introduction, Clarke recalls how many of the Black Loyalists left in frustration for Sierra Leone, where to this day there are settlements that maintain a strong sense of connection with Nova Scotia. There is likewise a strong sense in the Africadian community of a connection to Sierra Leone.

47 The text is widely available, perhaps most easily so at the African American Registry's site devoted to "The Merikins," another name for the refugees of the War of 1812: "The Merikins Community Is Established," accessed 23 April 2024, https://aaregistry.org/story/the-merikins-community-established/.

48 Robin W. Winks's seminal 1971 study *Blacks in Canada* offers wide-ranging discussion of the Black presence in Canada over the long term. In an appendix titled "How Many Negroes in Canada?" he writes that "[a]t no time have Negroes constituted more than five percent of the population of any one province" (484). This appendix includes summaries of census data going back to Nova Scotia in 1767; for the year 1931 Winks reports that Black people accounted for about 0.3 per cent of the Canadian population, that is to say 32,127 people out of a population of approx. 11,442,559 (487). Contrast this with Statistics Canada's 2023 estimation (offered on its website to commemorate Black History Month)

that "[t]he Black population now accounts for 4.3% of Canada's total population." It seems only fair to also point out that Clarke has been highly critical of
Winks's work, especially in the introduction to *Fire on the Water*, wherein he
writes that "[o]ne can almost detect in Winks' voice the tone of those who bulldozed Africville into the Bedford Basin in the name of liberalism, integration,
and progress" (14–15).

49 Daniel McNeill's 2005 article, largely based on the research for his MA at Dalhousie University, goes into these tensions between immigrant and indigenous
Black communities in some detail. One interviewee recalls that "[d]espite (or
perhaps because of) their wish to 'uplift' indigenous Blacks, immigrants can
seem condescending towards those who 'wallow' in poverty through attachment
to the demolished Halifax neighbourhood of Africville" (64). Another interviewee, however, laments how "these people in the diaspora are beginning to believe that Africans are expendable" (67).

50 MacLeod, "'The Little State of Africadia,'" 244–5.

51 Clarke, *Fire on the Water*, 14.

52 Ibid., 15.

53 Clarke, *Eyeing the North Star*, xvi.

54 Clarke, *Odysseys Home*, 10.

55 Ibid., 28–9.

56 Ibid., 46.

57 Ibid., 34.

58 Ibid.

59 Clarke, *Eyeing the North Star*, xxii.

60 NourbeSe Philip, *Frontiers*, 21.

61 Clarke, *Fire on the Water*, 23.

62 NourbeSe Philip, *Frontiers*, 19.

63 Ibid.

64 In 2004, Senegal's Doudou Diène, the UN special rapporteur on contemporary
forms of racism, racial discrimination, xenophobia, and related intolerance,
visited Canada and wrote a report on "Persons of African origin, particularly
Loyalists' descendants in Nova Scotia." The report stated in part: "In consultation with communities of African origin or their descendants, the Government
of Nova Scotia should re-examine the conditions of their relocation, particularly from Africville, taking particular account of their situation regarding
human rights and economic and social conditions with a view to granting them
reparation." UN Report E/CN.4/2004/18/Add.2, 1 March 2004.

65 Clarke, *Black*, 20.

66 Scargill et al., *A Dictionary*, 333.

67 Clarke, *Whylah Falls*, 35–6.

68 Clarke, *Odysseys Home*, 155.

69 Ibid., 187.

70 Walcott, *Black Like Who? Writing Black Canada*, 16–17.

71 Ibid., 147.

72 Ibid., 20.

73 It was based on his Du Bois lectures, given at Harvard University in 1994.

74 Hall, *The Fateful Triangle*, 158.

75 Ibid., 161.

76 Walcott, *Black Like Who?*, 15.

77 Clarke, *Odysseys Home*, 157.

78 Ibid.

79 Clarke, *Odysseys Home*, 187. He writes, "Walcott himself tacks towards a version of liberalism" in the original McGill version of the essay (4).

80 Walcott, *Black Like Who?*, 18.

81 Clarke, *Odysseys Home*, 27.

82 Here I feel an obligation to point out that Clarke has defined himself as "Afro-Métis" for some time, having stated in public fora that is he is "a card-carrying Afro-Métis of the Eastern Woodland Métis Nation Nova Scotia." He made that statement, for instance, in a *Toronto Star* op-ed of 16 January 2020, in response to the controversy around his publishing (on his website as Parliamentary Poet) work by a man who had been convicted of murdering an Indigenous woman in Regina (the CBC's coverage of this can be found here: Alex Soloducha, "Canadian Poet George Elliott Clarke Cancels Regina Lecture after Controversy over Convicted Killer's Poetry," CBC news, 3 January 2020, https://www.cbc.ca/news/canada/saskatchewan/pamela-george-u-regina-george-elliott-clarke-1.5413590). Clarke has been active in a movement to recognize the "Afro-Métis" of the Atlantic region. Details can be seen at http://afrometis.ca, which showcases his photo prominently. Both the Métis National Council and the Assembly of Nova Scotia Mi'kmaq Chiefs have been adamant that they do not recognize the presence of a Métis nation in Quebec or the Atlantic region. In 2018 they issued a joint Memorandum of Understanding making their shared position on this matter clear, to wit, "The Parties are concerned about individuals claiming Métis identity and declaring the presence of Métis Nations in the Province of Nova Scotia." The full document has been published in *Aboriginal Policy Studies* 8, no. 1 (2019): 115–16. For a thorough debunking of the claims of the "Eastern Métis," see Daryl Leroux, *Distorted Descent: White Claims to Indigenous Identity*; on the

Eastern Woodland Métis Nation, see 217, where Leroux also mentions that "[o]ver 23,000 people in Nova Scotia (or about 2.5 per cent of the province's population) identified as Métis in the 2016 Canadian census, while only 830 (or 0.09 per cent) did so in 1996." Also see Leroux's 2021 chapter "Outlining the Origin of 'Eastern Métis' Studies." Clarke has in turn critiqued Leroux and others' understandings of Métis identity in a 2022 article published in *Zeitschrift für Kanada-Studien*.

83 It is only fair to point out that it was the federal Conservatives who first enshrined multiculturalism in *law*, with the Brian Mulroney–era *Multiculturalism Act* (1988).

84 Walcott, *Black Like Who?*, 118.

85 Ibid., 60.

86 Clarke, *Odysseys Home*, 8.

87 Hountondji, "Producing Knowledge in Africa Today," 7.

88 Appiah, *In My Father's House*, 172.

89 Ibid., 92.

90 Ibid.

91 Ibid., 162.

92 Ibid., 177. Appiah doesn't give any bibliographical citation for this quote, so I honestly don't know under what circumstances Achebe said this. Google searches of excerpts from the quote only bring up sites that are connected to *In My Father's House*.

93 Achebe, *Home and Exile*, 3–4.

94 Ibid., 18.

95 Orwell, *The Lion and the Unicorn*, 5.

96 Appiah, *The Ethics of Identity*, 244.

97 Ibid.

98 Deneen, *Why Liberalism Failed*, 71.

99 Appiah, *The Lies That Bind*, 76.

100 Anderson, *Imagined Communities*, 145.

101 Appiah, *In My Father's House*, 180.

102 Hountondji, "Que peut la philosophie?," 67.

103 Hountondji, *African Philosophy*, 117.

104 Ibid., 129.

105 Appiah, *Cosmopolitanism*, 121.

106 Hountondji, "Que peut la philosophie?," 48.

107 Ibid., 52.

108 Senghor, *Poésie complète*, 19. The translation is Gary Wilder's, found in his *French Imperial Nation State*, 271.

109 Hountondji, *The Struggle for Meaning*, 83.

110 Ibid.

CHAPTER TWO

1 Taylor, *Philosophical Arguments*, 192.

2 Todorov, *La vie commune*, 84.

3 Ibid., 187.

4 Planes, *El petit llibre de Catalunya-Nord*, 23.

5 This is basically the argument I made in much greater depth in the long introduction that I wrote for the special section I edited of *Dalhousie French Studies* 113 (2019) devoted to "La France catalane." I argued there that the Catalans of France should be understood as *French*, and that this should not be taken as a challenge to that country's republicanism but rather as the logical product of its aspirations towards universalism.

6 Taylor, *Democracia Republicana / Republican Democracy*, 74.

7 Ibid., 78.

8 Deneen, *Why Liberalism Failed*, 29.

9 He wasn't the only head of government to take an interest. Upon meeting the Hungarian prime minister as part of a conference celebrating the translation of *Why Democracy Failed*, Deneen said that "I was very much impressed by Viktor Orbán's personality, intellect, the way he sees the world and explains what he thinks. He told me that he spends one day a week with reading. It's not only me he has met but also Rod Dreher or Yoram Hazony … I wonder how many other political leaders of the world find time for this." Deneen made those remarks in the context of his meeting with Orbán in the online magazine *Hungary Journal*, whose article about the rendez-vous has since been taken down. Rod Dreher offered his account of meeting Orbán (and spoke in similar terms) in his blog for *The American Conservative*, which is as of this writing in spring 2024 available as Rod Dreher, "Victor Orban among the Christians," *American Conservative*, 9 September 2019, https://www.theamericanconservative.com/viktor-orban-among-the-christians/.

10 I don't feel the same way at all about his follow-up work, which came out as I was doing final revisions on this book. *Regime Change: Towards a Postliberal Future* (2023) reads basically like a mass-market "political book" with a few dashes of classical, early mediaeval, and Renaissance political theory (in fairness,

its most widely quoted formulation about using "Machiavellian means to achieve Aristotelian ends" [167 *inter alia*] relies on a very wide reading of Machiavelli's body of work, something that has been largely ignored by a number of liberal critics who seem to have relied on their vague undergraduate memories of *The Prince* and thus taken "Machiavellian" as a synonym for "kind of sneaky and manipulative"). *Why Liberalism Failed*, on the other hand, is the inverse: at heart a serious work in political philosophy that also comes with an agreeable polemical edge. Having said that, it is worth noting that towards the end of *Regime Change*, Deneen writes that "[i]n the heat generated by contemporary divides, it is unsurprising that the liberal origins and progressive commitments to nationalism have been altogether forgotten or supressed by the various parties" (219). I agree wholeheartedly with the "progressive" piece of that formulation (one reason I do not like *Regime Change* is that unlike *Why Liberalism Failed* it plays a bit fast and loose with the distinction between "liberal" and "progressive"). This book is my effort to contribute to an undoing of such forgetting and suppressing.

11 That is the title of his 1993 book about the rise of nationalism in Europe and North America (there is also a chapter on Kurdistan). I respect the work that Ignatieff has done as a journalist, sometimes reporting from "hot" conflict zones. I also reject almost all of his analyses of nationalism, which he by and large presents in the form of patronizing appeals to a benevolent liberalism. The contemporary writer he is closest to comes from the right rather than the centre of such liberalism: Anne Applebaum. Much of what I said in the introduction about her work on eastern Europe could also stand for Ignatieff.

12 The *Quebec Act* (1774) basically brought Catholics into the fold of British North American life by making it possible for them to hold office, own property, proclaim Catholicism publicly, etc. Its UK Parliamentary fiche states that it "also preserved the seigneurial system of land tenure and French civil code." It is what arguably led to the creation of a publicly funded Catholic school system in Canada, an institution whose roots in attempts to keep the loyalty of Catholics in a changing British North American system are too easily forgotten, as is how progressive the *Quebec Act* was within the imperial context of the day. Consider, in contrast, the Irish penal laws, which remained in effect until Catholic emancipation in 1829. Ollivier Hubert and François Furstenberg's 2020 anthology *Entangling the Quebec Act* is a wide-ranging survey of the Act's effects; for a discussion of the Irish component of the Act, see Aaron Willis's chapter "Rethinking Ireland and Assimilation: Quebec, Collaboration, and the Heterogeneous Empire."

13 Deneen, *Why Liberalism Failed*, 82.

14 Public funding of Catholic schooling continues in Quebec, but in 1998, the province's school system was changed from a split based on Catholic and Protestant boards to one based on the divisions everyone knew those religious affiliations were stand-ins for: Francophone and Anglophone.

15 Taylor, *Philosophical Arguments*, 203.

16 "Ulster" is often taken to be a synonym for "Northern Ireland." This is a misunderstanding that I feel an ongoing obligation to correct whenever I encounter it. The island of Ireland has four provinces; these are historical entities, of no significance in the current Irish political regime. Ulster, the northernmost such province, has nine counties. Six of those counties make up Northern Ireland; three of them – Donegal, Monaghan, and Cavan – are part of the Republic of Ireland. I suppose I have a personal stake in this inasmuch as my Irish ancestry is partially connected to Co. Cavan and I have spent a fair bit of time studying the Irish language in Co. Donegal (if asked, I always say that I speak the Ulster dialect of Irish). Although it's basically sentimental, I feel genuinely invested in Ulster; at the same time I have relatively little experience of Northern Ireland (I've been to Belfast and Derry and had one particularly interesting trip to the Loyalist stronghold of Lurgan, but that's about it). Unionists and loyalists also tend to use "Ulster" in what reads to me as an attempt to downplay the artificiality of Northern Ireland, whose boundaries were drawn with the specific goal of creating a sustainable Protestant (and thus presumably unionist) majority. I don't consider myself a unionist when it comes to Ireland, but I can recognize that there were reasonable arguments for drawing the boundaries in this way. Habitually saying "Ulster" when you mean "Northern Ireland" doesn't give the impression that you understand or subscribe to those reasonable arguments.

17 Kearney, *Postnationalist Ireland*, 37.

18 Ibid.

19 "Gaeltacht" refers to areas in the Republic of Ireland that have been identified as at least 80 per cent Irish-speaking and are subsidized by the government with the aim of keeping them that way.

20 By which I mean Irish Gaelic, whose endonym is "Gaeilge." In Ireland, people generally call this language "Irish." To say "Gaelic" is generally to refer to Scottish Gaelic (Gàidhlig), which is about as close to Irish as Spanish is to Italian: more or less mutually comprehensible by fluent speakers, but by no means the same language. Irish is a mandatory subject in all twelve years of the Republic of Ireland's national school system, so it is rare to encounter someone from the Republic who has genuinely no knowledge of it (although it is common to encounter people from the Republic who insist that they remember no more

of the language than they do of trigonometry). Bona-fide mother-tongue speakers account for about 1 per cent of the population and are mostly found in Gaeltacht communities.

21 The constitution of Ireland has long guaranteed citizenship to anyone born on the island of Ireland. Article 2 used to read, in full, "[t]he national territory consists of the whole island of Ireland, its islands and the territorial seas." This article was one way that the independent State denied the legitimacy of the partition of Northern Ireland, and many unionists considered it highly offensive. Following the Belfast/Good Friday Agreement of 1998, Article 2 now reads, in part: "It is the entitlement and birthright of every person born in the island of Ireland, which includes its islands and seas, to be part of the Irish Nation. That is also the entitlement of all persons otherwise qualified in accordance with law to be citizens of Ireland." In 2004 the voters of the Republic amended Article 9 (part of the constitution that deals with "The State") to the effect that "Notwithstanding any other provision of this Constitution, a person born in the island of Ireland, which includes its islands and seas, who does not have, at the time of the birth of that person, at least one parent who is an Irish citizen or entitled to be an Irish citizen is not entitled to Irish citizenship or nationality, unless provided for by law."

22 Nairn, *Faces of Nationalism*, 133.

23 Weil's reputation as a philosopher was built almost entirely on essay-length material. Although there are a number of books under her name, none were published during her lifetime (1909–43). Her most famous works of religious philosophy, for instance, *La Pesanteur et la grâce* and *Attente de dieu*, first appeared in 1947 and 1950, respectively.

24 Sontag, *Essays of the 1960s & 70s*, 53.

25 Weil, *Need for Roots*, 191.

26 "… la transformation de la France libre en France combattante …"

27 Barré, "Simone Weil," 1176.

28 Sontag, *Essays of the 1960s & 70s*, 54.

29 Moi, "I Came with a Sword," 7.

30 Weil, *L'enracinement*, 99 / *Need for Roots*, 74–5; translation modified slightly.

31 "And as you know, there's no such thing as society. There are individual men and women and there are families. And no government can do anything except through people, and people must look after themselves first." She first made that statement to *Women's Own* in 1987; it was reproduced by *The Guardian* when she died: "Margaret Thatcher: A Life in Quotes," *The Guardian*, 8 April 2013, https://www.theguardian.com/politics/2013/apr/08/margaret-thatcher-quotes.

32 This is the subject of a longstanding critique from Thomas Flanagan, who has argued that on-reserve Indigenous people are unable to use their homes as capital, collateral, etc., and are thus marginalized by a mandatory adherence to collective ownership, an economic approach that has nothing to do with Indigeneity as such. See esp. *Beyond the Indian Act: Restoring Aboriginal Property Rights* (2nd ed., 2011), which he co-authored with Christopher Alcantara and André Le Dressay.

33 For more on the socialist roots of Alberta's Métis movement, see Murray Dobbin, *The One and a Half Men*. The title refers to the name a priest gave to Métis of the 1885 resistance at Batoche, whom he saw as dangerously radical: half Indian, half white, half devil.

34 Weil, *L'enracinement*, 129.

35 Weil, *The Need for Roots*, 99.

36 Ibid., 161.

37 Ibid., 112.

38 Ibid., 127.

39 My high school French teacher Christine Serna was born in Strasbourg, and her mother tongue was not French. I vividly remember her fondness for Germanic culture, but I remember just as vividly her fierce French patriotism. That was brought on by memories of wwii-era German occupation, when the pressure on families like hers to think of themselves as basically German must have been intense.

40 Jones, *Socialism in Georgian Colors*, 283.

41 Lee, *The Experiment*, 234–5.

42 This was the front-page story of the 30 June 1919 issue of the *Bulletin géorgien d'informations*, a four-page weekly newsletter published from Paris. We find the use of the term "République de Ciscaucasie" in its pages.

43 "Acte d'indépendance de l'Arménie unifiée," *Bulletin géorgien d'informations*, 10 July 1919.

44 It is no surprise that Kautsky would take an interest in Georgia, a "small nation" that had emerged into independence with a social-democratic government. Jean-Numa Ducange writes that "it is noteworthy that since at least 1910, Kautsky could be seen as being at the heart of the left of the [Austrian Social Democratic] party on national questions" (85, m.t.). Kautsky is a key character in Ducange's *Quand la gauche pensait la nation*, a book that is (as I discussed in the introduction) a focussed historical study of the German-speaking left in the *belle époque* but one with a lot of resonance with my discussions here.

45 Jones, *The Making of Modern Georgia*, 4.

46 "Président du gouvernement" is the term one generally sees in the aforementioned French discourse. For reasons that will become clear in this paragraph,
that is clearly meant to be read as "the one who presides over the government."

47 Matsaberidze, "The Georgian Democratic Republic," 142.

48 Ibid., 153.

49 Ronald Asmus's 2010 book *A Little War That Shook the World: Georgia, Russia,
and the Future of the West* is a highly readable history of the latter conflict,
written by a former US diplomat with the usual biases but a detailed sense of
the statecraft at play. Stephen Jones's 2006 anthology *War and Revolution in the
Caucasus: Georgia Ablaze* is a broad survey of the conflict. Jones has spent time
in Abkhazia as a consultant for the UN Development Programme.

50 The Israeli filmmaker Dover Kosashvili has made a number of films about this
community, such as *Late Marriage* (2001), about a young man who wants to
marry an older divorcée against his traditionalist family's wishes; and the French
co-production *Cadeau du ciel* (2003), a bawdy heist film about baggage handlers
at the Tel Aviv airport.

51 I think of the book as a bit dated because it is optimistic about Saakashvili.
Jones writes of him at one point, "[a]n educated pro-Western disciplinarian, he
would feel comfortable in US Tea Party circles. Yet alongside the promotion of
military-patriotic values and tough policies on crime, he advocates progams of
civic integration and decentralization more liberal than national minority policies in many European countries" (23). In those days Saakashvili did indeed
seem to be a real breath of fresh air, a Columbia-educated idealist keen to bring
Georgia into the European and western orbits. But matters turned dark during
his second term, with the spectres of corruption and state violence returning
under his oversight. Andrew Cockburn's 2023 dispatch from Georgia for the
London Review of Books, which I commend to those looking for a concise brief
on the situation of contemporary Georgia, notes that "[b]y 2012, Georgia had
the largest prison population per capita in Europe, and police torture was widespread" (41). Facing many criminal charges in the country of which he was
president until 2013, Saakashvili emigrated to Ukraine, where, in May 2015, he
was made a citizen and then, a day later, made governor of Odessa by Ukraine's
then-president Petro Poroshenko. This also fell apart, with Saakashvili resigning
a year later in the name of fighting corruption and initiating a stranger-than-
fiction *parcours* across eastern Europe that finally ended with his return to
Georgia, where he has since been confined in a series of locked hospital facil-
ities. He currently faces numerous charges in Georgia, in addition to the charges

of corruption, abuse of power, and conspiracy to commit assault that he was convicted of in 2018.

52 Jones, *Georgia*, 226.

53 Kandelaki, "The Democratic Republic of Georgia," 168.

54 Ibid.

55 Matsaberidze, "The Georgian Democratic Republic," 152.

56 Berber, *The Death of Communal Liberty*, 11.

57 Kearney, *Postnationalist Ireland*, 37.

58 Matsaberidze, "The Georgian Democratic Republic," 153.

59 Welt, "A Fateful Moment," 223.

60 Matsaberidze, "The Georgian Democratic Republic," 186.

61 Cited in Mamoulia, *Les combats indépendantistes*, 39.

62 Jones, *Georgia*, 44.

63 Sometimes this was explicit, as with Edgard Milhaud's 1926 pamphlet *Le Géorgie, la Russie, et la S.d.N.* The tone there is sometimes exasperated, with a section titled "La Russie et la Société des Nations" opening with the question "Que faire?" since the USSR would not officially join the league for another eight years.

64 The property was formally given as a gift from France to the Georgian state in November 2016.

65 Mamoulia, *Les combats indépendantistes*, 29.

66 Jordania, *Difficultés socialistes*, 189.

67 Jones, *Socialism in Georgian Colors*, 227.

68 Jordania, *Difficultés socialistes*, 24.

69 Lee, *The Experiment*, 119–20.

70 Jordania, *Difficultés socialistes*, 101.

71 Ibid., 189.

72 Matsaberidze, "The Georgian Democratic Republic," 152.

73 Tudor, *The Promise of Power*, 207.

74 For a broad and sympathetic survey of Nehru's socialist evolution (and Congress's along with him), see Jag Mohan's 1975 article "Jawaharlal Nehru and His Socialism." Perry Anderson's 2012 book *The Indian Ideology* is a thoroughgoing critique of this kind of idealism. I have more or less the same opinion of this assessment as the one he makes of British culture in *English Questions*, which I will discuss in chapter 4: I can see that he is on to something, but the tone and the overall assessments seem to me uncharitable, a sensibility that is driven by a wider (and at times blinding) antinationalism that is typical of the English left

(as opposed to their "opposite numbers" in Scotland or Wales). I am more persuaded by the critiques offered by Tariq Ali in his 1985 book *An Indian Dynasty: The Story of the Nehru-Gandhi Family*, wherein he explains the degree to which Indian and the politics of the Congress Party emerged in a way that was designed to benefit a relatively small inner circle, much of which was connected by family ties.

75 Ganti, *Bollywood*, 12.

76 Tudor, *The Promise of Power*, 21.

77 Ibid., 42.

78 Nehru challenges this position at some length in *The Discovery of India* (which I discuss below), wherein he argues that the term derives from the Persian word for people west of the Indus river, with the religion bearing the name "Hindu" springing up later. He writes that "'Hindi' has nothing to do with religion, and a Moslem or a Christian Indian is as much a Hindi as someone who follows Hinduism as a religion. Americans who call all Indians Hindus are not far wrong; they would be perfectly correct if they used the word 'Hindi'" (76). I can see the point that Nehru is making here, and it is closely connected to the sort of multicultural, multiconfessional republic that the Congress Party has always been committed to. But in twenty-first-century India I suspect that this point would be lost on someone using "Hindi" as a descriptor of all India, and that someone using "Hindi" in this way would more likely be taken for a Hindu chauvinist, something that is all but explicit in the policies of the currently ruling BJP.

79 Part of this refusal to see the Indian state as legitimate is driven by Pakistan's claim on Jammu and Kashmir, India's only majority-Muslim territory. Once a state with a special devolved status, it was relegated to a "Union Territory" as part of a wave of repression unleashed by Mr Modi's BJP government in 2019.

80 Weil, *Need for Roots*, 90.

81 Ibid., 92.

82 Nehru, *The Discovery of India*, 81.

83 Chatterjee, *Mother India*, 44.

84 Willemen and Rajadhyaksha, *Encyclopaedia of Indian Cinema*, 112.

85 This is from Rushdie's aforementioned program notes for the 2001 Telluride Film Festival. That year he was the guest director, and part of his contribution to the event was to bring both *Shree 420* and a program he called "A Mehboob Anthology." He also translates the lyrics in his famous 1982 essay "Imaginary Homelands" (11).

86 Khan, "The Song Picture Man," 28.

87 Kabir, *Guru Dutt*, 166.

88 McCarthy, *On the Contrary*, 239.

89 Deneen, *Why Liberalism Failed*, 132.

CHAPTER THREE

1 The 1987 television show *Frank's Place*, starring Tim Reid as Frank Parrish, a former history professor running a restaurant in New Orleans called Chez Louisiana, offered sensitive portrayals of Creole culture. The episode "Frank Joins the Club" (directed by Neema Barnette) centred on Frank being recruited for a social club for Black men, only to discover that he would be the token dark-skinned member. "Look, man, I'm not about to become the only Black in a Black club! That's going a little too far, don't you think?" he says at the end. At one point one of the waitresses even explains the difference between Creole and creole. *Frank's Place* lasted only one season; it is one of the unheralded masterpieces of 1980s American television.

2 Available from the United Nations' Digital Library at https://digitallibrary.un.org/record/689516?ln=en.

3 The award was an odd one in this case, because Kunuk had already enjoyed a long career as a video artist. This work was mostly made up of short pieces, but also included the 6½-hour, thirteen-part series *Nunavut* (1994). What he had not done before 2001 was make a feature-length work shot on 35mm film that was released theatrically. Even *Atanarjuat* only barely fit this description; it was originally shot on HD video and then blown up to 35mm, and rather than checking in at the usual length of 1½–2 hours, it ran 176 minutes.

4 I saw this film as part of writing the catalogue essay for the Merata Mita retrospective at the 2000 Taos Talking Pictures Festival. I was enormously impressed with it at the time, and thought of it as part of a lineage of global-south engagements with the legacy of colonialism and state formation brought on by the counter-celebrations of Columbus in 1992. This was begun by Patricio Guzmán's unjustly obscure *La Cruz del Sur* (1992); I saw this during my first year of working for the Philadelphia Festival of World Cinema. Perhaps *Te Pito o Te Henua: Rapa Nui* brought that period of engagement to a close, as filmmakers re-evaluated for the now fully globalized twenty-first century. Both films have largely disappeared from easy public access; *La Cruz del Sur* is no longer distributed by Icarus Films, as it was during those Philadelphia days, and I have never known of another chance to see *Te Pito o Te Henua: Rapa Nui*. Thus neither is in this book's works cited list.

5 Tunks, "Asia & Pacific," 16.

6 Anaya, *Report of the Special Rapporteur*, 1.

7 Possibly in answer to such criticism, Tunks notes that "[f]ive written versions of the treaty covenant entered into by Maori and the Crown now exist: four in English and one in Maori," going on to say that the Maori text was "signed by 512 Maori chiefs on behalf of their people" (15).

8 Jackson, "Changing Realities: Unchanging Truths," 124. She gets harsher as she moves forward, finally concluding that "[b]y promoting its new found awareness and sensitivity, the Pakeha law deludes many Maori into believing that it will indeed protect their rights and acknowledge the validity of their law, their authority, and their place in this land. Of course it will do no such thing" (128–9).

9 Anaya, *Report of the Special Rapporteur*, 2.

10 That is most clearly the case with the recent revisions to the *Metis Settlement Act* (1990) that the government of Alberta pushed through, over the objections of the Settlements and of their General Council, in 2021 (its official name is the *Métis Settlements Amendment Act* [2021]). These revisions reduced the size of the General Council executive as well as the councils of individual Settlements, mandated the charging of levies for utilities and infrastructure, etc. For details see the CBC's coverage of the passage of the act here: Janet French, "Alberta Métis Settlements Challenging Provincial Legislation in Court," CBC News, 28 July 2021, https://www.cbc.ca/news/canada/edmonton/alberta-m%C3%A9tis-settlements-challenging-provincial-legislation-in-court-1.6120299.

11 Valmaine Toki's 2017 article in the *Journal of Māori and Indigenous Issues* is a thorough survey of the legal and political issues that lead up to this process of constitutional reform.

12 The Independent Working Group on Constitutional Transformation, *Report of Matike Mai Aotearoa*, 104.

13 Ibid., 105.

14 Tunks, "Asia & Pacific," 18n34.

15 Dumont, *The Vigil of Quebec*, 34 / *La vigile du Québec*, 67–8; translation modified slightly.

16 Bouchard and Taylor, *Fonder l'avenir*, 119.

17 Bédard, "La République de Marcel Chaput," 296.

18 Available, via the Quebec newspaper *Le Devoir*, here: https://www.ledevoir.com/documents/pdf/constitution_martine_ouellet.pdf.

19 Parenteau, *L'indépendance par la République*, 146.

20 Ibid.

21 Ibid., 78n38.

22 For a critique of Chevrier's book and the Quebec republican position generally, see Gary Caldwell's 2015 article. Caldwell's critique of the Quebec republican position (one that is hardly surprising given that Chevrier dismisses him early in the book as one of "quelques conservateurs nostalgiques de la bonne vieille sagesse constitutionelle britannique" [23]) is utterly distinct from the one that I will offer going forward, even when he discusses the place of the Crown. Having said that, he is right when he says that "[Chevrier's] rhetoric has the effect of suggesting that 'monarchy' equals 'submission to the Crown'" (65). That is a simplification whose polemical value is clear (and thus part of what Caldwell calls the "republican temptation") but which betrays a naïve view of how Canada's constitutional monarchy serves to bind otherwise distinct nations together. I will explain this as I move forward into a discussion of treaties with Indigenous nations.

23 Chevrier, *La République québécoise*, 23.

24 Bock-Côté and Godbout, *Le tour du jardin*, 144.

25 Bastien, *The Battle of London*, 317.

26 Ibid., 311.

27 De Villers, *Multidictionnaire de la langue française*, 1105.

28 Michel de Certeau's 1975 book *Une politique de la langue* (written with Dominique Julia and Jacques Revel) is a comprehensive treatment of the meaning of this massive project of identity formation via language, focussing on the work done by Abbé Gregoire to survey the situations of various patois.

29 Ducharme, *Le concept de liberté*, 87. What Ducharme writes is "avait apporté des institutions libres aux Canadiens." As I mention above, in the context of the early nineteenth century, the word "Canadiens" broadly referred to Francophones north of the 49th; Anglophones would have been widely known as "les Anglais" or "les Britanniques."

30 These were originally published on the first two pages of the 21 February 1834 issue of *The Vindicator*, a Montreal newspaper with strong Irish affiliations. Quebec's Bibliothèque et archives nationales have produced a digital copy of this edition, available here: https://numerique.banq.qc.ca/patrimoine/details/52327/4202681. For an explanation of the newspaper's significance with special attention to the Patriotes context, see James Jackson's article "The Radicalization of the Montreal Irish: The Role of *The Vindicator*."

31 Durham, *The Report of the Earl of Durham*, 218.

32 Bouchard, *Genèse des nations et cultures du Nouveau Monde*, 105.

33 Bouchard, *The Making of Nations and Cultures in the New World*, 82.

34 Ibid., 83.

35 Ibid., 85.

36 The lead-up to the fiftieth anniversary of this event has inspired a great deal of scholarship on its cultural impacts. See Rhona Richman Kenneally and Joanne Sloan's 2010 anthology *Expo 67: Not Just a Souvenir*, Janine Marchessault and Monika Kim Gagnon's 2014 anthology *Reimagining Cinema: Film at Expo 67*, and Erin Hurley's *National Performance: Representing Quebec from Expo 67 to Céline Dion*.

37 The aforementioned Jacques Godbout had made the argument in his 2000 film *Traitre ou patriote?* that his uncle, Adélard Godbout, laid the groundwork for the Quiet Revolution when he was Quebec's premier during the wartime Liberal government of 1939–44.

38 Rudin, *Making History in 20th Century Quebec*, ix.

39 Couture, *Paddling with the Current*, 104.

40 Couture, *La loyauté d'un laïc*, 137.

41 Lévesque had been a cabinet minister in the Liberal government led by Jean Lesage, but left the party in 1967, sitting briefly as an independent. He forged the Parti Québécois out of a merger of his Mouvement Souveraineté-Association with the more militant Rassemblement pour l'Indépendance Nationale (RIN), both of which ceased to exist in 1968. The PQ fared badly in the 1970 elections, but became the official opposition in 1973 (albeit with only 6 of 110 seats) and then won their first government in 1976. Oddly, the date that René Lévesque won his first term as an MNA in 1960 (that is to say, the day that Lesage's Liberals were elected in Quebec, thus beginning the "Quiet Revolution") was the same day that the *Quebec Act* (1774) received Royal Assent: 22 June (see chapter 2, note 3). This is also the date that the Cinémathèque canadienne became the Cinémathèque québécoise in 1971.

42 Dumont, *The Vigil of Quebec*, 48–9.

43 Dumont, *La vigile du Québec*, 94.

44 Weil, *Need for Roots*, 74.

45 I rush to point out that "laïcité" does not simply mean secular. French has a perfectly good word for that: "séculaire." Rather, it means something like "acting in the manner of the laity, rather than the clergy." The French sociologist of culture Nathalie Heinich does a way better job of explaining this when she speaks of "*laïcité*, which does not mean 'secularism,' but rather, the abstention of any commitment to religion in the civil arena" (484). In terms of "secular," on the other hand, Charles Taylor has been most eloquent and precise on this term, writing in *Modern Social Imaginaries*, "Modernity is secular, not in the frequent, rather loose sense of the word, where it designates the absence of religion, but

rather in the fact that religion occupies a different place, compatible with the sense that all social action takes place in profane time" (194). His magnum opus *A Secular Age* proceeds from this definition.

46 Lévesque, *Option Québec*, 186.

47 Ibid., 187.

48 For a detailed proposal for a sovereign Quebec to bypass Canada altogether and join the Nordic League, see Luc-Normand Tellier, *Le Québec, état nordique* (1977). Jane Jacobs argues that Quebec is well-served by a comparison with Norway and its path to independence; see her 1979 Massey Lecture, published as *Canadian Cities and Sovereignty Association*. Both are basically following the Lévesque schema for independence.

49 Ibid., 190.

50 Ibid., 161.

51 Ibid., 173.

52 Mills, *A Place in the Sun*, 5.

53 Ibid., 88.

54 In this context it is worth noting that the majority language of Haiti is not French but Kreyòl ayisyen; French is, however, an official language there. Until about twenty years ago French would have been the exclusive language of education throughout Haiti, although that is changing. Benjamin Hebblethwaite's recent article in *Foreign Policy* lamented the slowness of this change, noting that "it is estimated that roughly 5 to 10 percent of Haitians are functionally bilingual in French and Haitian Creole. However, 100 percent of Haitians speak Haitian Creole, and, more critically, 90% of Haitians speak only Haitian Creole." He concludes with the following indictment: "People ask why Haitians struggle. The answer is simple. The Francophone Haitian state works against the Haitian Creole nation."

55 Bouchard, *Interculturalism*, 29.

56 Bouchard, *L'Interculturalisme*, 52.

57 Bouchard, *Interculturalism*, 32.

58 Poliquin, *René Lévesque*, 107–8.

59 Ibid., 91.

60 The *Jay Treaty* (1794) is explicitly designed to make this optional, inasmuch as it allows Indigenous people to enter the US or Canada by showing a status card or like identification. In principle this allows Indigenous people to be mobile on the continent of their Indigeneity without needing to formally adhere to either US or Canadian citizenship. In practice Indigenous people have a lot of difficulty exercising this treaty right, which in the US is linked to "blood quantum"

as a matter of policy. I discuss this in more detail in chapter 6, where I will draw on work by Audra Simpson and Ian Kalman on the Mohawk.

61 In English it is known as *The Agreement Respecting a New Relationship between the Cree Nation and the Government of Quebec* (2002).

62 Ibid., 42. The official English-language version of the text can be found here: https://www.legisquebec.gouv.qc.ca/en/document/cr/m-35.1.2,%20r.%201.

63 Chevrier, *La République québécoise*, 101.

64 In my limited experience, this kind of discourse is prominent among Irish immigrants to Canada and Quebec. I think they are acting on a generally admirable tendency to see in the cause of Indigenous peoples (and to a much lesser extent of Quebec nationalism) echoes of their own history with the Crown. But the Ulster Plantation does not have some equivalent of the numbered treaties; relations between northern Protestants and the "native Irish" whom they came to dominate were never governed by anything remotely like the Treaties of Peace and Friendship that to this day define settler-Indigenous relations in Canada's Atlantic region. I have recently observed a similar tendency on the part of Irish in New Zealand to assume that in the fullness of time, Kiwis will come to their senses and dump the monarchy and all other traces of their British history. Again, the gesture towards solidarity is admirable, but the tendency to ignore the clear historical differences (and, most importantly, the contemporary significance of those differences) is a problem. The lack of Indigenous political actors calling for an abolishment of monarchical ties alongside of these Irish immigrants is notable. Anti-monarchist activists should ask themselves why neither the Inuit Tapiriit Kanatami, the Assembly of First Nations, nor the Métis National Council are joining in their calls for the end of such practices as an oath to the Crown for legislators or new citizens.

65 Indian Chiefs of Alberta, "Foundational Document: Citizens Plus" (a.k.a. "The Red Paper"), 189. The *White Paper* was republished in full in the first issue of *Aboriginal Policy Studies*; the *Red Paper* appeared, in full, in the journal's second issue (both were published in 2011).

66 Bellegarde, "Crown-First-Nations Treaty Relationships," 23.

67 Ibid., 26.

68 Cuthand likely has Barbados in mind here. The CBC's coverage of that country's recent transformation into a republic was led by Jackson Weaver's story of 2 December 2021, which explains UBC law professor Gordon Christie's argument that "[i]f Canada were to transition to a republic tomorrow ... these treaties would likely be honoured in the same way as before – when one government supplants another, they inherit the treaties and agreements their predecessor made." The

phrase "would likely be honoured in the same way as before," common to much republican discourse in Canada, flows from an optimism whose source is opaque to me. The only other historical experience of a North American country becoming a republic after breaking ties with the British Crown is the United States, and their history of treaties "honoured in the same way as before" is, *ahem*, less than reassuring. See Jackson Weaver, "Barbados Just Cut Its Ties with the Queen. Should Canada Follow Suit?," 2 December 2021, CBC News, https://www.cbc.ca/news/world/barbados-canada-1.6270496.

69 Cuthand, "First Nations' Connection to Crown Endures," all quotes A9.

70 Tully, "The Crisis of Identification," 87.

71 He seems to have in mind here the creation of the province of Manitoba in the wake of the first Riel Resistance in 1870 and the emergence of the Métis Settlements of Alberta out of the ashes of the *Ewing Commission Report* (1934) right up to the *Alberta-Settlements Accord* (1989) and the *Metis Settlements Act* (1990), all of which I discuss in chapter 5.

72 I will discuss this in chapter 6.

73 Tully, *Public Philosophy in a New Key, Volume 1*, 226.

74 Éric Bélanger et al.'s 2018 book *The National Question and Electoral Politics in Quebec and Scotland* is the most wide-ranging survey I know of in English, although it is a work of highly descriptive political science. I discuss it in more detail in the next chapter, devoted to "Federations." In French the pace-setting work has been done by Stéphane Paquin; see his *La revanche des petites nations. Le Québec, l'Écosse et la Catalogne face à la mondialisation* (2001) and *Paradiplomatie identitaire en Catalogne* (2003).

75 *Scotland's Future: Your Guide to an Independent Scotland*, 22. The document more or less repeats this formulation in a section that also explains that it is not unusual for independent countries to share a monarch. "On independence Scotland will be a constitutional monarchy, continuing the Union of the Crowns that dates back to 1603, pre-dating the Union of the Parliaments by over one hundred years. The position of Her Majesty The Queen and head of state will form an intrinsic part of the constitutional platform in place for independence in 2016" (353).

76 The document explains this in its Q&A section: "How is this different from the existing position in the UK? Under current arrangements sovereignty – supreme authority – in the UK lies with 'the Crown in Parliament,' rather than the people. In practice this means that the Westminster Parliament has ultimate power to do anything that it decides, including to overrule the Scottish Parliament on any matter" (548).

77 For wholly unsympathetic coverage of this presence, see Philip Authier's article in the 16 September 2014 edition of the *Montreal Gazette*, "Quebec Sovereigntists Flock to Scotland to Witness Referendum." Authier recalls there how "Marie-Victorin MNA Bernard Drainville was in Scotland last summer, saying he returned 'pumped.' He said the PQ can learn a thing or two from the Scots about being clear in its sovereignty vision." Needless to say, nobody mentions the Crown even once.

78 The Independent Working Group on Constitutional Transformation, *Report of Matike Mai Aotearoa*, 104.

79 Tunks, "Asia & Pacific," 18n34.

CHAPTER FOUR

1 As I mention in the introduction and discuss later in this chapter and in the previous chapter, Tully has also been a serious contributor to debates about federalism and minority nationalism in Canada. The key book on this matter is probably 2008's *Public Philosophy in a New Key Volume I: Democracy and Civic Freedom*. Here he engages with many of the same issues dealt with by Charles Taylor in his work on federalism, nationalism, communitarianism, and liberalism, which I discussed in the introduction. Tully is noteworthy, though, for his head-on engagement with issues of Indigenous governance, to which he devotes an entire section. I also discussed his sense of the significance of the treaty relationship with the Crown in the last chapter.

2 Gagnon and Laforest, "The Moral Foundations of Asymmetrical Federalism," 101.

3 Ibid., 102.

4 I allude here to Pierre Perrault's very odd 1982 film, known in English as *The Shimmering Beast*.

5 Laforest, *Un Québec exilé dans la federation*, 267.

6 Brian Smith's 2022 article is consistent with Bastien discusses, but offers far more details on the personalities involved with this tension between a Trudeau-led federal government keen to push the new constitution through Westminster and provincial government figures who were trying to slow it down. In addition to serving as a negotiator, Smith was the attorney general of British Columbia from 1983 to 1988.

7 Bastien, *The Batttle of London*, 48.

8 Laforest, *Un Québec exilé dans la federation*, 146.

9   He also uses this formulation in his 2007 article "L'exil intérieur des Québécois dans le Canada de la Charte," 64.

10 Gagnon, *La Raison du plus fort*, 162.

11 Ibid., 98.

12 Beiner, *Philosophy in a Time of Lost Spirit*, 73.

13 Gagnon, *La Raison du plus fort*, 207.

14 Mitchell, *Devolution in the UK*, 218.

15 Henderson and Wyn Jones, *Englishness*, 46.

16 Parekh, *The Future of Multi-Ethnic Britain*, 38.

17 Bragg, *The Progressive Patriot*, 343.

18 For a summary of the dust-up, see Aamna Mohdin and Mattha Busby, "John Cleese Criticised for Saying London No Longer an English City," *The Guardian*, 29 May 2019.

19 Gilroy, *Small Acts*, 79.

20 Henderson and Wyn Jones, *Englishness*, 3.

21 Orwell, *The Lion and the Uniorn*, 29.

22 Ibid., 78.

23 Niven, *New Model Island*, 122.

24 Ibid., 122.

25 Ibid., 123.

26 Laffin and Thomas, *The United Kingdom: Federalism in Denial*, 90.

27 Ibid.

28 For a broad summary of the situation, see David Torrance's briefing report for the House of Commons library, *The Crown Dependencies*, wherein he writes that "[t]he Crown Dependencies are not part of the UK but are self-governing dependencies of the Crown" (5).

29 Mitchell, *Devolution in the UK*, 197.

30 Ibid., 197–8.

31 Ibid., 198.

32 Colley, *Britons*, 383.

33 Scruton, *England*, 49.

34 Anderson, *English Questions*, 68.

35 Nairn, *The Break-Up of Britain*, 282.

36 I discussed this matter of a Marxist approach to nationalism in the introduction, partially via Erica Benner's 1995 book *Really Existing Nationalisms* (revised 2018). I can summarize her overall critique of those who understand Marx as inherently anti-nationalist by recalling that she writes, "the prescriptive content of

Marx's early conception of 'nationality' appears considerably more radical than that of other democratic and republican concepts of the nation that have drawn on the legacies of the French and American revolutions" (34).

37 Elliot, *Scots and Catalans*, 10.

38 Ibid.

39 Kendle, *Federal Britain*, 59.

40 McCaffrey, "Isaac Butt and the Home Rule Movement," 79. For a more recent discussion also see Colin W. Reid, "Isaac Butt."

41 Pacificus, *Federalism and Home Rule*, xlix–l.

42 Nairn, *Break-Up of Britain*, 249.

43 Ibid., 250.

44 Ibid., 253.

45 Ibid., 209.

46 Ibid., 210.

47 Ibid., 210.

48 Bélanger, *The National Question*, 73.

49 Larner and Wyn Jones, "Progressive Home Rule," 236.

50 Ibid., 239.

51 Brennan, "The National Longing for Form," 57.

52 Fennell, *Heresy*, 178.

53 The Republic of Ireland's two historically dominant parties, Fine Gael and Fianna Fáil, are both centre-right. Fine Gael is more or less Christian-Democratic and was formed by people on the (victorious) pro-Treaty side during Ireland's Civil War of 1922–23. Fianna Fáil currently sits with the liberal Renew Europe group in the EU parliament and was originally formed by people who fought on the other (losing) side of the Civil War because they rejected that Treaty, a rejection that was mostly based in opposition to the partition of the island of Ireland and the acceptance of the status of "Irish Free State" rather than a full-blown republic (which, as I mentioned in my discussion of the Commonwealth, only came about with the *Republic of Ireland Act* [1948]).

54 They key text was his manifesto "Iosrael in Iarchonnachta," or Israel in West Connacht. This was published in the Irish-language newspaper *Inniu* in 1969. He wrote there that "Irish-language learners with trades and skills will go to Connemara, and they will make a 'New Israel' there … Many Irish learners must begin, through the colonies they establish in Connemara with the local people – alongside them – to issue a call from the West to the Irish both at home and abroad, as well as to the government (the *kibbutzim* provide an example)" (9, m.t.).

55 The back page of Fennell's 1972 pamphlet *A New Nationalism for the New Ireland*

states that "Comhairle Uladh seeks the establishment of Dáil Uladh – A Parliament of Ulster – within a New Irish Republic restructured with strong regional governments. In addition Comhairle Uladh – Council for Ulster – promotes co-operation with the Civil Disobedience Campaign in the North, endeavours to co-ordinate the relief of distress and suffering in that area, and works for the release of all political prisoners."

56 Fennell, *Towards a Greater Ulster*, 5.

57 Ó Cadhain, *Tone*, 129.

58 Ibid.

59 Kearney, *Postnationalist Ireland*, 37.

60 Fennell, *Beyond Nationalism*, esp. 176–82.

61 Fennell, "The Federation of Man 1," in ibid., 8.

62 Ibid.

63 Ibid.

64 In 1971 Sinn Féin (Kevin Street, also known as Provisional Sinn Féin, which is basically the version of the party we have today) published a short booklet called *Éire Nua: The Social and Economic Programme of Sinn Féin*, which called for a basically socialist (and explicitly anti-EEC) approach to Irish governance and economy. In 1972, the party published a short addendum in the form of a pamphlet called *Peace and Justice*, which called for a federal approach based on Ireland's historical four provinces. In his 1995 article Fennell writes about Republican Sinn Féin, a different and more extremist enunciation than the aforementioned Provisionals, saying that "[i]n 1989–90, in the booklet *Éire Nua: A New Democracy*, this party affirmed, with additional detail, the four-province federal policy, thereby placing it once more on the table of Irish politics" ("Solutions to the Northern Ireland Problem," 14).

65 Fennell, *The Revision of Irish Nationalism*, 31.

66 Fennell, "Sticking Together Two Partitioned Areas," 8.

67 Ibid.

68 He admits that this is a rough estimate, and it is debatable whether that would have been true of a nine-county Ulster that included Donegal, Cavan, and Monaghan.

69 For a particularly grumpy (although enjoyably on-the-nose) example of this tendency, see his 1993 essay "Getting to Know Dublin 4," part of his 1993 collection *Heresy*.

70 New Ireland Forum, *Report of Proceedings*, 34.

71 Ibid.

72 Fennell, "Solutions to the Northern Ireland Problem," 8.

73 O'Leary, *Making Sense of a United Ireland*, 158.

74 Ibid., 165.

75 Walker, *The Idea of the Union*, 70.

76 An endnote to Bassett's text in *The Idea of Union* also reads, "Although he believes Ireland should cultivate closer ties with the UK after Brexit, Dr. Bassett is not a unionist" (104).

77 Bassett, *The Idea of the Union*, 103.

78 Neill, *The Idea of the Union*, 370.

79 Gagnon, *La Raison du plus fort*, 207.

80 The parliament of Northern Ireland was officially opened by King George V on 22 June 1921.

81 Joan i Marí, *Els Països Catalans*, 150.

82 Today Catalan is spoken as a mother-tongue by about a quarter of the Sardinian city's 45,000 inhabitants.

83 Fennell, "A New Look at Federation," 8.

84 Pi y Margall, *Las Nacionalidades*, 87.

85 Barton, *A History of Spain*, 193–4.

86 This is the official translation, available at https://www.boe.es/legislacion/documentos/ConstitucionINGLES.pdf.

87 Stepan, Linz, and Yadav, "The Rise of 'State-Nations,'" 53.

88 Prat de la Riba, *La nacionalitat catalana*, 125.

89 Costa, *Cuba i el Catalanisme*, 33.

90 Ibid., 43.

91 The book is written in a pre-standardization Catalan, thus "polítich" as opposed to "polític."

92 Ibid., 111.

93 Junqueras, *Els catalans i Cuba*, 163.

94 As of May 2024, the PSOE was looking for coalition partners, but trouble was clearly ahead. The left party Comuns Sumar is agnostic on independence, but its support would not lead to a majority. The other unionist parties are on the right.

95 As I mentioned in the introduction, post-Franco Catalan nationalism has tended to be centre-right, until recently dominated electorally by a "Pujolist" coalition (named for Jordi Pujol, whose party Convergència Democràtica de Catalunya emerged in 1974, the year before Franco died, and quickly become the "big tent" party for Catalans). To return to a Quebec analogy, the Pujolist wing of Catalan nationalism looks a lot like a version of the Coalition Avenir Québec

that has been pushed towards actual separatism (something that the Pujolists were not in favour of until well into the twenty-first century).

96 Rovira i Virgili, *Nacionalisme i Federalisme*, 197.

97 Ibid., 199.

98 Ibid., 149.

99 Rovira i Virgili, *Escrits de l'exili*, 150.

100 Rovira i Virgili, *Viatge a la URSS*, 40.

101 Ibid., 81.

102 Rovira i Virgili, *L'Estat Català*, 51–2.

103 Ibid., 52.

104 Joan i Marí, *Els Països Catalans*, 51–2.

105 Canovan, *The People*, 41.

106 Pi y Margall, *Las Nacionalidades*, 89.

CHAPTER FIVE

1 Daniels, *We Are the New Nation*, 13.

2 Ralston Saul, *A Fair Country*, 1.

3 When I wrote the first draft of this chapter in autumn 2021, the Carrie Bourassa affair was unfolding at the University of Saskatchewan, my home institution. Bourassa was a professor running a large, federally funded Indigenous health institute, and claimed on various occasions to be Métis and Anishinaabe and to have a Tlingit grandmother, only to be revealed by the CBC (on 30 October 2021) as having no Indigenous ancestry at all. Since 2015 or so this sort of thing has happened at regular intervals in both the US and Canada. In the US it is often a matter of people (such as Senator Elizabeth Warren) claiming to be "part Cherokee." In Canada, the more common problem is people claiming to be "Métis," often on the basis of a single ancestor buried deep in a family tree. I discuss this in greater detail below when I engage with the notion of "Métis as mixed" so vigorously rejected by scholars such as Chris Andersen. I will also discuss it in the conclusion to this book as it pertains to the Mohawk and people with vague, blood-line-connected and ultimately liberalism-inflected senses of belonging to that nationality.

4 Ajzenstat, *The Once and Future Canadian Democracy*, 87.

5 This was completed by the Société Historique Métisse after de Trémaudan's death; there is a note to this effect in the book's appendices (402). Calling this group the "Old Wolves," Jean Teillet notes that they "decided to publish their

own history of the Métis Nation. The historical committee began to take sworn
declarations from Métis survivors, the men still alive who had played key roles
in the Red River Resistance of 1869–70 and the North-West Resistance of 1885.
There are affidavits taken in 1909, and twice in 1929 the committee visited
Batoche [Saskatchewan], the site of the last battle of the North-West Resistance.
Virtually the whole town came to their community meetings. They hired
Auguste de Trémaudan to be the author of their history" (6).

6 De Trémaudan, *Histoire de la nation métisse dans l'ouest canadienne*, 188.

7 Ibid., 192.

8 Dubois, *Constitutional Politics in Multinational Democracies*, 29.

9 De Trémaudan, *Histoire de la nation métisse dans l'ouest canadien*, 12.

10 Ibid., 152.

11 Duval, "The Catholic Church and the Formation of Metis Identity," 66.

12 Harry Daniels is important to my discussions here because he was so invested in
federalism, a real federalism, as the way forward for the Métis. I am aware of
criticisms of his legacy, including those around his tendency to speak of Métis-
ness as an identity that is blood-borne, something that a more fully realized
treatment of these issues would engage with. Suffice it for now to say that I take
Jennifer Adese's point, made in her 2016 article, that "Daniels and the NCC
[Native Council of Canada] were not considered the voice for Métis through
constitutional negotiations in the eyes of either the MNC [Métis National Coun-
cil] or Canada. An attempt to privilege his view of Métis over that of others,
such as [Clément] Chartier [at the time of patriation the vice-president of the
Association of Métis and Non-Status Indians of Saskatchewan and later to be
the president of both the Métis National Council and the Métis Nation of Sas-
katchewan], is problematically limited" (15). Any discussion that is only one part
of one chapter is indeed going to be limited, as this one is, problematically or
not. A more expansive discussion would indeed dig more deeply into Chartier's
understandings of Métis identity, including his efforts to reach out to places
such as Nicaragua during the 1980s, when he was the president of the World
Council of Indigenous Peoples. For discussion of his time in Central America,
see John Weinstein's *Quiet Revolution West*, 106–10.

13 Daniels, *We Are the New Nation*, 13.

14 Rovira i Virgili, *Nacionalisme i Federalisme*, 199.

15 Daniels, *We Are the New Nation*, 13.

16 Ibid., 47.

17 Ibid., 49.

18 Ibid., 51.

19 Jennifer Adese, "A Tale of Two Constitutions," 13.

20 This is actually a hotly contested topic in Métis studies. For the foundational statement, see Jacqueline Peterson's 1985 chapter "Many Roads to Red River: Métis Genesis in the Great Lakes Region, 1680–1815." For a sympathetic critique of this narrative of emergence, see Chris Andersen's 2014 book *"Métis": Race, Recognition, and the Struggle for Indigenous Peoplehood*, 44–58. I discuss both works in more detail later in this section.

21 Simply titled "Canadian Multiculturalism" and dated as "Revised 15 February 1999," this is available at https://publications.gc.ca/Collection-R/LoPBdP/CIR/936-e.htm.

22 This speech is reproduced in the anonymous and unpaginated document *Multiculturalism and the Government of Canada* (Ottawa: Minister of State for Multiculturalism, 1978). This is a document that is clearly intended to introduce the broad contours of the then-new multiculturalist programs of the federal government to a national readership.

23 Gagnon, *La Raison du plus fort*, 207.

24 Orwell, *The Lion and the Unicorn*, 5.

25 Weinstein, *Quiet Revolution West*, 75.

26 The full text of their 1936 reoprt is here: https://www.metismuseum.ca/media/document.php/03857.RoyalRep.Metis.Alta.pdf.

27 For details, see Catherine Bell's 1994 book *Alberta's Metis Settlements Legislation*, esp. 21–3.

28 See Bell, *Alberta's Metis Settlements Legislation*, 66–71.

29 I owe this formulation to Kai Woolner-Pratt, who in discussions about this book suggested that this seemed to be what I was hoping for in terms of this piece of Indigenous government.

30 The analogy is imperfect, for sure, but I think certain connections are enlightening. I tried to develop such connections in an article published in *Aboriginal Policy Studies* 9, no. 2 (2021), wherein I argued that the constitutional framework that Charlottetown would have created for the Métis Settlements of Alberta is somewhat akin to the UN admitting Andorra in 1993. I also argued that the status of the Turtle Mountain Chippewa Reservation in North Dakota (where the Michif language has historically been strong) is somewhat akin to the communities of Catalunya Nord, that is to say the parts of France that remain Catalan. For a survey of the latter, see Alà Baylac Ferrer, *Le Catalan en Catalogne Nord et dans les Pays Catalans: même pas mort!* or James Hawkey, *Language Attitudes and Minority Rights: The Case of Catalan in France*. For discussion of the US-Métis context generally (and some discussion of Turtle Mountain), see

Martha Harroun Foster's 2006 book *We Know Who We Are: Métis Identity in a Montana Community*.

31 The Métis filmmaker Gil Cardinal's two-part BBC documentary *Our Home and Native Land* (1992) is mostly about Ovide Mercredi, then the head of the Assembly of First Nations, and his role in negotiating Charlottetown. But it also includes a fair bit of detail about Clark's role, portraying him sympathetically. When Bill Beard and I interviewed Cardinal for our 2002 book *North of Everything: English Canadian Cinema since 1980* and asked him about that film and the Charlottetown process generally, he affectionately referred to Clark as "Uncle Joe." I do not think he had FDR's nickname for Stalin in mind, although I suppose it's possible that he was making a joke.

32 Peterson, "Many Roads to Red River," 64.

33 Andersen, *"Métis,"* 25.

34 This MOU has been published in full in *Aboriginal Policy Studies* 8, no. 1 (2019): 115–16. *APS* is edited by Chris Andersen.

35 De Trémaudan, *Histoire de la nation métisse dans l'ouest canadien*, 73.

36 Resnick and Latouche, *Letters to a Québécois Friend*, vii.

37 See "Trudeau's Canada, Again," *New York Times Magazine*, 8 December 2015.

38 Trudeau, *Le Fédéralisme et la société canadienne-française*, 161.

39 Bouchard, *Les nations savent-elles encore rêver?*, 196. I published a long, rambling essay on Englishness in the *Dorchester Review* 10, no. 1 (2020) that formed the basis for some of what I have to say in this chapter. In the course of that essay I had cause to use this quote from Bouchard, and when I did so I just left it in French in my manuscript. The *Review*'s chief Chris Champion was good enough to translate it in the process of editing, and so I've retained his translation here, partially because it gives me an opportunity to acknowledge the journal and the useful role it plays in Canadian intellectual discourse generally and for conservative-curious leftists such as myself.

40 Bastien, *The Battle of London*, 48.

41 I can also direct readers to Samuel Proulx-Chénard's entry on the term in the *Canadian Encyclopedia*, last updated on 22 June 2021, and available here: https://www.thecanadianencyclopedia.ca/en/article/interculturalisme.

42 Bouchard and Taylor, *Building the Future*, 40.

43 Howard Scott translated it in 2015 as *Interculturalism: A View from Quebec*. The chart I go on to mention is on p. 32.

44 Bouchard, *L'Interculturalisme*, 52.

45 Bouchard has also explained this in his contribution to a 2016 anthology edited

by English, Scottish, and Catalan scholars (and for which Charles Taylor provided a foreword); his chapter is titled "Quebec Interculturalism and Canadian Multiculturalism." For discussion of the concept in a more explicitly global context, see Bouchard's 2013 contribution to the Council of Europe publication *Interculturalism and Multiculturalism: Similarities and Differences*, "Interculturalism: What Makes It Distinctive?"

46 Joppke, *Is Multiculturalism Dead?*, 55–6.

47 Bouchard, *A View from Quebec*, 32.

48 Bouchard and Taylor, *Building the Future*, 40.

49 Taylor, "Interculturalism or Multiculturalism?," 420.

50 In some ways I am agreeing with the broad spirit of Lydia Perović's 2022 memoir *Lost In Canada: An Immigrant's Second Thoughts*. This is a spirited defence of Canadian culture; her final, stream-of-consciousness chapter is an especially moving collection of vivid images that capture this sense of a discernably Canadian experience. I disagree with a lot of her assessments – about Indigeneity especially, but probably also about Quebec – but Perović's wonderful book, along with the fact that she immigrated to this country only three years after me, and at the exact same age, really does make me want to call her "sister."

51 Bouchard and Taylor, *Building the Future*, 40.

52 Atwood, *Survival*, 32.

53 Ibid., 35.

54 Ajzenstat, *The Once and Future Canadian Democracy*, 110.

55 Atwood, *Survival*, 32.

56 José E. Iguarta's 2006 book *The Other Quiet Revolution: National Identities in English Canada, 1945–71* would seem to be relevant for my considerations here. But most of this book is given over to explanations of how narrow and unjustifiably British-centred English-Canadian identity remained during those decades. The basis for this is an admirably comprehensive survey of newspapers and school textbooks, and it is indeed valuable to see the degree to which an overly ethnic and often narrow concept of identity did seem to hold on in some quarters, until it suddenly and utterly collapsed in the 1960s, when, as Iguarta writes late in the book, "[t]he British reference, still invoked in the early part of the decade, yielded to expressions of national identity as the lack of national identity" (225). But it is very odd to find a book that engages this issue during these years and does not mention the name "George Grant" even once. Major historical and philosophical figures such as W.H. Morton and Harold Innis also come up either barely or not at all. I am tempted to chalk my disconnect with

this book up to what I have sometimes heard described as the old tension between political science and history, but Iguarta actually had a long career in the
History Department at Université du Québec à Montréal, so that can't be right.
Nevertheless, I think there is a "social science vs humanities" tension between
his work and the work I am trying to do here. From where I stand, the book
seems like a lot of really detailed description of trees; I imagine he would
respond that I am unduly taken with gazing at pretty landscape photographs
of forests. *Vive la différence*, I guess.

57 Resnick and Latouche are "characters" in the 1992 documentary *Le mouton noir*,
    by Jacques Godbout (as I discussed in the last chapter, a celebrated Quebec
    novelist and filmmaker, an intellectual giant of nationalism, and an eccentric
    monarchist). This is one of my all-time-favourite Quebec films, a sprawling
    (nearly four-hour), essayistic examination of the Meech Lake process and the
    aftermath of its collapse. Early in the film Godbout has Resnick meet Latouche
    at a large house on the shores of Meech Lake on 1 July 1990, basically as the
    British Columbian was finishing *Toward a Canada-Quebec Union*. In voiceover
    Godbout calls this "[une] rencontre entre deux frères ennemis qui, de chaque
    extrémité du pays, écrivent et s'écrivent, faisant le plus souvent le procès des
    politiciens." Latouche goes on to be a sort of "animateur" for many of the
    discussions in the rest of the film; we never see Resnick again.

58 Resnick and Latouche, *Letters to a Québécois Friend*, 49–50.

59 Ibid., 4.

60 Ibid., 47.

61 Ibid., 112.

62 Ibid., 94.

63 Ibid., 96.

64 Resnick and Latouche, *Letters to a Québécois Friend*, 118.

65 Resnick, *Toward a Canada-Quebec Union*, vii.

66 Ibid., 28.

67 Ibid., 29.

68 Zapata-Barrero, *Multiculturalism and Interculturalism*, 58.

69 Tully, "The Crisis of Identification," 79.

70 Resnick, *Thinking English Canada*, 67.

71 Ibid., 76.

72 Ibid., 105.

73 Rose, *A World After Liberalism*, 155.

CHAPTER SIX

1 The language of the *Constitution Act* is why terms such as "Indian" and "aboriginal" persist in both legal discourse and the arguments of political advocates,
even though they have been displaced by "First Nations" and "Indigenous" in
the polite Canadian English of the twenty-first century, including of course the
English of this book. In the introduction I discussed the shift from "aboriginal"
to "Indigenous" via the United Nations and correct usage of proper nouns.

2 Kalman, *Framing Borders*, 37.

3 Guilera, *Una història d'Andorra*, 26.

4 Simpson, *Mohawk Interruptus*, 64.

5 For notes on Komulainen and the circumstances of the photo, see Jennifer
Wells, "A Warrior, a Soldier and a Photographer – Remembering the Oka Crisis,"
Toronto Star, 22 August 2015.

6 Generally known as the SQ, this is the provincial police force for Quebec. They
have more or less the same role that the RCMP has in other Canadian provinces
(except for Ontario, which has the Ontario Provincial Police, and Newfoundland, which has the Royal Newfoundland Constabulary). That is to say, they
provide law enforcement for areas not covered by municipal police forces or
in communities that cannot organize their own police forces.

7 I am also at something of a loss as to how to refer to the group of armed supporters of the Mohawks of Kanesatake. The term "activist" isn't generally understood to encompass people with automatic weapons. The term "militant" in
French, which generally refers to people who are more intensely committed
than "activists" but not necessarily as intense as the English sense of "militant,"
seems about right as a description of the entire crowd behind the barricades,
whether or not they were carrying firearms.

8 "Kanehsatake" is the spelling the Obomsawin film uses. The territory's government uses the name "Mohawk Council of Kanesatake." I have favoured the latter
in this book.

9 At the time of the film's shooting Mitchell was a young activist who had invited
the NFB to come to film the protest he was organizing. The NFB considered him
a trainee on the film, and for years only Mort Ransen was credited as director.
Farbod Honarpisheh's chapter on the film in my anthology *The Cinema of
Canada* (London: Wallflower Press, 2006) identified both Mitchell and Ransen
as directors. In 2014 the NFB officially changed the film's credits, identifying
Mitchell as the sole director (nothing from Honarpisheh's contribution to my
anthology, published eight years earlier, seems to have had the slightest impact

on this). In any event, Mitchell would go on to be elected the band council chief in 1984 and again in 2012. This is ironic not only for the usual "young firebrand becomes respectable politician" sorts of reasons, but also because *You Are on Indian Land* is unsparingly critical of Akwesasne's chief, showing him asking the local police for a permit to carry a gun when he gets out of his car to meet the protestors, and talking in the voiceover about how he is Ottawa's man, how rather than bringing the community's concerns to Ottawa he brings Ottawa's concerns to the community, etc.

10 See Michelle Stewart's 2007 article for details of the connections between these two parts of the NFB.

11 Rosenthal, "You Are on Indian Land," 173.

12 In this book I am drawing on the revised 2009 edition.

13 Alfred, *Peace, Power, Righteousness*, 80.

14 Ibid., 91.

15 Ibid., 80.

16 Ibid., 138.

17 The Cayuga are an Iroquoian-language-speaking people who have historically been part, with the Mohawk (whose language is also in the Iroquoian family), of the Haudenosaunee Confederacy.

18 Kalman, *Framing Borders*, 77.

19 CBC coverage of the 2010 troubles is here: Associated Press, "Iroquois Lacrosse Team Denied Visas by UK," CBC News, 14 July 2010, https://www.cbc.ca/news/world/iroquois-lacrosse-team-denied-visas-by-u-k-1.869901. Their coverage of the 2018 voyage to Israel is here: Ka'nhehsí:io Deer, "Iroquois Nationals Arrive in Israel for World Lacrosse Championships after Passport Issues Resolved," CBC News, 12 July 2018, https://www.cbc.ca/news/indigenous/iroquois-nationals-arrive-israel-lacrosse-world-championships-1.4743850.

20 Ibid., 189.

21 Rosen, "The Right to Be Different," 256.

22 In fact the rule banning residents from marrying non-Mohawk people had been on the books since 1981, but it wasn't enforced in any serious way until almost thirty years later. For details see, *inter alia*, Salimah Shivji's CBC news story of 29 June 2016, "Mohawk Council of Kahnawake Hands Out More Eviction Letters," https://www.cbc.ca/news/canada/montreal/mohawk-kahnawake-marry-out-stay-out-eviction-notice-1.3658202.

23 Simpson, *Mohawk Interruptus*, 64.

24 Kalman, *Framing Borders*, 97.

25 Simpson, *Mohawk Interruptus*, 48.

26 Available at http://library.arcticportal.org/1895/1/Declaration_12x18_Vice-Chairs _Signed.pdf.

27 See Gidimt'en Clan, "We Are Wet'suwet'en and the Coastal GasLink Pipeline Protesters Do Not Represent Us," *National Post*, 7 December 2021, and J.P. Gladu, "Using Indigenous Peoples as Political Pawns in Resource Development Is Simply Wrong," *Globe and Mail*, 8 December 2021.

28 Note that I do not say "western ontologies." I object to the use of the term "western" to describe the position of the European-origin framework that has indeed been imposed by force on the peoples of the Americas. This is a matter of simple geography; Europe is *east* of, say, Nunavut, or Kahnawake/Kanesatake/ Akwesasne, or the Métis Homeland. This is not just linguistic fussiness on my part. Rather, this casual use of "western" indicates the unspoken assumption that the European colonial framework – where a large territory that stretched from Africa across Asia was dominated by a series of powers that were indeed *to the west* – is universally applicable to any colonial situation. The pattern of colonial domination that we can see in the British-South-Asian dynamic is not at all the same as the one that we see in the British-North-American one. I think that casual use of the term "western culture," "western domination," etc. is indicative of a casual assumption that it is basically the same. This strikes me as a historical error of significant proportions.

29 Rodon, "Inuit Diplomacy," 18.

30 The term "Eskimo" remains current in the United States partially because of the presence there of the Aleut and the Yupik, who like the Inuit have a circumpolar claim to Indigeneity. The Aleut are present on the Alaskan mainland, the Aleutian Islands, and the Commander Islands (part of Russia); the Yupik are present in Alaska as well as Siberia. Thus it is not correct to refer to the Aleut or the Yupik as "First Nations" or even "Native Americans" (whose claims to Indigeneity are continental, not circumpolar; there are no Tlingit communities in Siberia, no Cree communities in Greenland), but neither is it correct to refer to them as "Inuit."

31 English, "The Emergence of an Arctic Council," 224.

32 Shadian, "From States to Polities," 486.

33 Zellen, "Co-Management as a Foundation," 69.

34 Ibid., 66.

35 Wilson and Smith, "The Inuit Circumpolar Council," 921.

36 The full text, in Danish, is here: https://www.retsinformation.dk/eli/lta/2009/ 473. The official translation in English is here: https://www.stm.dk/media/11338/ 10-notifikation-af-7-oktober-2009-til-fn-s-generalsekretaer-om-selvstyrel oven.pdf.

37 Gerhardt, "The Inuit and Sovereignty," 10.

38 Ibid., 12.

39 Karl, "The Perils of the Petro-State," 36.

40 Gerhardt, "The Inuit and Sovereignty," 12.

CONCLUSION

1 Schama, *Dead Certainties*, 321.

2 Solzhenitsyn, *Rebuilding Russia*, 17.

3 Ermek Shinarbaev's luminous 1989 film *Revenge* (based on a novel by the Korean-Russian writer Anatoli Kim) deals with that community in a lot of lyrical detail. It is a meditation, really, on the Asian elements of Russian identity.

4 Hazony, *The Virtue of Nationalism*, 96.

5 Hazony has emerged as an intellectual leader of the movement known as "national conservatism," which seeks to use the power of the state to shore up common national values. The movement's "Statement of Principles" appears with the Edmund Burke Foundation logo and can be seen at https://nationalconser vatism.org/wp-content/uploads/mailings/2022/statement/?v=6. This, like the emerging "post-liberal" movement, is a loose grouping of actors on the American or American-adjacent right: some centre-right (Patrick Deneen, who did not sign the statement but whose writings are generally consistent with the movement's positions), some much further right than that (the Polish academic and MEP Ryszard Legutko, who did sign it). It is tempting to see National Conservatism as a useful movement for the left to ally with, especially since the statement includes points such as "2. Rejection of Imperialism and Globalism" and "7. Public Research," and "10. Race," the last of which features the statement "The cultural sympathies encouraged by a decent nationalism offer a sound basis for conciliation and unity among diverse communities," echoing thinkers such as Roger Scruton, an obvious influence on the movement. But the statement also includes points such as "4. God and Public Religion" (as a practising Catholic I strongly object to the statement "No nation can long endure without humility and gratitude before God and fear of his judgment that are found in authentic religious tradition"), and "9. Immigration," which concludes with the statement "Restrictive policies may sometimes include a moratorium on immigration." None of this has anything to do with the nationalism that I have been trying to defend in this book. Indeed, much of the statement has a very tenuous connection to nationalism at all (that is especially true of "6. Free Enterprise").

Thus I have avoided the movement in these discussions; some of its thinkers are genuinely useful to engage with, but as a whole it is far more conservative than it is national.

6 Hazony, *The Virtue of Nationalism*, 37.

7 Ibid., 219.

8 One unexpected joy of the critical edition of Léopold Senghor's *Poésie complète* (on which more in chapter 1, devoted to "Ethnos") is Jean-René Bourrel's critical note to Senghor's cycle "Camp 1940," which begins by saying that the poem "Africanizes and ennobles General de Gaulle," and goes on to say, "A man of synthesis and conciliation, Senghor had no problem squaring his socialist convictions and his Gaullist sentiments. In de Gaulle, Senghor admired the chief of the Free French, the statesman who sought to return his country to the place that it had lost on the international scene, the decolonizer who understood, from 1944 onward, that the time had come to accompany the countries who had made up the French empire to their independence. He told Mohamed Azia in 1970 that 'In my opinion, it's de Gaulle who, as a statesman, will have left the greatest mark on the second half of the 20th century. And if colonialism is about to pass from history, it may be General de Gaulle who has done the most for that'" (189, m.t.).

9 Ferro, *Colonization*, 13.

10 It is common to come across this pun in Canadian media discourse, especially on the neo-liberal end of the spectrum. Matthew Lau's opinion piece in the 2 September 2021 issue of the *Financial Post* – which bore the headline "The State Has No Place in the Boardrooms of the Nation" – is only the most recent example.

11 Berlin, *Four Essays on Liberty*, 24.

12 Tamir, *Liberal Nationalism*, 83.

13 Tamir, *Why Nationalism?*, 140.

14 Gilroy, *Against Race*, 53.

15 Anderson, *Imagined Communities*, 145.

16 During the 1990s and 2000s, my wife held various jobs with the Métis Settlements General Council, in Edmonton.

17 One of the only places in the United States where the Métis could be said to have a land base is the Turtle Mountain Reservation, in North Dakota. The legal name of the nation that resides there is the Turtle Mountain Band of Chippewa Indians, but there is a substantial Métis component to their identity. For a highly readable and detailed scholarly treatment of the modern emergence of

the government there, see Keith Richotte Jr, *Claiming Turtle Mountain's Constitution*. Richotte is a legal historian at UNC-Chapel Hill and also serves as an associate justice on Turtle Mountain's Court of Appeal. Also see chapter 5, note 29.

18 I'd like to state for the record that I do not have my aforementioned former student in mind here. He understands what it means to be Métis in Canada; we just disagree about the degree to which that applies to my sons.

19 This exists in two English-language translations: Alan Titley's *The Dirty Dust* (the more bawdy and easily readable version) and Liam Mac Con Iomaire and Tim Robinson's *Graveyard Clay* (closer to the original in some ways but more "foreignizing," to borrow a term from Lawrence Venuti's *The Translator's Invisibility*).

20 Clair Wills's book *That Neutral Island*, which devotes substantial discussion to Ó Cadhain, is the definitive cultural history of this period.

21 Ó Cadhain, *Gluaiseacht na Gaeilge: Gluaiseacht ar Strae?*, 10.

22 Weil, *The Need for Roots*, 213.

23 Ó Cadhain, *Gluaiseacht ar Strae?*, 9.

24 Weil, *Œuvres*, 268.

25 See the description for M/2/29, "A lecture by MÓC concerning his trip to Kirghizia with An Cumann Cairdis Éireannach Sóivéadach (Irish Soviet Society)," in the catalogue of the Máirtín Ó Cadhain papers at Trinity College Dublin (TCD MS 10878).

26 Weil, *Waiting for God*, 8.

27 In the original: "J'aime les six ou sept catholiques d'une spiritualité authentique que le hasard m'a fait rencontrer au cours de ma vie" (*Attente de Dieu*, 34).

28 Ó Cadhain, *Irish above Politics*, 11.

29 Weil, *Need for Roots*, 27.

30 Weil, *On the Abolition of All Political Parties*, 5.

31 Ó Cadhain, *Irish above Politics*, 11.

32 Weil, *On the Abolition of All Political Parties*, 25.

33 Ibid., 35.

34 See chapter 2, note 39.

35 Fustel de Coulanges, *L'Alsace est-elle allemande ou française?*, 96.

36 The government of France once included part of this quotation on its webpage devoted to the history of Ernst Renan's famous Sorbonne lecture, but that page now seems to have been taken down.

37 Chesterton, *The Napoleon of Notting Hill*, 17.

Bibliography

COURT CASES AND LEGAL DECISIONS

Effect of Cherokee Nation v. Nash and Van v. Zinke, etc. Case No. SC-17-07. Supreme Court of the Cherokee Nation. 22 February 2020. https://turtletalk.files.wordpress.com/2021/02/sc-17-07-37-final-order-2-22-21.pdf.

Daniels v. Canada (Indian Affairs and Northern Development). 2016 SCC 12, 2016, 1 SCR 99. https://decisions.scc-csc.ca/scc-csc/scc-csc/en/item/15858/index.do?site_preference=normal&pedisable=true&alternatelocale=en.

R. v. Powley (2003). 2 SCR 207, 2003 SCC 43. https://caid.ca/PowDec2003.pdf.

Sentencia 31/2010, de 28 de junio de 2010. Tribunal constitucional de España. https://boe.es/diario_boe/txt.php?id=BOE-A-2010-11409.

FILMS AND BROADCASTS

Barnette, Neema. *Frank's Place*, season 1, episode 5. Viacom Productions, 1987–88. https://www.youtube.com/watch?v=KU0f8ApQ-Ao.

Cardinal, Gil. *Our Home and Native Land*. BBC, 1992. VHS copy held as part of the Gil Cardinal Fonds (collection number PR3684), Provincial Archives of Alberta.

Curtiz, Michael. *White Christmas*. Paramount Pictures, 1954. https://www.primevideo.com/dp/amzn1.dv.gti.72af5d34-9c7e-a69e-72f4-c86b0d8703eb.

Dash, Julie. *Daughters of the Dust*. American Playhouse / Geechee Girls, 1991. https://www.kanopy.com/en/product/daughters-dust.

Deer, Tracey. *Beans*. Mongrel Media, 2021. https://tv.apple.com/ca/movie/beans/umc.cmc.ak20gqas726eu3coyrpeood.

Dutt, Guru. *Pyaasa*. Guru Dutt Films Pvt. Ltd, 1957. https://www.amazon.com/Pyaasa-Guru-Dutt/dp/B07HMFXCMC.

– *Kaagaz ke Phool*. Guru Dutt Films Pvt. Ltd, 1959. https://www.amazon.com/ Kaagaz-Ke-Phool-Guru-Dutt/dp/B07L449KGD/.

Godbout, Jacques. *Traitre ou patriote?* National Film Board of Canada, 2000. https://nfb.ca/film/traitor_or_patriot/.

– *Le Mouton Noir*. Office national du film du Canada, 1992. https://onf.ca/film/ mouton_noir/.

Greaves, William. *Wealth of a Nation*. United States Information Service, 1964. https://unwritten-record.blogs.archives.gov/2015/07/14/wealth-comes-in-many-forms-william-greaves-usia-films/.

– *The First World Festival of Negro Arts*. William Greaves Productions, 1972. http://www.williamgreaves.com/first-world-festival-negro-arts/.

– *Black Journal*, episode 56. National Educational Television, 1972. https://www. youtube.com/watch?app=desktop&v=KWTkuLDy760.

– *Nationtime*. William Greaves Productions, 1972. https://www.amazon.com/Nation time-William-Greaves/dp/B08T6C154L.

Hurston, Zora Neale. *Commandment Keeper Church, Beaufort South Carolina, May 1940*. Zora Neale Hurston Trust, 1940. Released on DVD by Kino as part of the collection *Pioneers of African American Cinema*.

Jenkins, Horace. *Cane River*. H.B.J. Productions, 1982. https://www.amazon.com /Cane-River-Richard-Romain/dp/B08B2H8N3V.

Kapoor, Raj. *Shree 420*. R.K. Films, 1955. https://www.amazon.com/Shree-420-Nargis/dp/B08IGKMYVL/.

Kiarostami, Abbas. *First Case, Second Case*. Kanoon, 1979. https://www.criterion channel.com/videos/first-case-second-case.

Kosashvili, Dover. *Late Marriage*. Transfax Film Productions, 2001. https://www. amazon.com/Late-Marriage-Lior-Ashkenazi/dp/B004D783L4.

– *Cadeau du ciel*. Transfax Film Productions, 2003. Released on DVD by Wild Side Vidéo (Paris).

Kunuk, Zack. *Atanarjuat: The Fast Runner*. Igloolik Isuma Productions, 2001. https://www.nfb.ca/film/atanarjuat_the_fast_runner_en/.

Obomsawin, Alanis. *Kanehsatake: 270 Years of Resistance*. National Film Board of Canada, 1993. https://nfb.ca/film/kanehsatake_270_years_of_resistance/.

McQueen, Steve. *Small Axe*. BBC Films, 2021. https://www.amazon.com/Small-Axe-Season-1/dp/B08J4HRR4P.

Mehboob. *Mother India*. Mehboob Productions, 1957. https://www.amazon.com/ Mother-India-Nargis/dp/B08CRSNR7B/.

Mita, Merata. *Patu!* Awatea Films, 1983. https://www.nzonscreen.com/title/patu-1983.

– *Mauri*. Awatea Films, 1988. https://kanopy.com/product/mauri.

Mitchell, Michael Kanentakeron. *You Are on Indian Land*. National Film Board of Canada, 1969. https://nfb.ca/film/you_are_on_indian_land/.

Shinarbaev, Ermek. *Revenge*. Kazakhfilm Studio, 1989. https://criterionchannel.com/videos/revenge.

Sidiq, Mohammad. *Chaudhvin Ka Chand*. Guru Dutt Films Pvt. Ltd, 1960. https://www.amazon.com/Chaudhvin-Ka-Chand-Guru-Dutt/dp/B07NBKHTJB.

Thornton, Warwick. *Samson and Delilah*. Madman Entertainment, 2009. https://www.amazon.com/Samson-Delilah-Rowan-McNamara/dp/B01MXRS88R/ref=sr_1_4?crid=1P50RNTEZZUZM.

Walker, John. *Quebec My Country Mon Pays*. John Walker Productions, 2016. https://vimeo.com/ondemand/quebecmycountrymonpays.

SECONDARY SOURCES

Achebe, Chinua. *Home and Exile*. New York: Anchor Books, 2001.

Adams, Christopher, Gregg Dahl, and Ian Peach. *Métis in Canada: History, Identity, Law and Politics*. Edmonton: University of Alberta Press, 2013.

Adese, Jennifer. "A Tale of Two Constitutions: Métis Nationhood and Section 35(2)'s Impact on Interpretations of *Daniels*." TOPIA: *Canadian Journal of Cultural Studies* 36 (2018): 7–19.

The Agreement Respecting a New Relationship between the Cree Nation and the Government of Quebec (2002). https://www.legisquebec.gouv.qc.ca/en/document/cr/m-35.1.2,%20r.%201.

Ajzenstat, Janet. *The Once and Future Canadian Democracy: An Essay in Political Thought*. Montreal and Kingston: McGill-Queen's University Press, 2003.

Alberta Federation of Metis Settlement Associations. *Metisism: A Canadian Identity*. Edmonton: Alberta Federation of Metis Settlement Associations, 1982.

Alfred, Taiaiake. *Peace, Power, Righteousness: An Indigenous Manifesto*. Oxford, UK: Oxford University Press, 2009 [1999].

Anaya, S. James. *Report of the Special Rapporteur on the Situation of Human Rights and Fundamental Freedoms of Indigenous People, James Anaya: Addendum*. Geneva: United Nations, 26 August 2010. https://digitallibrary.un.org/record/689516?ln=en.

Andersen, Chris. *"Métis": Race, Recognition, and the Struggle for Indigenous Peoplehood*. Vancouver: University of British Columbia Press, 2014.

Andersen, Chris, and Nathalie Kermoal, eds. *Daniels v. Canada: In and Beyond the Courts*. Winnipeg: University of Manitoba Press, 2021.

Anderson, Benedict. *Imagined Communities: Reflections on the Origins and Spread of Nationalism*. London: Verso, 1991 [1983].

Anderson, Perry. *English Questions*. London: Verso, 1992.

– *The Indian Ideology*. London: Verso, 2012.

Appiah, Kwame Anthony. *In My Father's House: Africa in the Philosophy of Culture*. Oxford, UK: Oxford University Press, 1992.

– *The Ethics of Identity*. Princeton, NJ: Princeton University Press, 2005.

– *Cosmopolitanism: Ethics in a World of Strangers*. New York: Norton, 2006.

– *The Lies That Bind: Rethinking Identity*. New York: Norton, 2018.

Applebaum, Anne. "A Warning from Europe." *The Atlantic*, October 2018: 53–63.

– *Twilight of Democracy: The Seductive Lure of Authoritarianism*. New York: Signal Press, 2020.

Aquin, Hubert. *Blocs erratiques*. Montreal: Quinze, 1982.

– *Writing Quebec: Selected Essays by Hubert Aquin*. Translated by Anthony Purdy. Edmonton: University of Alberta Press, 1988.

Asmus, Ronald. *A Little War That Shook the World: Georgia, Russia, and the Future of the West*. London: Palgrave, 2010.

Atwood, Margaret. *Survival: A Thematic Guide to Canadian Literature*. Toronto: House of Anansi, 1972.

Bag, Kheya, and Susan Watkins. "Structures of Oppression: Querying Analogies of Race and Caste." *New Left Review* 132 (November–December 2021): 55–82.

Baraka, Imamu Amiri. *It's Nation Time*. Chicago: Third World Press, 1970.

Barber, Benjamin. *The Death of Communal Liberty: A History of Freedom in a Swiss Mountain Canton*. Princeton, NJ: Princeton University Press, 1974.

Barré, Jean-Luc. "Simone Weil." In *Dictionnaire de Gaulle*, edited by Claire Andrieu, Phillipe Braud, and Guillaume Picketty, 1175–6. Paris: Robert Lafont, 2006.

Barton, Simon. *A History of Spain*. London: Macmillan, 2009.

Bassett, Ray. "Britain and Ireland after Brexit." In *The Idea of the Union*, edited by Foster and Smith, 89–104.

– "After Brexit, Is Ireland Next to Go?" *Globe and Mail*, 3 March 2017: A11.

– *After Brexit, Will Ireland be Next?* London: Policy Exchange, 2017.

Bastien, Frédéric. *The Battle of London: Trudeau, Thatcher, and the Fight for Canada's Constitution*. Translated by Jacob Homel. Toronto: Dundurn, 2014.

Baylac Ferrer, Alà. *Le Catalan en Catalogne Nord et dans les Pays Catalans: même pas mort!* Perpignan, France: Presses universitaires de Perpignan / Institut Franco-Català Transfronterer, 2017.

Bédard, Éric. "La République de Marcel Chaput." *Bulletin d'histoire politique* 26, no. 1 (2017): 296–312.

Beiner, Ronald. *Philosophy in a Time of Lost Spirit: Essays on Contemporary Theory*. Toronto: University of Toronto Press, 1997.

Bélanger, Éric, Richard Nadeau, Alisa Henderson, and Eve Hepburn. *The National Question and Electoral Politics in Quebec and Scotland*. Montreal and Kingston: McGill-Queen's University Press, 2018.

Bell, Catherine E. *Alberta's Metis Settlements Legislation: An Overview of Ownership and Management of Settlement Lands*. Regina: Canadian Plains Research Centre, 1994.

– *Contemporary Metis Justice: The Settlement Way*. Saskatoon, sk: Native Law Centre, 1999.

Bellegarde, Perry. "Crown-First-Nations Treaty Relationships." In *Royal Progress: Canada's Monarchy in the Age of Disruption*, edited by D. Michael Jackson, 19–29. Toronto: Dundurn, 2020.

Benner, Erica. *Really Existing Nationalisms*. London: Verso, 2018.

Berlin, Isaiah. *Four Essays on Liberty*. Oxford, uk: Oxford University Press, 1969.

Berry, Dawn Alexandrea, Nigel Bowles, and Halbert Jones, eds. *Governing the North American Arctic: Sovereignty, Security, and Institutions*. London: Palgrave, 2016.

Bock-Côté, Mathieu, and Jacques Godbout. *Le tour du jardin*. Montreal: Boréal, 2014.

Bouchard, Gérard. *Les nations savent-elles encore rêver? Les mythes nationaux à l'ère de la mondialisation*. Montreal: Boréal, 2019.

– "Quebec Interculturalism and Canadian Multiculturalism." In *Multiculturalism and Interculturalism: Debating the Dividing Lines*, edited by Nasar Meer, Tariq Modood, and Ricard Zapata-Barrero, 77–103. Edinburgh: Edinburgh University Press, 2016.

– "Interculturalism: What Makes It Distinctive?" In *Interculturalism and Multiculturalism: Similarities and Differences*, edited by Martyn Barrett, 93–110. Brussels: Council of Europe, 2013.

– *Interculturalism: A View from Quebec*. Translated by Howard Scott. Toronto: University of Toronto Press, 2015 [2012].

– *L'Interculturalisme. Un point de vue québécois*. Montreal: Boréal, 2012.

– *The Making of Nations and Cultures in the New World*. Edited by Michelle Weinroth and Paul Leduc Browne. Montreal and Kingston: McGill-Queen's University Press, 2008.

– *Genèse des nations et cultures du Nouveau Monde*. Montreal: Boréal, 2001.

Bouchard, Gérard, and Charles Taylor. *Fonder l'avenir: Le temps de la conciliation*. Quebec City: Gouvernement du Québec, 2008.

– *Building the Future: A Time for Reconciliation*. Quebec City: Gouvernement du Québec, 2008.

Bragg, Billy. *The Progressive Patriot*. London: Black Swan, 2007.

Brennan, Timothy. "The National Longing for Form." In *Nation and Narration*, edited by Homi Bhabba, 44–70. London: Routledge, 1990.

Brière, Jean-F. "Black Soul." In *Anthologie de la nouvelle poésie nègre et malagache de langue française*, edited by Léopold Senghor, 124–8. Paris: Presses Universitaires de France, 2015.

Burke, Edmund. *Reflections on the Revolution in France*. Edited by Conor Cruise O'Brien. London: Penguin, 1982 [1790].

Caldwell, Gary. "The Republican Temptation." *Dorchester Review* 5, no. 1 (2015): 61–9.

Canovan, Margaret. *The People*. Cambridge: Polity, 2005.

Césaire, Aimé. *Cahier d'un retour au pays natal*. Paris: Présence africaine, 1983 [1956].

– *Les Fondements de l'africanité. Ou, négritude et arabité*. Paris: Présence africaine, 1967.

– *Return to My Native Land*. Translated by John Berger and Anna Bostock. Brooklyn, NY: Archipelago Books, 2013 [1969].

– *Ce que je crois. Négritude, francité et civilisation*. Paris: Gallimard, 1988.

– *Discours sur le colonialsime, suivi de Discours sur la négritude*. Paris: Présence africaine, 2004 [1955].

– *Discourse on Colonialism*. Translated by Joan Pinkham. New York: Monthly Review, 1972 [1955].

Chastenay, Pierre. "Facebook et le mot en b." *Le Devoir*, 17 April 2021.

Chatterjee, Gayatri. *Mother India*. London: British Film Institute, 2002.

Chesterton, G.K. *The Napoleon of Notting Hill*. New York: Dover, 1991 [1904].

Chevrier, Marc. *La République québécoise. Hommages à une idée suspecte*. Montreal: Boréal, 2012.

Clarke, George Elliott, ed. *Fire on the Water: An Anthology of Black Nova Scotian Writing*, vol. 1. Halifax: Pottersfield Press, 1991.

– ed. *Eyeing the North Star: Directions in African-Canadian Literature*. Toronto: McClelland and Stewart, 1997.

– *Treason of the Black Intellectuals?* Montreal: McGill Institute for the Study of Canada, 1999.

– *Odysseys Home: Mapping African-Canadian Literature*. Toronto: University of Toronto Press, 2002.

– *Black*. Vancouver: Raincoast Books, 2006.

– "Assembling the Afro-Métis Syllabus: Some Preliminary Reading." *Zeitschrift für Kanada-Studien* 42 (2022): 10–41.

Cockburn, Alexander. "Diary." *London Review of Books*, 4 May 2023: 40–1.

Colley, Linda. *Britons: Forging the Nation, 1707–1837*. New Haven, CT: Yale University Press, 2012.

Costa, Lluis. *Cuba i el Catalanisme. Entre l'autonomia i la independència*. Barcelona: Rafael Dalmau, 2013.

Couture, Claude. *La loyauté d'un laïc: Pierre Elliott Trudeau et le libéralisme canadien.* Montreal and Paris: L'Harmattan, 1996.

– *Paddling with the Current: Pierre Elliot Trudeau, Étienne Parent, Liberalism, and Nationalism in Canada.* Translated by Vivian Bosley. Edmonton: University of Alberta Press, 1998.

Crenshaw, Kimberlé. "Mapping the Margins: Intersectionality, Identity Politics and Violence Against Women of Color." *Stanford Law Review* 43, no. 6 (1991): 1241–99.

Cuthand, Doug. "First Nations' Connection to Crown Endures." *Saskatoon Star-Phoenix*, 4 June 2022, A9.

Dahl, Greg. "A Half-Breed's Perspective on Being Métis." In Adams, Dahl, and Peach, *Métis in Canada*, 93–139.

Daniels, Harry. *We Are the New Nation.* Ottawa: Native Council of Canada, 1979.

de Certeau, Michel, Dominique Julia, and Jacques Revel. *Une politique de la langue. La Révolution française et les patois: l'enquête de Grégoire.* Paris: Gallimard, 1975.

Deneen, Patrick. *Regime Change: Towards a Post-Liberal Future.* New York: Penguin Random House, 2023.

– *Why Liberalism Failed.* New Haven, CT: Yale University Press, 2019.

De Trémaudan, Auguste-Henri. *Histoire de la nation métisse dans l'ouest canadien.* Montreal: Éditions Alberta Lévesque, 1936.

De Villers, Marie-Éva. *Multidictionnaire de la langue française.* 4th edition. Montreal: Québec-Amérique, 2003.

Diouf, Boucar. "Le mot en 's' pour systémique." *La Presse*, 20 February 2021.

Dobbin, Murray. *The One and a Half Men: The Story of Jim Brady and Malcolm Norris.* Vancouver: New Star Books, 1981.

Dubois, Janique. "What's the Deal? Canada's Constitutional Relationship with the Métis Nation." In *Constitutional Politics*, edited by Laforest, Lecours, and Brossard-Dion, 23–43.

Ducange, Jean-Numa. *Quand la gauche pensait la nation.* Paris: Fayard, 2021.

Ducharme, Michel. *Le concept de liberté au Canada à l'époque des révolutions atlantiques, 1776–1838.* Montreal and Kingston: McGill-Queen's University Press, 2010.

Dumont, Fernand. *La vigile du Québec.* Montreal: Bibliothèque québécoise, 2001 [1971].

– *The Vigil of Quebec.* Translated by Sheila Fischman and Richard Howard. Toronto: University of Toronto Press, 1974.

Durham, Earl of [John George Lambton]. *The Report of the Earl of Durham.* London: Methuen, 1930 [1902/1839].

Duval, Jacinthe. "The Catholic Church and the Formation of Metis Identity." *Past Imperfect* 9 (2001–03): 65–87.

Edgerton, David. *The Rise and Fall of the British Nation: A Twentieth-Century History*. London: Penguin, 2019.

Elliot, J.H. *Scots and Catalans: Union and Disunion*. New Haven, CT: Yale University Press, 2018.

English, John. "The Emergence of an Arctic Council." In *Governing the North American Arctic*, edited by Berry, Bowles, and Jones, 217–32.

Fanon, Frantz. *Peau noire, masques blancs*. Paris: Seuil, 1998 [1952].

– *Black Skin, White Masks*. Translated by Richard Philcox. London: Penguin, 2008.

Fennell, Desmond. *The Changing Face of Catholic Ireland*. Washington, DC: Corpus Books, 1968.

– "Iosrael in Iarchonnachta." *Inniu*, 28 February 1969, 9.

– *Sketches of the New Ireland*. Galway, Ireland: Association for the Advancement of Self-Government, 1973.

– *Towards a Greater Ulster: 1969–72*. Indreabhán, Ireland: Comharchumann Chois Fharraige, 1973.

– "A New Look at Federation." *Irish Times*, 23 March 1974.

– "The Federation of Man 2." *Irish Times*, 25 March 1974.

– "Sticking Together Two Partitioned Areas Is Unlikely to End Conflict." *Irish Times*, 24 February 1978.

– "'Unity by Consent' Requires a Federal Irish Constitution." *Irish Times*, 27 February 1978.

– *Beyond Nationalism: The Struggle against Provinciality in the Modern World*. Dublin: Ward River, 1985.

– *Heresy: The Battle of Ideas in Modern Ireland*. Dublin: Blackstaff, 1994.

– "Solutions to the Northern Ireland Problem: A Federal Ireland and Other Approaches." *Canadian Journal of Irish Studies* 21, no. 1 (1995): 1–24.

Ferro, Marc. *Colonization: A Global History*. New York: Routledge, 1997.

Fetzer, Joel S. *Luxembourg as an Immigration Success Story: The Grand Duchy in Pan-European Perspective*. Lanham, MD: Lexington Books, 2015.

Flanagan, Thomas, Christopher Alcantara, and André Le Dressay. *Beyond the Indian Act: Restoring Aboriginal Property Rights*. 2nd ed. Montreal and Kingston: McGill-Queen's University Press, 2011.

Foster, John Wilson, and William Beattie Smith, eds. *The Idea of the Union: Great Britain and Northern Ireland*. Belfast: Belcouver Press, 2022.

Foster, Martha Harroun. *We Know Who We Are: Métis Identity in a Montana Community*. Norman, OK: University of Oklahoma Press, 2006.

Frazier, Robeson Taj P. "The Congress of African People: Baraka, Brother Mao, and the Year of '74." *Souls: A Critical Journal of Black Politics, Culture, and Society* 8, no. 3 (2006): 142–59.

Fustel de Coulanges, Numa Denis. *Questions contemporaines*. Paris: Libraire Hachette, 1916.

Gagnon, Alain-G. *La Raison du plus fort: Plaidoyer pour le fédéralisme multinational*. Montreal: Québec-Amérique, 2008.

Gagnon, Alain-G., and Jorge Cagiao y Conde, eds. *Fédéralisme et sécession*. Bern: Peter Lang, 2019.

Gagnon, Alain-G., and Guy Laforest. "The Moral Foundations of Asymmetrical Federalism: Normative Considerations." In *Federalism, Plurinationality and Democratic Constitutionalism: Theory and Cases*, edited by Ferran Requejo and Miguel Caminal, 85–107. London: Routledge, 2012.

Gagnon, Alain-G., André Lecours, and Geneviève Nootens, eds. *Contemporary Majority Nationalism*. Montreal and Kingston: McGill-Queen's University Press, 2011.

– eds. *Les nationalismes majoritaires contemporains: Identité, mémoire, pouvoir*. Montreal: Québec-Amérique, 2007.

Gagnon, Alain-G., and Ferran Requejo-Coll, eds. *Nations en quête de reconnaissance: Regards croisés Québec-Catalogne*. Bern: Peter Lang, 2011.

Gagnon, Alain-G., and James Tully, eds. *Multinational Democracies*. Cambridge: Cambridge University Press, 2001.

Ganti, Tejaswini. *Bollywood: A Guidebook to Popular Indian Cinema*. London: Routledge, 2004.

Gardin, Matias, Ragnhild Barbu, and Barbara Rothmüller. "Educating Future Citizens in between Mischkultur Nationalism and Authorities: Traces from Teachers' Journals." *History of Education* 44, no. 5 (2015): 537–52.

Gerhardt, Hans. "The Inuit and Sovereignty: The Case of the Inuit Circumpolar Conference and Greenland." *Politik* 14, no. 1 (2011): 6–14.

Gibson, Dale. *Law, Life and Government at Red River*. 2 vols. Montreal and Kingston: McGill-Queen's University Press, 2015.

Gilda, Sujatha, and Alan Horn. "Caste, Race – And Class." *New Left Review* 131 (2021): 15–35.

Gilroy, Paul. *There Ain't No Black in the Union Jack*. Chicago: University of Chicago Press, 1987.

– *The Black Atlantic: Modernity and Double Consciousness*. Cambridge, MA: Harvard University Press, 1993.

– *Small Acts: Thoughts on the Politics of Black Cultures*. London: Serpent's Tale, 1993.

– *Against Race: Imagining Political Culture beyond the Color Line*. Cambridge, MA: Harvard University Press, 2000.

Giroux, Dalie. *L'Œil du maître*. Montreal: Mémoire d'encrier, 2020.

Graham, Brian Russell. *On a Common Culture: The Idea of a Shared National Culture*. London: Zero Books, 2022.

Grant, George. *Lament for a Nation: The Defeat of Canadian Nationalism*. Carleton Library Series 50. Ottawa: Carleton University Press, 1995 [1965].

– *Technology and Empire*. Toronto: Anansi, 1969.

– *Technology and Justice*. Toronto: Anansi, 1986.

Guilera, Josep M. *Una història d'Andorra*. Barcelona: Edicions Rústica, 1993 [1960].

Hall, Stuart. *The Fateful Triangle: Race, Ethnicity, Nation*. Cambridge, MA: Harvard University Press, 2017.

Harvey, Louis Georges, et al., eds. *De la république en Amérique française: Anthologie pédagogique des discours républicains au Québec, 1703–1967*. Quebec City: Éditions du Septentrion, 2013.

Hawkey, James. *Language Attitudes and Minority Rights: The Case of Catalan in France*. London: Palgrave, 2018.

Hazony, Yoram. *The Virtue of Nationalism*. New York: Basic Books, 2018.

Hebblethwaite, Benjamin. "Haiti's Foreign Language Stranglehold." *Foreign Policy*, 3 August 2021. https://foreignpolicy.com/2021/08/03/haiti-language-education-school-french-haitian-creole/.

Heinich, Nathalie. "On Academic Activism: A French Perspective." *European Review* 31, no. 5 (2023): 479–88.

Henderson, Ailsa, and Richard Wyn Jones. *Englishness: The Political Force Transforming Britain*. Oxford, UK: Oxford University Press, 2021.

Horowitz, Gad. "Conservatism, Liberalism, and Socialism in Canada: An Interpretation." *Canadian Journal of Economics and Political Science* 32, no. 2 (1966): 143–71.

Hountondji, Paulin. "Que peut la philosophie?" *Présence africaine* 119 (1981): 47–71.

– "Producing Knowledge in Africa Today: The Second Bashorun M.K.O. Abiola Distinguished Lecture." *African Studies Review* 38, no. 3 (1995): 1–10.

– *African Philosophy: Myth and Reality*. Translated by Henry Evans and Johnathan Rée. Bloomington, IN: Indiana University Press, 1996.

– *Combat pour le sens. Un itinéraire africain*. Cotonou, Benin: Éditions du Flamboyant, 1997.

– *The Struggle for Meaning: Reflections on Philosophy, Culture, and Democracy in Africa*. Athens, OH: Ohio University Press, 2002.

Hubert, Ollivier, and François Furstenberg, eds. *Entangling the Quebec Act: Transnational Contexts, Meanings, and Legacies in North America and the British Empire*. Montreal and Kingston: McGill-Queen's University Press, 2020.

Hurley, Erin. *National Performance: Representing Quebec from Expo 67 to Céline Dion.* Toronto: University of Toronto Press, 2011.

Hurston, Zora Neale. *Their Eyes Were Watching God.* London: Virago, 2020 [1937].

– *Barracoon: The Story of the Last "Black Cargo."* New York: Amistad, 2018.

Ignatieff, Michael. *Blood and Belonging: Journeys into the New Nationalism.* New York: Farrar, Strauss and Giroux, 1993.

Iguarta, José E. *The Other Quiet Revolution: National Identities in English Canada, 1945–71.* Vancouver: University of British Columbia Press, 2006.

The Independent Working Group on Constitutional Transformation. *Report of Matike Mai Aotearoa.* 2016. https://nwo.org.nz/resources/report-of-matike-mai-aotearoa-the-independent-working-group-on-constitutional-transformation/.

Indian Chiefs of Alberta. "Foundational Document: Citizens Plus" [a.k.a. "The Red Paper"]. *Aboriginal Policy Studies* 1, no. 2 (2011): 188–281.

L'Internationale socialiste et la Géorgie. Paris: Édition du comité central du Parti ouvrier social-démocrate de Géorgie, 1921.

Jackson, James. "The Radicalization of the Montreal Irish: The Role of *The Vindicator.*" *Canadian Journal of Irish Studies* 31, no. 1 (2005): 90–7.

Jackson, Moana. "Changing Realities: Unchanging Truths." *Australian Journal of Law and Society* 10 (1994): 115–29.

Jacobs, Jane. *Canadian Cities and Sovereignty-Association.* Toronto: Canadian Broadcasting Corporation, 1980.

Jessop, Bob. *The State: Past, Present, Future.* London: Polity, 2015.

Joan i Marí, Bernat. *Els Països Catalans: Un projecte articulable.* Barcelona: La Busca, 2013.

Jones, Stephen F. *Socialism in Georgian Colors: The European Road to Social Democracy, 1883–1917.* Cambridge, MA: Harvard University Press, 2005.

– *Georgia: A Political History since Independence.* London: I.B. Taurus, 2012.

– ed. *The Making of Modern Georgia, 1918–2012: The First Georgian Republic and Its Successors.* London: Routledge, 2014.

Joppke, Christian. *Is Multiculturalism Dead? Crisis and Persistence in the Constitutional State.* Cambridge: Polity, 2017.

Jordania, Noe. *Difficultés socialistes.* Paris: Éditeur D. Khéladzé, 1933.

Junqueras, Oriol. *Els catalans i Cuba.* Barcelona: Pòrtic, 1998.

Kabir, Nasreen Munni. *Guru Dutt: A Life in Cinema.* Oxford, UK: Oxford University Press, 1996.

Kalman, Ian. *Framing Borders: Principle and Practicality in the Akwesasne Mohawk Territory.* Toronto: University of Toronto Press, 2021.

Kandelaki, Giorgi. "The Democratic Republic of Georgia: Forgotten Lessons for Our Democracy." In *The Making of Modern Georgia*, edited by Jones, 161–74.

Karl, Terry Lynn. "The Perils of the Petro-State: Reflections on the Paradox of Plenty." *Journal of International Affairs* 53, no. 1 (1999): 31–48.

Kautsky, Karl. *Georgia: A Social Democratic Peasant Republic*. Translated by H.J. Stenning. London: International Bookshops, 1921.

Kearney, Richard. *Postnationalist Ireland: Politics, Culture, Philosophy*. London: Routledge, 1997.

Kelly, Stéphane, ed. *Les idées mènent le Québec: Essais sur une sensibilité historique*. Ste.-Foy, QC: Les Presses de l'Université Laval, 2002.

Kendle, John. *Federal Britain: A History*. London: Routledge, 1997.

Kennedy, James. *Liberal Nationalisms: Empire, State, and Civil Society in Scotland and Quebec*. Montreal and Kingston: McGill-Queen's University Press, 2013.

Khan, Perviz. "The Song Picture Man." *Sight and Sound*, October 1994: 26–8.

Koshy, Yohann. "The Last Humanist: How Paul Gilroy Became the Most Vital Guide to Our Age of Crisis." *The Guardian*, 5 August 2021.

Kymlicka, Will. *Multicultural Citizenship: A Liberal Theory of Minority Rights*. Oxford, UK: Oxford University Press, 1996.

Laffin, Martin, and Alys Thomas. "The United Kingdom: Federalism in Denial?" *Publius* 29, no. 3 (1999): 89–107.

Laforest, Guy. *Un Québec exilé dans la fédération: Essai d'histoire inellectuelle*. Montreal: Québec-Amérique, 2014.

– "L'exil intérieur des Québécois dans le Canada de la Charte." *Constitutional Form / Forum constitutionnel* 16, no. 2 (2007): 63–70.

Laforest, Guy, and André Lecours. *The Parliaments of Autonomous Nations*. Montreal and Kingston: McGill-Queen's University Press, 2016.

Laforest, Guy, André Lecours, and Nikola Brossard-Dion, eds. *Constitutional Politics in Multinational Democracies*. Montreal and Kingston: McGill-Queen's University Press, 2021.

Laforest, Guy, and Michel Seymour, eds. *Le fédéralisme multinational: Un modèle vivable?* Bern: Peter Lang, 2011.

Larner, Jac, and Richard Wyn Jones. "Progressive Home Rule: What Progressives Can Learn from Two Decades of Welsh Devolution." *Progressive Review* 27, no. 3 (2020): 235–45.

Lasch, Christopher. *The New Radicalism in America, 1889–1963: The Intellectual as Social Type*. New York: Vintage 1965.

– *The Culture of Narcissism: American Life in an Age of Diminishing Expectations*. New York: Norton, 1979.

– *The True and Only Heaven: Progress and Its Critics*. New York: Norton, 1991.

– *The Revolt of the Elites and the Betrayal of Democracy*. New York: Norton. 1995.

Laverdure, Patline, Ida Rose Allard, and John C. Crawford. *The Michif Dictionary: Turtle Mountain Chippewa Cree*. Winnipeg: Pemmican, 1983.

Lee, Eric. *The Experiment: Georgia's Forgotten Revolution, 1918–1921*. London: Zed, 2017.

Leman, Marc. *Canadian Multiculturalism*. Ottawa: Political and Social Affairs Division, 1999. https://publications.gc.ca/collections/Collection-R/LoPBdP/CIR/936-e.htm.

Leroux, Daryl. *Distorted Descent: White Claims to Indigenous Identity*. Winnipeg: University of Manitoba Press, 2019.

– "Outlining the Origin of 'Eastern Métis' Studies." In *Daniels v. Canada*, edited by Andersen and Kermoal, 188–209.

Lévesque, René. *Option Québec*. Montreal: Typo, 1997 [1968].

Locke, John. *Political Writings*. London: Penguin, 1993.

MacDonald, Scott, ed. *William Greaves: Filmmaking as Mission*. New York: Columbia University Press, 2021.

MacLeod, Alexander. "'The Little State of Africadia Is a Community of Believers': Replacing the Regional and Remaking the Real in the Work of George Elliott Clarke." In *Africadian Atlantic: Essays on George Elliott Clarke*, edited by Joseph Pivato, 227–56. Toronto: Guernica, 2012.

Macpherson, C.B. *The Real World of Democracy*. Toronto: CBC / Anansi, 1992 [1965].

– *Democratic Theory: Essays in Retrieval*. Oxford, UK: Clarendon Press, 1973.

Mamoulia, Georges. *Les combats indépendantistes des Caucasiens entre URSS et puissances occidentales. Le cas de la Géorgie (1921–1945)*. Paris: L'Harmattan, 2009.

Marantz, Andrew. "The Illiberal Order: Does Hungary Offer a Glimpse of Our Authoritarian Future?" *New Yorker*, 4 July 2022: 36–47.

Marchessault, Janine, and Monika Kim Gagnon, eds. *Reimagining Cinema: Film at Expo 67*. Montreal and Kingston: McGill-Queen's University Press, 2014.

Matsaberidze, Malkhaz. "The Georgian Democratic Republic of Georgia (1918–1921) and the Search for the Georgian Model of Democracy." In *The Making of Modern Georgia*, edited by Jones, 141–60.

McCaffrey, Lawrence T. "Isaac Butt and the Home Rule Movement: A Study in Conservative Nationalism." *Review of Politics* 22, no. 1 (1960): 72–95.

McCarthy, Mary. *On the Contrary: Articles of Belief, 1946–1961*. New York: Farrar, Strauss and Giroux, 1961.

Mikaberidze, Alexander. *Historical Dictionary of Georgia*, 2nd ed. Lanham, MD: Rowman and Littlefield, 2015.

Mills, Sean. *The Empire Within: Postcolonial Thought and Political Activism in Sixties Montreal*. Montreal and Kingston: McGill-Queen's University Press, 2010.

– *A Place in the Sun: Haiti, Haitians, and the Remaking of Quebec*. Montreal and Kingston: McGill-Queen's University Press, 2016.

Mitchell, James. *Devolution in the UK*. Manchester, UK: Manchester University Press, 2011.

Mohan, Jag. "Jawaharlal Nehru and His Socialism." *India International Centre Quarterly* 2, no. 3 (1975): 183–92.

Moi, Toril. "I Came with a Sword: Simone Weil's Way." *London Review of Books*, 1 July 2021: 7–9.

Moore, Celeste Day. "William Greaves, *Black Journal*, and the Long Roots of Black Internationalism." In *William Greaves*, edited by MacDonald, 217–84.

Moreno, Luis. *The Federalization of Spain*. London: Routledge, 1997.

Morton, W.L. *The Canadian Identity*, 2nd ed. Madison: University of Wisconsin Press, 1972 [1961].

Moyn, Samuel. *Liberalism Against Itself*. New Haven, CT: Yale University Press, 2023.

Nairn, Tom. *The Break-Up of Britain: Crisis and Neo-Nationalism*. Champaign, IL: Common Ground, 2015 [1977].

– *Faces of Nationalism: Janus Revisited*. London: Verso, 1997.

Nehru, Jawaharlal. *The Discovery of India*. New Delhi: Jawaharlal Nehru Memorial Fund, 1982 [1946].

Neill, William J.V. "Reaching Out: Reimagining Post-Centenary Unionism." In *The Idea of the Union*, edited by Foster and Smith, 356–73.

New Ireland Forum. *Report of Proceedings*. Dublin: Stationary Office, 1984.

Niven, Alex. *New Model Island: How to Build a Radical Culture beyond the Idea of England*. London: Repeater, 2019.

NourbeSe Philip, M. *Frontiers: Essays and Writings on Racism and Culture*. Toronto: Mercury Press, 1992.

Nussbaum, Martha, and Amartya Sen. *The Quality of Life*. Oxford, UK: Oxford University Press, 1993.

Ó Cadhain, Máirtín. *Cré na Cille*. Dublin: Sáirséal agus Dill, 1979 [1949].

– *The Dirty Dust*. Translated by Alan Titley. Indreabhán, Ireland, and New Haven, CT: Cló Iar-Chonnachta / Yale University Press, 2015 [1949].

– *Graveyard Clay*. Translated by Tim Robinson and Liam Mac Con Iomaire. Indreabhán, Ireland, and New Haven, CT: Cló Iar-Chonnachta / Yale University Press, 2017 [1949].

– *Tone: Inné agus Inniu*. Dublin: Coiscéim, 1999 [1963].

– *Irish above Politics*. Galway, Ireland: Gaelic Weekly, 1964.

– *Páipéir Bhána agus Páipéir Bhreacha*. Dublin: An Clóchomhar, 2003 [1969].

– *Gluaiseacht na Gaeilge: Gluaiseacht ar Strae*. Dublin: Misneach, 1969.

O'Leary, Brendan. *Making Sense of a United Ireland: Should It Happen? How Might It Happen?* London: Sandycove Penguin, 2022.

Orwell, George. *The Lion and the Unicorn: Socialism and the English Genius*. London: Penguin, 2018 [1941].

– *Notes on Nationalism*. London: Penguin, 2018 [1945].

O'Sullivan See, Katherine. *First World Nationalisms: Class and Ethnic Politics in Northern Ireland and Quebec*. Chicago: University of Chicago Press, 1986.

Pabst, Adrian. *Postliberal Politics: The Coming Age of Renewal*. London: Polity, 2021.

– "Is Liberal Democracy Sliding into 'Democratic Despotism?'" *Political Quarterly* 87, no. 1 (2016): 91–5.

Pacificus. *Federalism and Home Rule*. London: John Murray, 1910.

Paquin, Stéphane. *La revanche des petites nations. Le Québec, l'Écosse et la Catalogne face à la mondialisation*. Montreal: VLB Éditeur, 2001.

– *Paradiplomatie identitaire en Catalogne*. Ste-Foy, QC: Presses de l'Université Laval, 2003.

Paré, Étienne. "Fossé culturel à CBC / Radio Canada." *Le Devoir*, 10 July 2022, A1.

Parekh, Lord Bhiku. *The Future of Multi-Ethnic Britain: The Parekh Report*. London: Profile, 2000.

Parenteau, Danic. *L'indépendance par la République*. Montreal: Fides, 2015.

Patterson, Orlando. "Four Modes of Ethno-Somatic Stratification: The Experience of Blacks in Europe and the Americas." In *Ethnicity, Social Mobility and Public Policy: Comparing the USA and the UK*, edited by Glenn Loury, 67–121. Cambridge: Cambridge University Press, 2005.

Pelletier, Francine. *Au Québec, c'est comme ça qu'on vit. La montée du nationalisme identitaire*. Montreal: Lux, 2023.

Perović, Lydia. *Lost in Canada: An Immigrant's Second Thoughts*. Toronto: Sutherland House, 2022.

Peterson, Jacqueline. "Many Roads to Red River: Métis Genesis in the Great Lakes Region, 1680–1815." In *The New Peoples: Being and Becoming Métis in North America*, edited by Peterson and Jennifer S.H. Brown, 37–72. Winnipeg: University of Manitoba Press, 1985.

Pi y Margall, Francisco. *Las Nacionalidades*. Madrid: Alba, 1996 [1876].

Planes, Llorenç. *El petit llibre de Catalunya-Nord. Lluita per un "Rosselló" català*. Perpinyà, France: Edicions "La Falç," 1974.

Poliquin, Daniel. *René Lévesque*. Toronto: Penguin, 2009.

Prat de la Riba, Enric. *La nacionalidad catalana / La nacionalitat catalana*. Madrid: Biblioteca nueva, 1998 [1910/1906].

Ralston Saul, John. *A Fair Country: Telling Truths about Canada*. Toronto: Penguin, 2008.

Reid, Colin W. "'An Experiment in Constructive Unionism': Isaac Butt, Home Rule and Federalist Political Thought during the 1870s." *English Historical Review* 129 (April 2014): 332–61.

Resnick, Philip, and Daniel Latouche. *Letters to a Québécois Friend*. Montreal and Kingston: McGill-Queen's University Press, 1990.

– *Toward a Canada-Quebec Union*. Montreal and Kingston: McGill-Queen's University Press, 1991.

– *Thinking English Canada*. Toronto: Stoddart, 1995.

Richman Kenneally, Rhona, and Joanne Sloan, eds. *Expo 67: Not Just a Souvenir*. Toronto: University of Toronto Press, 2010.

Richotte, Keith, Jr. *Claiming Turtle Mountain's Constitution: The History, Legacy, and Future of a Tribal Nation's Founding Documents*. Chapel Hill, NC: University of North Carolina Press, 2017.

Rodon, Thierry. "Inuit Diplomacy: Reframing the Arctic Space and Narratives." In *The Internationalization of Indigenous Rights: UNDRIP in the Canadian Context*, edited by Terry Mitchell, 17–22. Waterloo, ON: Centre for International Governance, 2014.

Rose, Matthew. *A World after Liberalism: Philosophers of the Radical Right*. New Haven, CT: Yale University Press, 2021.

Rosen, Lawrence. "The Right to Be Different: Indigenous Peoples and the Quest for a Unified Theory." *Yale Law Journal* 107, no. 1 (1997): 227–59.

Rosenthal, Alan. "You Are on Indian Land: An Interview with George Stoney." In *Challenge for Change Activist Documentary at the National Film Board of Canada*, edited by Thomas Waugh, Michael Brendan Baker, and Ezra Winton, 169–79. Montreal and Kingston: McGill-Queen's University Press, 2010.

Rovira i Virgili, Antoni. *Nacionalisme i Federalisme*. Barcelona: Edicions 62 i "la Caixa," 1982 [1917].

– *L'Estat Català: Estudi de dret public*. Tarragona, Spain: Publicacions URV, 2016 [1947].

– *Viatge a la URSS*. Barcelona: Edicions 62, 1968.

– *Sobre història de Catalunya: Escrits de l'exili (1939–1949)*. Barcelona: Cossetània Edicions, 2012.

Rudin, Ron. *Making History in Twentieth-Century Quebec*. Toronto: Toronto University Press, 1997.

Rushdie, Salman. *Imaginary Homelands: Essays and Criticism, 1981–1991*. London: Granta Books / Penguin, 1991.

Scargill, M.H., et al. *A Dictionary of Canadianisms on Historical Principles*. Toronto: W.J. Gage, 1967.

Schama, Simon. *Dead Certainties: Unwarranted Speculations*. New York: Vintage, 1992.

Schwartz, Antoine. "Prenez garde à la jeune garde du libéralisme." *Le Monde Diplomatique*, December 2021: 20–1.

Scotland's Future: Your Guide to an Independent Scotland. Edinburgh: Scottish Government, 2013.

Scruton, Roger. *Philosopher on Dover Beach*. South Bend, IN: St Augustine's Press, 1998 [1990].

– *England: An Elegy*. London: Continuum, 2006 [2000].

– *England and the Need for Nations*. London: Institute for the Study of Civil Society, 2006.

– "What Trump Doesn't Get about Conservatism." *New York Times*, 5 July 2018: A19.

Sen, Amartya. *Identity and Violence: The Illusion of Destiny*. New York: Norton, 2006.

Senghor, Léopold. *Poésie complète*. Edited by Pierre Brunel. Paris: CNRS Éditions, 2007.

Shadian, Jessica. "From States to Polities: Reconceptualizing Sovereignty through Inuit Governance." *European Journal of International Relations* 16, no. 3 (2010): 485–510.

Simpson, Audra. *Mohawk Interruptus: Political Life across the Borders of Settler States*. Durham, NC: Duke University Press, 2014.

Smith, Brian. "Behind the Constitutional Curtain." *Dorchester Review* 12, no. 1 (2022): 88–92.

Solzhenitsyn, Aleksandr. *Rebuilding Russia: Reflections and Tentative Proposals*. London: Harvill, 1991.

Sontag, Susan. *Essays of the 1960s & 70s*. New York: Library of America, 2013.

Stepan, Alfred, Juan J. Linz, and Yogendra Yadav. "The Rise of 'State-Nations.'" *Journal of Democracy* 21, no. 3 (2010): 50–68.

Stewart, Michelle. "The Indian Film Crews of Challenge for Change: Representation and the State." *Canadian Journal of Film Studies* 16, no. 2 (2007): 48–81.

Symons, Scott. *Combat Journal for Place d'Armes*. Edited by Christopher Elson. Toronto: Dundurn, 2010 [1967].

Tall Bear, Kim. "The Political Economy of Tribal Citizenship in the U.S.: Lessons for Canadian First Nations?" *Aboriginal Policy Studies* 1, no. 3 (2011): 70–80.

Tamir, Yael. *Why Nationalism*. Princeton, NJ, and Oxford, UK: Princeton University Press, 2018.

– *Liberal Nationalism*. Princeton, NJ: Princeton University Press, 1993.

Taylor, Charles. *Sources of the Self: The Making of Modern Identity*. Cambridge, MA: Harvard University Press, 1989.

– *Multiculturalism and "The Politics of Recognition."* Edited by Amy Gutmann. Princeton, NJ: Princeton University Press, 1992.

– *Philosophical Arguments*. Cambridge, MA: Harvard University Press, 1997.

– *Modern Social Imaginaries*. Durham, NC: Duke University Press, 2004.

– *A Secular Age*. Cambridge, MA: Harvard University Press, 2007.

– "Afterword: Apologia pro Libro suo." In *Varieties of Secularism in a Secular Age*, edited by Michael Warner, Jonathan Vananterwerpen, and Craig Calhoun, 300–21. Cambridge, MA: Harvard University Press, 2010.

– *Democracia Republicana / Republican Democracy*. Santiago: LOM Ediciones, 2012.

– "Interculturalism or Multiculturalism?" *Philosophy and Social Criticism* 38, no. 4–5: 413–23.

Teillet, Jean. *The North-West Is Our Mother: The Story of Louis Riel's People, the Métis Nation*. Toronto: Harper Collins, 2019.

Tellier, Luc-Normand. *Le Québec, état nordique*. Montreal: Quinze, 1977.

Tilly, Charles. "National Self-Determination as a Problem for All of Us." *Daedalus* 122, no. 3 (1993): 29–36.

– "States and Nationalism in Europe 1492–1992." *Theory and Society* 23, no. 1 (1994): 131–46.

– "The Time of States." *Social Research* 61, no. 2 (1994): 269–95.

– "Citizenship, Identity and Social History." *International Review of Social History* 40 (supplement 3): 1–17.

– "Political Identities in Changing Polities." *Social Research* 70, no. 2 (2003): 605–20.

Todorov, Tzvetan. *La vie commune: Essai d'anthropologie générale*. Paris: Seuil, 1995.

Toki, Vamarie. "Māori Seeking Self-Determination or Tino Rangatiratanga? A Note." *Journal of Māori and Indigenous Issues* 5 (2017): 134–44.

Torrance, David. *The Crown Dependencies*. London: House of Commons Library, 2023.

Treps, Marie. "Accidents de parcours: L'assimilation des termes culturels empruntés à des langues étrangères." *Communications* 77 (2005): 211–33.

– *Maudits mots. La fabrique des insultes racistes*. Paris: Le gout des mots, 2020.

Trudeau, Pierre. *Le fédéralisme et la société canadienne-française*. Montreal: HMH, 1967.

Tudor, Maya. *The Promise of Power: The Origins of Democracy in India and Autocracy in Pakistan*. Cambridge: Cambridge University Press, 2013.

Tully, James. "The Crisis of Identification: The Case of Canada." *Political Studies* 42 (1994): 77–96.

– *Public Philosophy in a New Key Volume 1: Democracy and Civic Freedom*. Cambridge: Cambridge University Press, 2008.

Tunks, Andrea. "Asia & Pacific: Pushing the Sovereign Boundaries in Aotearoa." *Indigenous Law Bulletin* 4, no. 23 (August/September 1999): 15–18.

Venuti, Lawrence. *The Translator's Invisibility: A History of Translation*. New York: Routledge, 1995.

Wacquant, Loïc. "Resolving the Trouble with 'Race.'" *New Left Review* 133/134 (2022): 67–88.

Walcott, Rinaldo. *Black Like Who? Writing Black Canada*. Toronto: Insomniac Press, 1997.

Walker, Graham. "The Scottish Dimension of the Union." In *The Idea of the Union*, edited by Foster and Smith, 65–77.

Weil, Simone. *On the Abolition of All Political Parties*. Simon Leys, trans. New York: NYRB Classics, 2013.

– "The Iliad, or, the Poem of Force." Translated by Mary McCarthy. *politics*, November 1945: 321–31.

– *L'enracinement: Prélude à une déclaration des devoirs envers l'être humain*. Paris: Gallimard, 2016 [1949].

– *Attente de dieu*. Paris: Albin Michel, 2016 [1950].

– *Waiting for God*. Translated by Emma Craufurd. New York: Perennial, 2001 [1951].

– *The Need for Roots*. London and New York: Routledge, 2002 [1952].

– *Œuvres*. Edited by Florence de Lussy. Paris: Gallimard, 1999.

Weinstein, John. *Quiet Revolution West: The Rebirth of Métis Nationalism*. Calgary: Fifth House, 2007.

Welt, Cory. "A Fateful Moment: Ethnic Autonomy and Revolutionary Violence in the Democratic Republic of Georgia." In *The Making of Modern Georgia*, edited by Jones, 205–31.

Wilder, Gary. *The French Imperial Nation-State: Negritude and Colonial Humanism between the Two World Wars*. Chicago: University of Chicago Press, 2005.

Willemen, Paul. *Looks and Frictions: Essays in Cultural Studies and Film Theory*. London: British Film Institute, 1994.

Willemen, Paul, and Ashish Rajadhyaksha. *Encyclopaedia of Indian Cinema*. London and New Delhi: British Film Institute / Oxford University Press, 1994.

Willis, Aaron. "Rethinking Ireland and Assimilation: Quebec, Collaboration, and the Heterogeneous Empire." In *Entangling the Quebec Act*, edited by Hubert and Furstenberg, 165–94.

Wills, Clair. *That Neutral Island: A Cultural History of Ireland during World War II.* London: Faber and Faber, 2008.

Wilson, Gary N., and Heather A. Smith. "The Inuit Circumpolar Council in an Era of Global and Local Change." *International Journal* 66, no. 4 (2011): 909–21.

Winks, Robin. *Blacks in Canada: A History.* 50th anniversary edition. Montreal and Kingston: McGill-Queen's University Press, 2021 [1971].

Woodard, Komozi. "Imamu Amiri Baraka (LeRoi Jones), the Newark Congress of African People, and the Modern Black Convention Movement: A History of the Black Revolt and the New Nationalism, 1966–1976." PhD dissertation. Philadelphia: University of Pennsylvania, Department of History, 1991.

– "Imamu Baraka, the Newark Congress of African People, and Black Power Politics." In *Black Power in the Belly of the Beast,* edited by J.L. Jeffries and Tiyi Makeda Morris, 43–66. Urbana: University of Illinois Press, 2006.

Younge, Gary. "What the Hell Can I Call Myself Except British?" *New York Review of Books,* 29 April 2021: 8–10.

Zapata-Barrero, Richard. "Theorizing Intercultural Citizenship." In *Multiculturalism and Interculturalism: Debating the Dividing Lines,* edited by Nasar Meer, Tariq Modood, and Ricard Zapata-Barrero, 53–76. Edinburgh: Edinburgh University Press, 2016.

Zellen, Barry Scott. "Co-Management as a Foundation of Arctic Exceptionalism: Strengthening the Bonds between the Indigenous and Westphalian Worlds." *Yearbook of Polar Law* 13 (2022): 65–92.

– *On Thin Ice: The Inuit, the State and the Challenge of Arctic Sovereignty.* Lanham, MD: Lexington Books, 2009.

Zerofsky, Elisabeth. "The Orban Effect." *New York Times Magazine,* 24 October 2021: 22–9.

Index